South Africa in the
Global Imaginary

Imagined South Africa

Unisa Press celebrates ten years of democracy in South Africa with a range of books entitled *Imagined South Africa*. To publish is to name reality; it is to mark identity and to confer the status of valid knowledge on the opinions, views and knowledge of a mass of voices once denied a hearing. This series chronicles the multiple ways in which South Africans of all colours and ideological persuasions have been responding, either critically or creatively, to the numerous contradictions in ten years of democracy.

Abebe Zegeye
Director: Unisa Press

Chabani Manganyi
On Becoming a Democracy

Dial Ndima
The Law of Commoners and Kings:
Narratives of a Rural Transkei Magistrate

Reitu Mabokela
Hear Our Voices: Race, Gender and the Status of
Black South African Women in the Academy

Betty Govinden
'Sister Outsider': The Representation of Identity and
Difference in Selected Writings by South African Indian Women

Peter Stewart
Segregation and Singularity: Politics and its Context Among White
Middle-Class English-Speakers in Late-Apartheid Johannesburg

Keith Beavon
Johannesburg: The Making and
Shaping of the City

Ari Sitas
Voices that Reason: Theoretical Parables

Ashraf Jamal
Predicaments of Culture in South Africa

Michael Titlestad
Making the Changes: Representations of Jazz
in South African Literature and Reportage

Chris Ledochowski
Cape Flats Details: Life and Culture
in the Townships of Cape Town

Andries Oliphant (ed.)
Democracy X: Marking the Present
and Representing the Past

South Africa in the
Global Imaginary

Edited by
Leon de Kock,
Louise Bethlehem &
Sonja Laden

UNIVERSITY OF SOUTH AFRICA PRESS
PRETORIA

KONINKLIJKE BRILL NV
LEIDEN

© 2004 University of South Africa
First edition, first impression

ISBN 1-86888-260-8

Published by Unisa Press
University of South Africa
PO Box 392, Unisa, 0003

Editor: Finuala Dowling
Book series designer: André Nel
Electronic origination: Elsabé Viljoen
Printer: Interpak, Pietermaritzburg

Cover image: Dia!kwain and Jan Rondebout, Bleek and Lloyd archive, National Library (Cape Town). See also p. 39.

Copyright 2004 (with the exception of David Attwell's essay), the Porter Institute for Poetics and Semiotics, publishers of *Poetics Today*, Tel Aviv University. Reprinted with permission. Thanks also to The Storyteller Group (storyteller@icon.co.za) for permission to reprint illustration material from *Heart to Heart* in the essay by Loren Kruger and Patricia Watson Shariff. Further thanks to Macmillan SA for permission to republish pictorial material from *Roxy* (Story Circle) in the same essay.

CONTENTS

PREFACE

The volume in hand derives from a special issue of the journal *Poetics Today* carrying the same title, which was named Best Special Issue of 2001 by The Council of Editors of Learned Journals, a body affiliated with the Modern Languages Association. At the time, the judges strongly recommended that the issue be published as a book.

We have made one change: David Attwell's essay, 'The Experimental Turn in Black South African Fiction', has been added to the original collection. The addition of this fine essay is not arbitrary: Attwell was meant to have contributed to the special issue in the first place, but was prevented from doing so by unforeseen circumstances.

ONE

South Africa in the Global Imaginary:
An Introduction

Leon de Kock

1 The Elements in Play

> What I want to write about is the penetration, expansion, skirmishing, coupling, mixing, sepa-
> ration, regrouping of peoples and cultures – the glorious bastardisation of men and women mu-
> tually shaped by sky and rain and wind and soil . . . And everywhere is exile; we tend to forget
> that now. The old ground disappears, expropriated by blood as new conflicting patterns emerge.
> Breyten Breytenbach, *Dog Heart*

Introductions to South African literary culture conceived as an entity have a peculiar
trademark: They apologise for attempting to do the impossible and then go ahead any-
way.[1] This gesture, ranging from rhetorical genuflection to anxious self-examination to
searing critique of others who have dared to undertake what should not be attempted
lightly, reveals a significant fault line in the field of South African literary studies, although *field* is a problematic metaphor here, like almost every other metaphor one cares
to use. Literary 'fields' – entities, groupings – require some reason other than the mere
convenience of geography for their existence: they need minimal convergence in the
domains of origin, language, culture, history, and nationalism (contested or not) to become, in some sense, cohesive and inter-referential. But in the South African case each
of these domains fragments into heterogeneity the moment one looks more closely at
the literary objects at hand. As I argue later in this introduction, cultural heterogeneity
is nothing new or surprising in a context of globalisation, but the South African case is
peculiar because it remains to this day a scene of largely *unresolved* difference.

Arguments about the origins of South African 'literature' still shuttle between
different languages, different nationalisms, and different notions of culture, history,
and belonging in mutually excluding series and genealogies. For example, a symbolic
source object of the field might variously be given as the oral bushman song, the epic
account of Portuguese seafaring around the Cape, the Dutch register of occupation, the
English travel diary, the Xhosa praise song, the French pastoral narrative of Africa, or
the Scottish romantic ballad. These objects of culture have seldom been aware of each
other, despite their geographic contiguity. *And take note: the above list is not exhaustive.*

In saying this, as I must, I too bend to the rhetorical necessity that marks the field as something beyond the limits of singular description.

The evidence of such referential fracture in the signifier 'South African literature' is visible in day-to-day literary practice. Anthologists and writers of general histories of South African literature, because of the contingencies of publishing, markets, and marketing, tend to work within one language and to write for particular audiences. These audiences almost always exclude some of the other groups and individuals who, in the final analysis, must also be regarded as part of the thoroughly polyglot South African scene with its eleven 'official' languages. It is usually with such an awareness of the complexity of the field in mind that the trademark apology is proffered. So, for example, when André Brink and J. M. Coetzee (1986:7) published their anthology of South African writing, *A Land Apart*, they immediately genuflected as follows: 'It has not been our ambition to give a full picture of the wealth and range of contemporary writing, by writers both black and white, working in English, Afrikaans, Xhosa, Zulu, Sotho and the other languages of South Africa. The collection is offered as the personal choice of the editors.' Note that, even within the broadest possible description, such as that above, the telltale ellipsis remains, *'and the other* languages of South Africa', as if not even at the level of macrodescription, not even in catalogue terms, do these two doyens of South African writing feel it is possible to 'cover' the field. In this case as in most others, the ritual nod to an always-greater diversity occurs at a particular moment of publication and for a particular context. For Brink and Coetzee it is Faber and Faber, London and Boston. (A large proportion of the country's English writing continues to be published outside the country, usually in the United Kingdom.) Almost always the publishing context is regarded as precluding, in a supposedly provisional and unfortunate manner, the greater range, scope, and diversity of the *real* totality of South African literature. But always the power of the book is such that the provisional articulation, despite its apologies, becomes totemic. What the apologies and spatial gestures about *more, elsewhere*, and *other* tend to conceal is the fact that the body of literature is given shape – monumentalised, in a sense – not in gestures pointing to supplementarity but in the supposedly provisional selections immortalised in print, decorated between covers, and marketed from the global nerve centres of the publishing industry. In the colonies and the ex-colonies the imprints London, Boston, New York, Amsterdam, and Harmondsworth, among others, continue to import a considerable sense of awe and achievement. In the process the scales remain unevenly balanced against orality, as has been the case ever since the advent of print culture and colonisation in southern Africa.

Historically, for reasons originating in the politics and power of the English missionary-colonial project in South Africa, English-language publishing has seen by far the greatest number of works, whether 'South African' by origin, theme, or content. As a result the most visible corpus of South African writing occurs in the English language. This work includes, in its early phases, the imperial travelogue (e.g., John Barrow's *An Account of Travels into the Interior of South Africa* [1801]), clearly written within and for a metropolitan gaze; English lyrical forms that seek to inscribe strange territory within pastoral or romantic verse (e.g., Thomas Pringle's *African Sketches* [1834]); tales of otherness, in which wild animals, Boers, and blacks are depicted as the marvellous and dreaded stuff of strangeness objectified in the amber of the reasoned English tongue (e.g., Alfred W. Drayson's *Tales at the Outspan* [1862]; Percy Fitzpatrick's *The Outspan: Tales from South Africa* [1897]; and W. C. Scully's *Kafir Stories* [1898]); exotic adventure stories that utilise the mythography of a 'dark' and 'mysterious' continent for thrilling bedtime or fireside entertainment (e.g., Rider Haggard's *King Solomon's Mines* [1886] and *She* [1887]; and John Buchan's *Prester John* [1910]); polemical writings about slavery, settler conflicts, missionary endeavours, and the wars of appropriation and dispossession at the centre of South Africa's always violent history (e.g. Dr John Philip's *Researches in South Africa* [1828] and Robert Moffat's *Missionary Labours and Scenes in Southern Africa* [1842) and early black writing in derived English forms under the tutelage of missionaries (e.g., Sol T. Plaatje's *Mhudi* [1930]; and H. I. E. Dhlomo's *The Girl Who Killed to Save: Nongquase the Liberator* [1935]).

The later forms of South African English writing, both before and after the formal introduction of apartheid in 1948, into genres such as the story, the novel, the poem, the play, the film script, and others, become increasingly explicit treatments of a land sundered at the heart by the politics of race and tortured by impossible trials of conscience. Here obvious examples come to mind: Nadine Gordimer, Peter Abrahams, Alan Paton, Es'kia Mphahlele, Athol Fugard, Mongane Wally Serote, J. M. Coetzee, Breyten Breytenbach, André Brink, and Zakes Mda, represented by work published internationally in English, written in English, or translated into English. This, for a great many international readers, is 'South African literature'. If a country's literature can be measured by what is most visible and most obvious on the shelves of, say, the Library of Congress, then the South African example begins to look overwhelmingly English.

However, a rider attaches here: it is a literature in English that, especially in its early forms, exists to demonstrate its otherness to what may be expected in the English language. It is a literature that historically has often strained to demonstrate the variance, the strangeness, and the curiosity value of comically uncultivated people, wild animals, tragically doomed heathens, illiberal Boers, greedy prospectors – the list goes on – in a place whose otherness to the great English mainlands, whose imitativeness and backwardness, must perpetually be alleged as the literature's very raison d'être. In that sense it is a literature deeply rooted in its coloniality. In addition, as I argue later with regard to the thematics of the seam, it is a literature that has been, almost by definition, *other to itself*. That is, the literature carries with it a sense of being steeped in a culturally hybrid (for Breytenbach 'bastardised') context, a context so shot through with (dreaded) intermixture that expressions of Self are often marked by a simultaneous setting apart from various Others. And yet it is precisely such attempted setting apart that marks the South African subject as fractured. So, for example, in a quintet of *South African Short Stories* published in South Africa by *Reader's Digest* in 1973, every story narrates a key component of South African otherness from the perspective of an English speaker. Three of the narratives are about Afrikaners, one tells the story of a Zulu, and one relates the adventures of a seal. In another example, most of the short stories written by the country's most popular English writer, Herman Charles Bosman, deal with self-deluding Afrikaner backvelders and their comical views about the 'kaffirs' and animals that surround them. In the case of the *Reader's Digest* book, that a South African book published in South Africa feels the necessity to describe itself as *South African* short stories demonstrates to what extent the balkanised ex-colony sees its own terrain as a scene of perpetual tourism – a place in which one repeatedly encounters the marks of cultural difference and riven identity despite all attempts to step back from the scene of bastardisation. Ironically, it is the very act of stepping back, with eyes mesmerically fixed on the object of difference that confirms the dreaded – or perhaps desired – cultural bastardisation.

Literature in Afrikaans, on the other hand, has seldom wavered from a firm sense of its own, unique form of South African indigenity, although it, too, has historically defined itself as a fenced-off terrain (usually the farm) surrounded by threatening forces in the main, hostile natural elements, British imperialists, and the various avatars of 'nonwhite' otherness. Afrikaans South Africans have generally exhibited a desire to inhabit the land in a fuller and more nationalistic sense than their English-speaking counterparts. Contrary to the English-speaking establishment, Afrikaners developed a strong, self-sustaining publishing industry inside the country coterminously with the rise to power of Afrikaner nationalism. Although Afrikaans writing has received international exposure only in limited quantities (in translation), the institutions of Afrikaans power inside South Africa ensured that a robust culture of publication, criticism, dissemination, and teaching at all levels was promoted and maintained. The same cannot be said for literature in the indigenous African languages of South Africa. Various missionary and Afrikaner nationalist regimes of educational and cultural hegemony across at least two centuries have relegated African-language literature to a lesser status and deprived it of primacy in the cultural and educational domains. The importance of oral culture similarly was downgraded, as was an entire context of indigenous culture, which either was frowned upon (by missionaries) or reified in artificial Bantustans but was deprived of any real autonomy (by the social engineers of apartheid).

The result of such blatantly uneven development has been that 'South African literature' has shown many different faces but has seldom been regarded in its totality as an integrated field by all practitioners. At least four levels of stratification can be observed. (1) For Afrikaners, the rubric South African literature largely comprises the canon of Afrikaans literature and so continues to be taught inside the country. (2) For white English speakers, 'South African literature' has often appeared to consist of its most visible monuments, mostly in English and mostly endorsed by the gaze of metropolitan approval. (3) For African-language writers the once-revered oral performance traditions, although never obliterated, were superseded to some extent by works written for the curriculum boards of education departments that needed setworks for their many separate language classrooms under apartheid and after. Literary works in African languages, oral or written, have remained mostly invisible in the international profile of the field known as 'South African literature' except in rare cases of translation. (4) For writers politically exiled under apartheid, both black and white, 'South African literature' has been a site of struggle, often set in contradistinction to what was perceived as the smug complacency of the uncommitted writers inside the country (although by no means can it be said that all the writers who remained in the country were politically uncommitted). In the longer view, as more recent scholars have repeatedly emphasised (cf., Gray 1979; Van Wyk Smith 1990; Chapman 1996; Smit et al. 1996), the 'field' has consisted of an infinitely greater diversity of objects and forms – in many languages, in both oral and written forms, and in popular as well as belletristic modes – than any of these partial representations allow. Critically, as Malvern van Wyk Smith argues in his important essay 'White Writing/Writing Black: The Anxiety of Non-Influence' (1996), it cannot be shown conclusively that South African writers who have inhabited *different* domains of culture, language, and epistemology at the same time nevertheless created their works within a consciousness of 'one literature' in the way the more recent, anti-apartheid critics would wish to see the field. Rather, Van Wyk Smith (1996: 83), marshalling convincing evidence to support his point, avers, 'Southern African writers have deliberately [kept] their distance from cultures other than their own.'

Van Wyk Smith's argument brings to mind the possibility that 'South African literature' as a field is little more than its empirical base; that its unity resides less in its being a self-aware and interreferential field than in its being yoked together by geography and circumstance and by alphabetical-numerical arrangement. Alternatively, and this paradox surfaces frequently in South African literary historiography, the field's greatest unity lies in its history of division (Gray 1989; Chapman 1996). In Chapman's argument (1996: xvii), the moments of conflict and division are precisely what give the field its special character:

> In looking at frontier clashes in early nineteenth-century South Africa, for example, we might want to ask ourselves whether Xhosa literature would have taken the directions it did had there been no colonial settlement in Xhosa space; obversely, whether early South African literature in English would have followed its particular course had it not encountered indigenous people around its early settlements . . . the Xhosa bard and the settler journalist, though divided by language, literacy, race and probably sentiment, were both part of the same story – a story which remains open, of course, to different interpretations.

Similarly for Gray (1989: 20–21) the key figure is the cultural translator:

> A proposition: our literary system is similar to other literary systems . . . and it is different (*unlike* other literary systems, the total literary production of our system stretches across a vast spectrum of cultural manifestations, from Stone Age to TV . . .). *Therefore* our system does have some norms peculiar to it. For one, the writer is always forced into a position of having to negotiate between extremes, into crossing the language-colour barrier; he or she can only be a syncretist and hybridiser. And *therefore* the basic act of writing is one of carrying information across one or another socio-economic barrier, literally of 'trading' . . . I propose, thus, a new identikit portrait: the writer exists at any of several boundaries (*not* at the centre of one self-enclosed

group); his or her act of making literature is part of transferring data across that boundary, from one audience to another – an act which in its broadest sense may be termed 'translation.'

Many would argue that Gray's 'identikit' is idealistic; South African writers may occasionally have seen their roles in the way Gray describes, but his identikit is hardly universal. Certainly Van Wyk Smith's own extensive researches have led him to conclude that most South African writers do not resemble Gray's portrait. Nonetheless, Gray's historiographical work, especially his *Southern African Literature: An Introduction* (1979), was the first in many decades that surpassed the typically amateurish, Anglocentric survey-type approach. Seeking a suitable historiographical method for writing about southern African literature in English, Gray critiqued the various classificatory models used in the past to unify the field: those that proceed by general survey, by genre, by time periods, by alphabetical entry, and by the utterances of writers themselves. Yet he noted that in 1976 the 'whole' of the literature showed precisely how divided it was. South Africa's writers-in-exile met in Holland; South Africa's English writers, white and black, along with their 'vernacular' associates not in exile met in Johannesburg; and Afrikaans writers met in Broederstroom near Pretoria (Gray 1979: 14). To talk of 'unity', Gray felt in 1979, was chimerical. The best provisional conceptualisation Gray felt able to offer at that time, in the face of such apparent division, was a cartographic metaphor that allowed a semblance of unity within disparateness – the archipelago:

> The guiding metaphor for this introduction is that Southern African literature is like an archipelago. The islands with their peaks protrude in set positions, even if one does not readily see the connections between them beneath the surface. Like most archipelagoes, it is related to adjacent landmasses: in this case there are three of them – most importantly, the mainland of English literature, by language and historical circumstance; diminishingly, the British Commonwealth of literature; and increasingly, the continent of Africa which gives it its actual nourishment.

Almost twenty years later Louise Bethlehem (1998) offered a comprehensive critique of various cartographic tropes in the historiography of South African literature, including those of Gray. But Gray was one of the first to conceive of the possibility of strong conceptual unity in the field, a claim, as we have seen, van Wyk Smith's 'anxiety of non-influence' argument later questioned. Nonetheless, Gray's work in the 1970s was significant because it acted as a spur to a whole new generation of scholars taking the field seriously and placing it on the South African research agenda, which, in literary studies, had until then been smugly Anglophile and dismissive of the 'local'. The process generated a great amount of unease about earlier models and assumptions regarding South African writing. The new generation of scholars was also broadly anti-apartheid: they argued strenuously against classificatory division along ethnic-language lines, a balkanisation that until then had been the most predominant form of systematisation. They – in sympathy with their exiled colleagues – called for the unbanning of anti-apartheid works, such as André Brink's *Looking on Darkness* (1975; originally published as *Kennis van die Aand* [1973]), and the return from exile of banned writers, such as

Breyten Breytenbach, Dennis Brutus, Alex La Guma, Bessie Head, and many others, and they flew into attack against bourgeois-humanist complacencies about the universality of the (Western-modelled, belletristic) artwork in a context of political oppression and grassroots struggle. The period from the mid-1970s through to the 1990s, when formal apartheid finally began to disintegrate, therefore saw a great amount of intellectual fervour around South African literary material. Vibrant local publishing houses came into being (although often subvented by foreign-donor funding), and the literature began to develop more of its own critical machinery – symposia, publication series, prizes – leading to heightened self-awareness.

With the collapse of institutional apartheid in the 1990s and the gradual disappearance of the rallying cry of political liberation, a certain energy was lost to the literature in its guise as a 'site of struggle'. Local publishers without links to multinational houses came under pressure as funding dried up. The breakdown of the cultural boycott against South Africa and the country's reintegration into a rapidly globalising world led to a dissipation of that special interest associated with apartheid in the eyes of people inside and outside the country. Indeed the newfound permeability of 'inside' and 'outside' itself meant the literature emanating from South Africa could no longer take for granted its status as a global allegory of the struggle against racial injustice. Yet within the country's institutions, both economic and cultural, stratifications inherited from apartheid have been slow to disappear. The country's universities, with some exceptions, have continued to conduct studies in 'South African literature' under the auspices of separate departments of English, Afrikaans, and African languages with separate genealogies and distinct reading lists. While this is slowly beginning to change as universities embark upon restructuring exercises, the intellectual work of comparison, translation, and integration heralded by the 1994 conference entitled 'Rethinking South African Literary History' has hardly begun in any significant way.[2] The most serious recent attempt in literary history to integrate the field, Michael Chapman's *Southern African Literatures* (1996), has been widely faulted (despite much applause) for its omissions, its foreshortening, and its assumptions.[3] To this day it therefore remains problematic to regard 'South African literature' as a singular or unified field, although a vast amount of writing has taken place in or about the country. If anything, 'South African literature' is an area of enquiry that raises a multiplicity of questions about the colonisation of culture; about canonisation and tradition formation; and about literary-critical historiography, identity, objects of literature, the materiality of discursive regimes, the construction of culture, and the relations of power to cultural production. Such diversity of interest, I hope, is evident in the collection of essays presented in this book.

2 Different from Ourselves

It was a dull narrow little life enough, lived there among the flat-roofed houses, far removed from the currents of life and thought of the great world beyond.

Olive Schreiner, *From Man to Man*

From the above discussion it should be clear that, in telling the story of South African literature, there is greater sense in starting at the beginning than *in medias res*. Before the country's literature can be meaningfully appreciated, in other words, one needs, at a theoretical level, to understand the multiple constructions of identity in the country as a consequence of which the various literary subsystems came into existence. The rubric 'South Africa in the global imaginary' was identified because it captures both the impositions, from without, of various identity-forming global discourses upon the territory and its people as well as forms of self-fashioning, from within, either in the image of a greater world 'out there' or in defiance of it. In southern Africa, since the advent of colonisation more than three centuries ago, identity has all too often been mediated by the sense of that bigger, more powerful domain, as evidenced by Olive Schreiner's yearning evocation in 1926, from her desk in the colonial eastern Cape, of a 'great world beyond'. Modern South Africans, too, have been inclined to signify this other, more promising place, metonymically and with no less yearning, as 'overseas'. The dialectics of 'here' and 'there' have haunted South Africans for so long now that one may justifiably talk of it as a country that is neither here nor there but a place of 'glorious bastardisation' (Breytenbach 1998: 41), a country of thoroughly interstitial identities.

This is because South Africa, like so many other African states, came into existence historically within the clasp of the local and the imperial, a physically and epistemically violent conjunction that irrevocably changed the course of the territory's history. The various acts of provisional synthesis consequent upon this conjunction – that is, the various constructions of the 'nation' – have tended to compromise all identities, some more than others (see, for example, Pippa Skotnes's account of the bushmen in this volume). To be 'South African' has meant no longer fully to be something else, whether that 'something else' was Xhosa, English, Zulu, Dutch, Tswana, or any of the other language and cultural formations making up the country's brimming residual fund of identities. The scale of heterogeneity (suggested by the country's eleven 'official' languages) has tended to defeat the various statist models of social organisation attempted so far; or perhaps one should say these models, in the short term, have defeated the recognition of difference. But always, such defeat has been temporary. The return of the repressed is an all-too-common theme in the country's political and cultural development. Only in 1994, after more than three centuries of repressive segregation of one form or another, and after multiple acts of human slaughter on the battlefields, on the gallows, and in the torture chambers, did a formally democratic order come about that seeks ambitiously to recognise the full extent of the region's diversity.

In such a context it should not be surprising that writing – understood here as the efforts to establish an identity within the determinate sociocultural habitus of 'South Africa' – has been an extremely vexed occupation. From the earliest of times colonial authors either imported outlandish notions of the exotic as an ill-fitting template for the region's intractable realities or struggled to become less colonial and more 'South African' by expressing the integrity of the land and its people. However, for the greater part of the country's history writers have been compelled to do this without the help of an organic matrix, such as a common notion of the nation, a common language, or a common culture (the exemplary cases here are Schreiner and Sol T. Plaatje). As suggested in part 1 of this introduction, schisms, barriers, and misperceptions have been the rule, so that even today it is highly problematic to shift from the first-person singular to the first-person plural when talking South African – to move from 'I' to 'we' or 'us'. Unlike 'settlers' in certain other colonies, such as Canada, Australia, and the United States, the South African 'settlers' of European origin have remained in the minority throughout the country's history, and they have been divided among themselves, to boot. Unlike India and certain other former colonies, such as Kenya and the Congo, however, the minority 'settlers' in South Africa have stuck fast, retaining key stakes in the culture and the economy and in the economy of culture.

Such unresolved heterogeneity has long been evident in the sense of crisis attendant upon writing about 'South Africa', whose very nature as a signifier has been slippery and recalcitrant. Ironically, in a country where engagement with poststructuralist paradigms has been belated and grudging, 'South Africa' itself remains a sign under erasure – the question who 'speaks' for South Africa is as vexed today as it ever was. Much of the violence witnessed over the past three centuries has been epistemic in nature: the many acts, during the missionary-colonial period and then during apartheid, of forcibly reassigning indigenous people's cosmologies, identities, and culture from one signifying system to another, as though these people were little more than bedraggled, uninvited guests in the occupied colony/union/republic. The crisis of the sign thus belongs as much in the country's history of suffering as it does in university seminar rooms, and an exploration of South African signifying economies appears essential to an understanding of its literary and cultural production. Since none of us – I am speaking now provisionally as a 'South African' – can claim an unproblematic relation to our field of reference, my comments in this section seek not to describe the country or its written culture in a plural and comprehensive sense but to sketch some of the styles and manners in which a plurality of South African identities have been represented over time. The move into meta-rhetorical description, in which I take a view of the concatenation of self-inscription and othering in the midst of difference, is consistent with my view that textual production has long been integral to attempts to 'make' South Africa itself, or different from itself.[4]

Briefly, to go back to the beginning then: Before the country became a 'settled' state, before 'it' was incorporated into the first of many colonial dependencies and subsequent statehoods, the precolonial area we now know as South Africa encompassed a diversity of oral cultures whose verbal representations may be thought of as a shifting, aural palimpsest.[5] The evidence of the historians points to a plurality of communities occupying the land of southern Africa in societies that were neither static nor necessarily egalitarian.[6] Writing entered the scene only after the arrival of Europeans, particularly after the first encounters with the Cape landmass in the fifteenth and sixteenth centuries. At this point a crisis of inscription takes hold in the history of southern Africa. From the earliest of times the South African crisis of inscription has translated into a profound insecurity or a severe arrogance among writers when performing – or not performing, as the case may be – the pronominal slippage from 'I' to 'we' or 'us'. It has been a representational slippage – a slippery slope, one might say – that has haunted all manner of writers in and about South Africa. It is a slippage that has marked the always alluring but ultimately quixotic attempt to bring a certain order of composure, of settlement, to a place of profound difference. But no matter how much fictional composure is imported into the text, much of the writing that sets itself up as *covering* South Africa and its people, in a plural sense, remains marked by various mechanisms of homogenisation and erasure.[7] The peculiar quality of this writing has often been a sense of overextension, enervation, fabulation, or fixity as the crisis of inscription encircles the text and renders its relation to its referent, let us say the realia and the people of southern Africa, increasingly problematic. Many of the essays in this book deal precisely with that crisis and its many forms over the past three centuries in southern Africa (see, for example, the chapters by Jonathan Crewe and Louise Bethlehem).

One of the great examples of such problematic literary representation is the sixteenth-century epic *Os Lusiadas* [The Lusiads] by the Portuguese poet Luis de Camoens. Camoens's text, which has been called both '*our* portion of the Renaissance' (John Purves in Gray 1980: 2; emphasis added) and 'the white man's creation myth of Africa' (Gray 1979: 15–37), established a classic precedent for later writers by transforming the experience of Portuguese mariners rounding the Cape in the late fifteenth century into an epic footnote to Greco-Roman mythology. In his epic narrative Camoens recasts the figure of Cape Town's Table Mountain as Adamastor, a fallen titan. The broken-backed Adamastor has been turned to stone and left to writhe in the southern seas as punishment for his hubris in lusting after the divine Thetis, bride of Peleus. Adamastor, as various critics have noted (Crewe 1997; van Wyk Smith 1988; Gray 1979), then comes to stand for the pathos and brooding vengefulness of the (southern) African continent in its dealings with European explorers and settlers. Adamastor is the myth of nemesis for all those 'outsiders' who dare to trespass upon the land, and many of the (mostly white) writers who followed in Camoens's wake, making South Africa their home, have seized upon Adamastor as a rich trope for articulating a sense of ambivalence and division about their adoptive country. For Gray (1979: 18) the mythopoeic encounter with Adamastor sets up an Apollonian-Dionysian dichotomy that, he says, 'represents the basic tension of white-black confrontation as depicted in much of white South African literature'.

Whether or not Gray's claim is accurate, it seems crucial to note that what several critics have seen as a founding moment in the written literature of southern Africa is in fact an intertextual fragment in a larger work that more properly belongs to Portuguese epic literature. In addition, it is a fragment of literature marked by crisis and confrontation, and significantly it is a fabulous, mythic enactment of representational fixity. The scene of physical encounter in Camoens's epic is matched by a crisis of inscription, a full-blown crisis of representation. So much is clear from the cumbersome mythical overlay that effectively erases the intended referent at this point, the Cape of Good

Hope, and behind it the populous interior of southern Africa, leaving in its place a fairy-tale giant. If anything, it is this crisis that the supposed 'white man's creation myth of Africa' carries forward into the cultural memory encoded in South African letters: a crisis of writing in and about one of the great seams of the modern world.

I borrow the term 'seam' from Noel Mostert (1992: xv), who in his large historical work *Frontiers* claims that 'if there is a hemispheric seam to the world, between Occident and Orient, then it must lie along the eastern seaboard of Africa'. Nowhere else, says Mostert (ibid.) does one find such a 'confluence of human venture and its many frontiers, across time, upon the oceans and between the continents'. More pertinently Mostert (ibid.) claims, 'It was the Cape of Good Hope specifically that symbolised for many centuries the two great formative frontiers of the modern world', which he characterises as the oceanic barrier to the east on the one hand and on the other the more intangible frontier of 'consciousness', represented by Europe gaining a foothold at the tip of Africa. The American frontier, by contrast, was an optimistic one, Mostert (ibid.: xvi) argues, but 'more than at any other settlement point during the ages of oceanic expansion of Europe, it was along the frontier line of confrontation in the Cape Colony that uneasy questioning of the dark side of universal involvement became lodged'.

No doubt many of Mostert's claims are disputable in degree and emphasis. But as a scholar cum popular historian he nonetheless trenchantly rearticulates the trope of the *frontier* as a mainstay of historiographical mapping that is legend in South African written culture and has been the subject of vigorous argument among academic historians.[8] Partly to avoid the predictability of the frontier theme but also to make problematic its seeming stability, I choose here to explore the metaphor of the 'seam', which Mostert himself quickly jettisons in favour of the 'frontier'. I believe it is the representational dimension of cross-border contact that has received relatively short shrift in South African studies, while the material dimensions of the 'contact zone' (cf. Pratt 1992: 6–7) have been studied extensively. To see the crisis of inscription in South African writing following colonisation in terms of a 'seam' is to regard the sharp point of the nib as a stitching instrument that seeks to suture the incommensurate. The *Oxford English Dictionary* (2nd ed.) defines *seam* as a 'junction made by sewing together the edges of two pieces . . . of cloth, leather, etc.; the ridge or the furrow in the surface which indicates the course of such a junction'. The seam is therefore the site of a joining together that also bears the mark of the suture. For my purposes, it needs to be noted that my postulate of a crisis of inscription is characterised by a paradoxical process: on the one hand the effort of suturing the incommensurate is an attempt to close the gap that defines it as incommensurate, and on the other this process unavoidably bears the mark of its own crisis, the seam.

The seam is therefore not only the site of difference (as one might say of the more traditional 'frontier' metaphor), but it necessarily foregrounds the representational suture, the attempt to close the gap and to bring the incommensurate into alignment by the substitution, in the place of difference, of a myth, a motif, a figure, or a trope. (As we shall see, the trope of the binary pairing is especially prevalent here.) The seam is also the place where attempts are made to *renounce* social and cultural conjunction, as one may argue in the case of Afrikaner identity formation. But such renunciation nevertheless occurs in a constitutive relationship with the undesirable 'other side(s)' to which one turns one's back. For the seam is the site of both convergence and difference. It is a representational 'ridge or furrow' whose sudden turns bring about the manifold aporia that J. M. Coetzee (1988) has shown to be characteristic of what he calls 'white writing'. The suture marked by the seam – the representational 'translation' of difference, or its denial – flattens out the incommensurate only by virtue of the strain that the ridge of the seam marks and continues to mark for as long as the suture holds. Not only is the strain palpable in the many instances in which cultural inscription carries across its burden of crisis, I argue, but also the act of returning to the zone of the seam appears to be compulsive. It is the place where the divided culture must return time and time again, where the impossibility of origin and unity is staged repeatedly (indeed as I myself am doing in this essay). In Afrikaner identity formation, for example, the myth of a chosen people taking possession of a promised land is a compulsive restaging of a narrative of origins (du Toit 1983). South African missionary representations, too, are obsessed with restating the founding claims of a unitary providential destiny that, by implication, flattens the (ever-recurring) marks of difference in the missionaries' midst (Comaroff and Comaroff 1997: 33).

I suggest then, following Mostert, that the ubiquitous South African 'frontier', as much cultural and psychological as territorial, has historically constituted one of the great meeting points: a place, in my own terminology, of simultaneous convergence and divergence and where a representational seam is the paradox qualifying any attempt to imagine organicism or unity.[9] Further, as I suggest above, a compulsive tendency in cultural assertion appears to be the attempt to flatten the seam or to imagine it differently. Finally, I propose that the seam is the place where difference and sameness are hitched together – where they are brought to self-awareness, denied, or displaced into third terms.[10]

The key element in the process is desire. It is an incessant mark of desire that cultural inscription in the divided country seeks the site of lost origins, a lost or never-realised wholeness.

As suggested by John L. Comaroff and Jean Comaroff (1997: 27), missionaries in South Africa, those bearers of a new order's signs to the supposedly benighted indigenes, were caught in a contradiction: they spoke incessantly of *removing* difference (in the guise of non-Christian cultural practice) but were part of a colonial 'inscribing machine' (Deleuze and Guattari 1988: 7) that, in the Comaroffs' (ibid.) expression, 'engraved . . . ever more deeply onto the social and physical landscape' the very difference they sought to remove. The Protestant drama of 'rebirth', say the Comaroffs (ibid.: 33), was meant to be an induction into a 'universal moral community' in which natives would become 'sovereign citizens of empire' (ibid.), one and the same, like everyone else in the universal Protestant community.

Yet this process of flattening out difference was supported by what the authors call a 'grammar of distinctions' that affected the way the colonised 'inhabited their destinies' (ibid.: 25).

It is worth pondering this paradox, which I regard as typical of the poetics of the seam. The 'grammar of distinctions', highly dualist in nature, is noted as evident in colonial discourse *despite* the internal complexity of colonial society. In the Comaroffs' (ibid.) argument, colonial societies tended to be perceived and re-presented, from within, in starkly dualist and oppositional terms that solidified the singularity of, and distance between ruler and ruled, white and black, modernity and tradition. 'The objectification of this order of differences,' they write, 'was intrinsic to the gesture of colonisation itself' (ibid.). This is despite – perhaps even because of – the observable fact that, on the ground, identities increasingly were becoming hybrid and mixed.[11] Such dangerous fluidity of categories was countered by the establishment of a foundational order of representation in which ironclad binaries operated as metatropes in the long and arduous process of inducing new forms of subjectivity in colonised people.[12] It should immediately be noted, first, that the grammar of Manichean inscription – the overwhelming iteration of an order of terms that reinvented people as 'civilised' or 'savage' – was resisted, negotiated, used, and transformed by African subjects and in many cases subverted from within. Second, the colonisers themselves were afflicted by the necessary partiality of their representations and by the unacknowledged but haunting sense of not being quite the universal subjects they thought they were (de Kock, 1996a: 155–159; 1997b: 224). For indigenous subjects, though, discursive resistance in the late nineteenth century was ineluctably 'from within'; only within the seam could such subjects find a speaking position in colonial society. In other words, to become the so-called universal subject of God and Empire, it was necessary first to declare apparent allegiance to a binary scheme and to acknowledge that universal destiny (in Victorian parlance, 'manifest destiny') inhered in a partiality toward Empire's conception of 'civilisation', despite the looming paradox that such partiality was anything but universal. The only available speaking positions within the orthodox colonial order, then, where material gain, status, and political influence were to be won, demanded that 'native' subjects speak in the language of 'civilised' discourse and from within the physical conformity of Victorian apparel. Naturally a speaking position such as this was cramped into the either-or limitations of the seam as a site of self-recognition. But there was little choice in the matter. In the final frontier war of 1877–1888 in the Eastern Cape, for example, military resistance was smashed, and every subsequent act of protest, petition, complaint, or plea was necessarily mediated by the demands of the seam as a site of self-constitution, where alterity had to be transposed into third terms, stitched into something no longer quite itself (just as the coloniser's identity was by now compromised by its perpetual, ever-recurring defence *against* difference).

The issue for colonised subjects who were seeking the necessary legitimation in colonial society to advance socially and economically therefore was no longer whether or not one's identity would be sutured into missionary-colonial versions of personhood, no longer whether or not difference would be translated into the new representations of universal destiny, but simply the manner in which this would be done. And the manner in most cases, after the war option had been exhausted in the Hundred Years' War on the Eastern Cape frontier and in the wake of tumultuous losses of land and sovereignty, was necessarily polite. Hence Sol T. Plaatje, the first black South African novelist in English who is still revered for his acts of civil resistance against British imperialism, felt constrained to respect the ambit of his speaking position when he eulogised, on the occasion of Empire Day 1915, 'the happy reign of Queen Victoria, during which they [Transvaal chiefs and a number of provincial delegates to the Transvaal Native Congress] were led from the thraldom of heathenism and their native darkness into the enjoyments of social, economic, and spiritual benefits through missionary enterprise' (Plaatje 1915; see my companion essay in this volume).

I have written elsewhere (de Kock 1996a: 105–40) of the covert, subversive potential of statements such as these, despite their seeming subservience. The more immediate point I wish to make here is that Plaatje, and many others like him, appeared deliberately to *suppress* difference, suppress the precolonial identity, and recast it into the third term – 'the thraldom of heathenism and their native darkness' – in his rhetorical and, I would argue, strategic reaching after a civil imaginary (which Plaatje here characterises as the 'enjoyments of social, economic and spiritual benefits').[13] As the discursive site of 'rebirth', the civil imaginary is the place where a newly sutured organicism or unity is sought. But its price is a seeming suppression of difference, a suppression such as that so avidly given rhetorical expression by Plaatje in the example above.

Tomes of textual evidence in the record of South African colonial history show just such an apparent stifling of difference in which, on the face of it, indigenous subjects demand, in the name of justice and equality, a paradoxical 'sameness' with other subjects of empire. It is 'a sameness' in the guise of equal civil opportunities as a citizen of empire, a pseudo-universality of being in which the colonised African subject seems willingly to forego claims to cultural difference. Black colonial subjects often regarded such apparent rejection of cultural difference as necessary because to be 'different', within the prevailing discourse in colonial society, meant being less than that putative universal moral subject so assiduously touted by the legions of largely Protestant missionaries and missionary-teachers in the country.[14] Needless to say, employment and status in the civil institutions of colonial society followed from adherence to the civilisational model. In my argument Plaatje, a mission-educated subject who was nonetheless a proto-African nationalist, was thus enfolded in the colonial seam along which difference had been pressed into an uneven alignment with a pseudo-universal model of singularity. The only means open to him to legitimate claims to equal treatment for his people was via an appeal to the foundational 'civil' virtues of empire that had been so closely aligned, by missionaries, with the universal reign of God.

At the same time, however, Plaatje's appeals are embedded in an implicit knowledge of the colonial 'grammar of differences' – he was at this time also campaigning against the notorious Land Act of 1913, whose basis was racist and exclusionary. This is a crucial point to keep in mind when considering the possible meaning(s) of statements by black subjects of missionary education.

Plaatje's markedly strained position strikes me as typical of the poetics of the seam in South African cultural refractions of identity, an example of how the first-person singular begins to seek ways of slipping across or into the seam joining it with the first-person plural. The process, though, manifests a crisis of inscription. In seeming to foreclose the African subject's difference in an appeal to universal Christian virtue, Plaatje is in fact seeking an assurance that he and his brethren will not be *differentiated against*; in other words, his very act of claiming oneness carries with it the knowledge of doubleness, a doubleness that is the defining quality of the representational seam in which Plaatje is caught. His plea is that his people will not be held to a fixed conception of their difference, despite their own disavoval of difference in favor of citizentry in the British Empire. Plaatje's enunciations therefore encode an implicit awareness of the makeshift nature of identity as constituted in cross-cultural representation. Indeed scholars have suggested that the public, rhetorical positions of figures such as Plaatje often encoded complex modalities of subjectivity, in which multiple strands of allegiance to different orders of discourse are evident, despite the fact that in speech, dress, schooling, and general demeanour they appeared to be elitist 'gentlemen' of bourgeois-colonial persuasion (Odendaal 1984: 17–18; Marks 1986: 100).

It seems, then, that public enunciations of identity such as Plaatje's, which professed allegiance to the terms of a sutured identity, nonetheless concealed a mobility of self that shuttled between the paradoxes created when sameness and difference are unevenly pressed together. If people who were demonstrably different from the Victorian gentleman prototype had, at great cost to themselves, been required to put on the starchy garments of such a prototype in the name of a putatively *universal* identity, then they were not easily going to allow themselves to be enclosed in social structures of *fixed* difference – in other words, discrimination or, as the Comaroffs (1997: 25) put it, a submerged or explicit 'grammar of distinctions'. Such structures increasingly confirmed, for people of Plaatje's ilk and for the newly established South African Native National Congress (later to become the African National Congress (ANC)), that the promise of a universal empire of God was being degraded by a discriminating, ethnocentric conception of difference. Yet in this act of defending themselves against hypostatized, ethnocentric difference and claiming for themselves 'universal' subjectivity, they were also implicitly confirming variability, adaptability, and flexibility of identity.

In the long history of civil protest that followed, the ANC tradition of unity and nonracialism was born (cf. Frederikse 1990). This tradition testified to the desire for equal treatment in the modernising, industrial economy of the twentieth century, in which indigenous South Africans could not afford to be sentimental about a romanticised version of precolonial Africa. But also the tradition carried with it the representational strain that occurs when unity and oneness are professed in a place of disunity and difference. Nonracialism necessarily carried with it that crisis of inscription following colonisation, in which difference was seemingly suppressed, first by missionaries (in the interests of universal moral destiny), then by African nationalists (in the interests of a nonracial future). But it carried with it, too, the shadow of doubleness, an unsettling sense of us and them and of here and there, a grammar of distinctions lodged in its stitches of a great world out *there*, a place of science, invention, and discovery, against a locality *here*, a little place where claims of superstition, backwardness, and cultural aridity continued. (This discourse of provincialism was also internalised as a distinction between levels of 'civilisation' within the country, and it has remained with us in one form or another to the present, both in relation to the 'outside' world and in terms of internal stratification.) Paradoxically then, nonracialism has been rooted in, and defined by, an awareness of its opposite.

I believe that it is in the poetics of the seam where one may begin to look for continuity between pre-apartheid negotiations of identity and the attempted 'settlement' of identities in the apartheid era proper. The continuity, that is, might be found despite a seeming reversal of the order of terms from the one period to the next. While the missionary-influenced version of a collective South African identity may have been founded on a suppression of difference in favour of the universal empire of God and Britain, and while the more racist sector of colonial society sought, instead, to keep the natives in their place, the apartheid state officially *reinvented* difference in the name of equality. That this was a wholly spurious version of so-called 'equality' is now common cause, but it was a representation of reality that the apartheid state nonetheless went to enormous lengths to justify in the public domain.

It remains a great irony that, in theory, the apartheid state applied what would today be called a multicultural policy of restoring difference to a collection of 'nations' who, the apartheid ideologues would have argued, had been falsely homogenised in the colonial period as one and the same, as universal humans subject to a single, godly destiny. In a stark perversion of contemporary politics of difference, the white supremacist National Party of South Africa created an order of 'plural nations' with parallel destinies in 'parallel' and semi-autonomous social polities. In theory the Nationalists were trying to restore South Africa to its precolonial geography, creating 'homeland' states that supposedly would eventually become 'independent', sovereign political and social entities. That all this was based on a cynically skewed distribution of land and capital is common knowledge, and that it was one of the great confidence tricks of modern history is equally well known, since people were abandoned to stateless labour reservoirs ('locations') within the 'white' areas of the country. Others, again, were dumped in pseudostates with no economic viability whatsoever. But the more immediate point is that the apartheid design continued the tradition of inscription, the representational crisis upon which the very existence of a *unified* South Africa has always seemed to depend. For it merely took the terms inherited from an earlier, compromised era of English liberalism and changed the pattern of the seam. It never for a moment considered rupturing the seam, restoring the country to its primordial randomness and disunity. Instead, it resutured the conception of organicity in terms of 'difference' rather than 'sameness'. Where an earlier, quasi-liberal era had claimed a spurious oneness whose grammar remained inflected with differentiated orders of value, the South African National Party claimed a fraudulent plurality whose inner workings nonetheless pressed people together in a singularly oppressive unitary statehood.

In the resistance to apartheid, a keen awareness of the doubleness of representation – an awareness that, I believe, implicitly anticipated later theoretical critiques of the sign – led to a deep and enduring suspicion of the idea of formalised difference. In the most influential stream of anti-apartheid resistance, that of the Charterists or Alliance partners now consolidated in South Africa's African National Congress government, nonracialism became a key policy. During the years of resistance to apartheid, an alternative, revolutionary South Africa was represented – for we are here still firmly enclosed in the seam, in the crisis of self-representation – as a place of *non*-difference, a place of equality for all, despite race, class, or gender, and a place where difference is vigorously disavowed in favour of the one, seamlessly open society. Since the country's 'negotiated revolution' and the inception of full democracy in 1994, nonracialism has remained the government's pivotal philosophy, although it has been put under considerable strain by the demands of accelerated equity in all sheres, which necessarily mobilise race as a category.

I shall return in due course to the present-day representation of South Africa as a place of *non*-difference; however, two ancillary points demand mention. First, South Africa as a 'case' seems to offer one of the most acute examples of the crisis of the sign in colonial and postcolonial identity formation in the wake of imperialism. Historically, 'South Africa' as a third-person singular entity came into being only by virtue of tumultuously clashing modalities, the modernity of a globally expanding Western culture intermeshing with an irreconcilable heterogeneity of cultures and epistemologies. It required a series of extraordinarily violent ruptures – genocide of the bushmen and massive slaughter of Nguni-speakers in the frontier wars of the nineteenth century, to name just two examples – before hegemonic political entities preceding the creation of 'South Africa' could come into being.[15] But the violence witnessed on the grounds of the territory was equalled by a violence of representation,[16] a violence of such proportions that it is no wonder contemporary South African cultural politics has experienced what Louise Bethlehem (elsewhere in this issue) calls a 'rhetoric of urgency', a pervasive attempt to weld signifier to signified, to bypass the fraudulent contingencies of the sign and seek a place where things mean what they say. On a primary level the country has witnessed enormous volumes of crassly ethnocentric cross-cultural representation of the kind common to colonial occupations and racist mentalities. In that sense the sign has all too often been used as a stabbing needle. On a secondary level a more subtle and unavoidable doubleness has inhabited every representational act ever made in the efforts to stitch difference into sameness (as in the missionary colonial example) or to pretend that sameness – equality – actually inheres in formalised difference (as in apartheid ideology). My postulate is therefore that a crisis of representation has been endemic to the geographical and cultural conjunction that has become South Africa and that 'it', the country conceived as a third-person singular entity, is a seam that can be undone only at the cost of its existence. Its very nature, its secret life, inheres in the paradoxes of the seam.

Second, it follows that in a place of such interstitial identity, literary culture – the everyday, quotidian texts of self-constitution as well as the more belletristic traditions – will also be characterised by doubleness and representational crisis. That these two elements characterise the work of the country's foremost self-reflexive novelist, J. M. Coetzee, is therefore no accident. Indeed it is only those South African authors who 'hit the seam' as directly and truly as Coetzee and a few others have done (among them Nadine Gordimer, Alan Paton, Es'kia Mphahlele, Dennis Brutus, Athol Fugard, Mongane Wally Serote, Breyten Breytenbach, and André Brink) who get taken up in the world of letters at large – who become global South African writers. Perhaps to be a 'South African writer' in the full sense requires imaginative inhabitation of the seam as a deep symbolic structure. Indeed what has at times disparagingly been referred to as the white South African English 'canon' – Thomas Pringle, Olive Schreiner, Roy Campbell, Pauline Smith, Guy Butler, Alan Paton, Nadine Gordimer, J. M. Coetzee – usually consists of writers who have been intensely preoccupied with cultural doubleness, either of the home (Britain) versus outpost (South Africa) kind, or related to the tortured politics of Black and White and here and there (the *here* of gender and racial oppression and the *there* of a larger, more liberal-cosmopolitan world). Writers in non-English languages, whether Afrikaans or the Sotho or Nguni languages, have not been taken up into global consumption unless their work is available in translation and speaks to the great South African themes of duplicity and social conflict. Seams and boundaries predominate, and hence prominent writers are aware that social and cultural divisions are so deep as to make the organicism of a 'national' literature impossible (Gordimer 1976: 118–19) and a 'great South African novel' unlikely (Coetzee 1983: 74–79).

It therefore should not be surprising that South Africa has been a fertile ground for foundational binary inscription, a place of blatant dualisms, such as civilised and savage, settler and indigene, White and Black, oppressed and privileged, rich and poor. Given the slippery treacheries of signification and identity formation I have suggested, as well as the inherently paradoxical divisiveness of the seam as a site of self-constitution, the binaries always have been to hand. The literature of 'settlement' that comes in the wake of Adamastor struggles to reconcile opposites and irreconcilables. Olive Schreiner's South African classic, *The Story of an African Farm* (1883), for example, finds its form in seeking to conjoin the ameliorative spirit of the liberal novel with a degrading, rapacious colonial society; Pauline Smith's *The Beadle* (1926), as another example, displaces the unsayable conflicts between white and black anterior to land 'settlement' onto the divisions between Boer and Briton (Anthony 1998). During the period of apartheid rule, writers of any note were by definition 'dissident,' and like their predecessors' view, their view of things was starkly divided into home as a scene of debasement, of deformity and misrule, against the bigger picture internationally, a more capaciously conceived humanity, to whom writers could make appeals and to whom they bore witness of an internally unfolding series of social and governmental crimes. Often South African authors were in exile, following the forced division of the country's literature into a home component and an exile counterpart, an inside-outside polarity (Brink 1996: 146; Gray 1979: i). Writing in 1998, Lewis Nkosi still saw what he called an 'unhealed ... split between black and white writing' (1998: 75). In her essays and appeals to the world, the apartheid era's most influential literary opponent for many years, Nadine Gordimer, frequently called upon a standard of universal decency: the country's progressive forces wanted South Africa to cease being exceptional, different from the rest of the 'civilised world'; they wanted it to be the same, to belong again to the family of nations.[17] Meanwhile, the cleavages of 'local' and 'international', of home and exile, became deeply engraved by the cultural boycott of the 1980s (Nixon 1994: 155–72). Ironically, in the decades of isolation from the world at large ushered in by Hendrik Frensch Verwoerd's sundering of South Africa from the British Commonwealth in 1961, 'South African' literature and publishing began to flourish as a result of the artificial hothouse environment created by enforced isolation. Our writers could assume a sense of grave importance by virtue of writing from within one of the great crisis points of the world. They were witnesses to one of the final, most embattled scenes of a global struggle against neocolonialism. South Africa became one of the world's great allegories of racial strife, of the struggle for humane justice in the wake of successive waves of imperial, colonial, and neocolonial misrule.

To return to my main point, then: doubleness and representational crisis have been endemic not only to the higher callings of literature but also to the most everyday acts of identity formation. The country, in all of its various guises as a collective 'state', has been dogged by a crisis of naming, either a naming of people as other than what they might conceive themselves to be, or a naming of oneself in a constitutive (oppositional or identificatory) relation to others. Whether the naming of people was to strip them of one order of difference, in the name of a universal and providential destiny, only to impose a new grammar of *differentiation,* as I suggest happened in the colonial era; whether people named themselves as a singular entity of hardened difference and therefore as a rule unto themselves, despite convergence, as in Afrikaner identity formation; or whether the naming of people was to enclose them in fraudulently hypostatized categories of difference in the guise of equality, as evidenced in the apartheid era, one of the results has been an overwhelming desire, in the struggle against apartheid, for a unitary political identity and for the *suppression* of difference. This desire has been formally translated into the new South African constitution, which does indeed enshrine equality for all regardless of race, gender, or class, does make us all the 'same' legally and constitutionally. In the television broadcasting revolution that ran parallel to the country's democratisation, 'oneness' became a national jingle: '*Simunye* – We Are One!' The 'Simunye' slogan, selling the oneness of the new nation, was heard incessantly on one of the country's main television channels, telling us everyday that we are one and the same.

But we are not, as President Thabo Mbeki sought to remind South Africans in his 'two nations' speech to the South African Parliament in 1998 (cf. Krog 1998: 15).[18] Racial and class cleavages persist. Political rivalries of the past continue to re-emerge. Debates about affirmative action and employment equity cannot but mobilise racial particularity as a category of identity.[19] University campuses and workplaces have continued to witness clashes of a physical and philosophical nature predominantly about the assertion of *black* entitlement, where *black* is broadly defined in the South African manner (Black, Coloured, Indian), but nonetheless exclusionary, black as *against* others.[20] Alternatively, the assault is led by the campaigners for *Afrikaner* identity, Afrikaner as against other forms of identity. Or we have those who see themselves as connected to an 'English' world, either the old motherland England or one of its newer ex-colonies (Australia, New Zealand, Canada, the United States), whose shores continue to beckon for thousands of émigrés and would-be émigrés. We are, I believe, still fully in the seam, still restaging our identities in a place of converging difference – a place where neither oneness nor difference can be maintained without reference to the knowledge of its double, its constitutively cross-hitched character. In such a context representation must bear the strain. '*Simunye* – We Are One' will necessarily be met with a snort of derision or an impatient switch to the next channel. The 'rainbow nation' will necessarily become the butt of acidulous comments by citizens, intellectuals and writers alike. Protestations of primordial Afrikaner exclusivity will be regarded with wry irony, as will claims to liberal innocence among English speakers. People will know better. What endures, it seems, is not a successful suppression of difference – whether to be *one* or to be *none but oneself* – but that shadow of doubleness, that ingrained weariness with unitary representation, with national narratives, whether they offer a singularity of representation insisting on a glorious unity within difference (the 'rainbow' narrative) or differentiated oneness despite convergence (the argument for cultural exclusivity). What endures, it seems, is a sense that identities can never be that singular, that our representations of ourselves will always carry the mark of the seam.

Perhaps what is to be desired is that the value of difference be fully recognised in its guise as *différence*, as a representational differential offering liberation from imprisoning fixations of identity rather than as an imputation of fixity (being told *how* one is different, *how* one is the same). Once the representational basis of the ongoing crises of identity in South Africa is acknowledged, we may be able to shift from disputing *what* it is our fellows say we are to *how* it is that they say such things in the first place. In that case we may qualify the perception of ontological crisis (identity fixation) with the memory that identity has always been contingent upon representation and is likely to remain so. This requires a mobile sense of language and its referential complexities. It strikes me as a great irony, therefore, that anti-intellectualism is rife in South Africa and that the Plain and Simple English movement finds fertile ground for its campaign to install a public discourse of monosyllabic banalities.[21] Instead, we need to cultivate the very mobility of selfhood and representation that I have suggested was evident in the mannered and ambivalent language of Sol T. Plaatje and in many of his compatriots, of all races and persuasions, in the long history of discursive struggle in South African history. This mobility of identity may also account for the seeming contradictions in such a figure as Nelson Mandela, who conjoins a reverence for things British and missionary education with a continuing engagement in polyglot cultural traditions and the politics of postcolonial emancipation.[22] In cultural politics we need to be wary of the teleology of liberal justice, which seemingly culminated in the democratic elections of 1994, holding us to oppressive fixations of oneness and sameness.[23] Nor should we hold ourselves to be absolutely different and therefore occlude mobility of identity or glorify blackness in the way whiteness used to be sanctified, except as a specific contingency of equity consciously adopted as a medium-term measure. Now that representational tyrannies of racial essentialism have been eradicated from the statute books, we should not forget the lessons we have learned about the paradoxes and complexities of representation in a place of continuing convergence and difference. Ironically, in a country where historical materialist intellectuals have sought to belittle the poststructuralist critique of the sign as irresponsible to the demands of 'real' struggles, the sign has been an exceptionally contested and abusive item of exchange.[24] If ever there was a need for vigilant scepticism about the verities of reference and for that vigilance to continue beyond the illusions of revolutionary unity, it is here, enfolded in the convergence of identity and difference, where every protestation of singularity (whether of difference or of sameness), every representational fixity is felt in the seams of language, which is perhaps after all our only common *doppelgänger*, our most persistent, most betraying comrade. And so my only recourse to the first-person plural, my only path from 'I' to 'we' or 'us', is via this knowledge. 'We' is a tenuously created category, stitched together with deep ambivalences of signification. May 'we' at least remember *that*, if nothing else. May 'we' be different from ourselves, if South Africans are allowed to be; if they are to be the sole arbiters of their identities. But the global imaginary will come back to haunt them. Just as South Africans have, over the past three centuries, fashioned themselves in response to projections of a bigger world out there, so their collective struggles have come to assume a certain allegorical significance for that world. At a colloquium on the theme 'Living Difference: Towards a Society of Communities' at the University of the Witwatersrand in Johannesburg in August 1998, such figures as Richard Rorty, Nancy Fraser, and Jörn Rüsen forcefully suggested to South African delegates that they, as South Africans, *needed* a master narrative, a 'rainbow nation' type of governing motif that would frame everyone's energies within the miraculous new nation. At one point the venerable Professor Rüsen thundered, 'It is imperative for us that you succeed!' And therein lay the key. For many reasons, it is imperative for *others* that South Africans succeed at the democratic, multiracial miracle that *they* (the non-South Africans) have yet to see realised in their own countries. South Africa must carry this burden of moral example, just as in earlier times it carried the burden of having to be a moral pariah of the larger world. And so the dismay on the faces of international guests at the colloquium was palpable as South African speaker after speaker, black and white, expressed disillusionment with or sounded warnings about precisely the new master narrative that the assembled global academics were pressing on them. This master narrative amounted to little more than the project of the 'new nation' in South Africa. For the South African speakers at the colloquium, the memory of master narratives (the grand designs of colonialism, of apartheid, and of other forms of forcible conjunction or separation) was nothing short of bloody nightmares, literally. Many South African delegates had misgivings about a virulent ('affirmative') counterracism, about corruption, and about the new intellectual orthodoxy of the 'African Renaissance', which for some looked like a prelude to a one-party state, a government by wealthy elites that abandons the poor to market forces in a relentlessly globalising economy. These and other concerns about the direction the new nation was taking were regarded by the international delegates as misstruck, mistimed notes in that otherwise euphonious symphony of the democratic 'miracle' in South Africa. And so returns the spectre of oppressive representational singularity governing perceptions of the country. The *desire* from without to believe in that unlikely 'miracle' can be marshalled in support of a frightening orthodoxy within the country, in which 'those who are not with us are against us' and in which the totalising fictions (and factions) of the nation are given credence above the other lessons South Africans by now should have learned: namely, that they have been constituted in a fold, a doubleness of representation that should forever give them pause about any form of imagined singularity. Let doubt return. Let the tatty, patchwork 'rainbow nation' (in Breyten Breytenbach's description, a 'pot of shit') become once more, in representation, the normal thing that it is in the streets, the shacks, and the bloody intellectual parlours of the old 'new' South Africa.

3   Contributions to This Volume

As if to confirm the predominant position of the contested object of representation in South African cultural life and the impossibility of reducing it to any particular master narrative of national meaning, Pippa Skotnes, in '"Civilised off the Face of the Earth": Museum Display and the Silencing of the /Xam', illustrates to what extent representations of identity can, in the South African context, eclipse the country's 'reality' almost completely. In the case of the bushmen, arguably the 'first South Africans', this is a literal truth. Bushmen were all but wiped out by the late nineteenth century in an orgy of ethnocentric massacre (they were hunted down and shot like dogs), and the continued existence of a bushman culture – the trace of its memory – swiftly became a matter of intermediation and written record. Skotnes's essay shows how South Africa's 'seamed' (and seeming) condition ineluctably came into play the moment an attempt was made to rescue something of the near-destroyed culture: it took two European intermediaries, working across entirely different language systems and transposing orality into the written medium, to make the attempt to resuture bushman culture into a semblance of its previous state. Symbolically this is perhaps one of the most central gestures of the 'South African' condition: the attempt (as described earlier in this essay) to bring a certain order of composure, of settlement, to a place of profound difference. However, as

Skotnes so carefully explains, the strain of this particular act of suturing would always be felt. It would be felt in the wretched politics of cultural (mis)appropriation, in the misrecognition of identities, and in the uneven alignment of people and power held together by the precarious fabric of (selective) cultural representation. Skotnes's essay is crucial because, to a large extent, it conveys the sense of a root condition in South African cultural practice from time immemorial through to contemporary engagements.

In a similar vein Peter Merrington's essay, 'A Staggered Orientalism: The Cape-to-Cairo Imaginary', presents a detailed case history in which global discourses effectively wipe clean all indigenous signifying systems in southern Africa and provide instead a new imaginary overlay or, in the author's words, a 'colonial projection.' This immense and quite spectacular imposition, which Merrington describes in terms of fantasy and pageant, is also ultimately an act of longing for a 'national sign system'. Yet even here multiple threads and lines of influence challenge the metanarrative in Hegel's tableau of history as a march of progress from civilisation to civilisation and from continent to continent. Merrington's essay demonstrates in great detail just how copious and varied were the cultural fantasies that reconfigured South Africa in terms of a global imaginary and how pervasive the representational catalogues of imperial imposition were, so much so that the Cape-to-Cairo idea continues to exercise a hold even on contemporary imaginations. Yet the Cape-to-Cairo route remains essentially symbolic rather than feasibly geographic. It has long functioned as a kind of code for imperial signifying systems that imprinted themselves so deeply upon the face of Africa that nothing could ever remove them entirely.

In view of this long history of skewed signification, it is not surprising that the literature of political engagement under apartheid manifested a desire to bypass the contingencies of the sign. Indeed as Louise Bethlehem argues, a 'rhetoric of urgency' came to characterise South African literary criticism: what Bethlehem describes as the 'trope-of-truth' quickly becomes the 'trope-as-truth'. Bethlehem's essay provides a long-overdue critique of the widespread attempt to effect closure between the word and the world in South African literary criticism – in Bethlehem's description, a 'stenographic bent' that delivers a practice of 'representational literalism'. Such a practice has debilitating consequences in that the mediatory function of language is made to atrophy in the interests of social agency. Dangerously, History becomes a stable referent. The agendas of Marxist and/or liberal critics are seemingly safeguarded by the retrieval of History as an unmediated referent, but in the process language is once again instrumentalised. Bethlehem's quite revelatory critique brings one to the realisation that the earlier, imperial fantasies of imposition are not all that far removed from supposedly 'radical' attempts by critics of apartheid to 'weld' signifier to signified and to circumvent the lateral slopes of signification. However, Bethlehem persuasively reads the 'Need' of South African English literary criticism to invoke the 'immediately compelling, compellingly unmediated' as 'Desire': in this case, the desire for a kind of ethical agency in criticism that is not overly involved with the complexities and that cannot countenance the possible opacities of representation as understood by poststructuralism. Yet this fear of the vertiginous possibilities of a further deferral of meaning renders such criticism blind to the greater faults in and complicities of the field as a whole

My own essay, 'Sitting for the Civilisation Test: The Making(s) of a Civil Imaginary in Colonial South Africa', explores precisely some of the complicities of the 'English' project in colonial South Africa. The essay reviews the paradox that acculturated black South Africans under the colonial order were compelled to look to English as a site of universal selfhood in the image of Empire, lest they be consigned to 'native' or 'tribal' backwardness by the prevailing registers of social Darwinism. English was the site, I argue, of a civil imaginary, yet it also encoded a potentially damaging colonising ideology. How, the essay asks, did educated black South African subjects navigate their way between a more global imaginary of freedom and universal justice, implicit in the claims of empire on the one hand, and on the other a colonising ethic inherent in the actual deployment of English rule in the empire's territories. The essay argues that conventional notions of postcolonial oppositionality are unable to provide an adequate explanation for this paradox, in which identity politics were often based on the desire for Western acculturation instead of resistance to it. However, such identification with the 'colonial mirror' reinvoked the founding claims and the millenarian promise of the project of 'civilisation' in such a way as to act as a site of antagonism and a more subtle edge than outright opposition. In this way some of the brutal dualities of segregationist discourse were undermined.

The 'colonial mirror' is also seen to provide a few nasty surprises in Jonathan Crewe's articulate response to a white psychoanalyst's reading of the 'mind' of a black subject in South Africa in the early part of the century. Crewe's essay, '*Black Hamlet*: Psychoanalysis on Trial in South Africa', delineates a deeply ironical situation in which a universalising Freudian psychoanalysis, while apparently placing a native subject's mind under scrutiny, actually puts itself on trial not only methodologically and epistemologically but politically and morally as well. In Crewe's analysis, under South African conditions analytic interrogation comes uncomfortably close to police interrogation, and as the anomalous position of the analyst in propounding a global, universalising discourse in a situation of acute repression becomes more pronounced, the tables are turned. The human recognition putatively conferred on the black subject, concurrent with a Hamlet identification, increasingly becomes the recognition sought by the analyst as an alien. 'In the very act of invoking a Eurocentric, universalising psychoanalysis,' Crewe writes, 'to which [Frantz] Fanon would later object for its erasure of cultural and political difference, [Wulf] Sachs [the analyst-author] subjects the universal to powers of cultural contingency, mobility, and even locality.' The results, in Crewe's conclusion, are revelatory in a way that speaks volumes about the paradoxical refractions of global discourse under conditions of unexpected cultural contingency.

If the imposition of an oppressive psychoanalytic interrogation in the name of healing is one problematic area, another is the insistence by literary critics that black writing under apartheid and beyond has been trapped within a narrow 'realist' literalism shorn of literary experimentalism. This is the critical shibboleth that David Attwell confronts

– and convincingly refutes – in his key essay, 'The Experimental Turn in Black South African Fiction'. Taking as read Bethlehem's point that ethical imperatives have often led South African critics into an impoverishingly instrumentalist view of literature, Attwell demonstrates that black writers themselves have appropriated – and refashioned – experimental modes of fictional narrative in their quest to recalibrate political and historical agency for their own purposes. Attwell shows that the act of disregarding or failing to see what he calls 'the experimental line' in black South African fiction is demeaning and inaccurate. He argues, in addition, that such experimentalism is not merely a repetition of the subject-construction of European literature, but carries with it a 'posthumanist historicity'. Attwell's essay marks a significant correction in what has become an embarrassingly stock-in-trade conception of black South African fiction. It is a correction that is long overdue.

Another, similar but distinct reappropriation of existent representational modes occurs in the work of Breyten Breytenbach, where the institutional monolith of Afrikaans power is 'translated' – both into English and back into Afrikaans's bastardised origins. This is the view of Simon Lewis, whose 'Tradurre e Tradire: The Treason and Translation of Breyten Breytenbach' carefully sketches the background, context, and significance of Breytenbach's Afrikaner dissidence. If translation is betrayal, as the Italian idiom tradurre e tradire suggests, then the question, according to Lewis, is whether or not betrayal can be an act of translation. For the author, Breytenbach's work exemplifies a condition of cultural/political appropriation facing all Afrikaans writers. To write in Afrikaans is to be 'seen as' belonging, to have one's work assimilated to a compromised signifying system. Although Breytenbach continued to use Afrikaans, he also began 'translating' Afrikaans content into English prose as an act of betrayal against appropriation by monolithic cultural and political forces. Lewis concludes that Breytenbach has performed meaningful work in his various acts of stripping away and reassembling notions of identity as an Afrikaans dissident writer.

Dirk Klopper, in 'Narrative Time and the Space of the Image: The Truth of the Lie in Winnie Madikizela-Mandela's Testimony before the Truth and Reconciliation Commission', considers the possibility that South Africa's Truth and Reconciliation Commission (TRC) may have operated in a manner not dissimilar to Walter Benjamin's 'angel of history' in that an incapacitating melancholia (fixation on the wreckage of the past) characterises its dream of a redeemed mankind. The angel of history, Klopper argues, both invokes and punishes the desire for imaginary plenitude, endlessly reiterating the catastrophic events severing him from paradise. For Klopper, one of the most interesting points of splitting in the discourse of the TRC occurs in the testimony of Winnie Makidizela-Mandela, former wife of Nelson Mandela, who was associated with grave crimes in the course of South Africa's political struggle against apartheid. Two frames of reference became evident, argues Klopper: an appeal to familial/tribal/ethnic plenitude on the one hand, and on the other, the assumptions surrounding the modern subject, amenable to narrative and rational logic. By means of a linear teleology, the TRC narrative tried to bring closure to this threatening ambivalence and in so doing sought transcendence for the fragmented South African body politic. However, Klopper raises the possibility that the ANC, South Africa's ruling party, was compelled to sacrifice Makidizela-Mandela in its quest to heal this rupture. In her silence, he writes, the ANC found its speech. But in such a process the spectre of the double does not disappear, and reconciliation is compromised. Returning to the notion of melancholia, Klopper concludes that perhaps only through elegy can melancholia be turned into mourning. However, where the sense of loss exceeds verbalisation, there is only what Derrida calls 'an incinerating blaze where nothingness appears'.

It is to the post-apartheid scene of competing popular cultures that Loren Kruger and Patricia Watson Shariff turn in their essay, '"Shoo – This Book Makes Me to Think!" Education, Entertainment and "Life Skills" Comics in South Africa'. As the authors argue, the clear-cut opposition between 'state' and 'the people', so sustaining to the earlier political struggle, has given way to varied forms, practices, and habits of consumption, such that the designation 'the people' has become acutely problematic. South Africans, the authors argue, now have the opportunity to redefine the popular dimension of education and entertainment and to mediate in different ways between the understanding of cultural practices as global, metropolitan, or urban. The essay looks at the use of comics – two projects in particular – in nonformal education, and it raises important issues concerning the deceptive binary of 'local' and 'global'. Kruger and Watson Shariff argue that 'theoretical' or 'global' implications of 'local' conditions should not be seen to eclipse the 'local' as though it were merely a site for 'empirical' material. Indeed the virtue of Kruger and Watson Shariff's essay is that it shows that educational literacy is hardly a panacea or 'passport to success' but rather a means of reinventing identity through mediation and intervention. Localisations such as 'rural' and 'urban' or 'global' and 'local' often fail to account for unpredictable choices actually made by people who shuttle discursively between and around such imaginary locales. In their examination of the 'edutaining' graphic story, the authors draw attention to a significant degree of tension between manipulation and communication and between critical intervention and outside imposition in the staging of projects that seek to conscientise people via popular media. Ultimately, they argue, the production, distribution, and consumption of these goods contribute to a more differentiated understanding of modernity.

The final essay in this volume, Sonja Laden's '"Making the Paper Speak Well", or, the Pace of Change in Consumer Magazines for Black South Africans', also finds its focus in forms of popular culture, here the consumer magazine targeted at black middle-class South Africans. Laden regards such magazines as significant 'cultural tools' in which urban, middle-class repertoires are codified, disseminated, and legitimised for and by black South Africans. Examining magazines such as *Drum*, *Bona*, *Tribute*, and others, Laden makes the case that consumer magazines facilitate and help define sociocultural identity and change. The 'sociosemiotic work' of such magazines, Laden argues, goes far beyond their immediate or apparent use value. Neither should such magazines be regarded as a form of cultural imperialism. Instead, argues Laden, they constitute a kind of 'local knowledge.' Because they enable one to trace practices that may be regarded as part of a social 'unconscious', the magazines offer more acute insight into the dialectical workings of sociocultural entities than do, for example, overtly political publications. Moreover the manner in which magazines combine verbal and visual modes of representation provides a means for integrating and transforming oral traditions, such as public debate, oral poetry and song, storytelling, and historical narrative, into literate modes of print culture.

Laden's argument, like that of Kruger and Watson Shariff, consolidates a frequent theme in this issue as a whole: that the dialectics of South Africa in the 'global imaginary' speak of reversals and paradoxes rather than straight development. Several of the essays in this volume demonstrate a persistent rejection in South African life and cultural practice of simple binaries or trajectories of 'global' influence vis-à-vis 'local' culture, despite the fact that, as a colonial dependency, the country in its earlier forms came into being in the clasp of the predictable imperial dichotomies. If this book helps invigorate revisionary perspectives on less obvious complexities of cultural articulation in a global frame and on the specificities of the South African case, then it will have served a useful purpose.

Notes

1   See, for example, Gray (1979: 13); Van Wyk Smith (1990: i–iii); Chapman (1996: xx); Wade (1996: 1–9); and Jolly and Attridge (1998: 1).

2   See the book that grew out of this conference, Smit, van Wyk and Wade 1996.

3   See, for example, Crehan 1996; de Kock 1997a; Gray 1999.

4   See my position paper, 'Becoming Different from Ourselves' (de Kock 1997b), and *Civilising Barbarians* (de Kock 1996a). See also Robert Thornton (1996: 150), 'The politics of boundaries, and the boundaries of the political, and of the political community, all combine in South Africa to create a discourse that goes well beyond the political to the meta-political.'

5   For an overview of studies in this regard see Opland 1983: 32.

6   This formulation is partly borrowed from Worden 1994: 7. It should be noted that precolonial cultures persisted into the colonial period.

7   See Louise Shabat Bethlehem (1998), who deals with processes of homogenisation and erasure at length in her doctoral thesis on literary historiography in South Africa. See also my critiques of literary historiography that seek emphatic 'coverage' (de Kock 1996b, 1997a).

8   Famously, see Legassick 1980.

9   Thornton (1996: 150) writes: 'South African identities cross-cut each other in multiple ways and in multiple contexts. There is no fundamental identity that any South African clings to in common with all, or even most other South Africans.'

10   This is the gist of Dipesh Chakrabarty's 1996 argument that difference is represented only by virtue of the violence done to its integrity by rendering it as something other than itself – a third term.

11   See, for example, the case cited by Charles van Onselen (1996: 351): 'Jack Adamson was an "English" Afrikaner and Kas Maine an Afrikanerised MoFokeng. Paul Molapo, Piet Phopho and Jantjie Nku, respectively a MoTshweneng, a MoTswana and an UmXhosa – as their first names and religious affiliations indicated – were already partly deracinated and Afrikanerised. As usual on highveld farms, time and social isolation undermined notions of cultural purity.'

12   See de Kock 1996a.

13   See my essay elsewhere in this volume, which deals extensively with the idea of a 'civil imaginary.'
14   For a full treatment of this subject see de Kock 1996a.
15   For general history see Peires 1981, 1989 and Mostert 1992.
16   This is the underlying theme of de Kock 1996a.
17   See, for example, Gordimer 1989: 90–91.
18   Results of the first census after the 1994 elections – held in1996 – showed what the Johannesburg newspaper called 'a land still divided' (*Johannesburg Star*, October 21, 1998). Releasing the results, former South African president Nelson Mandela was reported as saying the statistics showed 'a society in which the lines between rich and poor [are] the historical lines of a racially divided society.'
19   The Employment Equity Act of 1998, for example, introduces racially defined employee quotas for large businesses.
20   See, for example, the comments of Peter Vundla, a leading black South African executive in the media industry. Vundla is quoted in *After Hours* (supplement to *Business Day*, July 24–26, 1998: 7) as saying: 'Apartheid was about racial domination in all spheres and race was at the cornerstone of the apartheid policy. How do you undo that without making race a cornerstone of transformation?'
21   See, for example, Jane-Anne Hobbs, 'Say It in Plain and Simple English,' *After Hours*, (Supplement to *Business Day*), June 19–21, 1998: 1. The strength of this movement is dubious, but the fact that its opinions were given front-page prominence in a leisure supplement to a national daily is evidence enough of the attractiveness of its ideas to media executives.
22   See my discussion in de Kock 1996a (195–96 and Note 4).
23   See my discussion of this problem in de Kock 1997a.
24   See, for example, Nicholas Visser (1993: 19), who sees 'postness' as 'purely gestural', '[substituting] textual for practical political endeavour'; and Kelwyn Sole (1997: 147), in whose opinion South African postcolonial scholars allow 'areas of structural conflict' to be 'downplayed'.

References

Anthony, Loren
    1998 'Buried Narratives: Representations of Pregnancy and Burial in South African Farm Novels.' M. A. diss., University of South Africa.
Barrow, John
    1801 *An Account of Travels into the Interior of Southern Africa* (London: Cadell and Davies).
Bethlehem, Louise Shabat
    1998 'Literary Historiographic Discourse Under Apartheid: 1976–1985.' Ph.D. diss., Tel Aviv University.
Bhabha, Homi K.
    1994 *The Location of Culture* (London: Routledge).
Breytenbach, Breyten
    1998 *Dog Heart: A Travel Memoir* (Cape Town: Human and Rousseau).
Brink, André
    1973 *Kennis van die Aand* (Cape Town: Buren).
    1975 *Looking on Darkness* (New York: Morrow).
    1996 *Reinventing a Continent: Writing and Politics in South Africa 1982–1995* (London: Secker and Warburg).
Brink, André, and J. M. Coetzee, eds.
    1986 *A Land Apart: A South African Reader* (London and Boston: Faber).
Buchan, John
    1910 *Prester John* (London: T. Nelson and Sons).

Chakrabarty, Dipesh
  1996 'Realist Prose and the Problem of Difference: The Rational and the Magical in Subaltern Studies.'
  Paper presented at the Shakespeare-Postcoloniality Conference, University of the Witwatersrand, Johannesburg, July.

Chapman, Michael
  1996 *South African Literatures* (London: Longman).

Coetzee, J. M.
  1983 'The Great South African Novel', *Leadership* 2 (4): 74-79.
  1988 *White Writing: On the Culture of Letters in South Africa* (New Haven: Radix and Yale University Press).

Comaroff, John L., and Jean Comaroff
  1997 *Revelation and Revolution: The Dialectics of Modernity on a South African Frontier,* vol. 2 (Chicago: University of Chicago Press).

Crehan, Stewart
  1996 'Broken English,' *Southern African Review of Books* 18(4): 16–17.

Crewe, Jonathan
  1997 'Recalling Adamastor: Literature as Cultural Memory in "White" South Africa'.
  Paper presented at the Languages of Poetry Conference, University of the Witwatersrand, Johannesburg, August.

De Kock, Leon
  1996a *Civilising Barbarians: Missionary Narrative and African Textual Response in Nineteenth-Century South Africa* (Johannesburg: Witwatersrand University Press and Lovedale Press).
  1996b 'The Pursuit of Smaller Stories: Reconsidering the Limits of Literary History in South Africa', in *Rethinking South African Literary History,* edited by Johannes A. Smit, Johan van Wyk, and Jean-Philippe Wade, 85–92 (Durban: Y Press).
  1997a 'An Impossible History: Michael Chapman's *Southern African Literatures*', *English in Africa* 24 (1): 103–17.
  1997b 'Becoming Different from Ourselves'. Panel discussion paper presented at Literary Studies at the Crossroads, University of South Africa, Pretoria, February. Published in *Journal of Literary Studies/Tydskrif vir Literatuurwetenskap* 13 (1/2): 223–26.

Deleuze, Gilles, and Félix Guattari
  1988 *A Thousand Plateaus: Capitalism and Schizophrenia* translated by Brian Massumi (London: Athlone).

Dhlomo, H. I. E.
  1935 *The Girl Who Killed to Save: Nongquase the Liberator* (Lovedale: Lovedale Press).

Drayson, Alfred W.
  1862 *Tales at the Outspan; or, Adventures in the Wild Regions of Southern Africa* (London: Saunders).

Du Toit, André
  1983 'No Chosen People: The Myth of the Calvinist Origins of Afrikaner Nationalism and Racial Ideology', *American Historical Review* 88 (4): 920–52.

Fitzpatrick, Percy
  1897 *The Outspan: Tales from South Africa* (London: William Heinemann).

Frederikse, Julie
  1990 *The Unbreakable Thread: Non-Racialism in South Africa* (Johannesburg: Ravan).

Gordimer, Nadine
  1976 'English-Language Literature and Politics in South Africa', in *Aspects of South African Literature,* edited by Christopher Heywood, 99–120 (London and New York: Heinemann).
  1989 *The Essential Gesture: Writing, Politics and Places*, edited by Stephen Clingman (London: Penguin)

Gray, Stephen

    1979 *Southern African Literature: An Introduction* (Cape Town: David Philip).

    1980 Camoens and the Poetry of South Africa. Camoens Annual Lectures no. 1 (Johannesburg: Oppenheimer Institute for Portuguese Studies).

    1989 'Some Problems of Writing Historiography in Southern Africa', *Literator* 10 (2): 16–24.

    1999 'Southern African Literatures' (Review of Chapman, *Southern African Literatures*), *Research in African Literatures* 30 (1): 207–15.

Haggard, H. Rider

    1886 *King Solomon's Mines* (New York: Cassell).

    1887 *She: A History of Adventure* (London: Macdonald).

Jolly, Rosemary, and Derek Attridge, eds.

    1998 *Writing South Africa: Literature, Apartheid, and Democracy, 1970–1995* (Cambridge: Cambridge University Press).

Krog, Antjie

    1988 'Risk Is the First Step to Reconciliation', *Johannesburg Star*, July 24, 15.

Legassick, Martin

    1980 'The Frontier Tradition in South African Historiography', in *Economy and Society in Pre-Industrial South Africa*, edited by Shula Marks and Anthony Atmore, 44-79 (London: Longman).

Marks, Shula

    1986 *The Ambiguities of Dependence in South Africa: Class, Nationalism, and the State in Twentieth-century Natal* (Johannesburg: Ravan).

Moffat, Robert

    1842 *Missionary Labour Scenes in Southern Africa* (London: John Snow).

Mostert, Noel

    1992 *Frontiers: The Epic of South Africa's Creation and the Tragedy of the Xhosa People* (London: Jonathan Cape).

Nixon, Rob

    1994 *Homelands, Harlem and Hollywood: South African Culture and the World Beyond* (New York and London: Routledge).

Nkosi, Lewis

    1998 'Postmodernism and Black Writing in South Africa', in Jolly and Attridge 1998: 75–90.

Odendaal, André

    1984 'Mayibuye I Afrika Nakwimbali Yelizwe: Towards Decolonising the History of Early African Politics in South Africa.' Paper presented at a departmental seminar, Department of History, University of South Africa, Pretoria.

Opland, Jeff

    1983 *Xhosa Oral Poetry: Aspects of a Black South African Tradition* (Cambridge: Cambridge University Press).

Peires, J. B.

    1981 *The House of Phalo: A History of the Xhosa People in the Days of Their Independence* (Johannesburg: Ravan).

    1989 *The Dead will Arise* (Johannesburg: Ravan).

Philip, Dr John

    1828 *Researches in South Africa* (London: Duncan).

Plaatje, Sol T.

    1915 'The late Allan King', *African World Annual* December. Reprinted in *English in Africa* 3(2): 26–27 (1976).

1930 *Mhudi: An Epic of South African Native Life a Hundred Years Ago* (Lovedale: Lovedale Press).

Pratt, Mary Louise

1992 *Imperial Eyes: Travel Writing and Transculturation* (London: Routledge).

Pringle, Thomas

1834 *African Sketches* (London: Edward Moxon).

Reader's Digest, eds.

1973 *South African Short Stories: A Selected Quintet* (Cape Town: Reader's Digest).

Scully W C

1898 *Kafir Stories* (London: Unwin).

Smit, Johannes A., Johan van Wyk, and Jeans-Philippe Wade, eds.

1996 *Rethinking South African Literary History* (Durban: Y Press).

Sole, Kelwyn

1997 'South Africa Passes the Posts', *Alternation* 4 (1): 116–51.

Thornton, Robert

1996 'The Potentials of Boundaries in South Africa: Steps Towards a Theory of the Social Edge', in *Post-colonial Identities in Africa*, edited by Richard Werbner and Terence Ranger (London: Zed Books).

Van Onselen, Charles

1996 *The Seed is Mine: The Life of Kas Maine, a South-African Sharecropper, 1894–1985* (New York: Hill and Wang; Cape Town: David Philip).

Van Wyk Smith, Malvern, ed.

1988 *Shades of Adamastor: An Anthology of Verse* (Grahamstown: Institute for the Study of English in Africa).

1990 *Grounds of Contest: A Survey of South African English Literature* (Cape Town: Jutalit).

1996 'White Writing/Writing Black: The Anxiety of Non-Influence', in Smit, van Wyk, and Wade 1996: 71–84.

Visser, Nicholas

1993 'The Epoch of Post-Everything', *Southern African Review of Books*, September/October, 19–20.

Wade, Jean-Philippe

1996 'Introduction: Disclosing the Nation,' in Smit, van Wyk, and Wade 1996: 1–9.

Worden, Nigel

1994 *The Making of Modern South Africa: Conquest, Segregation, and Apartheid* (London: Blackwell).

TWO

'Civilised off the Face of the Earth': Museum Display and the Silencing of the /Xam

Pippa Skotnes

When I was a child, my parents took me to see the bushman diorama at the South African Museum. This is a collection of exquisitely cast and painted plaster figures enacting a domestic scene in a nineteenth-century hunter-gatherer camp. It is framed by a finely painted stretch of Dolerite Mountains lit by a winter sun on a karoo morning. I remembered it as a compelling, dramatic scene – a fantastic glimpse into a primitive and silent past forever preserved in a small, dark hall in Cape Town. Many years later I hiked in the Poelela river valley in the Drakensberg Mountains and slept in the caves that were the last retreat of the bushmen in the eastern part of the country. These shelters were painted with the bushmen's own images of their destruction – British soldiers on horseback firing rifles and, near them, the white-bodied figure of the shaman snapping

South African Museum diorama, a bushman camp set in the Karoo around 1800

his fingers to harness the magical power that in the end, was powerless to avert his inevitable, tragic annihilation.

Not only did these images frame my encounter with representations of and by the Bushmen; they also represented the two extremes in the whole corpus of bushmen representations. At the one end, the interests of scientific enquiry and public curiosity (twinned with the needs of colonialism and later of apartheid) were served by alienating the bushmen from history and therefore from humanity. At the other, far less visible end, the bushmen left their own contrasting trace of how they saw themselves – as garnering all their political and symbolic power to participate, through resistance, in the progress of their own (and South Africa's) history. These images, products of the history and the political and scientific interests of the time, became inextricably bound up with the circulation of ideas about the bushmen and thus had an enormous impact on their fate. Just as Robert Gordon (1992a) argues that the 1980 film *The Gods Must Be Crazy*, which played to packed houses in the United States, South Africa, and elsewhere, had a disastrous impact on bushmen in Namibia, so too did nineteenth-century representations of bushmen play a devastating role in developing South African policy toward bushmen.

EGYPTIAN HALL,
PICCADILLY.

EXHIBITING DAILY,
The most Extraordinary

EXHIBITION OF ABORIGINES,

THE

BOSJESMANS,

Or *BUSH PEOPLE,*

They are the most SINGULAR SPECIMENS of that decreasing

RACE OF HUMAN BEINGS,

THE BUSHMEN OF SOUTH AFRICA,

CONSISTING OF

TWO MEN, TWO WOMEN, and A BABY,

Of the Bosjeman Tribe, from the interior of South Africa; a race that, from their wild habits, could never before be induced to visit a place of civilization. This opportunity of gratifying the man of science and the student in Zoology has only been obtained by great personal exertion on the part of the gentlemen who have brought them to England, at an immense outlay of capital. On the passage to Europe a baby was born at sea, thus adding to the great interest that must be excited by their appearance. From Moffat the Missionary's Work, on Southern Africa, page 53:—"Poor Bushman! thy hand has been against every one, and every one's hand against thee. For generations past they have been hunted like partridges in the mountains. Deprived of what nature had made their own, they became desperate, wild, fierce, and indomitable in their habits. Hunger compels them to feed upon everything edible. Ixias, wild garlic, mysembry anthamams, the core of aloes, gum of acarias, and other plants and berries, some of which are extremely unwholesome, constitute their fruits: whilst almost every kind of living creature is eagerly devoured, lizards, locusts, and grasshoppers not excepted. The poisonous as well as innoxious serpents they roast and eat. They carefully extract their bags or reservoirs of poison, with which they cover the points of their arrows."

From the "TIMES," May 19th, 1847.

"THE BOSJESMANS, OR BUSH PEOPLE."—A group of five of these 'interesting' people, was exhibited on Monday Evening at Exeter Hall, Strand, to a large assembly of the curious, and a lecture delivered on their nature, properties, propensities, and habits, by Dr. KNOX. They were landed in Liverpool by the brig, Fanny, Captain Wheeler, and this is their first appearance in Europe. Without saying that Europe will be, or not be, profited by their arrival, it may be affirmed that nothing, even in this age of 'strange and unnatural' importations is more curious than this stunted family of African Dwarfs. In appearance they are little above the monkey tribe, and scarcely better than the mere brutes of the field. They are continually crouching, warming themselves by the fire, chattering or growling, smoking, &c. They are sullen, silent, and savage—mere animals in propensity, and worse than animals in appearance. The exhibition is, however, one that will and ought to attract. The admirers of 'pure nature' can confirm their speculations on unsophisticated man, and woman also, or repudiate them, by a visit to these specimens. They are well calculated to remove prejudices, and make people think aright of the times when 'wild in his woods the noble savage ran.' In short, a more miserable set of human beings—for human they are, nevertheless—was never seen. They are about to perform, at the future exhibitions of them, some curious feats of activity, and of their modes of attack and defence, which will be worth attention."

Hours of Exhibition, from 11 in the Morning until 9 in the Evening.

ADMISSION, ONE SHILLING.

Poster of a kind common at the time in Europe, advertising the exhibition of exotic British subjects from distant colonies

Bushmen had been on show since the early nineteenth century and had been the recipients of a good deal of bad press. They were billed as 'bush people', curious creatures, the 'connecting link between man and the monkey',[1] one of 'the Wonders of the World', whose 'attempts to communicate with each other is more like the noise of Machinery or the Chattering of Monkeys than the language of Men'.[2] In 1858, following a series of such exhibits in England, Charles Dickens wrote:

> I call him a savage, and I call a savage something desirable to be civilised off the face of the earth. Think of the Bushmen. Think of the two men and two women who have been exhibited about England for some years. Are the majority of persons – who remember the horrid little leader of that party in his festering bundle of hides, with his filth and his antipathy to water, and his straddled legs, and his odious eyes shaded by his brutal hand, and his cry of 'Qu-u-u-u-aa!' (Bosjesman for something desperately insulting I have no doubt) – conscious of an affectionate yearning towards that noble savage, or is it idiosyncratic in me to abhor, detest, abominate, and abjure him! . . . the world will be all the better when his place knows him no more.[3]

Lying somewhere between the writer's pen and the painter's vision is an archive that became the focus of my own attempts to come to grips with who the bushmen were and what their paintings meant. I wanted, as did Stephen Greenblatt (1988:1), to speak with the dead. But these were the doubly dead, for all bushmen languages and the cultures they articulated were virtually wiped out by the early part of the twentieth century, and they had left so few clues as to what their painting symbolised and so little textual trace of themselves as to make it almost impossible to recreate a conversation. In fact, almost nothing at all would be left of the ideas of the bushmen were it not for the work in the 1870s of an English teacher, Lucy Lloyd, and German philologist Wilhelm Bleek. In the course of their remarkable and unique collaboration, Bleek and Lloyd acted as go-betweens, producing text from the performances of six /Xam bushmen prisoners, who knew they would not survive into the next century but who wanted their stories to.

Bleek and Lloyd had come to Natal and settled near the Drakensberg at the time the bushmen there were making their last paintings. In Natal, as in the Cape, colonists were struggling to wipe out bushman resistance, and as stories of bushman raids on white-owned property and their retreats into the mountains reached Bleek's ears, his interest grew.[4] He was convinced that they were a race destined to quick extinction but, unlike Charles Dickens, did not welcome this idea. With 'energetic measures,' he wrote '[we could] preserve, not merely a few "sticks and stones, skulls and bone" as relics of the aboriginal races of this country, but also something of that which is most characteristic of their humanity, and therefore most valuable – their mind, their thoughts and their ideas' (Bleek 1875: 2).

In South Africa at the time little was known or understood about the bushmen. There was no scholarly interest in them, and aside from a few recorded phrases, no one had ever written down a bushman language. Bushmen were seen as filthy beasts and barely human. Their heads were sometimes taken as trophies, stuffed and mounted, and their skins were collected and sold at auctions in Europe along with the skins of rabbits, hippopotamuses, and quaggas.[5] They had no familiar form of leadership, living in small bands, each band a law unto themselves. These were not people with whom the appropriation of their land could be negotiated, and since bushmen welcomed the colonists into their hunting grounds with poisoned arrows, the colonists in turn felt compelled to exterminate them.

While bushmen were paraded in English shows, bushmen back home were fighting a fierce war of resistance. In the Cape, where the bushmen were /Xam speakers, by the 1840s Dutch farmers had occupied their land all the way up the Orange River. But it was not only land the Dutch had stolen. For more than 130 years they had appropriated /Xam water holes, murdered /Xam families, and with their muskets and bloodlust, all but wiped out the game on which the /Xam depended for survival. From a cliff a bushman, Chief Koerikei, cried to a Dutch *veldwagmeester* in the 1770s: 'What are you doing on my land? You have taken all the places where the eland and other game live. Why do you not stay where the sun goes down, where you first came from?' (Penn 1995: 243). That cry echoed through the next century. The /Xam resisted with raids and the slaughtering of cattle. Indeed the archives are full of letters of complaint from farmers suffering from the crippling effects of stock thefts and fearful of the /Xam's poisoned arrows. The bushmen were described as 'the terror of the Aachterveld, being unerring marksmen and the swiftest runners in the country'.[6] But despite this, by the mid-nineteenth century /Xam resistance was all but over.

Bushman encounters with strangers to their land had begun some two thousand years earlier. Before then the hunters and foragers, medicine men and women, shamans, painters and storytellers, speakers of many different languages had lived in almost every part of the subcontinent, had explored an intellectual world that penetrated many complex levels of consciousness, and conducted an economy that relied on concepts of inclusiveness and sharing. Then African farmers began to move into the eastern parts of the country, bringing with them new concepts of space, amplified ideas of storage, and expanded settled villages. Pastoralism arrived in the Cape, bringing with it animal domestication and ceramics. Soon after, metalworking was introduced in the north. By the sixteenth century Europeans were regularly stopping over at the Cape and, staying for longer periods, they competed for resources and traded with the pastoralists, whom they called Hottentots or Khoikhoi. As their settlements expanded and the Dutch gained control, these most recent strangers became colonists and moved further inland to expand the colonial frontier and establish farmlands in areas previously thought not fit for agriculture or grazing. There they met bands of hunter-gatherers, who recognised no authority and did not welcome them. The Europeans called these people bushmen or San. The colonists, known as Trekboers or simply Boers, embarked on a process of exterminating all they could not subdue. The /Xam suffered most.

The central mechanism of Dutch expansion was the commando system, which instituted a strategy of bloody reprisals in the wake of bushman and Khoikhoi resistance (Moodie 1960 [1838]). /Xam families were hunted, killed, or captured and distributed

Preis-Verzeichniss

der

zoologischen Sammlung, von C. F. Drege in Süd-Afrika zusammengebracht

und in Hamburg für beigesetzte Preise zu beziehen.

July 1840.

Spalte I

Das Stück in Hamb. Ct.	ℳ	ß
I. Säugethiere.		
Buschmann Frau.	400	
Cercopithecus pygerythraceus	20	—
Cynocephalus ursinus	35	—
" " jun.	8	—
Vespertilio frons	2	—
Sorex capensis	2	—
" spec.	2	—
Bathyergus capensis	5	—
" caecutiens	8	—
" maritimus	10	—
" Hottentottus	6	—
" spec.	4	—
Chrysochloris aurata	4	—
" holosericea	5	—
Rhynomus jaculus	6	—
Lutra lapensis	15	—
" s. C.		
Canis mesomelas	20	—
" " jun.	6	—
Proteles Lalandii	50	—
Hyaena villosa	50	—
Viverra Genetta	8	—
" " s. Cr.	5	—
Herpestes griseus	8	—
" s. Cr.	5	—
" madagascariensis	10	—
" s. Cr.	5	—
" jun.	1	8
" paludinosus	10	—
Mephites Zorella	8	—
Felis capensis (Tigerboschkat).	20	—
" caligata (roode Kat)	10	—
" Leo fem.	150	—
" " masc. s. Cr.	100	—
" Leopardus	40	—
" jubata jun.	15	—
Sciurus capensis	5	—
" spec.	5	—
Mus pumilio	2	—
" spec.	2	—
" spec.	2	—
" spec.	2	—
" spec.	2	—
" spec.	2	—
" spec.	2	—
" rattus? spec. Natal	3	—
Otomis capensis	2	—
" spec.	2	—
" spec. (Vlakmaus)	3	—
Hypodeus spec.	2	—
" " (Klipmaus)	3	—
Dipus caffer	18	—
Hystrix cristata	25	—
" " jun.	4	—
Lepus capensis	5	—
" " jun.	1	8
" rufinucha (Kliphaas)	6	—
Sus aethiopicus (Vlaktevark)	35	—
" " jun.	10	—
Hippopotamus amphibius jun.	25	—
" s. Cr.		
Hyrax capensis	8	—
" " jun.	3	—

Spalte II

Das Stück in Hamb. Ct.	ℳ	ß
Equus Burchelli	150	—
" Quagga	80	—
" " jun.	10	—
" Zebra	150	—
" " jun.	15	—
Antilope Oryx (Gemsbock)		
" " jun.	100	—
" Pygarga (Boutebock)	60	—
" " jun.	15	—
" Gnu (Wildebeest)	90	—
" jun.	18	—
" Caama (Hartebeest)	80	—
" Oreas (Eland)	200	—
" " jun. s. Cr.	25	—
" sylvatica (Boschbock)	50	—
" albifrons (Blesbock)	100	—
" " jun.	20	—
" Euchore (Springbock)	35	—
" Oreotragus (Klippspring.)	40	—
" " jun.	10	—
" Eleotragus (Rietbock)	100	—
" Grimmia (Kuifduiker)	20	—
" " jun.	8	—
" Capreolus (Rehbock)	30	—
" " jun.	8	—
" Lalandii (roode Rehbock)	40	—
" melanotis (Grysbock)	20	—
" " jun.	8	—
" scoparia (Oribi)	25	—
" rufescens (Vlaksteenbock)	20	—
" " jun.	8	—
" pygmaea (Blaauwbock)	15	—
" " jun.	7	—
" spec.	40	—
Ovis steatopyga	30	—
" guineensis? (Damara Schaap)	40	—

Nachschrift:

Nur wobei s. Cr. bemerkt, fehlt der Schädel, die übrigen sind alle mit Cranium.

II. Vögel

in trocknen Bälgen.

	ℳ	ß
Vultur Kolbii	25	—
Cathartes percnopterus	10	—
Falco capensis	4	—
" chiquera	6	—
" ecaudatus	16	—
" exilis	6	—
" gabar	8	—
" Jackal	8	—
" melanopterus	10	—
" musicus	8	—
" niger	4	—
" voifer	15	—
" vulturinus	20	—
Milvus parasiticus	5	—
Gypegeranus-secretarius	50	—
Strix africana	2	—
" flammea	2	—
Bubo lactea	20	—
Lanius atrococcineus	6	—
" Bakbakiri	1	8

Spalte III

Das Stück in Hamb. Ct.	ℳ	ß
Lanius Bulbul	1	8
" colluris	1	8
" Cublan	1	8
" Fiscal	1	8
" icterus	2	—
" olivaceus	6	—
" senegalensis	2	—
Edolius forficatus	1	8
Muscicapa paradisi	2	—
" stricta	1	8
" torquata	1	8
" spec.	1	—
" spec.	1	—
" spec.	1	—
" spec.	1	—
" spec.	1	—
" spec.	1	—
Ceblepyris caesia	2	—
Turdus capensis	1	8
" erythacus	1	—
" griseus	1	8
" reposcens	1	8
" rupestris	1	8
" spec.	1	—
Lamprotornis Aenea	4	—
" bicolor	1	8
" morio	1	8
" nitens	2	—
Pastor galinacea	2	—
Oriolus auratus	3	—
" larvatus	2	—
Motacilla capensis	2	—
Saxicola cachinans	1	—
" pileata	1	8
" rubicola	1	—
" semirufa	1	8
" spec.	1	—
Crithagra chrysopyga	1	8
Sylvia madagascariensis	2	—
" spec.	1	—
" spec.	1	—
" spec.	1	—
" spec.	1	—
Malurus spec.	1	8
" spec.	1	—
Anthus capensis	1	—
Cypselus caffra	2	8
" pygargus	2	—
Hirundo capensis	2	—
" nigra	1	8
" panayana	2	—
" rufifrons	1	8
Caprimulgus infuscatus	2	—
Alauda africana	3	—
" capensis	2	—
" magnirostris	1	8
" rufocapilla	1	8
" spec.	1	—
" spec.	1	—
Parus afer	1	8
" capensis	1	8
" leucoptera	3	—
Emberiza flavigaster	2	—
Euplectes capensis	2	8

An auction sheet from 1842 advertising as its first item under 'Säugethiere' (mammals) 'Buschmann Frau' (Bushman woman) at a price of 400 marks – the highest price of any of the skins up for sale among the farmers as labourers or servants. The records tell of tobacco pouches made of women's breasts; children dragged from their mothers' arms to have their heads smashed on the stones;[7] shepherds tied to wagons and beaten to death.[8] Often the Xhosa, Koranna, and the Bastards – pastoralists whom a /Xam man had once described as 'the bloody-handed, the ticks on the backs of sheep'[9] – saw advantage in siding with the Trekboers and joined forces against the /Xam.

The English colonist and poet Thomas Pringle (1835: 238) described one adventure related to him by a Dutch colonist who had been out with a commando:

> I still often shudder, when I think of one of the first scenes of the kind I was obliged to witness . . . We had surprised and destroyed a considerable kraal of Bushmen. When firing ceased five women were still found living. The lives of these, after long discussion, it was resolved to spare, because one farmer wanted a servant for this purpose and another for that. The unfortunate wretches were ordered to march in front of the commando, but it was soon found that they impeded our progress – not being able to proceed fast enough. They were, therefore ordered to be shot . . . The helpless victims, perceiving what was intended, clung so firmly to some of the party that it was for some time impossible to shoot them without hazarding the lives of those they held fast. Four of them were at length dispatched.

The establishment of British rule at the Cape at the end of the eighteenth century brought efforts toward peace on the northern frontier. Farmers were encouraged to make presents of stock to the bushmen and to desist from attacking them, and missionaries tried to convert them to Christianity. At the same time bushmen families were captured and sent as curiosities of the empire – the strangest of British subjects – to exhibitions in England. But after so many decades of hatred, the efforts to 'civilise' the bushmen and appease the Boers soon failed. In 1863 the magistrate of Namaqualand, Louis Anthing, was sent to investigate reports of extreme violence and lawlessness along the northern frontier. Attacks against the bushmen were no longer excused as reprisals for stock theft. Farmers were hunting bushmen as they did wild animals; and those bushmen who were not attacked were starving to death. The many letters Anthing wrote to the Cape Parliament are a grim testament to the devastation wrought on bushman communities. They were, in any case, all but exterminated by then:

> The evidence I had obtained respecting the past and existing state of things on the Hartebeeste and Orange Rivers some years before, and that they had from time to time killed numbers of Bushmen resident there; that in some cases the latter had stolen cattle from the intruders, but that the killing of the Bushmen was not confined to the avenging or punishing of such thefts, but that, with or without provocation, Bushmen were killed – sometimes by hunting parties, at other times by commandos going out for the express purpose. That in consequence of the colonists having guns and horses, and their being expert hunters (the pursuit of game being their daily occupation), the wild game of the country had become so scarce, and almost inaccessible to the Bushmen, whose weapon is the bow and arrow, having a comparatively short range. That ostrich eggs, honey, grass-seed, and roots had all become exceedingly scarce, the ostriches being destroyed by hunters, the seed and roots in consequence of the intrusion of colonists' flocks. From these various causes, the Bushmen's subsistence failed him, and in many cases they

died from hunger. Those who went into the service of the new comers did not find their condition thereby improved. Harsh treatment, an insufficient allowance of food and continued injuries inflicted on their kinsmen are alleged as having driven them hack into the bush, from whence hunger again led them to invade the flocks and herds of the intruders, regardless of the consequences and resigning themselves, so they say, to the thought of being shot in preference to death from starvation.[10]

Anthing called for a magistracy to be set up in the area, for land to be put aside for the /Xam, and for punishment of crimes against the /Xam. But the British government failed to act until the /Xam who had escaped death or capture joined the Koranna War of 1868. To protect the Boers, not the bushmen, the Cape Parliament passed the Northern Border Protection Act to halt the massive losses of Trekboer cattle and sheep to both /Xam and Koranna (Strauss 1979). Within a year this war of resistance failed, and hundreds of Koranna and destitute /Xam were rounded up and tried for crimes committed or on suspicion of having acted against the colonists. Some were sentenced to jail terms with hard labour at the Breakwater Convict Station in Cape Town.

For Bleek and Lloyd, now increasingly interested in making a study of a bushmen language, the presence of /Xam at the Breakwater provided, in Bleek's words (1873: 2), 'an unprecedently rare opportunity of obtaining good instructors'. Two

Lucy Lloyd photographed around 1870 in Cape Town

prisoners, /A!kunta and //Kabbo, were placed in his custody, and Bleek and Lloyd began a project to 'achieve . . . a thorough knowledge of the bushman language and literature'. While Bleek concentrated on the language itself, Lloyd focused on the literature and the lore that was central to it. Their project resulted in more than 120 notebooks and 13,000 pages of interviews recorded in /Xam, phonetically notated, and translated into English.

Six principal /Xam contributed to Bleek and Lloyd's great collaborative work. They spoke two distinct dialects, and they lived, with members of their families, for varying periods of time at the Bleek home. Each had witnessed the destruction of their resources, and each was tragically touched by the violence which wrecked their homeland. /Han≠kass'o, the son-in-law of //Kabbo, commented on the senseless killing of game: 'The springbok resemble the water of the sea, . . . [they] come in numbers to the place, which is here, the springbok cover the whole place. Therefore the Boers' gunpowder becomes exhausted, that and the balls.'[11]

Dia!kwain, who stayed with Lloyd for two years after Bleek's death, had been convicted of culpable homicide for killing a farmer in defence of his family, whom the farmer had threatened to murder. Others told stories of beatings and assaults. /Han≠kass'o made the journey from Bushmanland specially to join Lloyd. During the nine months it took him to reach Cape Town, his baby died,

Dia!kwain, photographed with fellow inmate Jan Rondebout, who served six years in the Breakwater convict station for killing a farmer, then worked with Lucy Lloyd and was later murdered by friends of the farmer on his return home

his wife was savagely beaten by a policeman and also died, and he had to leave his elder son with friends. Some witnessed the murders of their friends by farmers. Other /Xam formed gangs that attacked farmers' property, and some related that shamanism, used to transform men into lions to attack farmers' stock, failed as a means of resistance against the theft of land and resources and the encroachment of European settlements.

For the /Xam this violence was not just about the destruction of individuals and families; it also amounted to the destruction of their own history, their own sense of connection to the land, and the ancestors who continued to inhabit it. In/Xam thought the first occupants of the country were 'the Early Race', a population of people who later became the stars, the animals, the wind, and the rain. All animals were, in that time, people. As the early race was dispossessed of its humanity, the /Xam, as they saw themselves, lived in the land and exploited its resources, but the memory of the early people lingered in their folklore and natural histories. In an important sense, these early mythical people had mapped the country for the /Xam and provided the basis for their understanding of the world and its workings. This mapping was a process of investing the natural features of the landscape and the heavens with human history and with evidence of their occupation and possession of the land. The /Xam described themselves in terms of the features of the land. They spoke of the Flat Bushmen, who lived between Kenhardt and Vanwyksvlei (on the pans), and the Grass Bushmen, who lived to the west between Kenhardt and Brandvlei (on the plains). Between those groups lived the River Bushmen, and to the south were the Berg Bushmen, who lived in the Kareeberg.

For the /Xam all things were sentient. All things marked place and referred to realities that existed beyond them. Stories were like lines drawn on the landscape to mark its passages and claim its features as home. Thus the history of /Xam occupancy of the land was invested in the land itself and was accessible to those /Xam who passed through it. //Kabbo (who was named Jantje by the Dutch and who was Bleek and Lloyd's first instructor) spoke of this presence of stories in the land and how stories moved from place to place. The third name he mentions, /Uh-ddoro, is the one he was given as a child:

> I do merely listen, watching for a story, which I want to hear;
> while I sit waiting for it; that it may float into my ear.
> These are those to which I am listening with all my ears; while I feel that I sit silent.
> I must wait (listening) behind me

> [//Kabbo explains that when one has travelled along a road and goes and sits down, one waits for a story to travel to one, following one along the same road],

> while I listen along the road;
> they (my three names) [Jantje, /Uh-ddoro, and //Kabbo] float along to my place;
> I will turn backwards (with my ears) to my feet's heels, on which I went; while I feel that a story is the wind.
> It (the story) is wont to float along to another place.

Then our names do pass through those people; while they do not perceive our bodies go along.
For, our names are those which, floating, reach a different place.
The mountains lie between (the two different roads).
A man's name passes behind the mountains' back;
those (names) with which he returning goes along.[12]

The /Xam also mapped the space between the land and the sky. In one of the most important of all /Xam rituals the rain !Kwa, a beast, was killed, and the body was symbolically dragged over the land so its blood would attract rainfall. For the /Xam the strangers' intrusion into the land was an intrusion into the delicate mapping of spaces and places that provided a web of connectedness to both their cultural heritage and the power the shamans (or !giten) drew from the land. A rainmaker shot by Boers in the 1860s described, with his last breath, how the Boers had destroyed his connection to the rain and the rain beast resident in the sky. He saw that connection as a physical thong, a string that bound him to his power. Elsewhere the /Xam spoke of 'thinking strings' as consciousness – at death these strings snap. The vibrating of these strings, which produced a ringing sound in the sky, enabled this shaman to communicate with the rain:

People were those who broke for me the string . . .
Therefore, the place became like this to me on account of it,
because the string was that which had broken for me . . .
the place does not feel to me as the country used to feel . . .
For [it] feels as if it stood open (empty) before me
because the string was broken for me . . .
For, things continue to be unpleasant to me;
I do not hear the singing sound I used to hear.
I do not feel any thing which vibrates in me.[13]

For this shaman the breaking of the string was the severing of his own life. In a symbolic sense the destruction of the fabric of/Xam society was a process of demapping the land, of snapping the threads that tied place to place and people to those places.

The wind was an important agent of this movement of stories and the process of drawing lines of connection between places and time. The wind was formerly a man but became a bird living in the mountains. The wind blew, telling of the coming of game or rain. Nothing was more pleasant than a warm wind, but a cold one was the wind of death. The wind cried for the dead, whose corpses filled the hollow of the new moon. Each person had his or her own wind, and when an individual died, that wind rose and blew away that person's footprints, leaving no trace of him or her on Earth.

This personal wind could act as a portent and an omen of death. Dia!kwain told Lucy Lloyd about a dream he had in which his father was killed by a Boer. When he awoke, he realised the wind had blown, begging him to hear its message of death. His father in fact did die shortly afterward and lay in a hut, watched over by Dia!kwain's mother. The tone of his story is elegiac, foretelling the death of the /Xam (symbolised by the springbok) as a people: 'The springbok had afterwards passed the hut, as if they

/Xam descendants photographed around 1810 by Dorothea Bleek in the Prieska region. It was from these people, amongst others, that 'pure-blooded Bushmen' were selected for the casting project at the South African Museum.

were not afraid. Mother did not know where the springbok came from, they were not a few and they came and played as they approached the hut where father lay dead. The springbok appeared to be moving away, and the wind really blew following them. They were running before that wind. It was really father's wind, and you yourself feel how it is blowing . . . As the wind blew past I felt my inside biting . . . I felt like that when one of my people was dying, my inside always ached when it was one of my people.'[14]

At one place in the Bleek and Lloyd archive, //Kabbo tells Lloyd that he should dearly love his stories to become known by way of books. He was, it seems, presenting his narratives to her for publication. This was a particularly bitter irony, for the Bleek and Lloyd records received no attention from anyone outside of the Bleek family for almost one hundred years. This fact somehow framed, for me, the whole history of loss to which the /Xam were subjected. When all /Xam resistance had failed, and just a few decades before the /Xam language ceased to be spoken, six /Xam individuals gave over their lore, endured the longing for their homes and the separation from their imperilled families, and worked on a common project to preserve all that was left of the ideas that made them uniquely who they were. When Dorothea Bleek (1929: 311-12), Wilhelm Bleek's daughter, visited the northern Cape to search for the descendants of //Kabbo, /Han≠kass'o, and the others, she noted:

Fifty years ago every adult Bushman knew all his people's lore. A tale begun by a person from one place could be finished by someone from another place at a later date. In 1910 I visited the northern parts of the Cape Colony and found the children, nephews and nieces of some of the former informants among the few Bushmen still living there. Not one of them knew a single story. On my reading some of the old texts a couple of old men recognised a few customs and said, 'I once heard my people tell that'. But the folk folklore was dead, killed by a life of service among strangers and the breaking up of families.

The twentieth century saw, if this were possible, a deterioration in the position of the bushmen. It saw the deaths of almost every bushman language within the borders of South Africa and, with language death, the deaths of oral traditions and cultural identity. Much of the destruction experienced by the bushmen was visited upon the Khoikhoi as well, and for most of the colonial period the distinction between dispossessed Khoikhoi and Bushman groups was blurred. This blurring has led to the belief by some (and to heated argument) that bushmen never had a distinct identity at all but were always an underclass of dispossessed pastoralists. The widespread use of the term *Khoisan* in the twentieth century acknowledges this shared fate (and these debates) and points to the tangled lines of inheritance that characterise Khoisan identity today. The final dispossession of the Khoisan came with their assimilation into Afrikaner life and their classification along with others of (as the state perceived it) 'mixed blood' as 'Cape Coloured'.

When I read the Bleek and Lloyd archive in the 1980s, I was particularly struck – bewildered in fact – by the knowledge that this material had existed side by side with the extraordinary mythology that had developed around the bushmen as primitive savages or the missing link. The distance between the beauty and depth of this collection of oral traditions, recorded in the words of the people who owned them, and the image constructed by the people who controlled their fate was so great that no knowledge of the former seemed to have leaked through to the latter. Like virtually all others, Charles Dickens, great champion of the underdog, was not prepared to look beneath that 'festering bundle of hides' to find the humanity of the bushmen that Bleek and Lloyd were so concerned to expose. I was also impressed by the collaborative nature of the project in an era when bushmen were given so little agency in the progress of their own lives, for not only prisoners worked with Bleek and Lloyd. Family members made the long journey from their homes in Bushmanland, often at great cost, to make their contributions (Skotnes 1999).

My response to this extraordinary archive, however, was governed less by my historical interests than by my role as artist and curator. The 1980s saw a major revision in bushman studies. Anthropologists working among the bushmen in Namibia and Botswana were engaged in often vitriolic debates on the nature of bushman identity and the role played by well-known authors, such as Lawrence van der Post, in infantilising and objectifying them. In South Africa in the 1970s Roger Hewitt became the first person outside of the Bleek family to write seriously about the Bleek-Lloyd archive (his thesis was published in 1986), and David Lewis-Williams published his groundbreaking thesis on rock art in 1981.[15] These works, crucial in recovering the narratives from their long obscurity, sired a small industry of papers and articles in which old-school authors and public alike tried but mostly failed to come to terms with the idea of symbolic complexity in bushman art. My own initial intervention, much informed by Lewis-Williams's ideas, was in a series of artists' books that combined text and visual interpretations of both folklore and paintings.

Despite this new spirit of revisionism in bushman studies, it became clear that, as long as scholarship was yoked to a study of the rock art, a shift in the image of the bushmen as unintellectual and ahistorical remained improbable. It appeared inevitable that, despite the attendant problems of mounting yet another exhibit about the bushmen, it would only be possible to confront these stereotypes through the medium of display. The power of the images and ideas conveyed by the diorama at the South African Museum and the multiple copycat dioramas in South Africa, such as the Cango Caves, the Natal museum, the Main Caves, and the Bloemfontein Museum, among others, was not in any way eroded by academic attempts to present a contrasting picture. My own studies of visitor responses to the diorama at the South African Museum show that little had changed in the ideas it generated since my first visit as a child. Indeed this continued to be a site where teachers and tour guides alike could enthusiastically re-create for their audiences the life and manners of the bushmen.

Almost every talk began with a physical description of a bushman. The language of these descriptions is inherited from more than two hundred years of European fascination with the bushman body. When Saartjie Baartman was exhibited in London and Paris in the early nineteenth century, the 'prodigious size of her buttocks' (as they were described by St. Hilaire of the Natural History Museum in Paris) was not the only great source of fascination; so was the imagined strangeness of her genitals. She was deemed to 'prove interesting to the naturalist'.[16] Travellers, such as Le Vaillant in the eighteenth century, had painted images of women flashing long pendulous labia. Captain James Cook had written that the 'Hottentot' women had labia that 'resembled the teats of a cow' (Gordon 1992b: 187), and reports had reached Victorian English ears that some women had labia that hung like an apron.

By the end of the nineteenth century bushman bodies had been the subjects of dozens of photographic 'essays'. Most of these photographs were part of scientific projects that examined racial differences. One such project, initiated by Thomas Huxley, president of the British Ethnological Society, required that photographs be taken of naked subjects from set vantage points so that the peculiarity of various races within the British colonies could be recorded.[17] Many of these photographs survive in museum collections and archives. Typically they depict men and women standing naked against a measuring stick, from both the front and side. Many collections also included images focused particularly on genitals; men were photographed most often to the side to show the tilt of the penis, while women were persuaded to grasp their labia to expose their length.[18]

While nudity in museums in post-apartheid South Africa is frowned upon, the diorama at the South African Museum still continues to provide for visitors' interest in bushman bodies. 'The male penis,' I once heard a guide bellow to an attentive group of tourists, 'is peculiar in that it stands erect at all times when at rest; the women's labia can hang to the knees.' Apart from genitals, hunting and lifestyle also were dealt with at length. Guides frequently characterised bushmen the same as predators, such as lions and leopards or as omnivores, such as baboons. Their hair was described as wool, and often it was suggested that the life of a bushman was nothing more than an endless pursuit of food and water. One teacher told her pupils that 'the bushman can run for three days non-stop in pursuit of game.' Another guide suggested that 'the bushmen were nocturnal,' sleeping in hollows in the ground during the day and coming out at night to hunt.

The stated purpose in the construction of the diorama in the South African Museum and its life casts was to preserve for the future what was understood to be a disappearing racial type. The museum had established early on an interest in the bushmen – its founder, Andrew Smith, started the bushman collection shortly after the museum's inception (in 1825). Until the end of the century bushmen were considered living fossils (a view still affirmed by Jan Smuts in 1925), physically distinct, and scientifically important for an understanding of racial difference.

In 1910 the museum's caster, James Drury, travelled with Dorothea Bleek to Bushmanland in search of specimens of 'undiluted blood' (Rose 1961) that would be suitable for life casts. Louis Péringuey, who became director of the museum in 1906, was particularly clear that the 'purity' of these 'specimens' should include the features considered at the time most characteristic of 'the Bush races', the male's semi-erect penis and the woman's elongated genitalia (Davison 1993: 169). Their cultural practices or social conditions were, for Péringuey, unimportant. What was to be cast for perpetuity was the ancient Bushman as a physical type, hunter-gatherers from our own distant past displaced from current culture and politics.

Dorothea Bleek's interest in this project was puzzling. She had grown up with the people and saw the commitment of her aunt and her father as they worked together to recover and preserve /Xam creative traditions. Nowhere did any of the /Xam who lived in her house comment on their stature or consider the shape of their own genitals worthy of discussion. Neither did they see the historical processes that had overtaken them, and their resulting social conditions, as irrelevant. On the contrary, these processes and conditions seemed to be the very reasons for their presence in Bleek's home. Yet her interest in these people was as 'specimens', examples of a 'vanishing racial type'. She wrote in a letter in 1911 that 'it is exceedingly difficult to get photos of the natives without clothes on'. Despite their reluctance, she managed to photograph some of her subjects naked, their tattered clothes seen lying in piles beside them.

The museum has acknowledged the false image this diorama represents and the stereotypes it perpetuates. In the late 1980s, responding to what was perceived as the perpetuation of a 'flawed anthropological notion of racial typology'

(Davison 1993:171), the museum mounted two smaller displays alongside the diorama. One display visually explains the technical methods used to make the life casts and has the unfortunate effect of further dismembering the bushman body, and the other display provides a historical context for the casting project. Nevertheless, like the emergence of a new academic discourse on the bushmen, these newer exhibits have done little to shift the ideas perpetuated by the oral tradition that continues in front of the diorama, passed down from one guide to the other and from indoctrinated visitors to their friends and children. These body casts have become for the public who the bushmen are, and the diorama is a place where, in Harvard professor of aesthetics Elaine Scarry's terms, the made-up has become the made real.

The contrast, not to say perceptual abyss, between the diorama at the South African Museum and the Bleek and Lloyd archive, as well as the narrative power of the form of display employed by the diorama, were among the factors motivating my authoring the *Miscast* exhibit. It was also true that, while museums chose to construct exhibits focused on bushman bodies, their storerooms, libraries, and archives were crammed full of objects, visual materials, and documents that told quite another story about the bushmen. Nowhere in any of the museum exhibits I saw was any evidence of the history and lore, the photographs, letters, narratives, and drawings richly present in the museum storerooms or any acknowledgement of the horrible encounters between Boers and bushmen. Nowhere were objects presented to focus on their creative achievements or to offer any insight into the fragments of rock paintings that lie unexplained in ill-lit display cases. Worse still, not a trace was found of bushman literature, which gave expression to their worldview and the uniqueness of their individuality. By the time I planned my own installation, my intention was to do two things: one was to confront visually the diorama, and the other was to put the archive and the storeroom on display. Central to this desire was the attempt to structure into the form of the exhibit a high degree of multivalence so it would be more about knowledge in the making than a presentation of the already known.

The South African National Gallery, situated in the same city garden as the South African Museum, was the chosen venue. The director, Marilyn Martin, had, for some years, been keen to cast aside the view of the gallery as colonial and elitist. She had previously encouraged the display of beadwork, basketry, and painted facades and participated in the debate scrutinising the historically determined roles of the various museums that housed material culture in Cape Town. An exhibit of this nature, she felt, would go a long way toward pooling resources and 'crossing traditional divides' (Martin 1996: 10).

The *Miscast* exhibition opened in April 1996 and became what the deputy director of the South African Museum has called 'a landmark in exhibition practice . . . stimulat[ing] unprecedented controversy' (Davison 1998: 145). It was structured around two oppositions. One figured a contrast between concepts of storage and display, and the other contrasted colonial images of the bushmen with those created by bushmen themselves. Along one wall of the exhibit in the main room of the gallery

Display section of the main room of the Miscast installation

were thirteen cases containing objects and many dozen photographs. Facing this wall was a semicircle of thirteen body casts, each a resin cast of a body section, such as legs and torsos. Each cast was headless. Produced from Drury's original field moulds, these represented the countless, nameless individuals reduced to racial types – a symbolic Last Supper in which the bushman body was the sacrifice. Continuing the symbolic theme, at the centre of the room was a grey brick structure, based on the ground plan of a centrally planned Renaissance church that referred to a fort, jail, and tomb as well as a church. On a central circle (a visual suggestion of the Eucharist) were twelve rifles, and in their midst was a taller metal flag, again making a total of thirteen objects.

In the 'back' section of the main room were two piles of casts, six metal shelves with cardboard boxes, and two cabinets of objects and instruments associated with nine-teenth- and early-twentieth-century physical anthropology. The cardboard boxes were designed to resemble those found in many museums for the storage of human remains. Each box was labelled with a particular dated event, sourced from historical narratives, from archives, and from comments and stories by //Kabbo, /Han≠kass'o, Dia!kwain, and others who participated in the Bleek and Lloyd project. With these boxes I present-ed a non-linear time line in which the processes of selecting information and gathering it into a narrative was problematised. The lack of chronology was also intended to evoke the nonlinearity of time present in the Bleek and Lloyd archive. I also tried to suggest that history is always fragmentary and incomplete and that histories are, like displays, always temporary and contingent, endlessly able to be reshaped by new insights. On each label, I used a system of double dating (date of event and date of publication), suggesting that historians are themselves characters in their own narratives. Thus

The second room of the installation, contained, on its walls, a series of photographs taken by Paul Weinberg between 1984 and 1996 in Bushmanland, Namibia, Botswana and South Africa, specifically Smitsdrift and Kagga Kamma. The photographs focus on dispossession and the vari-ous contemporary problems associated with limited access to land and resources. The floor of the room was laid with vinyl tiles which reproduce images and articles from newspapers, photo-graphs from archives, extracts from reports on commando raids and various official documents from archives and museum stores. In cases on the floor are three cameras.

history only begins to exist when its details are interpreted, and these interpretations are necessarily political.

The exhibit was framed by a quote from Greg Dening's remarkable book *Mr Bligh's Bad Language* (1992:178–79), which describes the consequence of a first encounter between native and stranger: 'There is now no Native past without the Stranger, no Stranger without the Native. No one can hope to be mediator or interlocutor in that opposition of Native and Stranger, because no one is gazing at it untouched by the power that is in it. Nor can anyone speak just for the one, just for the other. There is no escape from the politics of our knowledge, but that politics is not in the past. That politics is in the present.'

The exhibition opened to a flurry of media and political controversy. Bushman and Khoisan groups from all over southern Africa arrived for the opening and a forum for debate and discussion, which I had organised for the following day. I was aware of potential criticisms of the curatorial decisions I had taken and decided to provide an opportunity for their expression. Everyone was invited to the forum, and everyone came, including those who previously had declared themselves hostile to my initiative. Responses, perhaps surprisingly, were not divided along race or political lines, and people from all sides responded with shock, horror, sadness, anger, or wonder.

The preparation of the exhibition itself had been dogged by controversy. The strife began with a disagreement in which the British Museum (Natural History) allowed me access to a collection of putative trophy heads – bushman heads collected in the nineteenth century that had been dried and stuffed by a taxidermist–but then refused to allow me to make drawings of them or to take photographs. The museum's position was that the heads might 'cause offence'.[19] It was the museum's responsibility, the administrators felt, to preserve them for scientific experiment or use, for example DNA testing. Before they would even consider giving me (an artist) photographs of the heads for display or allowing the heads to be part of an exhibition, I would have to obtain the permission of 'the Khoisan', although the museum curator admitted that they could not really tell who all the Khoisan were and that the records of these heads were so poor that it would be impossible to trace descent. 'Besides,' someone whispered to me in the corridor, 'you'll never get these heads back or next we'll have to return the Elgin marbles.'

However, I wrote to the legal representative of the /Khomani;[20] to the newly established Khoisan Representative Council (KRC) and the Griqua National Conference, both in the Cape;[21] to the Kuru Development Trust in Botswana;[22] and to the Working Group of Indigenous Minorities in Southern Africa (WIMSA)[23] to canvas opinion on the exhibiting of human remains and the heads (or photographs thereof) in particular. Of those consulted in Botswana, none wished to see the heads themselves. At the same time they believed the heads should be shown so the world would know what happened. Similarly the /Khomani, through their legal representative, and the Khoisan Representative Council wanted the heads or photographs of the heads exhibited. In one of many press reports about this issue, Martin Engelbrecht of the KRC told the London Observer: 'I see no reason why the British are preventing us from exposing what

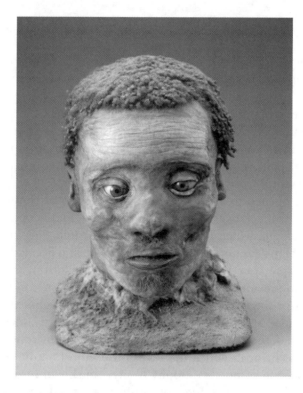

A stuffed 'Bushman' head with glass eyes in a collection in Europe. No details
are available as to how the head came to be collected.

happened to our people. We want to know how these remains came to be in the museum' (quoted in Van Niekerk 1996: 24).

Marilyn Martin, director of the South African National Gallery, made a formal
request to the British Museum (Natural History) for photographs of the heads. The
British museum never responded. Colonial control, it seemed, had once again been asserted over the gaze to whom the Bushman body should be subjected.

Of the other areas of controversy, many focused on the display of the casts. The
casts I showed – resin copies from the original moulds that had produced the painted
plaster copies in the South African Museum – were not articulated, and their surfaces
were not finished. These were yellowed, translucent parts of bodies, unlike the accurately rendered copies in the diorama. At the forum, on April 14, 1996,[24] a visitor from
Smitsdrift, a camp for displaced bushmen, who had served on the side of the South
African Defence Force in Namibia in the 1970s, expressed his displeasure: 'I do not believe that these things are true. All this plastic, they could have made it just to shock us.
Showing these naked bodies is a very, very bad thing . . . to show these things here is just
as bad as the people who did those things long ago. It is continuing the bad thing.' But
he continued, 'We are not angry with the people who are showing us these things, but

with the people who have done it to us.' Sixpence Hunter, another visitor from Kuru in Botswana, an Nharo organisation, said: 'We are shocked . . . these things are true . . . Although we are shocked and it is painful, we think it is good that people should see it. It strengthens our young people to stand up . . . the whole world should get a message from this exhibition. This should not happen to people ever again.'

A different response came from the Khoisan Representative Council. Struck by the elegiac nature of the exhibit, the council made a formal request to the National Gallery and me that forty skeletons, whose return they had recently negotiated from Professor Philip Tobias at the Wits Anatomy Department, be included in the exhibit as a kind of 'lying in state' before reburial. The gallery, nervous about any further controversy, turned them down.

Politically the installation became a rallying point and a focus of both Khoisan unity and disunity. At the opening a group of /Khomani came in traditional dress, wearing only loincloths and looking as if they had stepped out of the diorama. They attracted a great deal of press attention and were berated by the !Hurikamma Cultural Group (Afrikaans speakers who identify themselves as brown as opposed to black or coloured), who said they were 'sick and tired of naked brown people being exposed to the curious glances of rich whites in search of dinner-table conversation' (Roussouw 1996: 9). One Griqua group expressed concern about 'too many bushmen', and one of the Bushman representatives suggested that Afrikaans speakers could not claim to be Khoisan at all. Groups from Botswana and Namibia used the occasion almost exclusively to argue for political recognition and for access to their ancestral lands.

The installation also inspired a number of white Afrikaners to claim that they too were of Khoisan descent, which angered some other Afrikaners previously classified as 'coloured.' Similarly some groups, for example, the *Kleurlinge Weerstandsbeweging* (the Coloured Resistance Movement), were angered that a white person (myself) had chosen to interfere in the Khoisan past, that they were once again being 'represented' by whites and, worst of all, by white academics. 'Give us the money,' one member called out at the forum, 'so that we can make our own exhibit in our own way.' Yet others, such as the Khoisan Representative Council, valued the installation as a wake-up call for Khoisan communities. Some argued that the conflation of Khoi and San was insulting. 'We coloureds in the Western Cape,' one man told me in Afrikaans, are descended from the Hottentots [Khoi], not from the bushmen [San] – my people were never cattle thieves.' Contrastingly, some individuals expressed horror at the developing equation of 'coloured' with 'Khoisan' – a perceived 'tribal' category of the kind they had been at pains in previous years to escape.

The *Miscast* exhibition raised numerous other questions as well as insights offered by its viewers. The visitors book highlighted many of these. Many people, for instance, claimed that they had known nothing of this history. A diplomat from the Netherlands embassy resident in South Africa, for example, commented in the visitors book that back home 'little is known about the involvement of the Dutch in "early" South Africa. To my knowledge, just about nothing is known about their encounters with the Khoi and San people. They – we – should.' Another foreign visitor also characterised an aspect of the exhibition referred to many times in the visitor's book. He drew attention to the power of visual things to communicate differently from written things, saying: 'This is a challenging combination of text, materials and ideas. Thanks for bringing it all together, so that each of us can have the opportunity to confront our images/conceptions of a people who rarely have a chance to represent themselves to a western view. It challenges our knowledge – and the way that knowledge has been acquired about African peoples.' Many visitors, too, saw a relationship between this exhibition and the Truth and Reconciliation Commission in South Africa, which began its proceedings in the first part of 1996: 'This exhibit should be permanent – it is important that all South Africans see the genocide that was perpetuated. No truth and reconciliation commission is possible for the "bushmen".'

Subsequently a great deal has been written in the academic press about *Miscast* and the way the exhibition inserted itself into both South African politics of identity and museum practices in South Africa. A number of anthropologists accused me of aligning too closely with Lucy Lloyd and thus presenting myself as a spokesperson for the /Xam. More disturbingly, perhaps, they revealed that the techniques of display employed by *Miscast* provided them with the same opportunities to invent and re-create material as did and does the diorama. One anthropologist described photographs he saw dated to 1915, long before the invention of photography; another (in an uncorrected draft of her paper) saw rows of bottled genitals that did not exist; and others merely failed to see things they were standing in front or on top of. The process of making ideas real through display coupled with the politics of reception produced a simultaneous opportunity to make up ideas. At the same time, the diorama has been reappraised. While *Miscast* suggested that the diorama and the colonial gaze it promotes have been at least in part responsible for the suppression of bushman history and the denial of their cultural traditions, the South African Museum has used the controversy *Miscast* generated to suggest that the diorama still represents an acceptable alternative.

Patricia Davison (1998: 159), deputy director of the South African Museum, suggested: 'Controversy surrounding "Miscast" did not, however, extend to the South African Museum diorama. Skotnes' own response to the diorama had originally motivated the "miscast" concept but her indignation was not shared by Khoisan viewers. On the contrary the diorama tended to be favourably regarded. Perhaps a reason for this contradiction lies in the fact that, although problematic in other respects, the diorama does not represent the San [bushman] hunter-gatherers as victims.' The truth is, it does not represent the bushmen at all, if we understand that people are composed of more than just their physical attributes. The diorama, as a sanitised translation of the nineteenth-century freak shows, permits almost no contemporary identification, and those people who do identify with it are indeed, contrary to Davison's assertion, offended by it.[25] It is one of the strangest ironies of the *Miscast* exhibit that when, in 1999, the government invited Khoisan groups to prepare motivations for being granted political and land rights, first-people status, and representation on the South African Council of

Traditional Leaders, a newly organised group of /Xam descendants came to me to represent them. I asked them if they had seen or heard about the *Miscast* exhibit and whether or not they followed the controversy. 'Oh yes,' they said, 'it is through *Miscast* that we begin to know more about ourselves.'

Shortly after the close of *Miscast* the South African Museum invited me to install an exhibit in the room adjacent to the diorama that would conceptualise their rock art displays. I used the exhibit to reveal some of the legacy left by Bleek, Lloyd, //Kabbo, /Han≠kass'o, Dia!kwain, and the others. At the time I made a proposal for alterations to the diorama that would, while preserving its character and thus its own historical importance, nevertheless destabilise the narrative it presented and visually alert the viewers to its problematic lack of historicity. The museum is still thinking about this proposal. In the meantime the public still hears the echo of the ideas of Dickens, mediated by the diorama, and the bushmen continue to be represented as victims of the gaze of colonial museum practice.[26]

Notes

1   Opinions of the London press, Killie Campbell Afrikaner Library, Durban, SA: KC 12935 306.0896819 HIS.

2   Handbill for the 1852 exhibition 'Earthmen', Regent Gallery, London, in Museum Africa, Johannesburg, SA: 572:00 4388.

3   Killie Campbell Afrikaner Library, Durban, SA: PAM 306.0896819.

4   See, for example, John Wright's *Bushman Raider of the Drakensberg* (1977).

5   These auction sheets apparently were common in Europe in the mid-nineteenth century. A colleague provided me with one, which is reproduced in Skotnes 1996 opposite the title page. It was produced for the auction of the skin collection of C. F. Drege in Hamburg in July 1940. Item one under the heading *Saugethiere Buschmann Frau*. Drege had apparently waited until dark on the day this woman was buried to exhume and skin the body.

6   Letter to P. de Smit, resident Magistrate in Calvinia 30 March 1869. Cape Archives House of Assembly, HA 80.

7   Penn 1995 records in remarkable detail the onslaught of colonial expansion into the north and Khoisan resistance to it.

8   See, for example, 'Dia!kwain', in the unpublished notebook of Bleek and Lloyd, Bleek Collection BC 151, Book 23: 5872–80 (1876). Dia!kwain, a /Xam man, tells the story of Ruyter, who had been 'brought up by white men [and who had] died while he was with white men'. His death was at the hands of his employer, a farmer who had accused him of not herding sheep well and who tied Ruyter to a wagon wheel and beat him.

9   '//Kabbo', in Bleek Collection BC 151, Book 32: 2926 (1873), translated by Lloyd.

10   Message from his Excellency the Governor with Enclosures Relative to the Affairs of the North-Western Districts of the Colony. Letter by Louis Anthing 1863. Cape Archives A 39/63. Reproduced in Skotnes 1996 (162-78).

11   '/Han≠kass'o', in the Bleek Collection BC 151, Book 85: 7226r (1878), translated by Lloyd.

12   '//Kabbo', in the Bleek Collection BC 151, Book 34: 2876–78 (1873), translated by Lloyd.

13   'Dia!kwain', in the Bleek Collection BC 151, Book 60: 5101–5 (1875), translated by Lloyd.

14   'Dia!kwain', in the Bleek Collection BC 151, Book 60: 5110–46 (1875), translated by Lloyd.

15   Lewis-Williams developed what has become widely known as the 'trance hypothesis.' He proposed that bushman rock paintings were largely the product of the trance dance – the central religious ritual performed by most bushman groups. Images previously described as hunting or dance scenes were, in his theory, rather the visual expressions of trance experiences. This theory, at first aggressively debated, has become widely accepted. It also has implications for the interpretation of European Upper Paleolithic art.

16   'Private invitation to view Saartjie Baartman at Piccadilly from Hendrik Cezar', Museum Africa, 570:0 Hottentot.

17   Bleek Collection BC 151, D1.12, 1 (1871).

18   See, for example, the Haddon Collection at the Museum of Anthropology and Archaeology at Cambridge University.

19   Robin Cocks, head of paleontology, British Museum (Natural History), London, letter to author, 1995; Chris Stringer, Department of Paleontology, British Museum (Natural History), London, e-mail correspondence with author, January, October, and November 1995. Also see the discussion on the Web at www2.h-net.msu.edu/~africa/threads/trophyheads. html.

20   The Khomani are a small group of bushmen (two families), who were displaced from their home during the establishment of the Kalahari Gemsbok Park. They created a great deal of press and academic attention when they accepted an offer to live on a farm in Cedarberg, where they would dress in traditional dress and 'receive' paying guests. Some people felt this was no better than putting people on display and that they were being badly exploited by television and film crews, who used them in films and advertisements. At one stage Dawid Kruiper, leader of the group, claimed they were seeing none of the money they made. They have, however, instituted a land claim against the South African government.

21   The KRP represents Griquas and other Khoisan descendants in the Kimberley area under the leadership of Adam Kok. The GNC represents Griquas from the south of the country who do not recognise Adam Kok's leadership. These groups are demanding First Nation status and have taken the lead in calling for the return of Saartjie Baartman's remains from the Musée de l'Homme in Paris.

22   An organisation representing Nharo bushmen in Botswana.

23   An umbrella organisation based in Windhoek representing various southern African groups.

24   The curator planned a forum for the day after the opening to discuss both the exhibition and concerns common to many Khoisan groups. It was attended by over seven hundred people, including delegates from the Working Group of Indigenous Minorities in Southern Africa (WIMSA), comprising delegates from the Kuru Development Trust in Ghanzi and from Nyae Nyae, Bagani, and the Aminuis Corridor 17 in Namibia; the South African San Institute (SASI); the Griqua National Conference and South African Griqua Research and Development (SAGRAD); the Khoisan Representative Council, which includes Khwe, !Xu, and Griqua representatives; the /Khomeni of the southern Kalahari; the Richtersveld; the !Hurikammna Cultural Movement; and the *Kleurlinge Weerstandsbeweging* (KWB) or Coloured Resistance Movement of the Western Cape.

25   In a postgraduate museum course I teach, students, many of who are of Khoisan descent, consistently bring up the diorama as contentious and problematic. Students are particularly offended by the fact that the diorama continues to be exhibited in what is seen as essentially a natural history museum, while the Cultural History Museum a few steps away has relatively little space (and until 1997 virtually no space at all) allocated to exhibits of indigenous people.

26   After this article was written in early 2000, the leader of a group of more than twenty thousand /Xam descendants approached me to write their history for review by the South African government commission looking into the current status of the San (bushmen) and the reasons for their current settlement patterns. The Department of Constitutional Affairs has since begun to consider allowing bushman descendants the right of representation in the Council of Traditional Leaders and will address claims for compensation for the loss of land.

References

Bleek, Dorothea
> 1929 'Bushman Folklore'. *Africa* 2: 302–13.

Bleek, Edith, and Dorothea Bleek
> 1909 'Notes on the Bushmen', in *Bushman Paintings*, edited by M. H. Tongue, 36–44 (London: Clarendon Press.)

Bleek, W. H. I.
> 1873 'Report of Dr Bleek Concerning His Researches into the Bushman Language and Customs', *Report presented to the Honourable the House of Assembly by Command of His Excellency the Governor.* (Cape Town: House of Assembly.)
> 1875 'Second Report Concerning Bushman Researches, with a Short Account of Bushman Folklore', *Report Presented to both Houses of Parliament, by Command of His Excellency the Governor* (Cape Town: Saul Solomon.)

Bleek, W. H. I., and Lucy C. Lloyd
> 1869–1889 Unpublished Notebooks (BC 151 Jagger Library, University of Cape Town.)

Davison, Patricia
> 1993 'Human Subjects as Museum Objects: A Project to Make Life-casts of "Bushmen" and "Hottentots", 1907–1924,' *Annals of the South African Museum* 102 (5): 165–83.
> 1998 'Museums and the Reshaping of Memory', in *Negotiating the Past: The Making Memory in South Africa*, edited by Sarah Nuttall and Carli Coetzee, 143–60 (Cape Town: Oxford University Press).

Dening, Greg
> 1992 *Mr Bligh's Bad Language: Passion, Power and Theatre on the Bounty* (London: Cambridge University Press).

Dickens, Charles
> 1853 'The Noble Savage', *Household Words: A Weekly Journal*, June 11, 168–340.

Findlay, D. A.
> 1977 'The San of the Cape Thirstland and L. Anthing's "Special Mission"'. Honours essay, University of Cape Town.

Gordon, Robert
> 1992a *The Bushman Myth: The Making of a Namibian Underclass* (Boulder: Westview Press).
> 1992b 'The Venal Hottentot Venus and the Great Chain of Being', *African Studies* 51 (2): 185–201.

Greenblatt, Stephen
> 1988. *Shakespearean Negotiations* (Berkeley: University of California Press).

Hewitt, Roger L.
> 1986 *Structure, Meaning and Ritual in the Narratives of the Southern San*. Quellen zur Khoisan-Forschung 2 (Hamburg: H Buske).

Lewis-Williams, J. David
> 1981 *Believing and Seeing: Symbolic Meanings in Southern San Rock Paintings* (London: Academic Press).

Lloyd, Lucy C.
> 1889 'A Short Account of Bushman Material Collected', *Third Report Concerning Bushman Researches, Presented to Both Houses of Parliament of the Cape of Good Hope, by Command His Excellency the Governor* (London: David Nutt).

Martin, Marilyn
> 1996 'Foreword', in *Miscast: Negotiating the Presence of the Bushmen*, edited by Pippa Skotnes, 9–10(Cape Town: University of Cape Town Press).

Moodie, Donald
   1960 [1838] *The Record; or, A Series of Unofficial Papers Relative to the Conditions and Treatment of the Native Tribes of South Africa* (Cape Town: Balkema).
Penn, Nigel
   1995 'The Northern Cape Frontier Zone: 1700-c.1815' Ph.D. diss., University of Cape Town.
Pringle, Thomas
   1835 *Narrative of a Residence in South Africa* (London: Moxon).
Rose, Walter
   1961 *Bushman, Whale and Dinosaur: James Drury's Forty Years at the South African Museum* (Cape Town: H. Timmins).
Roussouw, R.
   1996 'Setting History Straight – or Another Chance to Gape', *Mail and Guardian*, April 19.
Skotnes, Pippa
   1991 *Sound from the Thinking Strings: A Visual, Literary, Archaeological and Historical Interpretation of the Final Years of /Xam Life* (Cape Town: Axeage Private Press).
   1996 'Running before That Wind: A Parallel Text', in *Miscast: Negotiating the Presence of the Bushmen,* edited by Pippa Skotnes, 26–354 (Cape Town: University of Cape Town Press).
   1999 *Heaven's Things: A Story the /Xam* (Cape Town: LLAREC and University of Cape Town Press).
Strauss, Teresa
   1979 *War along the Orange: The Korana and the Northern Border Wars of 1868–9 and 1878–9.* Communications 1 (Cape Town: University of Cape Town, Centre for African Studies).
Van Niekerk, Philip
   1996 'Skeletons in White Man's Cupboard', *London Observer*, February 18.

THREE

A Staggered Orientalism:
The Cape-to-Cairo Imaginary[1]

Peter Merrington

SYMBOLS OF RHODES' WAY FROM CAPE
TO CAIRO
The Southern Cross
Pilots stars to the Navigators of the Cape of Storms
The Stone Birds of Zimbabwe
Gleams in Darkest Africa of Northern Lights
The Mountains of the Moon
and the
Source of the Nile

> The sign – the monument-of-life-in-death, the sepulchre of a soul or of an embalmed proper body, the height conserving in its depths the hegemony of the soul, resisting time, the hard text of stones covered with inscription – is the *pyramid.*
>
> Jacques Derrida, *Margins of Philosophy*

This essay approaches the material from four broad emphases: first, the neo-Hegelian tropology of pre-World War I Oxford idealist philosophy, which celebrates the 'dawning of consciousness' in the subcontinent with the advent of union in 1910 and which the essay relates to Hegel's views on Africa and Egypt; second, the ubiquitous influence of Freemasonry in Britain and the British Empire at the turn of the nineteenth century, in particular Freemasonry's concern with Egyptology; third, the varied impulses behind the concept of the Cape as Mediterranean, from climate to architecture, tourism, and ethnography; and fourth, the mutually supporting roles of journalism, travel, and performance in rehearsing a national act of identity formation.

The Cape-to-Cairo idea coincides with the historical moment of the forging of union. It also coincides with a period of transition in Western culture from the late Victorian age to modernism. This essay suggests that these broad issues of national identity formation and of simultaneous transition between two different cultural milieus, which are evident as much in the dominant nations of Europe at the time as they are in the making of South Africa, may be tracked in a reconstruction of the complex of cultural epiphenomena that surrounded and propagated for several decades the fantasy of the Cape-to-Cairo axis.

The gloss in the epigraph by Derrida on Hegel's interpretation of the idea of the pyramid is intended to point toward three aspects of this essay – first, its argument that Hegelian tropology underlies much of the Cape-to-Cairo imagination; second, the general assumption as demonstrated by Partha Mitter (1977:190–205), Edward Said

(1978: 86–88), Martin Bernal (1987), and Robert Young (1995: 126–30) that for at least two centuries the West has exhibited a preoccupation with ancient Egypt as one source for the origins of Western culture (rivalled by the theories of the Indo-Aryanists); and third, the essay's emphasis on an imagined continent that was made to serve as an imperial sign system, a geographical space that was understood to be mysterious, a temenos or shrine, a sequence of monuments (natural or manmade) from the Gizeh Plateau to the Ruwenzori, to Great Zimbabwe and Cecil Rhodes's Matopos, the Union Buildings, and the numinous natural acropolis of Table Mountain. These are all emphases laid upon the continent by an imperial culture that sought avidly for a 'hard text of stones covered with inscription' and, when it failed to find this, built or imagined its own.[2]

The material on which this essay is based is largely the product of invention or imagination, a particular construction that was imposed upon the land by outsiders for reasons that were the consequence of 'colonial desire', to borrow Robert Young's phrase.[3] This desire is manifested in fiction and in speculative history and archaeology, as in the following two excerpts. In the first, from Rider Haggard's *King Solomon's Mines* (1985 [1885]: 21), the narrator fantasises about exogenous monuments in East Africa: '"Ay", said Evans, "but I will tell you a queerer thing than that;" and he went on to tell me how he had found in the far interior a ruined city, which he believed to be the Ophir of the Bible, and, by the way, other more learned men have said the same long since poor Evans's time . . . this story of an ancient civilisation and of the treasure which those old Jewish or Phoenician adventurers used to extract from a country long since lapsed into the darkest barbarism took a great hold on my imagination.' In the second, written twenty years later, R. N. Hall (1905: 15), in his book *Great Zimbabwe*, speculated: 'As one strays through the Sacred Enclosure, thoughts come: – . . . was Rhodesia the Havilah of Genesis; did it provide the Solomonic gold; of the close kinship of these successful ancient gold-seekers from Yemen or Tyre and Sidon to the Hebrews of Palestine; and of their intimate connection in origin, language, and neighbourhood which Holy Writ abundantly declares existed from the ninth chapter of Genesis until Paul preached in Phoenicia?'

Imperial stonemasonry in Africa is fundamentally monumental – and frequently mortuary – in its intentions, generating something like Derrida's paradoxical 'monument-of-life-in-death,' inflected perhaps as a dream of progress that manifests itself as a longing for antiquity. This dream and this longing are features of an international trend in the late nineteenth and early twentieth centuries, whereby modernising nationalisms and colonial identities alike were reinforced by recourse to mythologies, such as English 'Elizabethanism' or German Indo-Aryanism, national sign systems in the depths of which were supposed to be conserved the 'hegemony of the soul, resisting time'.[4] In South and southern Africa a variety of such colonial-national mythologies were mooted, and an 'Egyptian' or 'Phoenician' etiology enjoyed a popular persistence over many decades. This essay explores some of the cultural expressions of a colonial 'staggered orientalism' (to coin a phrase) whereby the Cape and southern Africa have been made out to be the naturalised allies of Mediterranean Africa. As suggested here, the reasons for this staggered orientalism are partially found in the desire by South Africans, circa 1910, for what Derrida calls a 'national sign system' that would help in the formulation – within the context of British imperial sentiment – of national history, identity, and heritage. Other causes and reasons exist for various aspects of the Cape-to-Cairo fantasy, but it is argued that these all contribute with cumulative force to the dominant idea.

The historical window surrounding the moment of South African union in 1910 reveals some graphic international perspectives on the new country. From the point of view of cultural and public history, we note in particular debates from the period that compare the constitutions, the founding histories, and the cultural identities of, for instance, Canada, Australia, and South Africa. The dominant topics in these debates are twofold: the nature of the emergent vernacular and national(ist) cultural identities of these colonies and dominions and their positions within the international structure of the British Empire. In South Africa the invention of a united vernacular tradition in terms of cultural and historical heritage and public works (in particular architecture) was intense and contested as both imperial or Loyal-Unionist and Afrikaner National-ist coteries lobbied for dominance.

In terms of a global imaginary, the cultural idea of South Africa was mooted, for instance, in the idiom of German and Dutch *Jugendstil* (the German equivalent of art nouveau), which promoted Nationalist interests, as in the work of the Dutch Transvaal painter and book designer J. H. Pierneef, or alternatively, in terms of the English Arts and Crafts movement and the Queen Anne vernacular revival in domestic architecture, where the Loyal-Unionists held influence. In other words, rival senses of public or national or clan identity were forming, depending on locale (the Anglo-Dutch imperial-loyalist Cape, or the avidly Anglophone colony of Natal, or the Germano-Dutch cultures that were emerging in the republics of the Orange Free State and the Transvaal), and these distinct identities were evident in the architecture and in numerous mundane cultural forms of expression, such as styles in publishing and the decorative arts.

One set of influences is emphasised in this essay, namely the role of 'Mediterranean' cultural forms in the making of an imperial South African public identity. At the time a considerable cultural interchange with England and Europe was motivated by the immense wealth of the Randlords (the proprietors and directors of the gold and diamond mining concerns, such as Cecil Rhodes, J. B. Robinson, and Abe Bailey) and by the frisson of imperial belle époque idealism that ended with the First World War. By this idealism one suggests the kind of expansive geographical and imperial missiological vision engendered in the popular imagination in Great Britain by authors such as Rudyard Kipling and Haggard or the more cerebral version of this vision, such as was propagated by the Oxford philosophical school of 'English idealists', the neo-Hegelians who taught to a generation of young men destined for the Indian civil service or for South Africa the ethical philosophy intended to inspire their idea of colonial civil society.

As regards the cultural interchange between South Africa, England, and Mediterranean Europe, the Randlord Sir Lionel Phillips and his connoisseur wife Florence Phillips are a case in point. He donated money to Amelia Edwards's Egypt Exploration Fund as well as to the excavation of the *Forum Romanum*; she founded the Johannesburg Art Gallery along with much else. The Phillips ménage toured Egypt in 1903, and their Edwardian photographic collection is preserved in the library of their Cape home, 'Vergelegen'. They hired the architect Herbert Baker to build for them a superb example of 'Mediterranean' domestic architecture in their 'Villa Arcadia' in Parktown, Johannesburg. The Mediterranean region, with its crucial strategic role for Britain and its cultural focus in terms of Greco-Roman antiquity, Etruscan and Minoan 'primitivism', Egyptology, and orientalism in its widest range of meanings, offered western Europe an accessible array of images of the exotic and archaic other. This array of images is drawn upon by writers, connoisseurs, performers, tourists, and travellers, in forging an Orientalist dimension to the cultural idea of Edwardian South Africa.[5]

The primary focus of this essay is thus on the interpretation of the Cape and at times of the general idea of South African as 'Mediterranean'. The argument links this understanding of the Cape to the period concept of the Cape-to-Cairo axis, an imagining of southern Africa largely associated with the ideas of Rhodes that once had implications for the continent as a whole and may well do so again in a postcolonial epoch with the evolution of South African president Thabo Mbeki's African Renaissance concept.[6]

This concept has been cited as the motivating philosophy behind various current transcontinental initiatives, such as the African Connection Rally (the 1999 information-technology project organised by the South African Telecommunications Ministry) and the Engen Oil Company's Open Africa tourism project.[7] This essay draws on material concerning architectural styles and the figuring of landscapes, colonialist ethnography, the history of tourism, and the Edwardian journalism that stitched these diverse interests into what might be regarded as a loose 'prospectus' for a great enterprise that never came about. Finally, all these aspects, the scenic backdrop, the typecast figures in the landscape, the efforts to forge meaning by chasing records and by rehearsing travellers' tales, are interpreted as a kind of pageant performance – a fancy-dress occasion in which the African orientalism of the Cape-to-Cairo fantasy is enacted. The script for this pageant-performance is underwritten by the meta-narrative of Hegel's *Lectures on the Philosophy of History* (1872 [1834]) with its grand tableau of the progress of history from civilisation to civilisation and continent to continent and his account of Egypt and Phoenicia in relation to greater Africa. A particular interlude in this figurative pageant is offered by the role of Freemasonry within British imperial ideology with its 'Egyptian' rituals and genealogy.

It needs to be borne in mind that Egyptological fashions are also evident in places that, strictly speaking, have nothing to do with the Cape-to-Cairo idea. Paris reflects considerable Egyptian influence in its architectural motifs, largely due to Napoleon's Nile campaigns of 1798–1799 and to the influence of Second Empire France in the Egypt of the Khedive Ismail. Egyptological motifs are commonplace in the urban architecture of most Western cities, and as demonstrated by Eric Grant (1988), from the 1830s Scotland became a late but avid exponent of the Egyptian revival movement in Britain. Nonetheless the fact of recurrent Egyptian revival trends in western Europe must be acknowledged as affording a cosmopolitan context of design and imagination that would enable and enhance in the public mind the idea of the Cape-to-Cairo link, just as would such features in the Cape as the Egyptian Building of the University of Cape Town, built between 1829 and 1841.

A reconstruction of what was meant by the Cape-to-Cairo idea needs to draw on a miscellaneous range of material that runs from the sublime to the bathetic. At one extreme we find Sir Henry Morton Stanley in his 1890 journal comparing the 'hoary' peaks of the 'Mountains of the Moon' to an 'Egyptian pyramid and sphinx'.[8] At the other extreme we encounter, in Cape Town sometime between 1910 and 1930, C-to-C cigarettes, a brand of petrol called Sphinx Motor Spirit, and, a little later, the C-T-C Building, which houses a popular department store in the city. In the mid-nineteenth century a pious band of Afrikaner trekkers, the *Jerusalemgangers*, heading into the far north toward what is now Polokwane in the Northern Province, encountered a river with a pyramid-shaped *kopje* and named it *Nylstroom* (that is, the Nile), believing that they had penetrated to the land of the pharaohs. The lush cultivated lands that run alongside the Orange River in the northern Cape amid the desolation of the Kalahari have prompted allusions to the fertile Nile Valley. In the town of Kakamas in this area (known as Gordonia) is a large building designed like an Egyptian pylon temple and built by a Swiss engineer in 1914 to serve as the town's first electrical 'transformater'.[9] Someone wrote a piece in the *Empire Review* (September 1938) entitled 'Cape to Cairo with an Ascot Hat'. In 1947 the aviator and author Cecil Lewis flew single-handedly from England to Johannesburg via Cairo and Nairobi to establish a colony of Theodore Gurdjieff disciples as the intended survivors of a projected world cataclysm.[10] The topic, as Robin Hallett (1975: 496) wryly comments, 'was an extravagant and in practical terms totally fatuous concept but . . . well calculated to appeal to Rhodes's perfervid imagination'.

This combination of the sublime and the ridiculous is accidental, but, when dealing with the totality of images of the Cape-to-Cairo idea as constituting a cumulative public imaginary, one notices a rhetorical pattern in which frivolity appears alongside items of imperial statesmanship. In 1922 the remarkable Victorian explorer and administrator Sir Harry Johnston wrote retrospectively on the origins of the Cape-to-Cairo concept:

> [It was] Stanley's letters home from Uganda to the *Daily Telegraph* in 1876 that first gave some definite impulse to British minds to establish an uninterrupted British control over South, Central, East, and North Africa which might link up Egypt within a series of peaceful, prosperous, well-governed states. The interpreters of the idea were [Sir] Edwin Arnold, principal leader-writer to the *Daily Telegraph*, and Colonel J. A. Grant, the veteran explorer, who had been [John Hanning] Speke's companion in the journey to the sources of the Nile.
> Edwin Arnold adumbrated the 'Cape-to-Cairo' idea in a pamphlet published in 1876.

From this pamphlet, and still more from Arnold's conversation, the writer of this chapter derived the idea and the phrase 'The Cape to Cairo,' and perhaps conveyed it to the mind of the Foreign Office, and especially to the imagination of the late Lord Salisbury, who, at any rate, allowed it to be used without disapproval in articles which I contributed to monthly reviews and the daily press in 1888 and 1889. The general policy of a North to South extension of British control was delineated in an article for the *Times* of August 22, 1888, a forecast of which Lord Salisbury thought might usefully prepare the public mind for coming developments in our African policy.

(Quoted in Weinthal 1922, 1: 65)

The following gem penned by W. T. Stead in the *Windsor Magazine*, September 1899, matches this:

The outer and visible reasons why the Cape to Cairo line is coming into being are simple and obvious enough. The first and dominating cause is the fact that the idea has fascinated the imagination of Mr Rhodes, and the second and hardly less potent reason is the fact that the Cape and Cairo both begin with the letter C. Possibly this second reason ought to have precedence over the first, for who knows how much of the fascination which has caught Mr Rhodes's fancy was due to 'apt alliteration's artful aid'? If the Cape and Cairo had possessed different initials, the suggestion of a through continental line might never have suggested itself to Mr Rhodes. But the notion of linking the two places, each of which commenced with the same capital letter, 'caught on', and the gigantic enterprise is already making progress from the realm of the imagination into the domain of accomplished fact.

(Quoted in Plomer 1984 [1933]: 142)

The concept of the Cape-to-Cairo link is so staggeringly vast and vague that it needs to be deprecated in this fashion even as the possibility is mooted. Perhaps the idea of yoking the two extremes of the continent generates a mimicking sense of giddy verbal syllepsis. More seriously, it seems that a rhetorical sylleptic logic might have been understood as necessary for the articulation of the totalising vision that emerged in the epoch of the new imperialism. The most frivolous formalism is blended with the colossal scale of Rhodes's imperial dream, as if the idea were thereby in some way domesticated, rendered self-evident or inevitably part of the scheme of things. Such vertiginous rhetoric is also a symptom of the jingo triumphalism that was evident in the British popular press at the time. Yoking together the heroic and sublime with the mundane and low transforms both factors in the equation, thereby taking a facile rhetorical control of them.[11]

Hegelian Tropology

Much public rhetoric in the period spoke of the 'sister states' of the British dominions, Canada, Australia, and South Africa – an 'organically' united 'family' of nations.[12] In South Africa the imagery of reconciliation after the SA War (the Anglo-Boer War) of

1899–1902 represented the Dutch and the English as 'brothers'. These metaphors obviously imply specific racial bonds, reflecting the kind of world order envisioned by the young Rhodes in his first will and testament of 1877, in which he spoke of a universal Anglo-Saxon world government that would reunite the British Empire and the United States of America and bring about world peace. Rhodes's universalist vision is not merely an expression of British imperialism. It is also an expression of a totalising concept of history as destiny, a typical later nineteenth-century amalgam of protestant teleology, nationalist sentiment, and evolutionary historicism.[13] When South African union was achieved, it was celebrated as a 'consummation', a hymeneal image for the 'marriage' of four colonies, and repeatedly in the dominions the concept of 'birth' was employed for the founding of new polities. Cape Town was described as the 'cradle' from which the new nation was 'born'. Similarly Quebec Province in Canada was described in the 1908 Quebec tercentenary celebrations – attended by a number of leading South Africans two years before South African union – as 'la berceau de Nouvelle France' (the cradle of New France). A tropology involving images of dawning and of crossing thresholds is common in the public rhetoric of the time. (The image of the rising sun is also adapted from union onward as a leading motif in Afrikaner nationalism, for instance, in the local school reader series, the *Dagbreek Reeks* or Daybreak Series.) This heliocentric tropology is central to Hegel's scheme of world history, the 'dawning' of human historic consciousness across the continents of the globe 'consentaneously' with the trajectory of the natural sun, from 'east to west'.

The Hegelian tropology is in itself not so much based on imperialism as on Enlightenment thought, a point that is borne out by the existence in the 1850s, a good few decades before the onset of the 'new imperialism', of Dutch heliocentric tropology in the Western Cape town of Paarl.[14] Here the imagery was a combination of Enlightenment and Protestant theological thought, but it became inflected later with imperialist implications. It involved, initially, a theological motto derived from the book of Malachi, 'the light of righteousness' (But for you who revere my name, the sun of righteousness will rise with healing in its wings, Mal. 4:2). This motto was adapted for the new boys' school in Paarl, the Paarl Gymnasium, in 1858. The school building was designed to resemble an Egyptian temple, providing a further inflection to the biblical motif with ornamental stucco sun discs or uraei on the outside walls of the building. Close by is a Masonic lodge, and it is very likely that this Egyptological version of a biblical sun motif was inspired by the Dutch Masonic tradition in the Cape, which stretched back to the early eighteenth century, again with a distinct Enlightenment or *Aufklärung* origin. In the period of the new imperialism and after, well into the 1920s, Masonic symbolism with its Egyptological and heliocentric motifs continued throughout the British Empire and dominions under what is known as the 'English Constitution' of Freemasonry.[15] This essay argues that the Cape-Cairene idea was propagated and popularly received partly because of this international male network, whereby a set of Enlightenment philosophical motifs was replicated and popularised. Further, the cultural and geographical aspects of these Egyptological motifs contributed to their adoption as motifs of global

British imperialism in that they served within the metropole itself (not only as Masonic symbols but also as common architectural ornamentation) to emblematise internally the antique and distant colonised other.

Returning, however, to Hegel, Andrew Nash (1985: 35) suggests that 'the question of how philosophy became possible in the colonial context of South Africa is also the question of "how Hegel came to Africa".' The initial answer to this question and the departure point for Nash's thesis is that the committed Oxford neo-Hegelian R. F. L. Hoernle, one of Benjamin Jowett's Balliol protégés, was in 1908 appointed the first professor of philosophy in the South African College in Cape Town (the forerunner of the University of Cape Town). Another Oxford neo-Hegelian of the period was Viscount Milner, the so-called Architect of Union, as were members of his 'Kindergarten' of administrators (so named because of their youth), whom he recruited for the task of rebuilding civil society in southern Africa after the war of 1899–1902. Milner was the British high commissioner for South Africa and governor of Cape Colony during the South African War and the four years immediately following the war. His unswerving policy was to direct events toward a political union, under the aegis of imperial Britain, of the British colonies and former Dutch republics that made up South Africa. He and his Kindergarten set about reconstructing the war-ravaged region with a continual eye to the political likelihood of bringing about 'loyal union'. Their application of neo-Hegelian philosophy was in terms of public ethics and of the idea of the state, the nation, and civil society as 'organic' (on the model of the 'organic' family), a concept taught them by the neo-Hegelian T. H. Green, whose 'gospel' 'of the organic nation . . . opened the door to social reform and to positive state action in all areas' (Semmel 1968: 20). To this end, members of the Kindergarten established a magazine titled *The State*, which ran from 1908 to 1912 to propagandise the concept of a united South Africa loyal to a greater empire. The contents of *The State* were intended to explore and create a new unified South African cultural identity. The leading members of the Kindergarten went on, after the conclusion of their South African experiment, to enact the same principles of organic unity and civic identity in the greater platform of the British Commonwealth, which was itself largely defined by their initiatives. The Commonwealth journal the *Round Table*, organ of their Round Table movement (the Commonwealth think-tank they founded after their South African experience), evolved out of their editorship of *The State*.[16]

As Nash points out, the late Victorian application of Enlightenment neo-Hegelianism to the new nation of South Africa argues an *occlusion* of local settler and native history, memory, and political identity. Hegelian globalism denies Africa's place in the sun of history. Instead, it lays an imaginary filter over the continent, attributing a thin skein of 'historically conscious' culture to the northern seaboard and – for the rest – celebrating at most the imposed 'consciousness' of a colonial 'dawn'. The Unionist magazine *The State* is a review or résumé of the admittedly rich and varied resources that were drawn upon to articulate this colonial identity, to which the Cape-to-Cairo set of ideas contributed.

For Hegel, Africa *had no history*. Africa was but 'on the threshold' of history. He made an exception, however, for two sites on the Mediterranean seaboard of Africa – Phoenician Carthage and Egypt. Said Hegel (1872 [1834]: 95) about Africa, 'Africa proper, as far as History goes back, has remained – for all purposes of connection with the rest of the World – shut up; it is the Gold-land compressed within itself, – the land of childhood, which, lying beyond the day of self-conscious history, is enveloped in the dark mantle of Night.' He continued:

> Africa is no historical part of the World . . . it has no movement or development to exhibit. Historical movements in it – that is in its northern part – belong to the Asiatic or European World. Carthage displayed there an important transition phase of civilisation; but, as a Phoenician colony, it belongs to Asia. Egypt will be considered in reference to the passage of the human mind from its Eastern to its Western phase, but it does not belong to the African Spirit. What we properly mean by Africa, is the Unhistorical, Undeveloped Spirit, still involved in the conditions of mere nature, and which had to be presented here only as on the threshold of the World's History.
>
> (Hegel 1872 [1834]: 103)

Again and again authors writing of the Cape at the time of union invoked this Hegelian structure in historical speculation, in travel writing, and in fiction. It is ironical that this adaptation of a Hegelian globalism should be in fact the basis for the evolution of a set of local traditions, for the invention of a local phylogenetic myth concerning southern Africa. The following passage from a long-serving school history textbook written by the Loyal-Unionist Cape author Dorothea Fairbridge (1917:16) exemplifies this myth:[17]

> It is possible that [the early travellers] made their way farther south than Punt, and eyes that looked on Moses may also have gazed on Table Mountain, but of this there is no record. What we do know is that Pharaoh Necho, who ruled in Egypt six hundred years before the birth of Christ, sent an expedition from the Red Sea, manned by Phoenician sailors, which sailed round Africa. Three years, the journey took, for the sailors landed at different places on the coast, dug the ground and sowed it with corn. When the crop had ripened it was gathered and sail was made for the next halting-place. Southward and southward they went, says the old chronicler, until, as they declared, the sun was on their right hand as they sailed. In the third year they doubled the Pillars of Hercules and came safe home. Think of the courage of it. Perhaps they put in at Table Bay or Durban or elsewhere on the coast, and made their temporary gardens in the kindly soil of South Africa. It is curious to think that the slender Egyptian explorers may have stood at the foot of Table Mountain and worshipped the Sun God as he rose over the Drakenstein. We may picture to ourselves their return after that three years' journey – how they sailed up the west coast and through the Pillars of Hercules and down the blue Mediterranean, until they came to the Rosetta mouth of the Nile and to the noble city of Sais, then the capital of Egypt.
>
> And after this the curtain falls for nearly two thousand years, to rise again in AD 1434, in which year that 'dreamer devout' Prince Henry the Navigator sent an expedition from Portugal which succeeded in rounding Cape Bojador and paved the way for the discovery of the sea-route to India.

Navigation, moral courage, sun consciousness, the realising act of the gaze, sowing seeds, gardens in kindly soil: here is a set of themes and motifs that epitomise the greater colonial project. This is not history but rather the imaginative figuring of a contemporaneous ideology. Time and space are more symbolic than real, written here as a sequence of acts on a stage. In his posthumously compiled *Lectures on the Philosophy of History*, Hegel represents history as an evolutionary process that took place not over a period of time but also across geographical space, running across the globe from east to west. Fantasies such as the one above reflect the symbolic use of these two dimensions. Here is another, this by the imperial writer, geographer, publisher, and diplomat John Buchan (1903: 146–48), who was briefly a member of Milner's Kindergarten in South Africa and a product of the same Oxford ethos of the 1890s:

> The romance which is inseparable from all roads belongs especially to those great arteries of the world, which traverse countries and continents, and unite different zones and climates, and pass through extreme variations of humankind . . . And it is a peculiarity of the world's roads that this breath of romance blows most strongly on the paths that point to the Pole-star. The Aemilian Way, up which the Roman legions clanked to the battlefields of Gaul and Britain, or that great track which leads through India to the mountains of the north and thence to the steppes of Turkestan, captures the fancy more completely than any lateral traverse of the globe. A way which passes direct through the widest extremes of weather, and is in turn frozen and scorched or blown in sand, has an air of purpose which is foreign to long tracks in the same latitude, and carries a more direct impress of the shaping and audacious spirit of man. Of all north roads I suppose the greatest to be that which runs from the Cape to Egypt, greatest both for its political meaning, the strangeness of the countries to which it penetrates, the difficulties and terrors of the journey, and, above all, for the fact that it is a traverse of the extreme length of a vast and mysterious continent . . .
>
>   With a profound respect for the road, I am constrained to admit that it makes bad going . . . and that it is apt to cease suddenly and leave the traveller to his own devices. But for the eye of Faith, that wonderful possession of raw youth and wise old age, it is as broad and solid as the Appian Way; the wheels of empire and commerce pass over it, and cities, fairer than a mirage, seem to rise along its shadowy course.

In this piece Buchan explicitly addresses the question of orientation – east-west or south-north. The Hegelian 'lateral traverse' is replaced by a south-north 'pilgrimage', a kind of staggered orientalism where the east (as Islamic Middle East) is no longer in relation to the Christian European West but rather a fulcrum from which a radius is swung southward.

Imperial Freemasonry

The glyph designed by Herbert Baker exhibited at the head of this essay is a symbolic statement of the Cape-to-Cairo axis, including the Southern Cross, the Zimbabwe Birds, the Mountains of the Moon, the source of the Nile, and the crescent moon of Islam.[18] The Zimbabwe Birds were alleged to have been the relics of a foreign (Semitic or Phoenician) culture that was supposed to have built the Great Zimbabwe (the elaborate and vast complex of dry stone walls dating back to roughly AD 800 in the fertile Mutirikwi Valley of Zimbabwe). Much has been written on this colonialist supposition.[19] Suffice it to make the point that for the imperialists built environments were, ideologically speaking, indices not of indigenous African culture but of lost 'white' or 'European' or 'Semitic' civilisations in Africa. Once again the motivations for this particular fantasy are to identify the traces of settler precedents in Africa as well as a racialist desire to diminish the cultural achievements of indigenous African peoples. The significant point for the purpose of this essay is that, again, links are made between southern Africa and the Middle East. The most apparent examples of this fantasy are the African novels of Haggard, in which lost cities, lost civilisations, and lost peoples are described with gestures at a composite Mediterranean (especially Egyptian) origin. Remarkably a South African Dutch novel, written by S. J. du Toit (1898), who was schooled at the Egyptological Paarl Gymnasium referred to above, addresses a similar topic, Solomon and the Queen of Sheba.[20]

Freemasonic lore makes more than evident that the development of this colonialist mythology surrounding Southeast Africa and the Great Zimbabwe depends on the widespread practice of Freemasonry in the British Empire. The eighteenth-century social adventurer Cagliostro introduced the 'Egyptian rites' into continental and British Freemasonry. Masonic lore holds that the 'wisdom' of the 'Craft' originated in Egypt and came to repose with the craftsman Hiram, 'Son of the Widow of the Tribe of Naphtali' (1 Kings 7:13), whom King Hiram of Tyre sent to Solomon for the construction of his temple. Hiram the 'Son of the Widow' (a standard encryption for Freemasons) was murdered by jealous apprentices, and his body was hidden and subsequently was resurrected – a parallel with the story of Christ and the Egyptian myth of Osiris. For Kipling, an avid Freemason, Queen Victoria was the 'Widow', and her 'sons' were the soldiers in her imperial regiments ('The Widow at Windsor', *Barrack-Room Ballads* [1892]). The figure of Isis, the sinister consort of Osiris, enters variously into the fiction of Kipling's friend Haggard as She, as Gagool, or as the dark queen Sorais in *Allan Quatermain* (1887). These figures are kin to the Queen of the Night in Mozart's Masonic opera *The Magic Flute*. The two pillars to Solomon's temple, mentioned in Chronicles, are named, in Hebrew, Jachin and Boaz, meaning 'strength' and 'beauty', a common Masonic pairing that seems to be personified by the rebarbative Horace Holly and his Apollonian companion Leo Vincey in Haggard's *She* (1886) and *Ayesha* (1905).[21] Many of Haggard's descriptions in his African yarns of symbolic landscape and of buildings and monumental masonry are either explicitly linked with ancient Egypt or Phoenicia or bear striking resemblance to eighteenth- and nineteenth-century Western Egyptological fantasies, such as the early stage sets for Emanuel Johann Schikaneder and Mozart's opera. The city of the sun in *Allan Quatermain* may be linked to representations of the Egyptian Heliopolis. Martin Bernal (1987: 176) cites Frances Yates's references to the utopian *Città del Sole* [City of the sun] (1602) by Renaissance writer Tommaso Campanella as an 'architectural memory system'. Campanella's city, says Bernal, is 'populated by white-robed, pure and religious Solarians who are transparently Egyptian, and its buildings form an ideal model for the universe or a heliocentric system of planets'. Bernal adds, 'Here it should be remembered that Masonic ideology was built around the notion of sacred buildings symbolising the universe.' These are distinct features of Haggard's East African city of the Zu-Vendi.

While on the subject of the city of the sun, it should be mentioned that circa 1905 private speculators built a new suburb of Cairo as housing for colonial and expatriate administrators and merchants and named it Heliopolis. It was designed according to Sir Ebenezer Howard's novel garden city concept (his Garden City Association, formed in 1899, introduced to urban planning the idea of greenbelts and satellite towns), with thematic ('Andalusian' and 'Moroccan') architecture and roads radiating in spoke-wheel clusters. At the very centre of this garden city the entrepreneur behind the scheme, Baron Edouard Empain (who designed the Paris Metro system), built for himself a fantasy palace that resembles a mixture of Hindu, Jam, Buddhist, and Mogul temples. This reminds us of the contemporary trend (held as a central tenet of Freemasonry) away from orthodox Christianity and toward a composite faith that would embrace Christian, Hebrew, Muslim, and other beliefs – an imperial and cross-cultural development from nineteenth-century Unitarianism.[22] Heliopolis enters into this Freemasonic creed as follows: its ancient Egyptian name was On, and this is included in the Freemasonic word for the Supreme Being or Grand Architect of the Universe, whom they term *Jabulon,* a composite of the Judeo-Christian Yaweh, the Carthaginian and Phoenician Baal, and the Egyptian On. Masonry's Grand Architect of the Universe is intended to embrace all religions. To this degree it is an ideal creed system for an empire as diverse as that of Britain in the late nineteenth and early twentieth centuries, and this inclusive aspect of the Craft seems to reflect a syncretic imperial idealism such as we encounter in the work of Kipling.

A South African historical novel published in 1910, the year of union, and set in the first decade of the eighteenth century, meditates (rather anachronistically) on the possibility of such an inclusive world creed. The governor of the Cape, Willem Adriaan van der Stel, is reading aloud a letter he has received from the Dutch governor of Ceylon, in which appears a translation of a passage of religious speculation by a Sri Lankan holy man:

> Oh God, in every temple I see people that see Thee, and in every language I hear spoken people praise Thee.
>
> Polytheism and Islamic feel after Thee. Each religion says, 'Thou art one, without equal.'
>
> If it be in a mosque people murmur the holy prayer, and if it be a Christian church people ring the bell from love of Thee. Sometimes I frequent the Christian cloister and sometimes the mosque. But it is Thou whom I search from temple to temple. Thy elect have no dealing with either heresy or orthodoxy, for neither of them stands behind the screen of Thy truth. Heresy to the heretic, and religion to the orthodox, but the dust of the rose-petal belongs to the heart of the perfume seller.
>
> (Fairbridge 1910: 155)

Van der Stel responds: "'[These lines] breathe of a faith which is above all creeds and embraces all. But I am afraid," and he smiled, "that some of our predikanten would think that my feet were set on the high road to perdition, did they hear me. It is strange," he added meditatively, "how the teaching of some of Calvin's followers dulls the ear and hardens the heart against the voice of God, except it sound on one note alone'" (ibid.).

The figure of Willem Adriaan van der Stel in this novel is supposed to represent both Cecil Rhodes and Sir Alfred Milner, who brought his experience of administration in Egypt to his governorship at the Cape during the critical period of the South African War.[23] Milner was a devotee of imperial closer union who wholeheartedly espoused the contemporary racial triumphalism, which claimed that Anglo-Saxons were the natural rulers of the world. He understood what we would now call multicultural societies to be the most serious obstacle to imperial closer union, and he believed quite simply, in the manner of his day, that interventionist rational progress (the total involvement of a liberal-reforming government) in the planning and execution of civil affairs would be the best means of integrating such societies.

In his *England in Egypt* (1894), for instance, he identifies what he terms the 'decrepit' and 'narrow and perverted' theology and the 'antiquated formulae and barren traditions' of the traditional learning at the *Madrassahs* as the reason for the lack of progress in popular education in Egypt (Milner 1894: 364–65). The imperial faction in South Africa was known as the 'progressive' faction. Imperial administration sought to establish principles of reason over and above sectarian orthodoxies, and it is evident that Freemasonry, with its architectural symbolism and its syncretic creed, served as a rather disingenuous vehicle for the propagation of this vision of society.

A fuller exploration of the Freemasonic underpinning to the Solomonic speculations about the Zimbabwe ruins must be done elsewhere. Suffice it for the moment to bear in mind that Solomon and his temple are at the root of Masonic myth and ritual, that Masonry was a primary vehicle for British imperial sentiment in the late nineteenth century, and that Haggard's literary friend and confidant Kipling drew widely and frequently on Masonic symbolism and myth for his own stories and poems. As far as literal Masonic connections between South Africa and Egypt are concerned, at the turn of the century we find evidence of numerous civilian and regimental Masonic lodges in both countries, as was the case also in India. The purpose of these lodges would have been to provide disciplined fellowship for British expatriates and to furnish them with a structured means of meeting selected local personalities across the spectrum of race, caste, and religious belief. In Egypt we find Freemasonry headed by such influential figures as Horatio Herbert Kitchener, and it is more than obvious that this imperial creed system afforded a means of propagating not only hierarchical social networks but also a set of imperial genealogies similar to those adopted by the popular fad known as the British Israelite Truth.[24] This cult and Freemasonry lay claim to the virtues of oriental antiquity in the name of imperial Britain.

The Cape as Mediterranean

Cairo is nearly on the equivalent latitude north to Cape Town's latitude in the south. Both Cape Town and Egypt were once clearinghouses for British eastbound travel and commerce as well as for expeditions into the interior of Africa, yet the Cape-Cairo axis is far more complex than commonsense geography. Both Fairbridge and Buchan refer to past civilisations, to the pharaonic, the Phoenician, and the Roman Empire. From this perspective the Middle East as the 'cradle of civilisation' lends itself readily to a reinterpretation as the 'cradle of imperialism'. By stitching the Cape-to-Cairo, the imperial travel writer forged a fictitious set of credentials for the colonisation of southern Africa in two ways. First, obvious parallels were struck between the eastern Mediterranean and the Cape: both were accessible to the English traveller en route to India, both at the turn of the century were contested territory (with rival claims from the British, other colonial powers, and existing local polities, such as Khedivial rule in Egypt and the Boer republics in South Africa), and both exhibited – in selective aspects – similar climatic, social, and touristic patterns. Both had Islamic communities, thereby displaying a kind of kinship between the Christian and Muslim 'people of the Book' over and against the 'animist' worship of greater indigenous Africa. Second, the ancient Mediterranean empires were a model for British imperial sentiment, and in particular the idea that Phoenicians first rounded the Cape in ancient history offered a distinct precedent for the modern colonial presence. This topic of an early Phoenician presence at the Cape has been for two centuries the focus of recurrent speculation concerning a find of carbonised timber on the Cape Flats.[25] At different times various figures advanced the possibility that this was the remains of one of Pharaoh Necho's Phoenician galleys, and archaeologists sustained the debate as recently as 1993. Thus the Cape-to-Cairo idea is argued here to be, in British colonial and imperial discourses, closely related to the idea of the Cape as 'Mediterranean'.

In numerous ways the topic of the Cape as 'Mediterranean' emerged over the past two centuries, largely since the first British occupation in 1798. The most common feature of this discourse concerns the climate and landscape and is reflected in the interpretation of Cape landscape as picturesque. In his memoirs the architect Sir Herbert Baker (1944: 32), Rhodes's protégé and the designer of the Union Buildings in Pretoria, made this point: 'The view from the Grotto, as it was called [a cottage on the Groote Schuur estate on the slopes of Table Mountain], was of great beauty; it was a narrow vignette of that seen from the garden above Groote Schuur, the firwoods of the Flats and the distant blue-grey mountains being framed and thrown back in perspective by the dark velvet-green stone-pines, as was Turner's use of the pine tree in the foregrounds of his Italian landscapes.' In the same text Baker speaks of 'the air on the top [of Table Mountain], as pellucid as that on Hymettus', and 'The calm sea [of False Bay], like a Venetian lagoon, [that] reflected the mountain peaks coloured by the low morning sun.' The tourist authorities in Edwardian Cape Town advertised their city as the 'Venice of the South Atlantic' and the 'Naples of the South'. In his memoirs, Buchan (1940:

35, 117) described the Cape landscape as follows: 'In the Cape Peninsula you have the classic graces of Italy, stony, sun-baked hills rising from orchards and vineyards and water-meadows . . . If you seek the true classical landscape outside Italy and Greece you will find it rather in the Cape Peninsula, in places like the Paarl and Stellenbosch.' Lord Randolph Churchill reportedly said, 'The lofty granite mass of Table Mountain, the distant ranges of hills stretching over half the horizon and the calm waters of Table Bay brought into the mind successively Gibraltar, the Riviera, and the Bay of Palermo' (quoted in Cape Town 1911: 2). Here is Fairbridge's (1928: 188-89) description of Cape weather:

> It is not always calm in the Cape Peninsula. If Pan still pipes among the flowers and reeds of Table Mountain, rude Boreas still rides the storm.
> Stand on the beach at Camp's Bay when the south-easter is blowing. How the wind shouts and exults as it sweeps down the valley and flings itself out to sea. Over the heads of the Twelve Apostles it soars, over the great mountain behind Cape Town, wrapped in its mantle of vapour. It hurls itself against the Lion's Head and is deflected out to sea, singing a wild paean of triumph as it beats down the poplars and tears the wild geraniums from their stems.
> Rude Boreas, did I say?
> Nay, here are Alecto, Megaera, and Tisiphone, shrieking down the blast, churning the green waves to foam, tearing the white sand from the beaches to fling it in your face, stinging and blinding you. Black Auster rides abroad tonight, with Eurus on his right hand. For the spirits of the Winds and the Furies are holding Saturnalia on the Camp's Bay beach.

These are perhaps commonplace tropes of late Victorian and Edwardian landscape writing, deriving from the example of John Ruskin, from the ubiquitous influence of travel guides such as Murray or Baedeker, or (lastly) the thespian spirit of art nouveau. The first tourist handbook published by the Corporation of Cape Town in 1911 adjures the traveller to 'bring your volumes of Ruskin when starting "Southward Ho!"' The editor of the guidebook quotes at length from *The Stones of Venice* to indicate how apposite this text is to the Cape.

The history of western tourism is very much the history of travel in Italy, Greece, and Egypt, and it is understandable that the experiences of these regions should be transposed into writings about the Cape. The following quotation from the published account of a journey to South Africa in 1894 illustrates this use of Mediterranean allusions as a frame of reference in English travel writing in the late Victorian and the Edwardian age:[26]

> CARE AMICE, – When I sent you word that I was going to South Africa in search of health, you first tried to dissuade me from my purpose . . . You urged me to come eastward; the Golden Horn alone was worth all the beauties of South Africa put together . . . In South Africa these charms would be conspicuous by their absence. The country had nothing in common with one's love of antiquity and beauty; no ancient towns, no architectural monuments; none of the refined atmosphere always surrounding places 'with a history' as with a halo ... You referred to our old Egyptian days; to Cairo, its tombs and mosques; the desert and its wonderful freedom:

to our delightful evenings, when you instructed me in the art of coffee-making, and conversation never flagged, and magic surrounded us, and the sands of life were gilded by the charms of a new-found friendship.

(Wood 1894: 48–50)

Despite this dissuasive start, the author then applies the same frame of reference to his newfound pleasure in the Cape coastal landscape: 'Point after point stretching out into a succession of lovely bays, and the sea today rolled over the white sand with a soothing, sleepy murmur: the most wonderfully green, transparent water imaginable. Not more lovely the waters of the Mediterranean which you have watched beating against the classic shores of Alexandria: not more lovely the waters which flow upwards to the mouth of your beloved Golden Horn' (ibid: 144). Finding a blue lotus flower in a pool on the road to Stellenbosch, this traveller waxed nostalgic for the Orient: 'Visions of a flashing sunlit Nile; of moonlit Pyramids steeped in the solemn silence of midnight, the solitude of endless plains; of wonderful mosques; of the tombs of the Caliphs, where we spent those magic hours under the moonbeams . . . We would have plucked and carried away this wonderful solitary lotus flower, but it was out of reach, and we had to leave it to blossom in its earthly paradise' (ibid.: 230). Finally, by a rather more violent effort of the imagination, he compared the new urban growth on the Rand to the phenomenon of the city of Memphis among the desert sands of Egypt:

> Here in the midst of a desert rose this wonderful hive. All building material had to be brought from an immense distance, reminding one a little of the Egyptians of old, building the Pyramids. And verily we might call Johannesburg a modern Cairo or Memphis, stripped of all beauty and romance . . . [In ten years time it will] be important and imposing, more nearly approaching the modern Memphis we have compared it to: and its temples will be underground, and its obelisks will be factory chimneys. These are the features of the 19th century; and in the year 4000 these will be its 'buried treasures.'

(ibid.: 310, 316)

Apparently material reasons explain why a Mediterranean frame of reference for the Cape (and indeed for South Africa at large) should have been so prevalent at the time, although this is a topic not yet broached by Cape cultural historians. The Islamic connection is one reason. Another is the perception in the mid-nineteenth century that the climate at the Cape was beneficial for consumption. Yet another was the Anglo-Indian habit of spending furloughs at the Cape, thereby ensuring that they did not fall onto half pay.[27] These perceptions gave rise to an interpretation of the Cape as a place for leisured activities on the existing model of popular continental and Mediterranean resorts. A report in the *Egyptian Gazette* of 5 July 1898, of a *conversazione* given by the British Balneological and Climatological Society, commends the health facilities in Egypt and South Africa as superior to those to be found on the Continent: 'Continental health resorts are often unsuited – stressful, costly, unhygienic, and bad . . . This must of necessity lead to the opening up of the unrivalled health resorts of the British colonies. Egypt and South Africa have already begun to reap the benefits, and Australia, New Zealand and Canada will no doubt soon do so.'

Perhaps the most celebrated Victorian consumptive at the Cape was Lucie Duff Gordon, who after a year went on to Egypt for her health. 'This climate,' she wrote about the Cape, 'is evidently a styptic of great power. I shall write a few lines to the *Lancet* about Caledon and its hot baths.' Her *Letter from the Cape* (1864 [1927]) was followed by the publication of *Letters from Egypt* (1865). In the letters of 1864 she exhibits a marked bias toward the Cape 'Malay' people, pronouncing them to be more skilled and industrious than the English, the Dutch, or any other social groupings at the Cape: '"Malay" means here Mohammedan. They were Malays, but now embrace every shade from the blackest to the most blooming Englishwoman. Yes, indeed, the emigrant girls turn Malay pretty often, and get thereby husbands who know not billiards and brandy – the two diseases of Cape Town. They risk plurality of wives, and profess Islam; but they get fine clothes and industrious husbands. I am going to see one of the Mullahs with Dr Chiappini soon, and to look at their schools and mosques' (quoted in Frank 1994:217). She befriends an elderly Muslim couple, emancipated slaves, who sent their son to study at Al Azhar Islamic University or *Madrassah* in Cairo. In a letter to her husband she requests him to ask Ross (her daughter's husband, working in Egypt) 'to cause inquiries to be made among the Mullahs of Cairo for a Hadji, by name, Abdul Rachman, the son of Abdul Jemaalee, of Cape Town'.

After a year at the Cape, Duff Gordon's condition required that she seek drier conditions, which she found in Egypt, where she became a celebrity on the banks of the Nile, living in a house built on top of the temple of Philae at Luxor. Duff Gordon was a leading figure in London literary society, a friend of George Meredith and of Alexander William Kinglake, author of the orientalist classic *Eothen*. Her writings about the 'Malays' and 'Mohammedans' are the mainstay of an orientalist tradition in the Cape, which we trace from Duff Gordon through Fairbridge (who edited a later edition of the *Letters from the Cape)* to I. D. du Plessis, the Afrikaans poet and self-appointed patron of the 'Cape Malays'. Duff Gordon's great-grandnephew Gordon Waterfield (1937: 4), author of a book on modern Egyptian history, paying tribute to her in 1937, emphasised her egalitarian spirit:[28] 'No one has described native life in South Africa and Egypt with such sympathy and penetration. Her views and her manner of life are of especial interest now when a technique of behaviour is being evolved to meet changes in political relations between Western and Oriental nations.'

Fairbridge's novel *Piet of Italy* (1913) vividly dramatises the Islamic and the Mediterranean connections. In this narrative a child washed up at Kalk Bay harbour is rescued by a Muslim family living in Cape Town's Malay Quarter of Schotsche Kloof. They believe the child is their son Piet, who drowned, restored to them by Allah. He is raised as a faithful Muslim trained in the Koran and speaking the Taal. He demonstrates an aptitude for drawing and sculpture, which gains him an apprenticeship with a Cape Town builder and stonemason. In his late teens he has an accident, and as he emerges from a prolonged coma, he recovers a long-lost identity, in which he is Pietro

Casanera, the Catholic scion of a noble Florentine family drowned in a shipwreck off the Cape coast. The accident arises from a necessary coincidence. Relatives of Pietro's lost family shipped an Egyptian obelisk from Italy to the Cape, intending that it be erected to the memory of the Casaneras. On the base of the obelisk are two inscriptions, one ancient and one new. One reads *'Neter mut, Bareniḳet'*, or 'Divine Mother, Berenice'. The other runs:

> *Pietro, Elena e Pietro Casanera.*
> *Nessum maggior dolore*
> *Che recordarsi del tempo felice*
> *Nella miseria*

> [Pietro, Elena and Pietro Casanera.
> There is no greater grief
> Than to record times of joy
> In the midst of sadness]

(Fairbridge 1913: 97)

Piet (or Pietro) stumbles and hits his head against this obelisk while assisting in its erection, and consequently this most Freemasonic of mnemonic devices becomes the means of his recovery of a lost identity, heritage, culture, language, and religion.[29]

Alongside the topic of the Cape Malays we encounter a recurring attempt to link the Cape 'bushmen' with *Ur*-people from northern Africa or southern Europe, such as the Hyksos or the Etruscans. As early as 1859 Frederick Maskew, writing in Cape Town, published *The History of Joseph* with an 'appendix on the analogy between the subjugation of the Egyptians to the Hyksos, and the Kafirs to the British'. Carl Peters (1902: 387-91), the German romancer of the Zimbabwe ruins, attempted to draw links between the Hottentots and the Egyptians. In her novel *The Uninvited,* set in England and in Egypt, Fairbridge (1926: 128) has the first-person narrator speculate in a similar fashion:

> Leaving out the revelation of the boy's soul, we could have traced the proportion of European influence as compared with that of the aboriginal Hottentots, together with the considerations of surroundings and their influence on the mother, as distinguished from heredity. Then, taking the Hottentots as a starting point, we would have pursued our investigations into the history of that curious race, debating whether the theory which links them (through the Bushmen) to the Cave Dwellers of ancient Spain, is tenable, and whether there is anything to be said in favour of those who assert that the Hyksos Kings of Egypt were in reality Hottentots, and that the so-called Egyptian type may be traced throughout Africa from north to south.[30]

This kind of speculation finds its place in the primitivist debates of the early twentieth century, in particular in the aesthetic primitivism of modern artistic and literary movements as typified by D. H. Lawrence in his 'savage pilgrimage' to Italy, Ceylon, Australia, and New Mexico. Lawrence's *Sea and Sardinia* (1927) was illustrated by the South

African artist Jan Juta, son of the Speaker of the Cape House of Assembly. Juta travelled in Mediterranean Europe with Lawrence, and his later writings, including speculative meditations on the provenance of the Zimbabwe ruins (1972: 182–93), are deeply influenced by Lawrence's themes and idioms. Primitivism is further expressed in the interest, during the 1920s, in the Kalahari bushmen, typically in Laurens van der Post's Jungian understanding of these people.[31] The *Ur* people discourse runs from Benin bronzes to Lawrentian primitivism, modernist ethnographic speculations, and Jungian theory. A distinct expression of the entire continent as a geographical equivalent to the idea of the human unconscious appears in Graham Greene's *Journey Without Maps*:

> The 'heart of darkness' was common to us both [Europe and Africa]. Freud has made us conscious as we have never been before of those ancestral threads which still exist in our unconscious minds to lead us back. The need, of course, has always been felt, to go back and begin again. Mungo Park, Livingstone, Stanley, Rimbaud, Conrad represented only another method to Freud's, a more costly, less easy method, calling for physical as well as mental strength. The writers, Rimbaud and Conrad, were conscious of this purpose, but one is not certain how far the explorers knew the nature of the fascination which worked on them in the dirt, the disease, the barbarity and the familiarity of Africa.
>
> (Greene 1957[1936]: 252)

Jan Juta's sister René Juta lived in the south of France, where she wrote two travel books in the Lawrentian dithyrambic style, illustrated by her brother. In her book *Cannes and the Hills* (1924), dedicated to Kipling, she makes the following statement, which is typical of this romantic primitivism: 'But gone are the old songs and dances, the dances of Provence wherein lay a literature of the people. In the late seventeenth century, the dance called Rigaudin was forbidden on pain of a beating, and later, on pain of death; it being regarded as a public disgrace, so curious were the gestures and figures of the dance. I suspect the Rigaudin of being the remains of a pagan, sacrificial, ritualistic dance, less bacchanalian, more like the curious obscene dances of the Hottentots of Africa, who so oddly resemble the small mountain race which lived in the caves above Nice' (Juta 1924:94).

Lawrence in Italy sported with the Pan cult prevalent at the turn of the century in writings set in Italy and Greece and which persisted into the 1920s – observable in short stories by E. M. Forster and in Buchan's novel *The Dancing Floor* (1926), which deals with the return of archaic ritual on a modern-day Greek island.[32] This Pan cult, alternatively a Dionysian cult, emerged in modernist literary discourses of the same period set in the Cape. The following scene from Fairbridge's *The Torchbearer* is a good example. The setting is a cellar on a Cape wine farm. A worker is crushing grapes with his feet:

> A mist hung before Katherine's eyes after a time, and the cellar seemed to have widened out until it was the width of the whole world. The little dancing figure had grown taller and more graceful. His hair was hair now – not pepper-corns – and it clustered over his ears and concealed them. Vine-leaves were wreathed round his head, a leopard-skin hung from his shoulders. And

still he sang and danced – and as he sang the meaning of the song was revealed to her. He sang of the life-giving sun and of the joy of existence, of the sparkle on the waves, of the song of the birds, the scent of flowers, the cool softness of the breeze, the ecstasy that is youth. And then he clashed together the cymbal that he held in his hands, and in a low voice that vibrated through every chord of Katherine's being, he sang of love. Of love of man for woman, of woman for man. Of love triumphant and rejoicing – and his voice rang out in rapture as he sang of the love that is the greatest thing in this world. And then the beautiful voice fell to deep, vibrant tones as he sang of the love that is sacrifice, of the love that knows no earthly fruition, of the love that is greater than death itself.

(Fairbridge 1915: 256)

Perhaps the most striking and typical of contemporary manifestations of the preoccupation with the Mediterranean were, however, architectural. Freemasonry, with its complex rituals and self-invented traditions and genealogies, lent during the period of the new imperialism a particularly powerful symbolism to the idea of the built environment. This was of course by no means the only set of meanings accruing to architecture at the time. Other major contemporary discourses around building derived from John Ruskin and his ideas concerning the historicity of architecture[33] and from the related revival at the turn of the century of vernacular architectural styles. At the same time, the architect Sir Herbert Baker recognised the value of the grand style of classical simplicity for the design of public spaces and buildings in South Africa, a country, (1909: 517) Baker wrote in an early essay, that 'the Arch-Architect has designed so essentially in the "grand manner". . . . It would be easy to imagine a Pergamos or Halicarnassus growing out of any semicircle of the cliffs that stretch from Muizenberg to Simon's Town, or rising from any of the encircling hills of Pretoria or Bloemfontein'. In the same essay Baker (522) clearly states the link between climate and architectural style: 'It is the South African architect's privilege, and one much envied by his fellow craftsmen in northern Europe, to have always at hand the most valuable of all materials for his craft (which the Greeks and Romans also had), warm sun-bathed wall surfaces contrasted with deep, cool shadows.' In 1900 Rhodes sent Baker 'to visit the old countries of the Mediterranean.' Baker (1944: 35) wrote in his autobiography, 'He wished me particularly to see "Rome, Paestum, Agrigentum, Thebes, and Athens", and to study other such great masterpieces of architecture and sculpture.' Baker subsequently travelled in Egypt, Greece, Italy, and Sicily and established an architectural scholarship at the British School at Rome for South African students to give them 'the opportunity of studying the great architectural and artistic traditions of classical art in the Mediterranean countries which have a similar range of climatic conditions to those which prevail in South Africa' (ibid.: 36). As is well known, in his own career he designed public buildings (other than in England) in Salisbury (Harare), Nairobi, Cairo, Khartoum, and – together with Sir Edwin Lutyens – the vast project of New Delhi in India.[34]

At the same time, the artist J. H. Pierneef, who was working in Pretoria in sympathy with emerging Afrikaner nationalist cultural traditions, gave lectures on the idea of a South African architectural idiom. His biographer (Nel 1990: 131) wrote that

Pierneef 'regularly pointed out parallels between South Africa and Egypt: the atmosphere with its intense heat, the contrast between desert and cultivated land, the enormous contrasts between plains and peaks which unexpectedly rise hundreds of meters without any gentle slopes. He showed how the Egyptians had used these circumstances in a monumental art form. Sharp verticals and horizontal lines laid the foundation for the austere Egyptian architecture, an art of great durability, majesty and harmony. Pierneef visualised a South African art of this kind: simple, and monumental on a grand scale.'

The final section of this essay will suggest that the architecture of the period, and the landscape, may be interpreted as the backdrop or stage setting for certain kinds of performances. In this colonial African mise-en-scène colonial identities were rehearsed and social or ethnic 'types' were enacted.

Tourism, Journalism, and Performance

'If it is not "Assouan" it is "Durbar"! Mostly you take your choice – a great many people take both. Among these are Mr and Mrs. Rochefort Maguire; but then the Durbar, in their case, is only one incident in a comprehensive tour of India. Sir George and Lady Farrar are also "Durbar-ing".'

African World and Cape-to-Cairo Express, 15 November 1902

This journalist adds that the Duke and Duchess of Connaught are leaving London for Egypt to attend the opening of the Assouan Dam, then afterward they will travel on HMS *Renown* to India for the Delhi Durbar; that the royal academician and painter of odalisques and harem scenes, Sir Lawrence Alma-Tadema, arrives in Cairo; and that Joe Chamberlain sails for the Cape on HMS *Good Hope* via Suez. The Duke laid the foundation stone of the dam with Masonic ritual; as the *Good Hope* bearing the colonial secretary neared Table Bay, the ship was welcomed by a mass performance on the flanks of the Twelve Apostles by thousands of school children manipulating tiny mirrors against the sun. In Edwardian public culture, travel, tourist performance, ritual, and fantasy were of a piece. Thomas Cook's *Traveller's Gazette, Excursionist and Tourist Advertiser* of September 1910 recommends the following:

Visitors to the Cape during the early part of November will be able to add an extra item of exceptional interest to the usual programme of sightseeing, viz., the Pageant at Cape Town, arranged in order to celebrate the opening of the Union Parliament, at which the Duke of Connaught will be present. The various scenes in this great spectacle will be presented at the foot of Table Mountain, on a scale closely resembling that held on the Plains of Abraham in Canada last year. The mastership of the Pageant has been entrusted to Mr Frank Lascelles, who is organising the Festival of Empire and Pageant of London to be held at the Crystal Palace next year.

In this final section this essay suggests that the Cape-to-Cairo idea was typical of Edwardian imperial sentiment in its emphasis on travel, tourism, exhibitionism, and performances of various kinds. The idea of performance will be the guiding motif in that tourism and the experience of the great exhibitions are both in some ways likened to theatrical productions with directors, casts, backdrops, and audiences. In all these cases illusions are maintained by a variety of techniques, in themselves as mundane and practical as railway schedules but designed to render the mundane into something special.

John Pemble (1987: 273) described the attitudes of English travellers in the Mediterranean: 'There was an unwillingness to allow the Mediterranean to become mundane and insipid; a desire to delay the dawn of common day and prolong the visitation of enchantment . . . Writers who would capture the genius loci felt the need to work fast, before novelty lost its power and nerves became too slack to vibrate.' The fact of the matter is that the mundane is ever-present, even in the midst of novelty and enchantment. The point was made earlier in this essay that the topic of the Cape-to-Cairo idea evinces a kind of sylleptic logic, a constant mingling of the sublime and the bathetic. The organisation of the touristic experience demonstrates just such a mixture with its unavoidable combination of picturesque description along with practical matters, such as shipping timetables and dietary precautions. The logistics of tourism and the kind of journalism that promotes tourism reveal basic social dynamics side by side with the heightened fantasies of 'colonial desire' that perceive exotic wonders.

Basing his argument on the new material culture that developed around the phenomenon of the nineteenth-century great exhibitions and *expositions universelles,* Timothy Mitchell (1988) has persuasively demonstrated that Westerners viewed Cairo during the colonial period as a living exhibition of antiquities, goods, and ethnic types. For Mitchell, the culture of ephemera, such as exhibition catalogues, guidebooks, souvenirs, maps, tables, and statistics, distinguishes between the exhibited and 'what it stands for.' 'These mediate between the visitor and the exhibition by supplementing what was displayed with a structure and a meaning' (Mitchell 1988: 20). Paul Greenhalgh (1988: 52-81) has indicated the role the great exhibitions from 1851 to 1940 played in reinforcing British imperial propaganda. It seems reasonable to suggest that the rise of popular tourism during this same period, in particular the activities of the pioneer Thomas Cook, reinforce and reflect these trends. Cook organised his first popular excursion in England in 1841. While in 1869 he took his first party of tourists to Egypt and the Holy Land, the chronicler of the company Piers Brendon (1991:120) points out that 'as early as 1835 Murray's initial *Handbook* for Egypt was published . . . precursor of 165 different guides printed in England and America over the next eighty years.'

Cook enjoyed a monopoly in running steamers on the Nile. Thomas Cook and Sons was appointed agent to the Cape Government Railways in 1890 but only ran their first tour in southern Africa in 1894, with a six-month round-trip from Southampton to the Cape and up to Bulawayo, in the aftermath of the Matabele War. During the Anglo-Boer War, Thomas Cook and Sons conducted battlefield tours (Brendon 1991: 248); in a 1908 travel brochure they advertised a 'Conducted Tour through the Highlands of British East Africa including Victoria Nyanza, the Source of the Nile, the Mau

Escarpment, and the Primeval Forest.' In the same year they mounted a 'Durban Season Excursion Program' and 'Circular Tours by Land and Sea Covering all the Principal Towns in Cape Colony, Orange River Colony, Transvaal, Natal, Portuguese East Africa, and Rhodesia, including the Victoria Falls and Zimbabwe Ruins.' In 1914 they arranged a four-month tour to South Africa by sea from Southampton down the west coast of Africa via the Canary Isles. The tour in the union included peninsula excursions, a train to Bloemfontein, Kimberley, Paardeberg, the Victoria Falls, Bulawayo, Rhodes's grave at World's View on the Matopos, Johannesburg, Pretoria, Ladysmith, Spioen Kop, Marianhill Trappist monastery, Umkomaas, and Durban. The return voyage up the east coast took in Beira, Zanzibar, Mombasa, Aden, Suez and Port Said, Naples, Marseilles, and Gibraltar. The first Cook trip from Cairo to the Cape took place in 1922. The editorial notes in Cook's *Traveller's Gazette* of January 1922 (1, 72: 10–11) comment: 'The party which will leave London on February 2nd for Cairo thence through the Sudan, Uganda and the Congo to the Cape (arriving back in England on July 3rd), is an epoch-making one, for it is the first organised tour traversing the whole length of the great African continent. It includes a month's safari in big-game districts around Lake Kiva, under the personal guidance and direction of Sir Alfred Sharpe, KCMG, the distinguished explorer and administrator, and will be accompanied throughout by a competent member of our staff who knows the principal African languages.' The *Egyptian Gazette* of January 12, 1925, wrongly describes a six-month journey from Cairo to the Cape that year, also conducted by Cook, as the 'first attempt from north to south.' This tour party, made up of four wealthy North American 'sportsmen,' was conducted by an expedition leader from Uganda, a German photographer and cinema operator, and an East African 'white hunter.' The idea, according to the *Gazette* article, was to indulge in big-game hunting and to make 'photographic and cinematographic records of wild animals in their native habitats'.

Leo Weinthal, a South African-born entrepreneur and journalist, rivalled the activities of Thomas Cook and Son and specialised in southern Africa and Egypt. In 1902 he founded a newspaper based in London, the *African World and Cape-to-Cairo Express.* His efforts to promote tourism in Egypt won him the Order of Osmanieh in 1909 and Commander of the Order of the Nile in 1929. He wrote two guidebooks, one on the *Deutsche Öst-Afrika* line's voyages around the continent, *Round Africa by the Deutsche Öst-Africa Line* (1902), and *Fascinating Egypt* (1908).

In 1922, after the British occupation of German East Africa, Weinthal produced a belated but substantial tribute to Rhodes's idea in a five-volume *Story of the Cape to Cairo Railway and River Route, 1887–1922.* As an advisory board for this Brobdingnagian project, Weinthal recruited every possible survivor with a connection to Rhodes and to colonial Africa, every likely expert on the continent, and every amenable viceroy, sirdar, and colonial governor, from the general manager of the South African Railways to Sir Abe Bailey, Flinders Petrie and Lord Lugard. The contents include essays on the history, society, and natural conditions of the African states to be traversed by the prospective railway; the mercantile potential of these states and the benefit of rail transport; the railway engineering feats undertaken in East Africa; tourist topics, such as ethnographic studies of tribespeople; big-game hunting; the 'mysteries' of the Great Zimbabwe; the progress of colonial society in Cairo; and genial fantasies concerning the future of an 'unlocked' continent that would be crossed by great silver airships stopping airily at new cities to disembark their passengers – merchants, mining engineers, and families of colonial administrators.

The mere bulk of this five-volume opus lent a kind of cogency to what was no more than a dream. Such fantasies as an all-red Cape-to-Cairo route belonged to a past age; the world after Versailles no longer had place for such imperial claims. The timing of this huge prospectus is bizarre unless it is read for what it is, a post-war nostalgic fantasy that, like the tourism industry, sought to invent a market for its own commercial success as a publishing project. This aspect of self-invention and self-advertisement is the abiding sense of the Cape-to-Cairo idea. Its artificiality ('apt alliteration's artful aid') is constantly if unintentionally pronounced.

In Egypt itself, the idea of the Cape-to-Cairo link is encountered periodically as a rather languid speculation in the main English-language newspaper, the *Egyptian Gazette*, founded in 1880. On 1 July 1893 the paper reported: 'The Honourable Cecil Rhodes arrived in Cairo yesterday coming from Italy, via Ismailia. Mr Rhodes leaves Cairo on Monday next for Upper Egypt for a Nile trip of two weeks, and then proceeds to the Cape via Zanzibar and the East Coast. The scheme for laying telegraph wire from Cape Town to Cairo . . . will be commenced from south and carried north as far as can be. If Soodan is not captured by British troops, then the cable will be diverted along the coast. At present the most northerly point is Fort Salisbury in Mashonaland.' The *Egyptian Gazette* dutifully records the various arrivals and departures of Rhodes and his associates, including Sir James Sivewright, Sir Leander Starr Jameson, Sir Charles Metcalf, Rochefort Maguire, and Alfred Beit, as well as such other figures in the history of colonial Africa as Carl Peters, Mary Kingsley, and Captain Jean-Baptiste Marchand. The pages of this newspaper are telling in their constant emphasis on the activities of society tourists; the social programs of the famous Cairene hotels of the day; fetes and balls; the movements and parades of troops; the ceremonies of the many Egyptian Masonic lodges; and the Khedivial receptions, processions, funerals, and other public events. Interrupting this constant social pageant are the military dramas of Khartoum, Fashoda, Omdurman, and the South African War – the lists of regiments and the names of their officers read as a version of the social page.

During the first year of the SA War, a series of informed articles on South Africa appeared, written by H. A. Bryden and covering the spectrum of colonial South African history, fauna, flora, and topography. One passage from these articles pays tribute to the 'trekking spirit' of the Boers:

> The trekking passion is still there, it yet burns deep within the breast of many of these strange people. They have reached, after incredible sufferings, Portuguese West Africa – the province of Angola. They are filtering into Rhodesia, Bechuanaland and the Kalahari. They are not

unknown in Portuguese East Africa. They talk of moving yet further North into Central Africa. Knowing the trekking spirit of these farmers of the wilderness, it is not too much to predict that within fifty years some of them, at all events, will have reached, in their wanderings, the sources of the Nile. The Boer of South Africa, in truth, with the romance of the veldt still deep within him, is at this day one of the strangest, most interesting, and most moving studies of human character to be found upon the face of the globe.

(Egyptian Gazette, July 8,1899)

Mostly, however, the recognition of others of any sort by the British was either cursory or fantastical. Frequently the 'other' served as the subject for entertainment in fancy dress balls and similar social occasions. One particularly glittering evening saw the Gaekwar of Baroda and his maharani, guests of Lord and Lady Cromer, and Baron von Richtofen (dressed as a mendicant friar) at a masked ball among 'savage warriors from the Soodan, Arab Sheikhs, Odalisques, Gypsies', and the like *(Egyptian Gazette,* February 21, 1895). During the season a programme of fêtes at Heliopolis Palace Hotel (a building designed in 1910 in 'Saracenic' style) included *Une Nuit chez les Maures, Grande Fête Japonaise, Une Nuit Montmartre,* and *La Grande Fête Orientale.* No less typecast and directed were the funeral arrangements for the Khedive Ismail in 1895. The procession through Alexandria to the railway station included:

> 1. Mounted Police. 2. 100 coastguardsmen with two officers. 3. Religious deputations with banners. 4. The Fighis. 5. Mourners chanting prayers for the dead. 6. Two companies of Egyptian infantry, and band. 7. Police on foot. 8. Corporation of Dervishes. 9. Students at Mussulman colleges. 10. Native merchants and notables. 11. European merchants and notables. 12. Officials of the Daira Sanieh Customs and Railway. 13. High civil and military functionaries. 14. The Municipality. 12. Judges of the Alexandria Native and Mixed Tribunals. 16. The clergy. 15. Officers of the Army of Occupation, followed by British and other European Naval Officers. 18. The Consular Body. 19. The Ministers. 20. His Highness the Khedive (Chief Mourner). 21. Princes of the Khedivial family. 22. Officials of the Palace. 23. Ulemas. 24. Pupils of the Musselman schools. 25. Bearers of incense and books. 26. Officers of the Egyptian Marine. 27. The Coffin, borne by Egyptian sailors. 28. Mounted police. 29. Carriages of the Harem.

(Egyptian Gazette, March 9, 1895)

Another annual procession regularly recorded in the pages of the *Egyptian Gazette* was the departure during the month of Ramadan of the Holy Carpet from Cairo to travel to Mecca. The careful observation of social, military, and religious ritual seems to have been a noted feature of late Victorian and Edwardian public life, and it appears that, in a multicultural city such as Cairo, punctilious attention to social ritual was a form of diplomacy between different castes and nationalities.

Tourism in the period under consideration is frequently represented – in tour brochures and in travel writing – as a form of itinerant exhibition or pageant. People and places become types and backdrops, and tour brochures provide a kind of script in which the unfolding pageant is narrated. During the same period this idea of pageantry emerged in fact as a major genre of large-scale public performance in which jubilees and inaugural moments were celebrated by means of historical re-enactments or allegorical masques and tableaux.[35] A hypothetical etymology of *pageantry* may be drawn from the Latin *pangere,* from which root is derived the Latin for a field and a page as well as peace. 'Pax Britannica' is a condition that is enacted or performed. The field is held, the page is inscribed, and the peace is kept. The following description of the various peoples of the continent was written long after the age of empire, yet it propagates what became most distinctly (in discourses about the continent that predated the anti-colonial move-ments) an accepted dramatis personae for a touristic pageant play:

> Rhodes's aim, to put it briefly, was to link together the Cape Town 1820 settler from Europe; the cross-bred remnants of the Hottentots; the stolid, independent Afrikaners; the Zulu and Basuto, the Rhodesian immigrants from Leeds, or Dublin; the Matabele of Lobengula, the fishermen on Lake Nyasa; the lonely, backward tribesmen on the fringes of the Congo; the fierce, lion-hunting Masai; the white coffee and sisal growers around Mount Kilimanjaro; the adaptable Kikuyu; the advanced community of Buganda's Kabaka; the missionaries of all creeds; the naked Acholi of the southern Sudan; the tribesmen who live in the swamps of the Sudd; the slave-trading Arabs of Khartoum; the fuzzy-wuzzies from the East; the diseased and down-trodden fellahin of the Nile; and the suave, elegant, intelligent, businessmen of modern Cairo.
>
> (Smith 1961: 16)

The geographical idea of the Cape-to-Cairo link itself became a topic for dressing up and for decorative design, as in William Plomer's (1984 [1933]: 155) description of a fancy dress costume in his biography of Rhodes:

> [The Southampton–Cape Town ocean voyages] had not been without a touch of fantasy. Dur-ing one of them an obscure young woman had appeared at the customary fancy-dress ball in a costume representing 'Cape to Cairo', with a picture of Table Mountain and Table Bay in water-colours at the bottom, and pictures representing the chief towns on the way to Cairo all the way up the skirt, all joined together with a string of telegraph poles and wire in black, while on her head was a fez and crescent, one breast being covered with a portrait of Kitchener and the other with a portrait of Rhodes himself.

As Benedict Anderson (1991:175) has pointed out in a different context, the map has been taken up as a form of symbol or 'logo': 'pure sign, no longer compass to the world. In this shape, the map entered an infinitely reproducible series, available for transfer to posters, official seals, letterheads, magazine and textbook covers, tablecloths, and hotel walls'. The map of Africa, with its gouache of imperial red and its spinal serpent of Rhodes's projected railway, a seeming extension of the uraeus-like Nile, entered into the realm of the iconic. It was adopted by the Africana bibliographer Sidney Mendelssohn as his bookplate, and it became a Cook poster and a design for dust jackets.

The idea of the Cape-to-Cairo link has been held before the public most commonly in terms of travel – expeditions by foot, motorcar, bicycle, motorcycle, or air. An early attempt at this journey was made by a Czech medical doctor and naturalist, Emil Holub, who worked in South Africa in the mid-nineteenth century. In the 1880s, accompanied by his wife, he unsuccessfully attempted a trip to Cairo. The first to claim this achievement on foot were two Cambridge students, Ewart Scott Grogan and Arthur H. Sharp, in 1899.[36] They asked Rhodes to write an introduction to their account of this journey, and he entered into the spirit of their 'lark' by saying that 'the amusement of the whole thing is that a youth from Cambridge, during his vacation, should have succeeded in doing that which the ponderous explorers of the world have failed to accomplish' (Grogan and Sharp 1902: vii).

Most typical of the 1920s and 1930s were the numerous automobile journeys across the continent in which drivers of different nationalities (French, German, British, South African) rivalled one another with regard to the marques they drove and the time they took. In 1924 a Citroën team made the first north-south crossing of the continent from Morocco to Mozambique, and a Renault team made the first crossing of the Sahara from Algeria to Niger in one week. Members of the latter expedition then attempted the first fully motorised north-south journey in 1925, covering 22,500 kilometres in eight months and building or repairing 129 bridges on the way. Major Court-Treatt and his wife, Stella Court-Treatt, made the first motor journey from south to north driving two Crossleys. Their journey (which was written up by Stella Court-Treatt in 1927) took sixteen months. In 1928 Gerry Bouwer, a South African racing driver, and Emil Millin, the motoring editor of the *Rand Daily Mail,* made the journey in three months, in a Chrysler. Bouwer and his wife did the return journey in a record forty days. Two Girl Guide officers, M. L. Belcher and E. C. Budgell, tackled the journey in 1930 in a six-year-old Morris Cowley nicknamed 'Bohunkus,' which they then drove on to Oxford (Belcher 1932).[37] In 1936, the same year Carl von Hoffman published a children's novel entitled *Jerry on Safari: A 7,000 Mile Journey from Cairo to the Cape,* two South African brothers, Jack Attwell and Eric Attwell, made the traverse by bicycle from Port Elizabeth to London via Cairo, Athens, and Budapest (Attwell 1997).

The numerous subsequent transcontinental journeys by cycle, on foot, or by motor vehicle deserve to be listed.[38] The point for this paper, however, is that, again, the attempt from Cape Town to Cairo or vice versa is a kind of performance – a feat, a heroic lark, an attempt at a record, a point to be proven, amid a set of legends rehearsed in travel. Other than by air, it has never been a practical itinerary for regular travellers. It is in effect a symbolic journey signifying a set of decidedly colonialist interpretations of the continent: the modernising prowess of technology pitched against the hazards of the land; the treating of indigenous Africans as a touristic or ethnological phenomenon; the idea that 'Africa' is an undifferentiated mass to be overcome, whether by heroism or facility.

Heroism or titanism were the associations attached to Rhodes as a person and to his imperial schemes.[39] This 'colossus' chose to be buried in the Matopos in Zimbabwe, as if these mountains were a great mausoleum and he the body proper. The progress of his funeral cortege from Cape Town to the Matopos was itself a kind of pageant performance, described by Sarah Gertrude Millin (1952 [1933]: 352) in her hagiography of Rhodes:

> The body of Rhodes passed along the path of his spirit: from Cape Town where he had ruled, through the Western Province of his vineyards, to Kimberley that had begotten his dreams and his wealth, along his own railway in Bechuanaland [a country that Rhodes called 'the Suez of the South'], through the country of his name, to the hills where he had made peace with the sons of Moselikatze.
>
> A gun-carriage, drawn by twelve oxen, carried the coffin up the black slope of his hill. It was lowered with chains into the rock. The hill was swarming with the Matabele he had won and betrayed and won again and succoured. 'Our father is dead!' they cried, and gave him, alone of white men before or since, the royal salute of 'Bayete!'

This theatrical description is the essence of the Cape-to-Cairo idea: the staging of particular scenarios subsequently rehearsed in murals and on monuments, in fiction and in speculation, and in modern-day theme parks; the wishful thinking or make-believe of the theatre; sleight of hand; the fanciful backdrops of architectural styles; the casting of explorers as principal actors and indigenous Africans as picturesque and type-cast extras,[40] an imperial mise-en-scène that rehearses a desire for a meaning that never was – a colonial projection upon the land.[41] As a coda to this essay, the following passage from Fairbridge's *The Pilgrim's Way in South Africa* (1928) epitomises this desire. The author sought to yoke the Cape to Mediterranean Europe, and she imagined that this link exhibited both a picturesque antiquity and progressive modernity. Like all writing of the period concerning the Cape-to-Cairo connection, it is both a prospect (a northward-oriented picturesque landscape) and a prospectus for projected schemes:

> Home again, up the winding road and over the Kloof Nek to where Cape Town glitters below you, as she lies in the lap of the mountains.
>
> The glow of moonlight still rests on the summits of the mountains across the bay, but the water is deep, dark grey now, with silver gleams where the lazy waves break at the city's feet. She is ringed with jewelled lights, as is Naples, and through the lights a long, straight road cuts northward, always northward, through smiling vine-lands and the parched Karoo to cities yet unborn, and – at long, long last – to Cairo.[42]

(Fairbridge 1928: 1890)

Appendix

'From the Cape to Cairo'

From Cape Town's mountain-minster, from Durban's lake of sleep
The steeds of steel are hasting, their inland tryst to keep;

From Inyak and Algoa, from rock-barr'd Buffalo –
For whereso'er the white men fare, those steeds of steel must go.

Across the tawny desert that slender thread is flung,
O'er arch'd and column'd granite the bridge of bronze is hung;
Beneath the Rainbow Forest 'tis washed with torrent spray,
And thru' the sand, one burning band, sparkles the living way.

By silent Tanganyika the thunder-wheel shall beat,
By all the land-bound waters shall press those flaming feet –
Shall pierce the central forests for many an endless mile,
Burst with their freight through Egypt's gate, and race beside the Nile.

The oldest of the cities shall see earth's newest things;
The oldest of the rivers shall feel their rushing wings.
Oh, messengers of magic, not vainly are ye spent;
The word ye give makes nations live, and binds a continent!

Lance Fallaw, 1909

Notes

1   Acknowledgments to Cy Reed, director of the Office of African Studies, the American University in Cairo, for a visiting fellowship in 1994 and to him and his wife Carol for hosting me on subsequent visits; M. Ali Ebrahim, editor in chief, for access to back numbers of the *Egyptian Gazette;* to Samir W. Raafat of Cairo for advice and support; to the archivist of the Thomas Cook archives, London; and to Keith Grenville of the South African Egyptian Society for the opportunity to air these ideas in the form of a public lecture.

2   The following quotation from a Freemasonic handbook (Gould 1911, 2: 85) is apposite: 'Mr Truter relates, that in the southern extremity of Africa, among the Betjuanas, he saw children busy in tracing on a rock with some sharp instrument, characters which bore the most perfect resemblance to the P and the M of the Roman alphabet; notwithstanding which, these rude tribes were perfectly ignorant of writing.'

3   Robert Young (1995:128) points out how Egyptology was used in the nineteenth century as a means of justifying (by the claim that ancient Egyptians were Caucasian) the belief that Caucasians were superior to Negro races. This usage of Egyptology is fundamental to my general thesis that the Cape-to-Cairo idea was motivated by colonialist racial fantasies.

4   'Elizabethanism' emerged at the beginning of the twentieth century as a nostalgic means of articulating English identity, evidently in the face of the traumas of modernisation. It appears to be a popular fashion that replaced late-nineteenth-century medievalising (as in the Gothic trend in design, the pre-Raphaelite movement, and the fashion for Arthurian legend). Elizabethanism is rampant in the modernist English literary culture (most obviously in the work of T. S. Eliot and aspects of Virginia Woolf) but enjoyed its major manifestation in the expansion of the Shakespeare Memorial Movement at Stratford-upon-Avon and in the phenomenon of the 'new pageantry' that swept England from 1905 until the 1930s. A contemporaneous preoccupation in Germany with Indo-Aryan national mythology is partially grounded in the romantic linguistic and folkloric school of Jacob and Wilhelm Grimm and partly, for example, in the speculative archaeology of Heinrich Schliemann, who sought evidence to link 'Aryan' Germany with ancient Sanskrit origins. For a concise history of the nineteenth-century German schools of comparative philology see R. H. Robins 1969: 164–84. And for a useful discussion of Indo-Aryan fantasy see Malcolm Quinn 1994: 22–46.

5   It is noteworthy that in 1910, the year of South African union, Sergey Pavlovich Diaghilev's Ballets Russes produced *Schéhérazade* at the Paris Opera with the orientalist choreography, libretto, and stage setting of Michel Fokine and Léon Bakst. The ballet had produced *Cleopatra* in the preceding year and the Hindu-styled *Le Dieu Bleu* in 1912.

6   It is difficult to trace any literature on the topic of the Cape-to-Cairo that is not strictly firsthand travel narrative, for instance by Anthony Smith (1961), or synoptic histories of the period that deal with the transcontinental idea in terms of international diplomacy, exploration, and missionary activity, such as by Lois Raphael (1936) or Mark Strage (1973). A fair number of early commentaries on the idea appear in such period journals as *Fortnightly Review, Empire Review, Contemporary Review, United Empire,* and the *Nineteenth Century.* Of course the five-volume opus published by the enthusiast Leo Weinthal (1922) remains a work to excavate for primary material, as are his London-based *Africa News* and *Cape-to-Cairo Gazette.* A recent chapter on the subject by James B. Wolf, 'Imperial Integration on Wheels: The Car, the British and the Cape to-Cairo Route' (1991), is full of factual errors, including mistaking intrepid women automobilists for men, but it has a helpful if incomplete bibliography. The cultural interpretation of the idea of the Cape as 'Mediterranean' apparently has not yet been addressed at all. As far as current interpretations of the idea of the 'Cape-to-Cairo' are concerned, interest in Africa tourism and in travel writing is experiencing a resurgence. The oil company Engen, for instance, has joined the Cape Metropolitan Tourism authority in launching a Web site entitled 'African Dream' (www.openafrica.org) to promote tourism in Africa. Apart from South African president Mbeki's continental vision of the African Renaissance, the Egyptian Ministry of Foreign Affairs has a blueprint for a Cairo-Gaborone Trans-East Africa Highway that, according to Ambassador Safwat Ayoub, director of the Research and Policy Planning Department, may be extended all the way to Cape Town now that apartheid has ended (Ayoub1997).

7   See the Engen newsletter *Pipeline* (July 1999) and the related Web site www.openafrica.org for an account of the launch of the Open Africa Cape-to-Cairo Afrikatourism project. Details of the African Connection Rally are accessible on www.africanconnection.org.

8   I am grateful to my colleague Hermann Wittenberg (2000: 237) for pointing this out in his essay on the 1906 Duca d'Abruzzi expedition to the Ruwenzori Mountains.

9   Thank you to Sakkie Cornelius of Stellenbosch University for drawing my attention to this building.

10   The Russian Theodore Gurdjieff was a Svengali-like figure who practised alternative and Eastern forms of psychic wholeness and spirituality in the early decades of the twentieth century, attracting a large following of converts. See Cecil Lewis (1984) for an account of the Gurdjieff cult and a description of the transcontinental flight over Africa.

11   Perhaps domestic economy is a good metaphor for taking control. In any event a fanciful book on domestic economy in colonial South Africa, Madeline Alston, *From an Old Cape Homestead* (1929), situates its final chapter in Egypt. The rest of this book is a series of essays on Cape domestic economy, South African society, immigration, the suitability of various races as domestic servants, links with Britain, Afrikaner nationalism, farming, flora, and South African poetry.

12   A later but exemplary instance of this trope by Conrad Lighton (1951) is a once-popular social and historical comparison of South Africa and Australia evidently timed for publication to make the most of the market created by the 1952 Jan van Riebeeck tercentenary, just as the moment of union in 1910 precipitated a spate of popular publications.

13   Rhodes's extravagant notion of an Anglo-Saxon world government is not peculiar to him. The cult of the British Israelite Truth propagated this idea widely and popularly from about 1870 to the early 1950s, claiming that Great Britain, the United States, and the British dominions were the lost tribes of Israel and would come into their own by inheriting the governorship of the earth. The British Israelites are in fact a further source of Egyptophilia within British imperial discourse. One of their number, the Astronomer Royal for Scotland, Charles Piazzi-Smythe, published a study of the Great Pyramid in which he argued

that this monument embodies clues to the destiny of Britain. A host of British Israelite books propagate their cult. One example claims that the two obelisks Egypt gave to England and the United States in the late nineteenth century are 'way marks' that prove these two nations are the descendants of the sons of Joseph borne in Egypt, Ephraim and Manasseh, the names of the two lost tribes consequently held to be Britain and America (MacKendrick 1921: 51).

14   The new imperialism is the phenomenon from circa 1880 to 1900 when (broadly speaking) national rivalry among Britain, France, and Germany spurred Britain to expand and consolidate colonial posses- sions in Africa and elsewhere.

15   Some countries have their own Freemasonic Constitutions or governing bodies, the most influential of which are the English Constitution or the Grand Lodge of England, the Scottish Constitution, and the Grand Orient of France. These national bodies are empowered to exercise authority over local lodges established under their respective constitutions in other countries, such as in the British colonies and dominions.

16   For information on this magazine see Peter Merrington 1997a.

17   Dorothea Fairbridge (1862–1931) was a prolific South African author described as a 'nation builder' whose work and reputation have been largely neglected due to her unfashionable imperial loyalties. She is referred to several times in this essay. The present author has published an essay about her (Merrington 1995).

18   From the title page of Baker's biography of Rhodes (1934).The same glyph appears with variations in stucco on the walls of Baker's London House and South Africa House in London and Rhodes House in Oxford, all built in the same decade.

19   See Peter Garlake 1982 and Wilfred Mallows 1985 for treatment of the history of the reception of the ruins by colonial authors.

20   This novel is discussed by Stephan Meyer (1996).

21   The columns that support the entrance to every Masonic lodge are named Jachin and Boaz, and their symbolism are central to Masonic ritual.

22   This trend was evident at the close of the nineteenth century in the popular fascination with spiritism (pursued with keen interest by Kipling and Sir Arthur Conan Doyle) and the emergence of new cults, such as Mary Baker Eddy's Christian Science, Annie Besant's Hare Krishna movement (with which the imperial architect and colleague of Herbert Baker, Sir Edwin Lutyens, became involved via his wife's theosophical interests), Madame Blavatsky's theosophical movement, Rudolf Steiner's anthroposophy, and the cult that developed around the person of Gurdjieff. See also Nicholas Goodrick-Clarke 1985 for links between occultism and Freemasonry in Austria-Germany in the late nineteenth and early twentieth centuries.

23   The figure of Van der Stel also reflects, in these religious views, the opinions of Rev. H. C. V. Leibbrandt, first archivist of the Cape government, to whom this novel is dedicated. As archivist Leibbrandt, himself a Unitarian and for that reason defrocked by the Dutch Reformed Church, made the life and work of Van der Stel his particular hobby. It should be added that as early as the late eighteenth century the Dutch church accused the oldest Masonic lodge in South Africa, the Lodge de Goode Hoop in Cape Town, of preaching deism. For a history of Freemasonry in South Africa see Alan Amos Cooper 1986.

24   The British Israelite Truth enjoyed its heyday as a cult movement in the years of the new imperialism, roughly 1870 to 1930. The cult held that the Anglo-Saxon race was one of the lost tribes of Israel, the British being the senior sept of this tribe and the Americans their cousins. The fullness of time would see Britain recognised as the head of Israel, as the chosen people and the inheritors of the lineage of King David, King Solomon, and Christ. The British Empire would then become, as a global organisation, the underpinning of the Kingdom of God. This cult enjoyed popular following among conservative Anglo- Saxon communities throughout the world well into the 1960s and still survives among extreme right-wing

movements in South Africa and in parts of the United States. The British Israelite Truth published such titles as Mary Hazell Gayer's *The Heritage the Anglo-Saxon Race* (1928), *The British Israelites; or, Evidences of Our Hebrew Origin Gathered from History, Genealogy, Philology, Etc.* (188–), and F. Wallace Connon's World *Government: The Drama of the Ages* (1946).

25   See Raymond Dart 1925, H. F. Sampson 1948, and Bernard O'Sullivan 1990.

26   I am grateful to my colleague, Professor Stan Ridge, formerly Department of English, University of the Western Cape, for this reference.

27   In the mid-nineteenth century British members of the prestigious Indian civil service received only half pay if they took their furloughs in Britain, whereas a sojourn at the Cape, on foreign soil, entitled them to full benefits.

28   Duff Gordon's family in some ways epitomises the orientalism and the Mediterranean preoccupations of British culture in the late nineteenth and early twentieth centuries. Her daughter Janet Duff Gordon married Henry Ross, a banker in Alexandria, who published Duff Gordon's *Letters from the East, 1837-1857* and who had been on the Nineveh expedition with the Assyriologist Sir Austen Henry Layard. Layard's brother Edgar Layard (born in Florence into an Honourable East India Company family) was the first curator of the South African Museum in Cape Town. As a friend of Kinglake, Duff Gordon was familiar with a variety of texts about North Africa and the Near East. Her daughter and descendants finally settled in Florence. Duff Gordon's granddaughter Lina Duff Gordon wrote six guidebooks on Perugia, Assisi, Rome, and Florence, and she published an autobiography, *Castle in Italy* (1961).

29   Freemasonry is largely preoccupied with funerary symbolism, and obelisks are a standard Freemasonic symbol. It is fairly common to note Freemasonic signs on obelisks in cemeteries of the late nineteenth century. The ceremonies of Freemasonry are also very much concerned with memory and mnemonic systems. See James Stevens Curl 1991 for a description of Masonic architecture and symbolism.

30   Sarah Gertrude Millin (1966: 30) makes a similar claim in *White South Africans Are Also People,* 'the blood of Hottentots and Bushmen who had been pushed down to the Cape from the regions of the Red Sea'.

31   See Van der Post's later syncretic comments on Jung and the Bushmen in Van der Post 1983 [1976]: 48–56 and 1986: 33–34.

32   Lawrence's short story 'The Funicular' is an account of confrontation between the archaic and the brashly modern in which a party of tourists that ascends a hill by funicular faces, during an electric storm, a numinous vision of a Pan-like figure.

33   See Ruskin's 'The Lamp of Memory' in *The Seven Lamps of Architecture* 1849.

34   Lutyens and Baker were commissioned by the British government to design a parliamentary building, a senate house, government buildings, a viceregal palace, and a residential garden city for the Indian government on a site outside Delhi known as New Delhi. For the definitive account of this massive project, which ran for nearly two decades, see Robert Grant Irving 1981.

35   For a description of the historical pageant staged in Cape Town to inaugurate the parliament of the Union of South Africa see Merrington 1997b.

36   Grogan's descendant Tony Grogan, a Cape Town artist, published a book of illustrations made in Malawi in 1994 entitled *Between the Cape and Cairo* (Grogan 1995).

37   I am grateful to the Automobile Association of South Africa for some of this information.

38   See, for instance, Dorothy Rogers 1959, Anthony Smith 1961, and Obie Oberholzer 1996.

39   See Baker's mythologising of Table Mountain as the spirit of Rhodes in which, drawing on Percy Shelley's *Prometheus Unbound* (1820), he laid over the myth of Adamastor (devised by the Portuguese poet Luis de Camoens) the antique myth of Prometheus (Baker 1934: 159-66). Rhodes was, for Baker, a Promethean figure. The myth also appears in stucco work in Baker's Rhodes House in Oxford.

40   This is not to deny the subjectivity of indigenous Africans in such events as the Rhodes funeral but rather to indicate that imperial and colonial writers such as Millin were, at one level, interested only in a coercive

discourse of appropriation and justification. To state the thesis of this paper reductively perhaps, the overall effect of the multitude of articulations of the imperial Cape-to-Cairo fantasy was meant to be just such appropriation and justification. As Leon de Kock (1996: 190) has stated, 'The larger text of English in colonial South Africa not only buttressed, but extended the work of a haphazard yet ultimately murderous imperialism in the country.' It is needful to reconstruct and examine the ambiguities of coercion, co-optation, and resistance as regards the subjective position of black Africans in such events as that described by Millin, and it is needful to pursue the question of a 'staggered orientalism' from perspectives other than the British imperial one, for instance, from the very significant point of view of reports by Cape Muslims of their *hajj* or pilgrimage to Mecca. But that is beyond the scope of this essay, which has the limited intention of sketching a discursive field generated from a largely British colonial and imperial complex of desires.

41   See Martin Hall 1995 for a discussion of the colonialist mythology invested in the late-twentieth-century hotel and casino complex of Sun City and the Lost City in South Africa's North West Province.

42   The significance of northern orientation in South Africa is partially that, to take best advantage of the sun in the Southern Hemisphere, 'desirable properties' are north-facing, but the idea of a northward orientation is also linked to the idea of colonial expansion.

References

Alston, Madeline
    1929 *From an Old Cape Homestead* (London: Bodley Head).
Anderson, Benedict
    1991 *Imagined Communities: Reflections on the Origin and Spread of Nationalism* (London: Verso).
Attwell, Eric
    1997 *The Road to London* (Port Elizabeth: Palladian Press).
Ayoub, Safwat
    1997 Interview with author, January 18.
Baker, Sir Herbert
    1909 'The Architectural needs of South Africa', *State,* May, 512–24.
    1934 *Cecil Rhodes: By His Architect* (London: Oxford University Press).
    1944 *Architecture and Personalities* (London: Country Life).
Belcher, M. L.
    1932 *Cape to Cowley via Cairo in a Light Car* (London: Methuen).
Bernal, Martin
    1987 *Black Athena,* vol.1 (New Brunswick, NJ: Rutgers University Press).
Brendon, Piers
    1991 *Thomas Cook: 150 Years of Popular Tourism* (London: Secker and Warburg)
Buchan, John
    1903 *The African Colony: Studies in the Reconstruction* (Edinburgh: Blackwood).
    1940 *Memory Hold-the-Door* (London: Hodder and Stoughton).
Cape Town
    1911 *The Cape of Good Hope: Being the Official Handbook of the City of Cape Town* (Cape Town: Corporation of the City).
Connon, F. Wallace
    1946 *World Government: The Drama of the Ages.* (London: Covenant Publishing).
Cooper, Alan Amos
    1986 *The Freemasons of South Africa* (Cape Town: Human and Rousseau).

Court-Treatt, Stella
    1927 *Cape to Cairo* (London: Harrap).
Curl, James Stevens
    1991 *The Art and Architecture of Freemasonry* (London: Batsford).
Dart, Raymond
    1925 'The Historical Succession of Cultural Impacts upon South Africa', *Nature* 115: 425–29.
De Kock, Leon
    1996 *Civilising Barbarians: Missionary Narrative and African Textual Response in Nineteenth-Century South Africa* (Johannesburg: Witwatersrand University Press).
Derrida, Jacques
    1982 [1968] 'The Pit and the Pyramid: Introduction to Hegel's Semiology', in *Margins of Philosophy,* translated by Alan Bass, 69-87 (Brighton: Harvester).
Duff Gordon, Lucie
    1865 *Letters from Egypt 1863-65* (London: Macmillan).
    1875 *Last Letters from Egypt* (London: Macmillan).
    1927 [1864] *Letters from the Cape,* annotated by Dorothea Fairbridge (London: Humphrey Milford).
Du Toit, S. J.
    1898 *Di Koningin fan Skeba of Salomo syn Goudvelde in Sambesia: Historiese Roman, met Prente* [The queen of Sheba; or, Solomon's ancient gold fields in Zambesia: A historical novel, illustrated] (Paarl: D. F. du Toit).
Engen Oil Company
    1999 *Pipeline* (newsletter) July.
Fairbridge, Dorothea
    1910 *That Which Hath Been* (Cape Town: Cape Times).
    1913 *Piet of Italy* (CapeTown: J. C. Juta).
    1915 *The Torch Bearer* (Cape Town: J. C. Juta).
    1917 *A History of South Africa* (Oxford: Oxford University Press).
    1926 *The Uninvited* (London: E. Arnold & Co.)
    1928 *The Pilgrim's Way in South Africa* (London: Oxford University Press).
Fallaw, Lance
    1909 *An Ampler Sky* (London: Macmillan).
Foster, Jeremy
    1996 'Landscape Phenomenology and the Imagination of a New South Africa on Parktown Ridge', *African Studies* 55: 93–126.
Frank, Katherine
    1994 *A Passage to Egypt: The Life of Lucie Duff Gordon.* (London: Hamish Hamilton).
Garlake, Peter S.
    1982 *Great Zimbabwe Described and Explained* (Harare: Zimbabwe Publishing House).
Gayer, Mary Hazell
    1928 *The Heritage of the Anglo-Saxon Race* (London: Covenant Publishing).
Goodrick-Clarke, Nicholas
    1985 *The Occult Roots of Nazism: The Ariosophists of Austria and Germany, 1840–1935* (Wellingborough: Aquarian Press).
Gould, R. F.
    1911 *A Library of Freemasonry,* 2 vols. (Philadelphia: Yorston).

Grant, Eric
> 1988 'The Sphinx in the North', in *The Iconography of Landscape,* edited by Denis Cosgrove and Stephen Daniels, 236–53 (Cambridge: Cambridge University Press).

Greenhalgh, Paul
> 1988 *Ephemeral Vistas: The 'Expositions Universelles', Great Exhibitions, and World's Fairs, 1851–1939* (Manchester: Manchester University Press).

Grogan, Ewart Scott, and Arthur H. Sharp
> 1902 *From the Cape to Cairo: The First Traverse of Africa from South to North* (London: Thomas Nelson).

Grogan, Tony
> 1995 *Between the Cape and Cairo: Tony Grogan Paints Malawi* (Blantyre, Malawi: Central African Books).

Haggard, H. Rider
> 1886 *She* (London: Longmans, Green).
> 1887 *Allan Quatermain* (London: Longmans).
> 1985(1885) *King Solomon's Mines* (Johannesburg: Ad. Donker).

Hall, Martin
> 1995 'The Legend of the Lost City, or, the Man with the Golden Balls', *Journal of Southern African Studies* 21(2): 179–99.

Hall, R. N.
> 1905 *Great Zimbabwe* (London: Methuen).

Hallett, Robin
> 1975 *Africa Since 1875* (London: Heinemann).

Hegel, G. F. W.
> 1872 (1834) *Lectures on the Philosophy of History,* translated by John Sibree (London: Bell and Deldy).

Irving, Robert Grant
> 1981 *Indian Summer: Lutyens, Baker and Imperial Delhi* (London: Yale University Press).

Juta, Jan
> 1972 *Background in Sunshine: Memories of South Africa* (New York: Charles Scribner's Sons).

Juta, René
> 1924 *Cannes and the Hills* (London: Martin Secker).

Lewis, Cecil
> 1984 *Gemini to Joburg: The True Story of a Flight over Africa* (Harmondsworth: Viking).

Lighton, Conrad
> 1951 *Sisters of the South* (Cape Town: Howard Timmins).

MacKendrick Lt.-Col. W. G. ('The Roadbuilder')
> 1921 *The Destiny of the British Empire and the U. S. A.* (London: Covenant).

Mallows, Wilfred
> 1985 *The Mystery of the Great Zimbabwe* (London: Hale).

Merrington, Peter
> 1995 'Pageantry and Primitivism: Dorothea Fairbridge and the "Aesthetics of Union"', *Journal of Southern African Studies* 21(4): 643–56.
> 1997a 'The State and the "Invention of Heritage" in Edwardian South Africa', in *The Round Table, the Empire/Commonwealth and British Foreign Policy,* edited by Andrea Bosco and Alex May, 127–33 (London: Lothian Foundation Press).
> 1997b 'Masques, Monuments and Masons: The 1910 Pageant of the Union of South Africa', *Theatre Journal* 49 (1): 1–14.

Meyer, Stephan
> 1996 'Fact (or) Fiction in Dominee du Toit's Inscription of the White Queen into the Origin of African Civilisation –Notes on an Extract from *Di Koningin fan Skeba*', *Alternation* 3 (2): 130-47.

Millin, Sarah Gertrude
    1952 [1933] *Rhodes* (Johannesburg: Central News Agency).
    1966 *White South Africans are also People* (Cape Town: H. Timmins).
Milner, Alfred
    1894 *England in Egypt* (London: Edward Arnold).
Mitchell, Timothy
    1988 *Colonising Egypt* (Cambridge: Cambridge University Press).
Mitter, Partha
    1977 *Much Maligned Monster: A History of European Reactions to Indian Art* (Chicago: University of Chicago Press).
Nash, Andrew
    1985 'Colonialism and Philosophy: R. E. Alfred Hoernle in South Africa, 1908–11'. M.A. thesis, University of Stellenhosch.
Nel, P. G., ed.
    1990 *J. H. Pierneef: His Life and His Work,* translated by Rose Malinaric (Cape Town: Perskor).
Oberholzer, Obie
    1996 *Beyond Bagamoyo: A Journey from Cape to Cairo* (Cape Town: Hotazel).
O'Sullivan, Bernard
    1990 'A Report on Drilling and Trenching on the Woltemade Flats, Cape Town in 1988 and 1989', *South African Journal of Science* 86: 487-88.
Pemble, John
    1987 *The Mediterranean Passion: Victorians and Edwardians in the South* (Oxford: Oxford University Press).
Peters, Carl
    1977 [1902] *The Eldorado of the Ancients* (Bulawayo: Rhodesiana Reprint Library).
Plomer, William
    1984 [1933] *Cecil Rhodes* Cape Town: David Philip).
Quinn, Malcolm
    1994 The *Swastika: Constructing the Symbol* (London: Routledge).
Raphael, Lois A. C.
    1936 *The Cape to Cairo Dream: A Study in British Imperialism* (New York: Columbia University Press).
Redgrave, J. J.
    194- *Africa: From Cape to Cairo* (Cape Town: Juta).
Robins, R. H.
    1969 *A Short History of Linguistics* (London: Longmans).
Rogers, Dorothy
    1959 *Jeopardy and a Jeep: Africa Conquered by Two Women Professors* (London: Robert Hale).
Ruskin, John
    1849 *The Seven Lamps of Architecture* (London: Smith, Elder).
Said, Edward
    1978 *Orientalism: Western Conceptions of the Orient* (London: Routledge and Kegan Paul).
Sampson, H. F.
    1948 'Phoenician Shipwreck on the Cape Flats', *South African Archaeological Bulletin 3* (10): 34-40.
Semmel, Bernard
    1968 *Imperialism and Socialism Reform* (New York: Anchor Books).
Smith, Anthony
    1961 *High Street Africa* (London: George Allen and Unwin).

Strage, Mark
  1973 *Cape to Cairo: Rape of a Continent* (New York: Harcourt Brace Jovanovich).
Van der Post, Laurens
  1983 [1976] *Jung and the Story of Our Time* (Harmondsworth: Penguin).
  1986 *A Walk with a White Bushman* (Harmondsworth: Penguin).
Von Hoffman, Carl
  1936 *Jerry on Safari: A 7000-Mile Journey from Cairo to the Cape* (Philadelphia: J. B. Lippincott).
Waterfield, Gordon
  1937 *Lucie Duff Gordon: In England, South Africa and Egypt* (London: John Murray).
  1967 *Egypt* (London: Thames and Hudson).
Weinthal, Leo
  1902 *Round Africa the Deutsche Öst-Afrika Line: A Guidebook* (London: A. Andrews).
  1908 *Fascinating Egypt: A Bilingual Guide Book to Nile-land and Its Wonders from the Delta to Uganda.*
  1922 *The Story the Cape to Cairo Railway and River Route, 1887–1922,* vols. 5. (London: Pioneer Publishing and *African World).*
Wittenberg, Herman
  2000 'Ruwenzori: Imperialism and Desire in African Alpinism', in *Spaces and Crossings: Essays on Literature and Culture of Africa and Beyond,* edited by Rita Wilson and Carlotta Von Maltzahn, 235–58 (Frankfurt: Peter Lang).
Wolf, James B.
  1991 'Imperial Integration on Wheels: The Car', the British and the Cape-to-Cairo Route', in *Literature and Imperialism,* edited by Robert Giddings, 112–27 (New York: St. Martin's Press).
Wood, Charles W.
  1894 Letters in *The Argosy,* vols. 57 and 58.
Young, Robert
  1995 *Colonial Desire: Hybridity in Theory, Culture and Race* (London: Routledge).

FOUR

'A Primary Need as Strong as Hunger': The Rhetoric of Urgency in South African Literary Culture Under Apartheid[1]

Louise Bethlehem

> The tradition of the oppressed teaches us that the 'state of emergency' in which we live is not the exception but the rule. We must attain to a conception of history that is in keeping with this insight.
>
> Walter Benjamin, *Illuminations*

1 The Trope-of-Truth; the Trope-as-Truth

Jeremy Cronin (1988: 13), poet-activist and former prisoner under apartheid, has suggested that the censorship trials conducted in apartheid South Africa of the 1980s led the state prosecutor to anthologise black poetry with a deeper understanding of its politicised aesthetic than was to be found in the contemporary anthologisings of the formal South African literary academy. The provocative substitution of courtroom for university classroom inverts the usual postcolonial and post-Foucauldian argument concerning the imbrications of literary studies in establishing the apparatuses of governmentality.[2] But if Cronin's observation is striking for its deliberately scandalous transgression of the boundaries between different forms of agency, the real scandal here is, it seems to me, that there is no scandal at all. After all, both professor and prosecutor, censor and critic, have adopted a pervasively 'stenographic' attitude to literary production in South Africa.[3] Writers and readers collectively assume that literature and life in South Africa maintain a mimetic or one-to-one relationship, that writing provides a supposedly unmediated access to the real, and that the transparent rendering of South African life is a type of 'resistance' to apartheid that can and often does trigger repressive state intervention. 'Telling the truth is bad for apartheid,' proclaims Rose Moss (1978: 48–49) in one characteristic formulation. 'The primary obligation is to tell the truth.' The writer's function, says fellow white South African author André Brink (1983a [1976a]: 152), in blunt corroboration, is to ensure that 'the terrible excuse of Nuremberg is not heard again'.

The commitment to literary truth-telling evident here constrains the range of discursive forms available to literary production in English, whether by blacks or whites. The resultant emphasis on documentation and testimony places a premium on various forms of literary realism. As Njabulo Ndebele (1991 [1984]: 37), an influential black academic and writer, observes, 'The visible symbols of the overwhelmingly oppressive South African social formation appear to have prompted over the years the development of a highly dramatic, highly demonstrative form of literary representation.' The word *dramatic* does not restrict Ndebele's comments to theatrical or performance-based representation alone. What anchors this form of literary representation – which Ndebele (ibid.) famously critiques in the controversial essay 'The Rediscovery of the Ordinary' – is the idea that the writer opposes apartheid through exposing it. Or, in the words of a key figure in African literary studies in the American academy, Bernth Lindfors (1968: 17), 'The picture alone indicts the society which permits such inhumane conditions to exist.' Lindfors's article is entitled 'Robin Hood Realism in South African English Fiction', and tellingly so. For him as for many others the political challenge of South African 'protest' literature is held to reside in the restoration to (white) consciousness of the social content the literature articulates – content the 'obscene social exhibitionism' of apartheid (Ndebele 1991 [1984]: 37) actively elides. Where apartheid 'exhibitionism' occludes reality, mimetic realism 'exposes' apartheid.

In the years preceding the 1994 transition to democracy in South Africa the revelatory thrust of South African literature was often glossed as an agenda of 'literary commitment,' most forcefully perhaps by black writers. Revelation befits revolution, runs an important subtext of South African literature in English. 'We need a writing that records exactly the situation we live in,' states Mothobi Mutloatse, 'and any writing which ignores the urgency of political events will be irrelevant' (quoted in Seroke 1988 [1981]: 305). 'In a situation of oppression,' confirms Keorapetse Kgositsile, 'there are no choices beyond didactic writing: either you are a tool of oppression or an instrument of liberation. It's that simple' (quoted in Lindfors 1985 [1975]: 81). As Mbulebo Vizikhungo Mzamane (1988: 10) states in a later article on black poetry: 'No barrier separates the new poetry from social and political reality. The words of the poets are as solid as their objectives: to build a new country and finish with the exploitation of man by man. They are socially and politically committed and write with this commitment in mind.'

For whites the notion of 'commitment', overtly politicised by Mzamane, is often sublimated through slightly more oblique, often tellingly depoliticised references to the truth-telling, shamanistic, or vatic role of the poet-writer (Haresnape 1988: 42; Brink 1983b [1976b]: 104). Retrospectively aligning South African writing in English with a humanist agenda, Leon de Kock (1989: 230) has spoken of its 'desire to tell, from the individual's point of view, to reveal the lie behind the moral sanctimony of separate development' – a state euphemism for apartheid. 'This was,' he adds, 'an immediate, primary need as strong as hunger.'

This set of attitudes, highly representative of the literary scholarship I have investigated,[4] may be restated as an adherence to what I term the *trope-of-truth*: a strenuous investment on the part of South African literary culture in the assumption that South African literature, in the words of one of its most celebrated practitioners, exists to expose 'the real meaning of the South African government's vocabulary of racist euphemisms' (Gordimer 1988 [1984]: 247). But the trope-of-truth is itself underwritten by an equally dominant investment in the notion of the *trope-as-truth* – or what I shall be analysing as a thoroughgoing disregard for the discursive codes that mediate between 'realism' as a literary construct and the over determined social 'reality' of apartheid, the lived substratum of individual and collective existence experienced as the real. If South African literary scholarship achieves for itself an 'essentially outward or moral or worldly thrust' (Attwell 1990a: 594) that provides it with a vicarious form of political agency, it does so partly by deploying various discursive mechanisms that repress recognition of the arbitrariness of signification. Discussions of literary function and value in South African literature in English, I claim, are refracted through an elaborate rhetoric of urgency that strains to effect a secular closure between the word and the world precisely to safeguard the ethical claims of South African literary culture. My analysis of the rhetoric of urgency begins with some of its most visible inscriptions: recurrent uses of the word *urgency* in black South African literary discourse.

2 Wrenching the Spiked Cactus with Bare Hands: Urgency and Agency in Black South African Literary Discourse

'The English we use in our poetry,' announces Oswald Mtshali (1976: 127), a black poet much beloved of white liberals, 'is not the Queen's language that you know as written by say Wordsworth and Coleridge. It is the language of urgency which we use because we have got an urgent message to deliver to anyone who cares to listen to it.' In Mtshali's statement the means of representation ('the language of urgency') stand as the mimetic correlative of that sense of urgency that is the desired outcome of the communicative interaction. An incipient tautology (the language of urgency delivers an urgent message) is averted through positing a causal relationship between the form of a literary statement and its pressing social content. As Mtshali (ibid.) elaborates, 'We have not got the time to embellish this urgent message with unnecessary and cumbersome ornaments like rhyme, iambic pentameter, abstract figures of speech, and an ornate and lofty style. We will indulge in these luxuries which we can ill-afford at the moment when we are free people.' In a variant on Mtshali's standpoint, the urgency of the form is said to have been dictated by 'the tyranny of place,' to use Es'kia (Ezekiel) Mphahlele's terms. 'The writer in South Africa packs his line with all he has,' says Mphahlele (1987: 54). 'He tends to document his physical and human settings in stark, grim detail, to document minute-to-minute experience. There is a specifically African drama in the ghettos that the writer cannot ignore. He must simply come to terms with the tyranny of place or grapple with it, because he *must* have place, because his writing depends on his commitment to territory.'[5]

Elsewhere Mphahlele (1983:14) reiterates: 'Mtutuzeli Matshoba is one of those Black writers of today who wrench the spiked cactus from the ground with bare hands, so to speak, in their attack on the [apartheid] system. He extracts experience from raw life and does little to impose an aesthetic structure on the material.' In an unmistakably Lukacsian formulation (see, for example, Lukács 1971: 110–48), Mphahlele (1983: 14) characterises black writing in South Africa from the 1960s onward as 'a response to the immediate, to the instant, and a direct, urgent confrontation with the dominant political morality. The dramatisation of a message is the major concern. The intention to *make* literature is either ignored or subdued'. But if the predominant function of black literature is documentary (the writer 'tends to document his physical and human settings . . . to document minute-to-minute experience'), what separates it from other modes of discourse, primarily journalism? My question is, of course, not original but gestures toward a particularly long-lived debate inaugurated in the mid-sixties by Mphahlele's fellow *Drum* magazine contributor Lewis Nkosi.

For Nkosi (1973 [1966]: 110) black writing's 'mere concern with telling the story' reflects the shortcomings of a black literary tradition wholly preoccupied with documentation. According to Nkosi, 'What we . . . get from South Africa . . . – and what we get most frequently – is the journalistic fact parading outrageously as imaginative literature.' What is found in South African literature, continues Nkosi, is 'a type of fiction which exploits the ready-made plots of racial violence, social apartheid, interracial love affairs which are doomed from the beginning, without any attempt to transcend or transmute these given 'social facts' into artistically persuasive works of fiction'. Nkosi suggests that black writing forfeits its properly literary status by a kind of premature submission to the exigency of what I have been calling *urgency*. Whereas in the late seventies and early eighties black criticism used the trope of urgency to counter the depoliticisation of black literature in the name of a rarefied 'aesthetic' allegiance, as we have seen, Nkosi disrupts this strategy by proposing to suspend the relation between black literature and politics altogether. 'To read a novel like Richard Rive's *Emergency* is to gain a minute glimpse into a literary situation which seems to me quite desperate. It may even be wondered whether it might not be more prudent to "renounce literature temporarily", as some have advised, and solve the political problem first rather than continue to grind out hackneyed third-rate novels of which [Rive's] *Emergency* is a leading example' (ibid.).

Stated in theoretical terms, the debate over imaginative literature versus journalistic fact is essentially a conflict over the means authors employ, in the given social context of apartheid South Africa, to achieve symbolic power. The question of the appropriate mimetic strategies of black South African writing is clearly central here, but to posit its centrality is not to restrict our discussion to the carefully delimited sphere of literary aesthetics. Rather, as Gunther Gebauer and Cristoph Wulf (1995:3) point out in their detailed historical investigation of the notion of mimesis, 'The history of mimesis is a history of disputes over the power to make symbolic worlds, that is, the power to represent the self and others and interpret the world. To this extent mimesis possesses a political dimension and is part of the history of power relations.' Gebauer and Wulf propose that it is the author's strategy in relation to the medium (linguistic or otherwise) that generates a codificatory system through which he or she gains symbolic power (ibid.:24). Mimesis in general, they hold, is 'a turn toward a world that is by no means identical with empirical reality' (ibid.: 9), since empirical reality – or the 'represented world' – is mediated through the intentionally structured correlatives of the 'representational world' (ibid.: 22), which is replete with its own discursive and generic codes. An adequate description, Susan Stewart (1993: 26) reminds us in a similar vein, is always a 'socially adequate description.'

If we keep this account of mimesis in mind, it is apparent that Nkosi's comments have direct bearing on the codificatory strategies that best serve the black South African writer. His stated aim is to carve out a space for black writing practice that evinces a responsibility to representational thickness – the crafting and constructing of the *vraisemblable* through conscious mastery of generic and discursive codes – that journalistic documentation and the work of his literary opponents supposedly do not share. Nkosi (1973 [1966]: 113–14) reviles what he sees as the flattening of the potential *formal* deftness of black writing:

> In the past what had always put me off Ezekiel Mphahlele's writing was a certain dullness of tone, much like the ponderous speech of a dull-witted person, so that it was often difficult to pursue the story to its ending. The gems were often embedded in a thick mud of cliché and lustreless writing: a succession of simple clauses, for instance, linked together by semi-colons. The texture of the prose had the feel and look of sweaty labour much like the stains of honest sweat on the cloth-cap of the toiling proletariat; but hardly congenial for being honest.

Similarly, Nkosi (ibid.: 15) complains: 'In Rive's novel, as indeed in most of the stories recently published in *Quartet* by four Cape coloured writers [*sic*], there are no real full-blooded characters with real blood to spill; no characters whose fighting or love-making has the stench of real living people: they are cardboard pieces and cardboard pieces don't spill any blood. Embarrassingly, what comes out of the apartheid machine when it has ground to a standstill is not human flesh but cardboard pulp.' 'Black South Africans write', he states bluntly, 'as though Dostoevsky, Kafka or Joyce had never lived' (ibid.:110).

Nkosi continued to elaborate such demands for what we have been calling representational thickness as a critique of black South African writing for the next three decades (see Nkosi 1986, 1998). In an article entitled 'South African Writers at the Barricades' published in 1986, he focused directly on the mediatory function of language in literary production:

Black South African writers attempt to reproduce or re-enact in their writings what is happening in the streets, as if language is ever capable of consuming reality, of digesting it, then of finally regurgitating it to us exactly as it was given without essentially changing it. The fact that what happens in the streets never actually happens in literature, not even in the most committed of socialist realist novels, is lost to many Black South African authors. The naive realism of Sipho Sepamla's and Mtutuzeli Matshoba's fiction, the succession of documentary novels such as Lauretta Ngcobo's *Cross of Gold* and Miriam Tlali's *Amandla* owe a great deal to this frustrated desire to abolish any space between literature and the horrible reality of life under apartheid.

(Nkosi 1986: 43)

Formal deftness, interpreted at the very least as a demand for stylistic sophistication, conscious awareness of intertextual models, and convincing characterisation, signals a writer's willingness to grapple with the mediatory dimensions of the linguistic medium and becomes the implicit antidote to the kinds of codificatory strategies that Nkosi associates with 'naive realism': a conflation to the point of coincidence of the representational with the represented world, so that the space between 'literature and the horrible reality of life under apartheid' is abolished.

But before we accept Nkosi's pronouncements at face value let us register a conflictual adherence on his part to crucial presuppositions of the naive realism he deplores. I refer you again to his criticism of Rive's supposed inability to deliver 'real full-blooded characters' or 'real blood,' 'the stench of real living people'. The fact that the adjective *real* asserts itself three times in the course of a single sentence betrays certain nostalgia on Nkosi's part for a form of language use in which language might efface itself to produce an otherwise unattainable proximity to the constituents (human or otherwise) of the empirical world. This mode of language use – which Ian Watt (1970 [1957]: 9–35) terms 'formal' realism and Damian Grant (1985 [1970]: 14–15) terms 'conscientious' realism – is of course employed by the novel as the exemplary medium of the emerging bourgeois subject. In short, Nkosi betrays a nostalgia for the 'representational literalism' (ibid.) of a realism anchored in 'positivist' or 'correspondence' theories of signification (ibid.: 9). Its ultimate goal, Roland Barthes (1995 [1986]: 141) reminds us, is to remake writing, notation, as the 'pure encounter of an object and its expression'.

Realism's submission to the 'purifying ravishment of fact' (Grant 1985 [1970]: 14) is read for its ideological agenda in the post-Althusserian Marxist critique of realism. It is widely conceded in this tradition that the reader of a realist text is, in Tony Bennet's (1979: 25) words, encouraged to 'read through the formal artistic devices without noticing them, in order to appropriate the story that rests beneath them'. The elision of the codificatory apparatus enables the realist text to present itself not only as a plausible simulation of the 'real' but also as providing immediate access to the constituents of the represented world. Thus realism constantly returns us to its 'ultimate etymological derivation from *res*, "thing"' (Grant 1985 [1970]: 43). It is precisely in the elisions that seek to invest the realist signifier with an ontologically grounded command over the realist signified that the workings of the realist sign redouble those of ideology in becoming an *ideology of form* (Coward and Ellis 1977: 34–44, 45–60; Eagleton 1984 [1976]: 8–86; Heath 1974; Macherey 1978). In one well-known critique of the manner in which classic realism serves as the 'accomplice of ideology', Catherine Belsey (1980: 73, 117) shows how the realist work of fiction 'installs itself in the space between fact and illusion through the presentation of a simulated reality'. It requires critical work of the magnitude of Roland Barthes's *S/Z* (1975) to demonstrate the naturalisation every-where deployed in the realist text – for realism seeks with particular intensity to elide all traces of its mediation through the sign, 'dissolving' its specific modes of production as signification into what Terry Eagleton (1984 [1976]: 85) terms 'the spontaneity of the lived'.

For all his concern with literary technique, Nkosi seems particularly anxious to harness precisely this dimension of textuality, 'the spontaneity of the lived'. Consider a phrase like 'thick mud of cliché', used with reference to Mphahlele, or the simile: 'The texture of the prose had the feel and look of sweaty labour much like the stains of hon-est sweat on the cloth-cap of the toiling proletariat'. Might not these figures stand as so much detritus of Nkosi's attempt to call forth the selfsame materiality of the social as is desired by the documentary novel? Nkosi's tropes at this point effect a kind of 'return of the repressed': they subvert his putative vigilance concerning the demands of the representational medium and reveal how the nostalgia for transparent and immedi-ate signification inheres even in critical pronouncements that state the impossibility of such signification. The turn to the world that motivates the figuration here does, of course, encode ironic intertextual allusion to the staples of black socialist realism Nkosi repudiates. Alex La Guma is the most pertinent target here. Literary rivalries aside, it is my argument that the 'worldliness' of Nkosi's criticism must also be read as a residue of the powerfully stenographic bent of black South African literature, its representational literalism, which he can only partially displace.

3   The Crime of Escapism: Urgency and Agency in White South African Literary Discourse

> Nadine Gordimer takes literary realism to its furthest limits, to the regions where it begins to intersect with reality. Because of this, the stories in *Something out There* provoke some extremely urgent questions about the sense we are making of our society right now.
>
>   Ménan du Plessis, 'Literary Realism at its Furthest Limits'

As my epigraph to this section suggests, the representational literalism of black South African writing under apartheid is held to be a central feature of that most canonical and most paradigmatic of South Africa's white literary opponents of apartheid, Na-dine Gordimer. With similar deference to the realist agenda as Ménan du Plessis, the academic critics Sarah Christie, Geoffrey Hutchings, and Don Maclennan (1980: 99) introduce the section of their volume devoted to realism in South African fiction with the statement that the texts under examination (all novels by white writers, Alan Paton, Doris Lessing, Dan Jacobson, and Nadine Gordimer, with the exception of Mphahlele's 1959 autobiography) are the 'most forthright and serious of all South African fiction'. Their power, the critics claim, 'comes from knowledge, and from deep concern for social and political change. The crime, for a writer of this group is to be in any way escapist, not committed to the greater human cause . . . Consequently most of this writing is by intention critical and protesting, for its main function is to present the truth and the truth is seldom pleasant' (ibid.: 99). Once again the transformation of the trope-of-truth into the trope-as-truth depends on the contiguity between text and sociohistorical context: a contiguity sustained by the postulate of an essentially mimetic literature on the one hand and the supposed feasibility of transparent signification on the other. The notion of urgency, implicit as an anxiety concerning 'escapism' (*let us not be found loitering without intent in the vicinity of revolution*),[6] is called into play to close the gap between commitment to 'the greater human cause' and its textual articulations. But it is exactly where they raise the question of ethico-political agency that Christie, Hutchings, and Maclennan's (1980: 100) analysis reinvokes representational literalism of a peculiar kind:

> Realist writing in South Africa lives in the shadow of a paradox, and such writers know that they are playing with divine fire, for they know that if people are hungry or suffering from persecution you feed them and free them from persecution. You do not first write novels about them. People come first, novels second. The main task of a realist writer, even though he knows thousands are starving and that the cost of the paper on which he writes his novel will feed a family for weeks, is to bring moral outrage and injustice to public attention, to turn his reader's conscience to ashes. Such is the mandate of this kind of writing, to effect a crisis of consciousness and, hopefully, to be an agent of change.

Ostensibly the authors' programme for social transformation has a breathtaking simplicity thanks to its melioristic faith in the individual's (read white liberal's) ability to transcend the repressive social conditions of apartheid South Africa. If the unadorned literalism of their exhortation 'you feed them and free them' seems reductive, it is worth noting that this reductionism renders the sociopolitical arena pliant to the goals of liberal humanism, as if the transformation of apartheid were a matter of loaves and the lone local conscience. In much the same way as we have seen Nkosi elide the differences between critical discourse and the official claims of the realist textual object for itself, so Christie, Hutchings, and Maclennan's exhortation is best seen as reduplicating the constitutive conditions of what they term the realist 'mandate'. Michael Vaughan (1982: 120) helps us understand why this might be so: 'If individuals hold potential mastery over the real world, it follows that a fiction which is concerned to promote this mastery must set an example in its own domain. Reality must be mastered, rendered amenable in every facet. This implies an ideal of transparency – of absolute clarity. Liberal fiction aims at clarity, ease and concreteness of exposition. It is fiction that works within the conventions of realism, whereby the perception of reality is treated as a non-problematic issue.'

Given Vaughan's problematisation of the fictions of liberalism, indeed the liberal fiction of transparent signification, it comes as something of a surprise to find him resolutely opposed to the work of J. M. Coetzee – the radicalism of whose textual practice, it has been argued, subversively rewrites not only what Benita Parry (1998: 149) calls South Africa's 'liberal novel of stricken conscience' but also the discursive and ideological codes that make a liberal subject position tenable in the first place (see Attwell 1990a, 1993; Dovey 1988; and Parry 1998: 149). But why should the early Coetzee's studied nonmimeticism immediately raise questions regarding the writer's 'commitment' to 'South Africa,' 'history', or 'the struggle'? It is my claim that Coetzee's critical reception is a useful point of entry for examining how a shared instrumentalist conception of language unites critics of South African literature in English, whether of 'liberal', 'Marxist', or 'populist' persuasions.

Coetzee was accused, with increasing vehemence over the course of the early 1980s, of what South African literary criticism construed as a 'dehistoricisation' of the 'real'. Vaughan's (1982) contrastive reading of Coetzee and Mtutuzeli Matshoba, framed by a discussion of South African literature's engagement with politics, inaugurated the Marxist critique of Coetzee later taken up by Peter Kohler (1987). While identifying Coetzee's problematisation of language as central to his fictional project, Vaughan uses this very aspect of Coetzee's practice to deny him any validity beyond his own (post)liberalism. Coetzee's language, says Vaughan (1982:128), 'can say next to nothing, and certainly nothing reliable, about experiences outside the modality of its own racial-historical dialectic'. Paul Rich was less restrained. Coetzee's vision of empire in *Waiting for the Barbarians* lacks 'any understanding of the historical forces that produce actual imperial systems at particular phases of history' (Rich 1984: 385). The novel indicates that 'literary postmodernism in a postcolonial context as South Africa . . . is a moral dead end' (ibid.: 389). For Abdul JanMohamed (1985: 73) Coetzee's *Waiting for the Barbarians* 'epitomises the dehistoricising, desocialising tendency of colonialist fiction'. The text's 'studied refusal to accept historical responsibility' renders it a mystification of the imperial endeavour (ibid.).

Gradually the Marxist position on Coetzee solidified into something like critical orthodoxy, reaching well beyond the Marxist camp – so much so that Michael Chapman's strident rejection of both Coetzee's poetics and some of the critical practices they generated seemed, upon its appearance in 1988, rather recuperatory. Published in response to Teresa Dovey's study of Coetzee issued that year (Dovey 1988), Chapman's contribution brings the matter of Coetzee to a climax – the libidinal metaphor is, as we shall see, entirely intentional.

Deprived of what Chapman (1988: 336), following Koestler, calls the 'responsibility of action', Coetzee is said to be lost to history. The literary-theoretical debates surrounding Coetzee's *Foe*, for instance, are held by Chapman (ibid.: 327) to be a specially pertinent evasion of responsibility for a South Africa where 'history may certainly be regarded, poststructurally, as discourse while to millions of the dispossessed it is more likely to manifest itself, concretely, as low wages or the police cell'. Equally culpable in Chapman's (ibid.: 339) eyes is criticism that, turning its back on the dual virtues he terms 'accountability and accessibility,' follows Coetzee into the poststructural web. In this instance Dovey's poststructuralist judgments on Coetzee are held to 'confirm the suspicions of many black writers that literary pursuit in white South Africa has rather more to do with the gratifications of libidinal language than the fulfilments of fighting political injustice' (ibid.: 338).

Note that the category of the erotic ('libidinal language') is now opposed to 'history' or to 'reality', and note also how 'reality' intrudes into the discourse as 'low wages or the police cell'. Riding on the implicit hierarchisation of values inherent in the libido-versus-lived-reality opposition, Chapman's criticism openly sides with the 'real.' 'In our knowledge of the human suffering on our own doorstep of thousands of detainees who are denied recourse to the rule of law,' insists Chapman (ibid.: 335), '*Foe* does not so much speak to Africa as provide a kind of *masturbatory release*, in this country, for the Europeanising dreams of an intellectual coterie' (emphasis added).

What might it mean, in this context, to 'speak' to Africa, and what form might such 'speech' take? Chapman (ibid.: 340) provides one answer through contrasting Dovey's poststructuralism, a form of criticism he holds to be 'distinctly limited in the urgent search for productive ways of moving forward in sociopolitical life' with the 'plain speech' of Mphahlele. '[Black people] need to be told now who they are, and where they come from, and what they should be doing about these things we're talking about. That's where the scholar comes in' (Mphahlele in Manganyi 1981: 44, cited in Chapman 1988: 339–40). The phrase 'plain speech' could have come from Mtshali or from Mphahlele himself, as could Chapman's (1984: 257) pronouncement, apropos the white South African poet Wopko Jensma, that 'urgency dictates form and the pressures of the moment seem so intense as to militate against "craftsmanship".' But so to privilege the representational literalism of a South African literary criticism that constantly defers to the dictates of the realist writing it valorises is to misrepresent the situated literary histories of crucial discursive constructs. Chapman well knows that the resonance, not to say historical constructions, of 'plain speech' are more complicated than his castigation of Dovey would have them seem. Chapman's 1984 work *South African English Poetry: A Modern Perspective* charts the influence of Pablo Neruda's theories on the value of 'simple speech' in South African poetry as well as the manner in which the Chilean socialist Nicanor Parra's theory of the 'anti-poet' informs the work of James Matthews (ibid.: 190), Peter Blum (ibid.: 189), Wopko Jensma (ibid.: 257), and others.

In one version of realist ideology a 'plain' or straightforward devotion to 'the truth' generates, as if inevitably, its own ethical authority (see Norris 1988: 106). This doctrine leads in a straight line of descent from George Eliot to South African appropriations of realism.[7] That Chapman is compelled to forget his own historicisation of the notion of 'plain speech' as literary construct is evidence of a desire for referential authority deriving from the plain, the plainly urgent. We are back in the province of the trope-as-truth. The mediatiory function of language is made to atrophy in order that fictional discourse might retrieve social agency and critical discourse might partake of this retrieval as a (vicariously) political speech-act.

4   A Political Economy of Forms

In a provocative article interrogating the 'politics of form' in black South African writing, Benita Parry (1994: 16) asks, 'Why is it that mimetic modes that are testamentary and documentary continue to be dominant in black South African fiction, given the fantastic congruence and incongruence of cultural forces, of the broken histories and disrupted traditions of dispossessed and persecuted communities?' Why, she continues, has black South Africa's writing, unlike its jazz and demotic poetry, not emulated the literatures of

> other struggling and dominated peoples who . . . have invented meta-fictional modes where parody and citation of native and Western discourses – the reinscription of fabulous and digressive oral storytelling and the performance of self-referential language-games – effect linguistic and narrative dislocations of both indigenous and metropolitan conventions? . . . Should we perhaps consider the influence of prevalent critical practices, observing how the restricted privilege of a liberal education in South Africa brought with it the constraining influence of a literary aesthetic valorising the organicism and coherence of a representational realism, a limitation reinforced on different grounds by political agendas for a purposeful literature depicting oppression and illuminating the struggle?
>
> (Parry 1994: 17)

Parry's explanation, phrased as a question, has the advantage of articulating between literary and social praxis – whether in the context of pedagogy or oppositional politics. I would certainly concur that 'representational realism', narrowed, on the pretext of urgency, to the restricted circumference of what we have referred to as a representational literalism, unites the otherwise divergent agendas of liberalism, revisionism, and radicalism in South African literary studies. But is the aetiology of this tendency to be sought chiefly in the sphere of History, in the history of liberalism/the history of oppositional politics, as Parry seems to imply?

I am wary of the *premature* imbrication of History into the literary historiographic narrative on two counts. First, the appeal to History itself can be what Andries Walter Oliphant (1996: 61), in a different but not unrelated discussion, terms 'the narrative pragmatism of social and historical referentiality associated with realism'. It reinstates the realist metanarrative precisely to the extent that History becomes a stable referent, the object of empirical rather than, say, tropological interrogation. It is largely the case that revisionist or radical history in South Africa during the later phases of apartheid, a practice on which the work of oppositional literary scholars such as Tim Couzens and Isabel Hofmeyr was partially modelled, retained a resolutely empirical dominant. In line with the thrust of my argument concerning the rhetoric of urgency as a vicarious means of laying claim to political agency, Tony Morphet (1990: 99) sees the empirical orientation of revisionist historical work as enabling the emplacement of culture 'in the struggle'. Similarly, David Attwell (1991:133–34) in his rebuttal of Hofmeyr's rebuttal (1990) of his defence of poststructuralism at the 1990 Wits History Workshop (1990b), speaks of literary criticism's desire to 'wrest from historical studies an achieved political potency, a desire, in other words, to be uplifted and transported on the wings of social power'.

Second and related, the confident retrieval of History as referent obscures the extent to which the master narratives, the master's narratives, liberalism and realism, are already in crisis with respect to the social, even as they enact their ascendancy. I have been arguing that the frequent recourse to the notion of urgency by both black and white South African writers and literary scholars in English reflects their thoroughgoing will to power over the exteriority, the concrete datum, of the lived social relations of apartheid South Africa. Precisely because the ethical claims or quest for social agency of the South African literary critic are rooted in an instrumentalist conception of language, the arbitrariness of the signifier-signified connection must be denied. This being so, it becomes possible to see the rhetoric of urgency as seeking to weld signifier to signified, a constitutive condition of all realism, one might argue. Granted. But the particular poignancy of this quest to suture a lack internal to the sign is exacerbated by that specific juncture 'under apartheid'. Writes Harry Bloom (1959: 200) in Transvaal Episode: 'Apartheid – a word with a potent appeal to the longing for racial exclusiveness. A word with a thousand meanings and no meaning, but with a curious power to change the meaning of other words.' Mafika Gwala (1984: 47) adds, 'In a divided society, words cannot be expected to carry the same value.'

The apartheid state's dislocations of signification are justly infamous, as when the textual articulations of forced displacements of populations from their land or coercive regimes of land use are apparently dignified by the title of 'betterment schemes' or when the Natives (Abolition of Passes and Co-ordination of Documents) Act of 1952 actually extends the pass law legislation to black subjects previously exempted from it. But try as it will to claim a high moral ground vis-à-vis apartheid and despite the underpinnings of the liberalism that motivates much of it, the language of academic literary scholarship cannot simply invert these disjunctions as a preliminary step, supposedly, in undoing them. For the shifting of signification, so cynically deployed by a host of apartheid functionaries, is a spectre that disrupts the liberal programme from within. Ironically, the liberal humanist vocabulary, based on the illusion of the unequivocal and universal applicability of such terms as freedom, justice, civilisation, or equality, turns out to be as slippery as the language of the apartheid bureaucrat. Liberalism is unequal to its own professions of political universality in that its exclusionary strategies drive a wedge between the 'natural individual equipped with universal capacities' (Mehta 1997: 70) and the necessary conditions, socially and politically encoded, for their actualisation (ibid.: 59–86). In the face of the ongoing deferral of the enlightened and Enlightenment promise contained in such terms, liberalism's langue and parole differ, shall we say, spectacularly.

We might find evidence of the spectacle of exclusion in the pivotal placing of the verb *to see* in the following impassioned letter written in 1942 by Azael Tsoai, a resident of the Orlando Township near Johannesburg, to John David Rheinallt Jones, a 'stalwart of the liberal establishment', adviser to the South African Institute of Race Relations, and for five years from 1937 one of two senators representing Transvaal and Orange Free State blacks in terms of the Representation of Natives Act of 1936 (Murray 1992: 127, 131):

> Today we are being called to sacrifice for freedom for what freedom then if we are not allowed to buy land or be given residence at the reserves only that one is not Barolong. Is there any justice then? If we cannot see justice shall we get it tomorrow never? The first Native to win a military metal [*sic*] in this war is a native from the OFS [Orange Free State] but I am afraid unless he is a Barolong what will he get from all his services if he is not a Barolong, nothing.
>
> (Quoted in Murray 1992: 166)

This is, it seems to me, a remarkably interesting passage. The disruptions of Tsoai's syntax, the dissolution of language into a series of syntagmatic oppositions at the point where he substitutes metal for medal, and the shifting of a conditional mode that moves between outright antithesis and non-equivalent equivalences ('unless he is a Barolong what will he get from all his services if he is not a Barolong, nothing') all dramatise a difference contingent on Tsoai's difference from his liberal addressee. 'If we cannot see justice shall we get it tomorrow never?' asks Tsoai. The suspicion that the lofty signifier has no perceptible signified leads Tsoai to despair of a justice he cannot quite antici-pate. The non-Barolong soldier, enlisted to defend against 'fascism' a country that fails to accord him the full rights of citizenship, embodies a doubleness that troubles Tsoai. The soldier's plight dramatises the failure of the Enlightenment charter based on the 'natural law' of equality formulated by Rousseau.

Tsoai's anguish is proleptic. As Nicholas Dawes has recently pointed out, *citizen* and what Dawes somewhat misleadingly terms *subject* will cease to coincide for the black man or woman under apartheid. In his words: 'The subject is consigned to a stateless, rightless existence as a mere body severed from its necessary (humanising?) connection with citizenship and thus mutilated. Forced beyond the pale of white South Africa to a Bantustan which no force of natural law will constitute, or can constitute as sovereign state, the black body politic cannot send itself the letter of the (properly constituted) law which will reinstate the proper subject/citizen identity' (Dawes 1997: 6). Aberrant in more than its grammar, unsutured, Tsoai's question disrupts the coincidence of unitary signifier and unequivocal signified fundamental to a restitutive agenda whereby, as if in conformity to Ernst Bloch's or Marx's own precedents, the very description of apartheid encodes its antithesis as an unwritten but clearly decipherable utopian complement – the future realisation of a postapartheid sublime. (See Jameson 1971 [148] on Bloch,

Hamilton 1996 [106–8] on Marx.) Let injustice be seen through its inscription on the page, implies critic after critic, and we shall get justice tomorrow ever.

Or not. Impervious to a liberalism that assigned 'English' a conciliatory role as the 'linguistic analogue of liberal politics' (Watson 1983: 17), the institutions of apartheid proved equally impervious to various shades of cultural radicalism, including populist constructions of 'writing as a cultural weapon' that sought to invest the signifier with a certain 'words-as-bullets' animism (Gwala 1984). 'I have been considering the millions of words that have been written on South Africa,' wrote Nkosi in 1965. 'You would think that the South African Government should have been written to death by now. It has not been' (1965: 35). The institutions of apartheid refused the imperative of the Word, the call to dismantle themselves, as it were, at the literary critic's behest so that 'justice' might once again take up residence in the signifier's shell /justice/ – and might continue to do so every time the signifier were to be used in such seemingly trivial linguistic contexts as, say, the designation of J. T. 'Jimmy' Kruger as 'minister of justice'.[8]

The disavowal of 'rhetoric' in the name of 'urgency,' I have been claiming, shields South African literary culture in English against the inadmissible: the recognition that the referential authority of the sign is contractual rather than immanent, ontologically founded, or constitutive (see de Man 1979a: 205). The referent, argues Bill Readings (1989: 230) in an elaboration of de Man, is the 'text's fiction of the absence of text, the text's fiction of its own outside'. The real, Readings's argument continues, is 'language's unjust fiction of an escape from rhetoric, from the linguistic, to the literal as the personified voice of the prelinguistic real itself' (ibid.: 231). Drawing on the poststructuralist precedent, I claim that the rhetoric of urgency in South African literary discourse functions to ward off the spectre that the vaunted mimesis of instrumentalist signification (whether liberal, Marxist, or otherwise) might prove merely specular – the site of opaque reflexivity rather than of transparent reflection. The rhetoric of urgency allays the suspicion that the inscription of the signifier involves a strange doubling, so the signifier is never present to the deferential presence that haunts it, the referential presence that taunts it behind the wall of language.

The democratic right to starve themselves to death.

'As long as a man looks for truth in the world,' claimed Nietzsche, '. . . he stands under the dominance of desire: he wants pleasure, not truth; he wants the belief in truth and the pleasurable effects of this belief' (quoted in de Man 1979b: 114). Mindful of Nietzsche's exhortation, I conclude that it is a primary conflict of South African literary criticism that what casts itself as Need – immediately compelling, compellingly unmediated – is properly Desire. My insistence on recasting South African literary critics' inscriptions of Need as allegories of Desire reverses the official priorities of South African literary scholarship for itself. It drives a wedge between the critical *énoncé*, or utterance, and its enunciation, the act producing the utterance (see Benveniste 1961). But to read the rhetoric of urgency in this manner is to disrupt the claims of South African realist novelists and their critical successors to such an extent that critical and fictional texts alike become unreadable on their own preferred terms. What emerges in the chasm critical intervention opens up between the realist/instrumentalist/utilitarian signifier and its signified(s) is the ideological function of the rhetoric of urgency for literary culture in apartheid South Africa.

5   The Erotic Structure of Morality

'Is the naked body really the truth?' asked Coetzee in an interview with Attwell, recognising that the pleasure of unmasking (the pleasure even of ideological unmasking) is prey to both a certain naïveté and misrecognition: 'a critical practice whose climactic gesture is always a triumphant tearing-off . . . begins to confine its attention to clothed subjects, and even to subjects whose clothes are easily torn off' (Coetzee 1992: 106).[9] The unmasking achieved through my tropological intervention therefore now must be coupled with the revelation of its interest, the rendering of its account.[10] My interrogation of the politics of form in South African literary studies should be seen as derivative of the larger theoretical question regarding the relationship between artistic or literary representation on the one hand and notions of lived truth or reality on the other but not merely derivative of this question. What is at stake is not the constructedness of textuality, all textuality, for such an argument might be taken to imply that all representation is equally fallacious with respect to that exteriority over which it exerts its will to power – effectively vitiating hereby the historicity of any claims I make about literary discourse under apartheid. In relation to the question of the appropriate literary 'rendering' of 'life' under apartheid, I would (need to desire to) state that the relations between word and world are both more and less causal than English South African literary culture suspects. That these relations subsume issues concerning the autonomy of language – played out in the deMan(d)ing hands of the tropological reader that I have become – is integral to my claim that South African literary critical discourse in English must be read for more than or in excess of its imperatives. My insistence that readings of the relations between apartheid and representation, between trauma and truth, be cognisant of a poststructuralist critique of the sign seeks to wrest the South African national corpus from its hegemonic renderings under realism. In my reading the substitution of tropology for preferentiality to decipher the social text of apartheid replaces the ethics of protest with notions of ethicity routed through the work of Paul de Man and J. Hillis Miller, that is to say 'a willingness to stick with the letter of the text, to follow out its formal or rhetorical complexities wherever these may lead' (Norris 1988:111).

My concern to historicise literary discourse under apartheid, however, demands a complementary movement. Instead of an undifferentiated critique of the 'metaphysics of presence', I would like to invoke Stephen Slemon's insight concerning a politically interested postcolonial praxis. Slemon (1990: 7) claims that 'the assumption of "natural" seamlessness within language has never taken hold within colonised territory; for when colonialism transports a language, or imposes it upon a differential world, a fracturing, indeterminate semantics becomes the *necessary* medium for verbal and written practice . . . Post-colonial cultures have a long history of working towards "realism" within an awareness of referential slippage'. It is the task of a correspondingly fractured postcolonial criticism, Slemon (ibid.: 5) argues, to 'draw on poststructuralism's suspension of the referent in order to read the social "text" of colonialist power' while simultaneously reinstalling the referent to serve colonised and postcolonial societies. Even as I repeat, am compelled to repeat, desire to repeat that *land*, *event*, *body* are never rendered free of rhetorical mediation, I also insist that the specific material imprints of apartheid be restored to the reified tropes of public and academic debate – lest we forget our own complicity in hegemonies (discursive or otherwise) 'won by blood' (de Kock 1996: 30).

It is in this spirit that I read Guiseppe Stellardi's (1990: 41) reflections, for a predominantly South African audience, on rendering the 'truth' of/in art and literature: 'This word [rendering] is still ambiguous (returning [something] to its rightful owner? reproducing it correctly? reflecting something as it truly is?), but the accent seems to fall, more than on mere technical exactitude, on a moral imperative directly related to an indebtedness.' Something exists, says Stellardi (ibid.), 'something which is due and owing and which must be returned.' *Mayibuye*!

The 'come-back!' charge of the slogan returns us to the apartheid subject who used to voice it: his engendering, her gendered body. *The democratic right to starve themselves to death*. Jessie Tamboer, the black South African woman who set herself alight and burned to death because she could no longer provide food for her children.[11] *She was immediately engulfed by flames but did not utter a sound as she walked around the yard burning*. A rendering, a terrible rendering – as one might say that lard is rendered. *Tamboer burns to death, and lards the lean earth as she walks along*. As one might say that our renderings render their indebtedness. *The ashes of one household are collected by another for the bits of coal*. If there is an urgency in my rhetoric here, and I believe there is, it lies precisely in the knowledge – Walter Benjamin's knowledge (1973: 256) – that the claims of the past on its would-be redeemers cannot be settled cheaply.

Notes

1   To Hannan Hever, Brian McHale, and Leon de Kock in full knowledge of my indebtedness. I would also like to thank Bob Griffin, Baruch Hochman, Sonja Laden, and Meir Steinberg for their attentive readings of this essay.

2   For a post-Foucauldian reading of this nexus, see Ian Hunter 1988 as well as Simon During's critique of Hunter (During 1992: 186–94). Gauri Viswanathan's treatment of literary studies and British rule in India explicates the Indian instance (1990). In South Africa, Christo Doherty (1989: 81–82) has shown that university-level education in English literature was instituted in response to the need for a standard qualification in the civil service. Similarly Leon de Kock (1996:188) forcefully reminds us that the textual inscription[s] and prescription[s] of 'English' are integral to a 'discursive machinery' that sought 'to cordon off the very souls of "barbarous" people, and to rewrite their subjectivity'. In other words, the deployment of English as an academic subject is deeply complicit with the strategies of subjectification of the civilising mission, that is, the transformation of indigenous consciousness through discursive and disciplinary inscriptions, material and symbolic signifiers in a historically situated field (Comaroff 1985; Comaroff and Comaroff 1991). De Kock's (1996: 192) project is motivated through the need to disabuse

'English' in its institutional forms of blindness to its own complicity in colonialism; its wish to present itself as 'innocent of a coercive colonial history for which it should bear any responsibility whatsoever'.

3   The phrase is Tom Conley's (1988: xv).

4   In Bethlehem 1998 I investigate a considerable – if diffuse – body of textual material, the literary historiographic significance of which is generally occluded by the shifting taxonomies of race, place, and genre: 'white writing' in J. M. Coetzee 1988 and Michael Wade 1993; 'black writing' in Ursula Barnett 1983, Piniel Viriri Shava 1989, and Jane Watts 1989; 'the Johannesburg genre' in Rowland Smith 1976; 'Soweto poetry' in Michael Chapman 1982; and 'exile writing' in Stephen Gray 1979: 1–2.

5   All emphases are in the original texts unless otherwise stated.

6   See Nkosi on Gordimer's *Sport of Nature*: 'A great part of the motivating force of this fiction is its fear of exclusion, the fear of loitering without intent in the vicinity of revolution' (1988: 46).

7   See Norris 1988: 106 on J. Hillis Miller's 1987 reading of George Eliot.

8   Kruger's justice was administered on September 12, 1977, when Bantu Stephen Biko died in police custody as a result of severe physical injuries inflicted by the South African Security Police. At the time of Biko's death Kruger was at a National Party conference in the Transvaal. In his first announcement reporting it, he said that Biko had died 'following a hunger strike, adding that "Biko's death leaves me cold" . . . A certain Christoffel Venter stood up among the sniggers of appreciation to commend Minister Kruger's "democratic principles". Venter added that Mr Kruger was so democratic that he allowed detainees "the democratic right to starve themselves to death"' (quoted in Wilson 1991: 7).

9   I borrow the phrase the 'erotic structure of morality' from Sara Suleri's reading of Salman Rushdie's *Shame* (Suleri 1997: 180).

10   On 'interest' see Gayatri Chakravorty Spivak 1988b: 205; Ania Loomba 1991: 183–89; and Ella Shohat 1992: 110.

11   I am citing Karen Press, who dedicated her found poem, 'Dispossessed Words', to Jessie Tamboer, using precisely this phrase. Her editors, Leon de Kock and Ian Tromp, noted elsewhere that the words from which Press constructed her poem (e.g., 'She was immediately engulfed by flames', 'the ashes of one household') were extracted from the Second Carnegie Report into Poverty in South Africa (de Kock with Tromp 1996: 118). The rewriting of the reference to Falstaff (I *Henry IV* 2.2.90–91) that follows is my own.

References

Attwell, David

1990a 'The Problem of History in the Fiction of J. M. Coetzee', *Poetics Today* 11(3): 579-615.

1990b 'Political Supervision: The Case of the 1990 Wits History Workshop', *Pretexts: Studies in Writing and Culture* 2 (1): 78–85.

1991 'Resisting Power: A Reply to Kelwyn Sole and Isobel [*sic*] Hofmeyr', *Pretexts: Studies in Writing and Culture* 3 (1–2): 130–34.

1993 *J. M. Coetzee: South Africa and the Politics of Writing* (Berkeley, Los Angeles, Oxford: University of California Press; Cape Town, Johannesburg: David Philip).

Barthes, Roland

1975 *S/Z*, translated by Richard Miller (London: Jonathan Cape).

1995 [1986] 'The Reality Effect', from *The Rustle of Language*, in *The Realist Novel*, edited by Dennis Walder, 258–61 (London: Routledge and Open University).

Belsey, Catherine

1980 *Critical Practice* (London: Methuen).

Benjamin, Walter

1973 *Illuminations*, edited with an introduction by Hannah Arendt, translated by Harry Zohn (London: Fontana).

1982 [1970] 'Theses on the Philosophy of History', in Benjamin 1973: 255–67 (Bungay, Suffolk: Fontana).

Bennet, Tony
1979 *Formalism, and Marxism* (New York and London: Routledge).

Benveniste, Emile
1961 *Problems in General Linguistics* (Bloomington: Indiana University Press).

Bethlehem, Louise
1998 'South African Literary Historiography Under Apartheid'. Ph.D. diss., Tel Aviv University.

Bloom, Harry
1959 *Transvaal Episode* (Berlin: Seven Seas).

Brink, André
1983a (1976a) 'After Soweto', in *Mapmakers: Writing in a State of Siege*, 128–53 (London and Boston: Faber and Faber).
1983b (1976b) 'English and the Afrikaans Writer', in Brink 1983a: 96–115 (London and Boston: Faber and Faber).

Burnett, Ursula A.
1983 *A Vision of Order: A Study of Black South African Literature in English (1914–1980)* (London: S. Browne).

Chapman, Michael
1984 *South African English Poetry: A Modern Perspective* (Johannesburg and Cape Town: Ad. Donker).
1988 'The Writing of Politics and the Politics of Writing: On Reading Dovey on Reading Lacan on Reading Coetzee on Reading . . .', *Journal of Literary Studies/Tydskrif vir Literatuurwetenskap* 4(3): 327–41.

—ed.
1982 *Soweto Poetry* (Johannesburg: McGraw-Hill Book Company).

Christie, Sarah, Geoffrey Hutchings, and Don Maclennan
1980 *Perspectives on South African Fiction: Critical Studies in South African Literature* (Johannesburg: Ad. Donker).

Coetzee, J. M.
1988 *White Writing: On the Culture of Letters in South Africa* (Johannesburg: Radix, in association with Yale University Press).
1992 'Interview', in *Doubling the Point: Essays and Interviews*, edited by David Attwell, 103–6 (Cambridge, MA, and London: Harvard University Press).

Comaroff, Jean
1985 *Body of Power, Spirit of Resistance: The Culture and History of a South African People* (Chicago: University of Chicago Press).

Comaroff, Jean, and John Comaroff
1991 *Of Revelation and Resolution: Christianity, Colonialism, and Consciousness in South Africa* (Chicago: University of Chicago Press).

Conley, Tom
1988 'For a Literary Historiography', in *The Writing of History*, by Michel de Certeau, translated by Tom Conley, vii–xxiv (New York: Columbia University Press).

Coward, Rosalind, and John Ellis
1977 *Language and Materialism: Developments in Semiology and the Theory of the Subject* (New York and London: Routledge and Kegan Paul).

Cronin, Jeremy
1988 '"Even under the Reign of Terror . . .": Insurgent South African Poetry,' *Research in African Literatures* 19 (1): 14–23.

Dawes, Nicholas
    1997 'Constituting Nationality in the Fold of the "Interim,"' *Jouvert* 2 (1–2): Online. Internet. November 3.
De Certeau, Michel
    1988 *The Writing of History*, translated by Tom Conley (New York: Columbia University Press).
De Kock, Leon
    1989 'A Prison-House of Mirrors?' *Journal of Literary Studies* [*Tydskrif vir Literatuurwetenskap*] 5(2): 229–31.
    1996 *Civilising Barbarians: Missionary Narrative and African Textual Response in Nineteenth-Century South Africa* (Johannesburg: Witwatersrand University Press; Lovedale: Lovedale Press).
De Kock, Leon, with Ian Tromp
    1996 '"The Heart in Exile": South African Poetry in English 1990–1995', *Ariel: A Review of International English Literature* 27 (1): 105–31.
De Man, Paul
    1979a 'Allegory (Julie)', in *Allegories of Reading: Figural Language in Rousseau, Nietzsche, Rilke and Proust*, 188–220 (New Haven and London: Yale University Press).
    1979b 'Rhetoric of Tropes (Nietzsche)', in *Allegories of Reading: Figural Language in Rousseau, Nietzsche, Rilke and Proust*, 103–118 (New Haven and London: Yale University Press).
Doherty, C. M. W
    1989 'A Genealogical History of English Studies in South Africa, with Special Reference to Responses by South African Academic Literary Criticism to the Emergence of an Indigenous South African Literature'. Unpublished M. A. diss. University of Natal.
Dovey, Teresa
    1988 *The Novels of J. M. Coetzee: Lacanian Allegories.* (Johannesburg: Ad. Donker).
Du Plessis, Ménan
    1985 'Literary Realism at Its Furthest Limits', *Contrast* 59: 84–92.
During, Simon
    1992 *Foucault and Literature: Towards a Genealogy of Writing* (London and New York: Routledge).
Eagleton, Terry
    1984 (1976) *Criticism and Ideology: A Study in Marxist Literary Theory* (London: Verso).
Gebauer, Gunter, and Christoph Wulf
    1995 *Mimises: Culture, Art, Society,* translated by Don Reneau (Berkeley, Los Angeles, London: University of California Press).
Gordimer, Nadine
    1988 [1984] 'The Essential Gesture', in *The Essential Gesture: Writing, Politics and Places*, edited and introduced by Stephen Clingman, 239-50 (Johannesburg: Taurus; Cape Town: David Philip).
Grant, Damian
    1985 [1975] *Realism* (London: Methuen).
Gray, Stephen
    1979 *Southern African Literature: An Introduction* (Cape Town: David Philip).
Gwala, Mafika
    1984 'Writing as a Cultural Weapon', in *Momentum: On Recent South African Writing*, edited by M. J. Daymond, J. U. Jacobs, and Margaret Lenta, 37–51 (Pietermaritzburg: University of Natal Press).
Hamilton, Paul
    1996 *Historicism* (London and New York: Routledge).
Haresnape, Geoffrey
    1988 'The Battle for the Books: The Evolution of the Academic Criticism of South African Literature in English 1956–1976', *English Studies in Africa: A Journal of the Humanities* 31(1): 41–49.

Heath, Stephen
   1974 *Vertige du deplacement* (Paris: Fayard).
Hofmeyr, Isabel
   1990 'Introduction: History Workshop Positions', *Pretexts: Studies in Writing and Culture* (2): 61–71.
Hunter, Ian
   1988 *Culture and Government: The Emergence of Literary Education* (London: Macmillan).
Jameson, Fredric
   1971 *Marxism and Form: Twentieth-Century Dialectical Theories of Literature* (Princeton: Princeton University Press).
JanMohamed, Abdul R.
   1985 'The Economy of Manichean Allegory: The Function of Racial Difference in Colonialist Literature,' *Critical Inquiry* 12 (1): 59–87.
Knox-Shaw, Peter
   1982 'Dusklands: A Metaphysics of Violence', *Contrast* 53: 26–39.
Kohler, Peter
   1987 'Freeburghers, the Nama and the Politics of the Frontier Tradition: An Analysis of the Social Relations in the Second Narrative of J. M. Coetzee's *Dusklands*'. Paper delivered at the University of the Witwatersrand History Workshop, The Making of Class, February 9–14.
Lindfors, Bernth
   1968 'Robin Hood Realism in South African English Fiction', *Africa Today* 15 (4): 16–18.
—ed.
   1985 (1975) *Contemporary Black South African Literature: A Symposium* (Washington, DC: Three Continents Press).
Loomba, Ania
   1991 'Overworlding the "Third 'World'"', *Oxford Literary Review* 13(1–2): 164–91.
Lukács, Georg
   1971 'Narrate or Describe', in *Writer and Critic and Other Essays*, edited and translated by Arthur D. Kahn, 110–48 (New York: Grosset and Dunlap).
Macherey, Pierre
   1978 *A Theory of Literary Production* (London: Routledge and Kegan Paul).
Manganyi. N. Chabani
   1981 *Looking though the Keyhole: Dissenting Essays on the Black Experience* (Johannesburg: Ravan).
Mehta, Uday
   1997 'Liberal Strategies of Exclusion', in *Tensions of Empire*, edited by Frederick Cooper and Ann Laura Stoler, 59–86 (Berkeley and Los Angeles: University of California Press).
Miller, J. Hillis
   1987 *The Ethics Reading: Kant, de Man, Eliot, Trollope, James and Benjamin* (New York: Columbia University Press).
Morphet, Tony
   1990 'Cultural Settlement: Albie Sachs, Njabulo Ndebele and the Question of Social and Cultural Imagination', *Pretexts* 2 (1): 94–103.
Moss, Rose
   1978 '"Telling the Truth": Interview by Jean Marquard', *Contrast* 47: 48–55.
Mphahlele, Es'kia
   1983 'South African Literature vs. The Political Morality 1', *English Academy Review* 1: 8–28.
   1987 'The Tyranny of Place and Aesthetics: The South African Case', in *Race and Literature* [*Ras en Literatuur*], edited by Charles Malan, *CENSAL* publication no. 15, 48–59 (Pinetown: Owen Burgess Publishers).

Mtshali, Oswald

  1976 'Black Poetry in South Africa', in *Aspects of South African Literature*, edited by Christopher Heywood, 121–27 (London, New York: Heinemann).

Murray, Colin

  1992 *Black Mountain: Land, Class and Power in the Eastern Orange Free State 1880s–1980s* (Johannesburg: Witwatersrand University Press for the International African Institute, London).

Mutloatse, Mothobi

  1981(1980) 'Introduction', in *Forced Landing – Africa South: Contemporary Writings*, edited by Mothobi Mutloatse, 1–7 (Johannesburg: Ravan).

—ed.

  1981 *Reconstruction: 90 Years of Black Historical Literature* (Johannesburg: Ravan).

Mzamane, Mbulelo Vizikhungo

  1977 'The Short Story Tradition in Black South Africa'. Address to the Writer's Workshop of the UBLS (Gaborone Campus), Which Way African Writing? April 2–4, 1976, *Marang* 1: n.p.

  1988 'New Poets of the Soweto Era: Van Wyk, Johennesse, and Mandingoane'. Special issue, 'Black South African Literature since 1976', edited by Tim Couzens and Stephen Gray, in *Research in African Literatures* 19(1): 3–11.

Ndebele, Njabulo S.

  1991 [1984] 'The Rediscovery of the Ordinary: Some New Writings in South Africa', in *Rediscovery of the Ordinary: Essay on South African Literature and Culture*, 37–57 (Johannesburg: Congress of South Africans Writers [COSAW]).

Nkosi, Lewis

  1965 *Home and Exile* (London: Longman).

  1973 [1966] 'Fiction by Black South Africans', in *African Writers on African Writing*, edited by O. D. Killam, 109–57 (London, Ibadan, Nairobi: Heinemann).

  1986 'South African Fiction Writers at the Barricades', *Third World Book Review* 2(1-2): 43-45.

  1988 'Resistance and the Crisis of Representation', in *South African Literature, from Popular Culture to the Written Artefact: Second Conference on South African Literature, December 11–13, 1987* (Bad Boll, West Germany: Evangelische Akademie).

  1998 'Postmodernism and Black Writing in South Africa', in *Writing South Africa: Literature, Apartheid, and Democracy, 1970–1995*, edited by Derek Attridge and Rosemary Jolly, 75–90 (Cambridge: Cambridge University Press).

Norris, Christopher

  1988 *Paul de Man: Deconstruction and the Critique of Aesthetic Ideology* (London and New York: Routledge).

Oliphant, Andries Walter

  1996 'Fictions of Anticipation: Perspectives on Some Recent South African Short Stories in English', *World Literature Today: South African Literature in Transition* 70 (1): 59–62.

Parry, Benita

  1994 'Some Provisional Speculations on the Critique of "Resistance Literature"', in *Altered State: Writing and South Africa*, edited by Elleke Boehmer, Laura Chrisman, and Kenneth Parker; 11–24 (Sydney and Mundelstrup: Dangaroo Press).

  1998 'Speech and Silence in the Fictions of J. M. Coetzee', in *Writing South Africa: Literature, Apartheid, and Democracy, 1970–1995*, edited by Derek Attridge and Rosemary Jolly, 149–65 (Cambridge: Cambridge University Press).

Pechey, Graham

  1994 'Cultural Struggle' and the Narratives of South African Freedom', in *Altered State: Writing and South Africa*, edited by Elleke Boehmer, Laura Chrisman, and Kenneth Parker; 25–36 (Sydney and Mundelstrup: Dangaroo Press).

Press, Karen
    1996 'Dispossessed Words', in *The Heart in Exile: South African Poetry in English*, 1990–1995, edited by Leon de Kock and Ian Tromp, 52–53 (London: Penguin Books).

Readings, Bill
    1989 'The Necessity of Politics', in *Reading De Man Reading*, edited by Lindsay Waters and Wlad Godzich, 223–43) Minneapolis: University of Minnesota Press).

Rich, Paul
    1984 'Apartheid and the Decline of the Civilization Idea: An Essay on Nadine Gordimer's *July's People* and J. M. Coetzee's *Waiting for the Barbarians*', *Research in African Literature* 15 (3): 365–93.

Seroke, Jaki
    1988 (1981) 'Black Writers in South Africa: Jaki Seroke Speaks to Miriam Tlali, Sipho Sepamla and Mothobi Mutloatse after a Steering Committee Meeting of the African Writers' Association at Khotso House in 1981', in *Ten Years of Staffrider 1978–1988*, edited by Andries Walter Oliphant and Ivan Vladislavic, 303–9 (Johannesburg: Ravan).

Shava, Piniel Viriri
    1989 *A People's Voice: Black South African Writing in the Twentieth Century* (London and New York: Zed Books).

Shohat, Ella
    1992 'Notes on the "Post-Colonial"', *Social Text* 31/32: 99–113.

Slemon, Stephen
    1990 'Modernism's Last Post,' in *Past the Last Post: Theorizing Post-Colonialism and Post Modernism* (Calgary, Alberta: University of Calgary Press).

Smith, Rowland
    1976 'The Johannesburg Genre', in *Exile and Tradition: Studies in African and Caribbean Literature*, edited by Rowland Smith, 116–31 (London: Longman and Dalhousie University Press).

Spivak, Gayatri Chakravorty
    1988a 'Can the Subaltern Speak?' in *Marxism and the Interpretation of Culture*, edited by Cary Nelson and Lawrence Grossberg, 271–313 (Urbana: University of Illinois Press).
    1988b 'Subaltern Studies: Deconstructing Historiography', in *Other Worlds: Essays in Cultural Politics*, 197–221 (New York and London: Routledge).

Stellardi, Giuseppe
    1990 'The Truth in the Shoe: Deconstruction and the Work of Art', *Pretexts: Studies in Writing and Culture* 2 (1) 39–51.

Stewart, Susan
    1993 *On Longing: Narratives of the Miniature, the Gigantic, the Souvenir, the Collection* (Durham and London: Duke University Press).

Suleri, Sara
    1992 *The Rhetoric of English India* (Chicago and London: University of Chicago Press).

Vaughan, Michael
    1982 'Literature and Politics: Currents in South African Writing in the Seventies', *Journal of Southern African Studies* 9(1): 118–38.

Viswanathan, Gauri
    1990 *Masks of Conquest: Literary Study and British Rule in India* (London: Faber and Faber).

Wade, Michael
    1993 *White on Black in South Africa: A Study of English-language Inscription of Skin Colour* (New York: St. Martin's Press).

Walden, Dennis, ed.
    1995 *The Realist Novel* (London: Routledge in association with Open University).

Watson, Stephen

    1983 'Recent White English South African Poetry & the Language of Liberalism', *Standpunte* 36 (2): 13–23.

Watt, Ian

    1970 (1957) *The Rise of the Novel* (Harmondsworth: Penguin).

Watts. Jane

    1989 *Black Writers from South Africa: Towards a Discourse of Liberation* (London: Macmillan in association with St. Anthony's College, Oxford).

Wilson, Lindy

    1991 'Bantu Stephen Biko: A Life', in *Bounds of Possibility: The Legacy of Steve Biko & Black Consciousness*, edited by N. Barney Pityana, Mamphela Ramphele, Malusi Mpumlwana, and Lindy Wilson, 15–77 (Cape Town: David Philip; London and New York: Zed Books).

FIVE

Sitting for the Civilisation Test: The Making(s) of a Civil Imaginary in Colonial South Africa[1]

Leon de Kock

1 Postcolonial, Tribal, National

Debates in postcolonial criticism about centres and margins and about the geopolitical distribution of power/knowledge stemming from the imperial project inevitably tend to regard *oppositionality*, at whatever level, as an axiomatic condition of postcoloniality. Indeed the notion of the 'postcolonial' rests to a large extent on the perception of antagonistic struggle that, at the cultural and political levels, manifests itself as a kind of Freudian 'return of the repressed' in the aftermath of imperialism and colonialism. Return, reply, writing back, revision, reformulation – these iterative processes of *counter*-assessment are widely regarded as being at the heart of the *post* in postcoloniality, from Edward W. Said's *Orientalism* (1978) to Bill Ashcroft, Gareth Griffiths, and Helen Tiffin's *The Empire Writes Back* (1989) and from Homi K. Bhabha's 'Sly Civility' (1994b [1985]) to Dipesh Chakrabarty's 'Postcoloniality and the Artifice of History' (1992), to name just a few well-known instances. Oppositionality as an axis on which unequal relations of power and representation turn is also fundamental to the conception of *subalternity*. The question of whether the authentic 'voice' of the colonial underclass is at all recoverable – a question central to Gayatri Chakravorty Spivak's 'Can the Subaltern Speak' (1988) and to J. M. Coetzee's *Foe* (1986) – rests on suppositions about *oppositional* classes, cultures, and economies (whether representational, cultural, or financial).

Given the widespread prevalence of oppositionality as an axiomatic condition of postcoloniality, then, the question arises whether all experiences of struggle within conditions of colonial supremacy are necessarily founded on outright opposition or, if direct opposition is not possible, on 'sly' or agonistic complicity. My essay answers this question in the negative. The essay presents, as an alternative to the by now ritualised invocation of oppositionality, evidence of *desired identification* with the colonising culture as an *act of affirmation*, a kind of publicly declared 'struggle' that does not oppose the terms of a colonial culture but insists on a *more pure* version of its originating legitimation.

Consider the evidence. In October 1936 eminent black South African writers gathered in Johannesburg for what they called an African Authors Conference, together with white liberals of the time – missionary fathers, 'Bantu studies' experts, and Christian benefactors.[2] Delegates to this conference included public figures of the stature of D. D. T. Jabavu, R. T. Caluza, B. W. Vilakazi, R. V. Selope Thema, and H. I. E. Dhlomo,[3] all of whom were integral members of the educated black elite, a group whose campaigns in the face of racial segregation – historians have come to agree – cannot be separated from the contemporaneous struggles of black South African working classes.[4] One of the several unanimous resolutions of the African Authors Conference was: 'Africans must write for Africans, but English is the medium through which Africans can be reached. It is impossible to produce a national literature through the use of a tribal language; only tribal literature will result' (Javabu n.d.).[5] By declaring themselves in favour of using English to the exclusion of indigenous languages, black writers were staking a claim to literary nationalism, in a colonial language, on behalf of a wide constituency of classes and indigenous groupings. The writers gathered at the African Authors Conference rejected outright any 'tribal' option, in terms of which pre-eminence might have been given to the precolonial in matters of literary representation. The leading black writers of the day instead chose to regard English as the vehicle of an inclusive, 'national' literature. This view encodes several paradoxical positions that, I believe, have the potential to tell us much about the peculiar torsions of colonial and late-colonial subjectivity in South Africa.

For one thing, the rejection of 'tribal' literature in favour of colonial English seems, on the surface, a profound negation of precolonial culture. The resolution could easily be construed as an indication of 'colonised' identity, in which an indoctrinated acculturation into Western forms has reached such an extent that the imperial language, English, is given ascendancy over the mother tongue. But matters are never so simple. By the time this sentiment was uttered, South African blacks were in what Saul Dubow (1995:116) calls an 'insidious climate of racial determinism' characteristic of the 1920s and 1930s. At the time of the African Authors Conference, public policy in favour of racial segregation in South Africa had appropriated the language of scientific racism, particularly eugenics, as a key part of its ideological discourse (Dubow 1989: 29), pinning newly reified racial 'groups' back into a 'tribal' status conceived as backward. This happened after the early missionaries in the first part of the nineteenth century had worked tirelessly to *detribalise* people and to offer them entry into a universal kingdom of God in the guise of a regal 'civilisation' led by Queen Victoria's British Empire. As V. Y. Mudimbe (1994:128) suggests: 'Colonisation cohesively binds the diverse, often antagonistic, collective memories of many African cultures. Offering and imposing the desirability of its own memory, colonisation promises a vision of progressive enrichment to the colonised.' Jean Comaroff and John Comaroff (1991: 59) remind us that

> the pathway along which [nonconformist missionaries in southern Africa in the nineteenth century] were to lead the heathen was to retrace their own journey through contemporary Brit-

ish society – or, rather, toward an image of that society as they wished to see it. And what they wished to see was a neat fusion of three idealised worlds: the scientific, capitalist age in its most ideologically roseate form, wherein individuals were free to better themselves and to aspire to ever greater heights; an idyllic countryside in which, alongside agrarian estates, hardworking peasants, equipped with suitable tools, might produce gainfully for the market; and a sovereign Empire of God, whose temporal affairs would remain securely under the eye, if not the daily management, of divine authority.

In sharp contrast to such visions of progressive enrichment via detribalisation and the unqualified acceptance of 'civilisation', however, a second wave of imposed 'tribalism' was now being orchestrated by white segregationists for the purposes of a crude racial capitalism, in which participation was racially skewed and in which ethnic reserves bore the costs of reproducing the urban labour force (Harries 1989: 98).

Discriminatory racial determinism in South Africa in the early part of the twentieth century, coded as European recognition of ethnic 'authenticity', was not the province of politicians alone. It existed in the fabric of civil and academic discourse. To give just one famous example, at the heart of South Africa's famous contribution to global anthropology in the early part of this century, Professor Raymond Dart's discovery of fossil remains of what he dubbed *Australopithecus africanus* in 1924, lay what Dubow (1995: 285) shows was a 'partially submerged discourse of race typology and essentialism.' In the common parlance of the day, the *Australopithecus* was known as the 'missing link between man and ape', underscoring a crudely evolutionist model of racial thinking. Academics of the day, not to mention 'liberals' and missionaries in the public sphere in general, were by no means innocent of the racial essentialism that supported segregationist ideology. Missionaries particularly had played a key role in social change. As the sign bearers of Victorian 'civilisation' and as agents of massive socio-cultural transition in the nineteenth century, missionaries had loomed large indeed. By the early twentieth century missionary 'knowledge', now less idealistically millenarian and more in line with racial capitalism, had become complicit with the relatively new 'science' of anthropology (including 'Bantu studies' and, in Afrikaans, '*volkekunde*'), at the core of which were the debilitating tenets of social Darwinism. In this nexus of purported knowledge, racial or 'tribal' provenance was seen as integral to the idea that Africans were 'naturally' inferior to and less intelligent than Europeans (Dubow 1989: 30–31). Language classification – the special preserve of missionary-linguist – was central to the typology of groups and 'national' (read 'tribal') characteristics (Harries 1989: 87), which lent segregationist thinking a pseudoscientificity. In the retribalisation process, missionaries played the lead role by creating an objectified taxonomy of languages and fossilised 'social customs'. As Leroy Vail (1989: 11) writes: 'Missionaries themselves were often instrumental in providing the cultural symbols that could be organised into a cultural identity, especially a written language and a researched written history . . . [Missionaries] had the skills to reduce hitherto unwritten languages to written forms, thereby delivering the pedigrees that the new "tribes" required for acceptance.' Such an ethnic conception of separate but unequal nationalisms later became the core justification for apartheid. South Africa in the late colonial period therefore saw a concerted effort to 'retribalise' black South Africans, from above, for the purposes of political and economic containment (Vail 1989:11 Harries; 1989: 87).

It should thus be clear that, when the African Authors Conference rejected 'tribal language' and 'tribal literature,' they in the deepest sense rejected an imposed ideology of racial essentialism that would set them apart from a common humanity and turn them into drawers of water and hewers of wood. Going against the stream of imposed tribalism was, however, no easy task. 'The new South African discourse of "native affairs",' writes Kate Fletcher (1996: 2) about the 'Native Question' in the wake of the Lagden Report of the South African Native Affairs Commission of 1903–1905, 'swept the entire, preponderant, Black population into a separate, homogeneous, category of "problemacy".' Even among so-called friends of the Native, the language and philosophy of racial essentialism were rife. J. D. Rheinallt Jones, for example, who was a 'liberal' delegate to the African Authors Conference of 1936, was at the centre of a group of white liberals who helped set up 'Bantu studies' as a discipline in the 1920s. Rheinallt Jones founded the journal *Bantu Studies*, which was affiliated with the Diedrich Westermann's International Institute of African Languages and Cultures. The executives of this institute included many of the major culture-contact anthropologists and apologists for indirect rule. Westermann, in a book called *The African To-Day* (1934), earnestly expressed, as purported knowledge, the idea that 'the Negro is largely ruled by his emotions' (44) and that 'the Negro has a tendency to imitate' (47). Westermann nevertheless sought to locate 'national genius' within ethnic enclosures: 'Each [nation] has its own genius which is . . . nowhere so clearly brought out as in language'. Similarly the leading South African missionary of the time, R. H. W. Shepherd (1945: 57), wrote in *Lovedale and Literature for the Bantu* that 'the vernacular must have a large place in African life and literature'.[6] The idea of the 'national' was therefore problematically cast within a racially deterministic philosophy that employed a static and reified sense of ethnicity. It was a schema of descending value, in which the European was positioned at the top and the African several steps below.

This then was what South African black leaders of the time were up against. In the light of widespread efforts by whites of both 'liberal' and non-liberal persuasions, backed by the pseudoscience of anthropology, by missionaries, and by the mechanisms of the state toward a repressive construction of ethnic typology, it is little wonder that black authors seeking the best deal for themselves and their people should emphatically reject 'tribalism' and declare the whole of English their terrain for national purposes: the notion of 'national' is reconfigured as transcending the externally imposed ethnic imposture. Seen against the background of segregationist desires to keep the Bantu in their place and in their prescribed 'tribal' enclosures, it was an act of political affirmation to declare oneself an inhabitant of nothing less than the English language and Western 'civilisation' at large.

However, for African authors to adopt the greater universalism of English as a bulwark against impositions of ethnic identity was a paradoxical and problematic exercise. The writing of 'literature' in English was an uneasy negotiation: in its dense web of textuality were multiple constraints and restraints. One didn't just take English and make literature in a vacuum. If one had undergone 'liberal' missionary education in English or instruction in literature at the single 'black' South African university in existence in the first half of the century, Fort Hare, as many African writers had, then one's sense of what was possible in literary English was constituted by the King James Bible, Shakespeare, Milton, Pope, Keats, Wordsworth, Browning, Tennyson, Dickens, Sir Walter Scott, and similar models.[7]

Many early works of black South African writing in English attest to this unease in the very forms, idioms, and registers employed in writing for a readership that did not really exist in any significant numbers except as an imaginary community where English and the values it was held to represent approximated the ideals of civil egalitarianism. Shula Marks (1986: 56) writes: 'The very access to print through the literacy and English language brought by missionaries made the new "imagined political community" implied by nationalism a possibility.'[8] If, then, English was a discursive site riven with contradiction – offering entry to a larger world, a more global imaginary, but hedged by the constraints of a colonising ideology – in what terms could such political imagining take place?

2   A Civilisation Test

Some indication is given by a resolution at the inaugural All African Convention (AAC) in 1935, which has been described as 'perhaps the most representative gathering of African political figures ever convened' by that time (Dubow 1989: 164) and as representing a 'genuine African consensus' (Walshe 1987 [1970]: 119), despite the restraints of limited political participation by South African blacks in the period. The convention, which took place just a year before 'tribal' literature was emphatically rejected in favour of English at the African Authors Conference, boasted more than four hundred delegates from a variety of organisations, including the Communist Party of South Africa, the African Political Organisation, the African National Congress, and the South African Indian Congress (Worden 1995: 85).

At this gathering a resolution was taken that, upon a superficial reading and in conventional postcolonial terms, seems peculiarly retrograde but that on closer consideration compels us to seek new vocabularies to describe situations of colonial negotiation. The resolution earnestly called upon the segregation-minded South African authorities of the time to institute a *civilisation test*[9] as a way of determining eligibility in the last remaining pocket of black enfranchisement in the country.[10] At the time the only blacks eligible to vote in South Africa were those in the former Cape Colony who, in terms of a restricted franchise inaugurated in 1853 (contingent upon wage and property qualifications) were eligible to vote for a *white* candidate (cf. de Kock 1996: 112).

The AAC was set up in response to the immediate threat posed by a new Franchise Bill, which sought to take away from black South Africans even this restricted, 'liberal' Cape franchise and to replace the wage/property criterion with the dreaded standard of eligibility conditional upon a white skin. The resolution passed by the AAC proposed that the 'civilisation test' consist in an 'educational or property or wage qualification, as a condition for the acquirement of political privileges' (Jabavu 1935: 6). Given the extreme restrictions on education for black Africans current in 1935 and the dependence of jobs and property ownership on a colonial education, all three terms here invoked as constitutive of 'civilisation' – education, wage, property – were in effect metonymies for a *missionary* primary and secondary education, since such was all that had been available to blacks for the preceding century. In many cases such missionary education would have included schooling at the famous Lovedale Missionary Institution or one of the other missionary schools and/or an education at the country's only university open to blacks on a wide scale, Fort Hare.

The AAC was chaired by Professor D. D. T. Jabavu, a prominent Fort Hare personality who was elected president of the convention. Jabavu favourably cites the words of his vice-president, Dr A. B. Xuma (who later became president of the African National Congress), at the AAC's closing ceremony as aligning the movement with the ideals of civilised dignity and gentlemanly behaviour: 'The vice-president, Dr A. B. Xuma said that the Bantu had reached a higher stage of civilisation than most people realised . . . They had behaved as ladies and gentlemen of Africa and true sons and daughters of the soil. More august bodies had not behaved so well when faced with such grave circumstances. He thanked all the delegates for their decorum' (Jabavu 1935: 35–36).

A *civilisation test? Ladies and gentlemen* of Africa who behave with *decorum?* In view of the rapacious political thievery South African blacks were subjected to, such sentiments do indeed sound quaint. Here we see a paradox typical of early African nationalism: the response to segregationist pressure is *seemingly* dressed in a language of complicity with colonial, 'civilising' discourse. The AAC's desire for a 'civilisation test' within the African Authors Conference's similarly imagined 'national' domain was somehow styled on what appears to be the model of a British gentleman. How else do we read the explicit call for the apparently degrading 'civilisation test' as a means to fend off Afrikaner and 'liberal' segregationists, when for decades 'civilisation' had been defined by missionaries, those message bearers of the High Victorian gentlemanly order (cf. Comaroff and Comaroff 1991; de Kock 1996)? Contrary to the appearance of capitulation in the AAC's submission to a 'civilisation test,' however, I suggest that it contained an emergent postcoloniality in which black subjects sought to transcend colonising impositions of backward-looking 'tribal' identity by the *desire to be the same* rather than different.[11] In this instance, what one commonly understands as 'difference' operated in its particular historical and public context as a *homogenising* force (reified, 'backward' tribal status) decidedly *against* the interests of black South Africans, while the ideal of the gentlemanly, civilising subject opened up the possibility of full participation in a civil society conceived as generous and just. The public desire for a 'civilisation test' therefore was driven by an impulse similar to that which declares 'tribal' literature less desirable than 'national' literature in English. Both sought assimilation because the segregationist policies of the day represented a backwater, and both sought inclusion in the world of civil justice founded on English constitutional norms and on the Bible's promise of equality as an alternative to the appalling option of complete disfranchisement in the South African state.

The AAC and its call for a 'civilisation test' as well as the African Authors Conference and its espousal of English as a medium of nationalism therefore appear to suggest that, in the South African context, we must seriously reconsider all binarist models of neatly apportioned *oppositional* resistance. Something else was at work in the history of the negotiation by Africans of what came to be known in twentieth-century South African history as 'internal colonialism' – a condition 'which combines the worst features of both imperialism and colonialism in a single national frontier,' making 'Non-white South Africa' a colony of 'White South Africa' (Kistner 1989: 35). On the surface we have an emergent African nationalist discourse framing its ideals in what postcolonial theory would normally regard as the language of complicity. Here is a genuinely representative postcolonising ethos, *not* driven by self-serving elitist or bourgeois sell-outs that seemingly *asks* to be measured by the standards of imperial 'civilisation.' Can postcolonial theory cope with such a non-oppositional strain of resistance that, in addition, is clothed in the language of seeming collaboration? How many postcolonial paradigms are able to unlock, *without* invoking elaborate, retroactively validated notions of 'sly' civility,[12] the paradox of colonised subjects resisting colonial political reduction by begging for a civilisation test in the white person's image? Must the colonial subject always *reject* the colonising episteme to circumvent its oppressive implications?

Anyone who cares to inspect the record pertaining to South Africa will find a massive paper archive of plea and petition by educated Africans against the erasure of the *Pax Britannica's* civil ideals in the years between the 1880s and the 1930s, when increasingly racist legislation repeatedly signalled the end of even the restricted Cape franchise for black South Africans.[13] In the early years of missionary conversion, from the beginning of the nineteenth century up until about the 1880s, a softer, millenarian brand of Christianity was taught that sincerely foresaw total equality and brotherhood between all God's people. Africans who had made the deeply traumatic conversion of identity from 'red people' (pagans) to 'school people' (converts) under military and other forms of pressure would never forget the millenarian basis of their conversion – it became an ethic revered and handed down from generation to generation. But the harsher winds of social Darwinism, scientific racism, and High Imperialism that began to blow in the later years of the century undermined the egalitarian basis of Christian conversion. Thus a protracted negotiation or conversation began in which the ideals and terms of 'civilisation' under the banner of Queen Victoria were contested between the colonising and the colonised classes themselves. Among those whose entire trajectory of identity had been altered by the emphatic experience of religious conversion, a vigilance was born that upheld the uncorrupted ideals of an imagined political and ethical community based on the ennobling ideals of civilised life – repeatedly figured as ideal imperial gentlemanly behaviour – where fair play and justice reigned supreme. This ideal found a wide representational reach and was widely regarded as foundational to African nationalism. Thus it was not for nothing that in 1912, before resolving to form the South African Native National Congress (later the African National Congress, which today presides over democratic South Africa), delegates sang Tiyo Soga's Xhosa hymn 'Fulfill Thy Promise, God of Truth' (Lodge 1983: 1), underscoring the millenarian basis of received African versions of missionary Christianity (cf. Willan 1996).

A suggestive documentary example of earnest but vigilant reverence for 'imperial' values, among the many such examples available, is a document entitled 'Questions Affecting the Natives and Coloured People Resident in British South Africa' (ca. 1903), which Thomas Karis and Gwendolen M. Carter (1972, 1: 18) attribute to the executive of the South African Native Congress and which is addressed to Joseph Chamberlain, secretary of state for the colonies. The writers affirm the 'loyalty' of the 'Native people' to the 'Mother Country'. The 'Gospel of Salvation' has been brought to people who 'sit in darkness and the shadow of death'. The document complains, however, that 'some' of the clergy in South Africa have not caught the 'spirit of the times,' defined as the 'spiritual blessings brought by the Messengers of Peace and good-will from the Church Catholic in fulfillment of the Divine commission'. It continues: 'The Natives have much to learn and unlearn, and the power of resistance to the will of the ruling caste having been effectually broken down, they are now applying themselves to the newer conditions imposed upon them by Christianity and civilisation with a common faith in the necessity of British rule, as the best and most liberal system for the Government of the various tribes and the settlement of their conflicting interests. There is, therefore, no longer a Native problem, but the Problem of the Ruling Caste, how to govern and educate on those broad and impartial lines' (ibid.). Later in the document the writers quote the judge president of the High Court of Kimberley as saying during a judgment in a murder trial that

> inflexible justice must be administered, not only between the European race in this country but between men of European races and those who were not. The basis upon which the Empire was built up was not material force or numerical strength and accumulated wealth. These things singly or collectively would not hold the Empire together. It was the fact that equal justice was meted out to all, irrespective of race or creed. The question of the administration of inflexible justice, irrespective of colour, was one in connection with which every citizen of the Empire, when called upon, must do his duty.
>
> (ibid.: 20)

This concept of *inflexible* imperial justice proved a highly effective rhetorical whip in the hands of African nationalists, since they found no end of illiberal flexibilities in the departure by South African authorities from their imperial mandate. Describing the African Political Organisation, led from 1905 by Dr Abdullah Abdurahman, Kate

Fletcher (1996: 20) comments that it was 'steeped in the Cape liberal tradition, desiring equal political rights and economic opportunities for all 'civilized' men . . . This message was echoed time and time again by Abdurahman and the African Political Organisation and was broadcast more widely by the Native Press Association, founded in late 1903 by newspaper editors Sol Plaatje and F. Z. S. Peregrino.' Fletcher continues:

> Significantly, these organisations also espoused a rhetoric and ideology of unity, primarily 'between the coloured races', but emphatically not to the exclusion of Whites . . . onto the old system of individualist enterprise and competition in the name of progress was imprinted a new emphasis on the reciprocal duties of state (and/or empire) and citizen. The realisation of these duties was seen as characteristic of 'civilisation', *a state of awareness of the conditions necessary for the advancement of the civic 'organism' as a whole:* that is, the collaboration of its constituents in the pursuit of the 'common good.'

> (ibid.: 20–21; emphasis added)

Tom Lodge (1990: 165), in a discussion of Plaatje's contribution to African National Congress historiography in Plaatje's novel *Mhudi* (1930), argues that the resolution of the novel's subplot 'expresses a Christian brotherhood in which "there is neither Greek nor Jew, bond nor free, male nor female, white nor black, but all are one in Christ Jesus". It reflects the African National Congress's concept of a racially inclusive nation based on common values, an ethic which for African intellectuals such as Plaatje found powerful historical resonance in the hospitable capacity of both the Barolong and Matabele to absorb outsiders.'

These examples of a recuperated sense of imperial *civitas*, rather than outright opposition or even subversive complicity, suggest that what may be described as a civil imaginary was deeply embedded in emerging texts of African nationalism. In Simon During's (1990: 142–43) description the civil imaginary, whose origins he locates in eighteenth-century England, 'reproduces everyday life in the public domain, reducing the gap between the divine/moral order and actual behaviour, thereby replacing the old science of casuistry by the modern domination of the life-world by style and civility . . . One might say that it replaces the law of the father, the absolutist order, with *autonomous subjects regulated by internalised representations*' (emphasis added). The 'internalised representations' of civility characteristic of the civil imaginary are replete in the public record of colonial politics in South Africa, in which black subjects enunciate their own viewpoints. These viewpoints are consistently marked by invocations of a millennial civilian order of free, autonomous, and gainfully employed modern subjects under the beneficent sway of Victoria, who represents justice, fairness, and equality within a gloriously conceived empire of God. The more obvious examples range from Tiyo Soga's 'transvaluation' of Enlightenment ethics for an emerging sense of national identity among South African black people in the 1860s (cf. Attwell 1997: 562) to John Tengo Jabavu and A. K. Soga's struggle in the 1890s for the 'true British principle' (de Kock 1996: 137), to Plaatje's hammering at the doors of Westminster over the iniquities of the 1913 Land Act, to the examples of the AAC and the African Authors Conference cited in this essay. In such instances a high degree of synchrony exists in the *rhetorical* substance of the civil imaginary. The question then arises as to how to regard this concept, given the paradox of seeming captivity in the coloniser's discourse of civility that, historically, cannot easily be characterised as 'sly civility.'

3   Imagining Civility

We know from countless studies and from the historical record that the imperial promise of a benign civitas was not kept. The ideals of ultimate justice were broken in making the Union of South Africa in 1910, which largely excluded black South Africans from meaningful political participation. The promise of Christian brotherhood was decisively undermined by the Land Act of 1913, which effectively excluded blacks from landownership in the greater part of the country. In the face of such treachery, the obvious options are resistance or acquiescence. But in the South African context, where black military resistance had been crushed in the Hundred Years' War, which ended in the late nineteenth century, and where simple acquiescence has never been embraced as a political strategy, the campaign for civil rights was taken up symbolically as a contest over the publicly held *terms* of the civil imaginary. Black South Africans did not fight *not* to become colonial subjects, they fought to *become* colonial subjects in the public realm, the *res publica,* in the fullest possible sense, and they did so in the image of unalloyed imperial promise. In the process they sought to hold to eternal shame the shoddy colonial compromises inflicted in the name of the civil imaginary.

In this particular articulation of discursive negotiation, the paradigms of straightforward oppositionality fail to provide adequate or even rudimentary explanatory value, especially when they become so generalised as to assume the status of transhistorical allegory. So, for example, Homi K. Bhabha's reliance on a sense of universalised antagonism as a prime category within colonial relations is simply inaccurate to the South African experience of postcoloniality. Bhabha's (1994a: 77) generalisation of a proposed universal antagonism is embodied in the statement that 'a repertoire of conflicting positions constitutes the subject in colonial discourse.' In his foreword to the English edition of Frantz Fanon's *Black Skin, White Masks,* Bhabha (Bhabha 1986: xiii) says, 'The colonial subject is *always* "overdetermined from without", Fanon writes' (emphasis added). Significantly the 'always' is Bhabha's interpolation and a potentially serious misrepresentation, since it is qualified by the phrase 'Fanon writes'. In truth the 'always' is added to Fanon's phrase outside the quotation marks.

From the point of view of situated scholarship in southern Africa, it seems necessary to resist the potential washing away of regional history by the potential force of such an 'always', particularly in the minds of regionally invested students whose sense of history should on no account be allegorised. We must insist, in all cases, on case-specific historicisation. To say that the colonial subject is *always* overdetermined from

without robs that subject of individual or group agency in a way that is difficult to reconcile with the historical record of South African colonialism.

I propose a different manner of thinking about the 'colonial mirror' (cf. Low 1996).
Despite the conflictual nature of the South African frontier wars in the nineteenth century and the consequent realignment of individual subjectivity under coercive conditions; despite, in other words, the horrors in the colonial mirror and the 'determinations
from without', the colonial mirror can also be seen to have served, paradoxically, as an
affirmation, as offering a conception of self provisionally tied to a conceptual ideal of
civitas that was not necessarily or invariably mediated by the gaze of the coloniser. In my
view 'native' subject formation under the sway of the civil imaginary came to hold its
own gaze fixedly on its *own* determinedly public appropriation of the values embedded
in the civil ideal, despite or perhaps because of the dislocations of colonial temporality,
of which Bhabha makes so much.[14] In this way what appears to be complicitous deferral
to the values of the civilised white master is a combination of strategic politeness and
the determination to see through the consequences of such politeness in socio-political
terms, in full awareness of the doubling of Enlightenment ideals in deferred colonial
contexts (cf. Bhabha 1994a; Attwell 1997; Ndebele 1984: 6–7). If my view is valid, it is
precisely the conflictual, oppositional quality of colonial subjectivity, allegorised as a
universal factor by Bhabha, that is *downplayed* by 'native' subjects in their embracing of
the undarkened ideals of civil community in the colonial mirror.

A vast rhetorical matrix exists in the record of colonial relations, particularly relating to the civilising mission in the nineteenth century, in which the key terms *rebirth*
and cultural *infancy* are repeatedly and, one should add, obsessively invoked by all parties. Conversion is viewed as 'rebirth,' and the assumption of Western cultural habits is
regarded in evolutionary terms, as a kind of 'infancy' (cf. de Kock 1996: 88–91,112). In
view of this, it does not seem at all far-fetched to propose that, in the imagined rebirth
of a public self under missionary guidance, a 'mirror-stage' imaginary fixation, analogous to Jacques Lacan's *imago,* was established in which both the missionary and the
missionary subject co-operated in creating a monologic public representation of the self
as a Christian convert. In the Lacanian schema, the infant is in a pre-symbolic phase.
Strictly speaking, the analogy is therefore impermissible, since any conception of newly
conceived self under colonial persuasion would perforce have to be linguistically transmitted. However, if one allows a secondary sense of the imaginary, such as that proposed by Fredric Jameson in his essay 'Imaginary and Symbolic in Lacan' (1977), one
may regard a term or an image as imaginary if taken absolutely but symbolic if taken as
a differential value correlative with other terms that limit it reciprocally (Jameson 1977:
377).[15] Following this schema, the civil imaginary in colonial South Africa is initially
struck in monologic, relatively unmediated, terms. The 'new self' that emerges from
missionary interaction, *reborn* into an originary sense of imaginary plenitude, is singularly imbued with the grace of God in rigidly millenarian language, and the metaphoric
support for this is characteristically Manichean, according all too well with the stark
dichotomies and binary oppositions of the mirror-stage – inside-outside, good-bad,

light-dark (cf. ibid.: 357, 369). In keeping with mirror-stage experience, the image of a new Christian self (entertained as much by the missionaries as their subjects in their own fixation with saving themselves by saving others) was saturated with polarities. The transverse reflection of self – in other words, the transformed subject as apprehended in the mirror of this imaginary – presented sharply idealised prospects of a gainful, free, justly administered *civil* life in the image of Protestant Britain.[16]

However, the twist occurs when, in Jameson's words (ibid.: 357), 'the Imaginary itself is assumed into the Symbolic Order by way of its alienation into language itself', or when the monologically conceived imaginary object is subjected to differentiation in value. The civil imaginary then is a fixation with an idealised transverse image of a public self in the colonial mirror, starkly imbued with a desired alterity as 'civilised' citizen and supported by an as yet unfractured narrative of civil freedom and progress. However, it is assumed into a Symbolic order, where the mirror image is shattered by the strictures of the colonial fathers and the prohibitions on absolute identification with what the civil imaginary was meant to offer subjects made in its image.

Before its fracture by the doubtful politics of colonial administration and later a white state, the civil imaginary is a seeming fixation with the projection of unfettered liberty under the reign of Christian egalitarianism, calling on the beneficent protection of the Mother of civilisation, Queen Victoria. In 1885 Elijah Makiwane, president of the Native Educational Association, described this queen as 'great and gracious'. In the same speech, in which Makiwane launched an incisive attack on the idea of a general notion of European superiority, he also uttered the following eulogy:

> Long may she live. Oh, Queen Victoria, thou shalt never know how many hearts even in this far off Africa thou hast cheered in their passage through 'the wilderness of this world.' Thou art not only a Queen, but a Mother. Prosper thou in all places; prosper thou in South Africa.
>
> *(Imvo Zabantsundu,* February 2, 1885)

Makiwane's sudden lyrical turn into biblical English serves to emphasise the passionate feeling of loyalty to a Queen who was an imaginary projection of imperial, civil rule.[17] In the context of Makiwane's speech this is important, since he is addressing the Native Educational Association in the 1880s, when the idea of one and the same civility for Africans as well as Europeans had begun to slide into treacherous deferral in a racist colonial society. Makiwane was invoking the idea of a queen in the guise of a 'mother', a queen of equality and civil rule in the philanthropic sense of the word.[18]

This example is richly illustrative because it shows how the alienation consequent on a civil imaginary's displacement into a colonial symbolic register – breaking the mirror – was both suffered and contested. The crucial point is that Makiwane, as a colonial subject, was not simply blinded in a naive way by a fixation with the imaginary transverse reflection of self in idyllic Western terms but that he entered into the referential fracture of the colonial Symbolic – in this case the allegation that Europeans were generally superior to Africans – as someone who clearly was wise to the treacheries of representation.

Before his eulogy to the queen, Makiwane proposed an intricate argument to demonstrate that Africans had been 'misapprehended and misrepresented' on the issue of equality with Europeans. The appeal to immemorial virtues of queenly civility comes *after* this argument as a kind of recuperation of an originary value. In this way the political argument of the day is brought under the sway of the civil imaginary, which in theory at least bound all parties to the imperial contract in South Africa. In my view Makiwane, the delegates to the All African Convention, and the many others who relied on the civil imaginary in rhetorical address through many years were aware that they were engaged in a discursive negotiation in which all was not what it seemed. In Maurice Merleau-Ponty's argument, one masters a language not by conquering it, but by infiltrating it, inhabiting it (Guetti 1993: 11).

Practitioners of the rhetorically deployed civil imaginary in the public realm understood precisely the fact that the social, and its orders of symbolic assertion, are precarious discursive fixations vulnerable to fracture. They rode the swells of public argument and politely joined the debates with their late-colonial 'fathers', except for one major difference. Their politics – and the politics of their increasingly dispossessed fellows – comprised a narrowing of material potential (land, spoils of power, wealth) and an inverse widening of imaginative capital. They were compelled to have recourse to that elusive civil imaginary, that blinding image of uncorrupted civil beneficence, and to use it as an evocation, potentially hovering in the midst of every argument, to illustrate that the politics of exploitation and inequality had captured material wealth at the expense of the imaginary, at the expense of that seemingly magical moment in the mirror.

Early African nationalists were frequently unwilling to resolve their identities in partial fixations of meaning, such as the heavily overdetermined discourse of race and ethnicity. How could they? The language of race enforced pseudo-literality on them as essences that their every intuition rejected as reductive and wholly false. In contesting such imputations of the self, African nationalists perforce recalled the *mutually* available preoccupation with a civil imaginary at the heart of the civilising mission, *not* because they were dupes buying into conformity with an oppressive order but because the civil imaginary was a *shared* site of memory, the moment in which coloniser and colonised were *joined* in a vision of plenitude. Paradoxically, the coloniser now faced the risk of becoming less than his own imaginary creation as he slipped into the casuistry of colonial deferral: into the deferral of equality and magnanimity, those values supposedly inherent in the Bible at his side; into the cultivation of a labour force instead of a celestial army; into the narcissistic convolutions of self-aggrandisement in every act of teaching a doctrine of equality from the vantage of cultural superiority. Marks (1986: 57) writes: 'By the time the African elite was so enthusiastically improving itself, the mid-Victorian faith in the prescriptive power of "civilisation" was waning. As the forces of production expanded in South Africa and made the mid-Victorian vision possible in a dramatically new way, both imperialists and Cape liberals retreated from the vision.'[19]

The pervasive, mutually understood language of civility could reopen discursive plenitude because it was constitutive of the colony's representational economy in the master language of English and of its symbolic relations of exchange. The act of recalling the civil imaginary reopened the intermediary zone in subject constitution, namely that between the imaginary projection of self as an ideally civilised other and the self that has passed through multiple metonymic displacements into imprisoned symbolic fixations of partial meaning: in short, the 'cheeky Kaffir'. The politics of an emerging African nationalism could not but reinvigorate itself imaginatively in the face of representational and material departures from the civilised ideal. The politics of white supremacy, to the contrary, required just such imaginative foreshortening to justify its cupidity.

To conclude, the seeming subservience of the leaders of the All African Convention in calling for a 'civilisation test' contained the seed of a richer sense of discursivity – a greater appreciation of the plenitude of the social – that eventually won the day in South Africa's first democratic elections in 1994.[20] (Other versions of nationalism, both Afrikaner and exclusivist Pan Africanism, failed to capture the critical mass of voter support in these elections.) The call for a 'civilisation test' was a call for that imagined wealth before its metonymic fracture. The process of gaining colonial subjectivity often involved the promise of ultimate goodness – represented by 'Christ the King' and the 'Great White Queen' of imperial hegemony (Marks 1986: 70). But this promise was all too often corrupted by countless deficits from the civil standard and therefore by the loss of that sense of wholeness imaginatively realised at the point of conversion to a new standard of 'public good.' Nevertheless, the loss was never allowed to slip into forgetfulness. It inspired a gnawing sense of absence and desire, and it prompted a ceaseless searching back for that evanescent sense of political and cultural promise figured in the civil imaginary.

This searching back, regardless of the seeming desire for bourgeois civilised respectability, became an edge, a site of antagonism in which the breaking of the colonial mirror in its vaunted, supposedly glorious plenitude was brought into remembrance as a source of shame and degradation. Since the advent of the civil imaginary in nineteenth-century South Africa, the recapture of legitimacy in the social polity has never been able to dispel the curse – or is it the blessing? – of that mirror.

Notes

1   An earlier, substantially different, version of this essay was read as a paper at the Shakespeare Postcoloniality Conference in Johannesburg in July 1996 and subsequently as a public lecture under the auspices of the Porter Institute for Poetics and Semiotics in Tel Aviv in March 1997. I am grateful to Greg Cuthbertson, Annamaria Carusi, Louise Bethlehem, Sonja Laden, Meir Steinberg, and Brian McHale for criticism and comment. I benefited also from having access to the D. D. T. Javabu Collection, in the archives of the University of South Africa Library, and to *Imvo Zabantsundu* 1885.

2   The gathering was convened and presided over by R. H. W. Shepherd in his capacity as convenor of the Committee on Christian Literature appointed in 1935 by the Christian Council of South Africa.

3   Davidson Don Tengo Jabavu was a linguist, poet, author, and first-ever lecturer at the Native College at Fort Hare (later Fort Hare University); Reuben Tolakele Caluza was a songwriter and lyricist, musician,

and teacher; Benedict Wallet Bambatha Vilakazi was a poet, novelist, scholar, and teacher; Richard Victor Selope Thema was a politician, journalist, and newspaper editor; and Herbert I. E. Dhlomo was a dramatist and poet.

4   See Gail M. Gerhart 1978; Alan Gregor Cobley 1990; Philip Bonner 1982; Bradford in Cobley 1990: 9–10, 15; and Shula Marks 1986. Bonner (1982: 276–77) shows that there was a 'small differential between the wages of the black petty bourgeoisie and the rest of the black working class'. Cobley (1990: 225) writes: 'In addition to their virtual monopoly of political leadership and their social eminence, the black petty bourgeoisie engendered a unique cultural consciousness. It was a culture inclusive of their 'African' and 'European' experiences and . . . it provided a basis for the new ideology of African nationalism in South Africa.'

5   As reported by J. D. Rheinallt Jones, editor of the journal *Bantu Studies*, published by the University of the Witwatersrand. Rheinallt Jones reported on the conference in a pamphlet published by the Lovedale Missionary Institution. The pamphlet is housed in the D. D. T. Jabavu Collection in the archives of the University of South Africa Library.

6   Shepherd (1945: 73) professed to find it 'extraordinary' that 'enthusiasm for the use and development of Bantu languages makes Europeans showing such enthusiasm objects of suspicion in a few African circles.' At this point Shepherd refers to the statement that it would be impossible to create a 'national' literature through the use of a 'tribal' language because only 'tribal' literature would result. Significantly, however, he fails to attribute this public sentiment to its source, the African Authors Conference of 1936, but derogatively attributes it to 'a small group who advocate the constant use of the English medium'. Shepherd's censorious proclivities, clearly demonstrated by Jeffrey Peires (1979), are evident in this deft elision.

7   The English department at Fort Hare in 1935 and 1939, for example, prescribed for undergraduate study Chaucer, Shakespeare, Milton, Pope, Keats, Wordsworth, Browning, Tennyson, Mrs. Gaskell, Henry James, Percy Bysshe Shelley, Sir Philip Sidney, and Coleridge, among others. Syllabi for 1944 and 1943 are similar. By 1954 'practical criticism' found its way into the syllabus as well as more modern authors, such as E. M. Forster, James Joyce and George Bernard Shaw, in addition to the more classical authors mentioned above (Calendars for the South African Native College at Fort Hare, Jabavu Collection).

8   Marks's quoted phrase is a reference to Benedict Anderson's *Imagined Communities* (1983).

9   Dubow (1989: 159) recalls that the 'civilisation test' idea was upheld by the Non-Racial Franchise Association (NRFA) founded in 1929 by Sir James Rose Innes and other prominent Cape liberals of what has been referred to as the 'great tradition' of Cape liberalism. The NRFA was determined to resist any differentiation of franchise rights on the grounds of colour and to make a 'civilisation test' the sole criterion of eligibility. However, as Dubow (ibid.) notes, 'If fears of black domination proved real, the franchise qualification could always be raised.'

10 The resolution is contained in *The Findings of the All African Convention* by D. D. T. Jabavu, a pamphlet (printed at Alice, December 1935: 6), in the D. D. T. Jabavu Collection, University of South Africa Library.

11 It is crucial to note that this 'desire to be the same' operated in declarative, public discourse and that, as Mastin Prinsloo (1998: 39) suggests, behind the declarative stance remained privately held senses of self-defined difference, illustrated by the adherence of noted black public figures to indigenous customs, such as circumcision and *lobola* (bride price), despite their public disavowals of 'heathenism' (cf. also de Kock 1996: 179–84).

12 For the argument on 'sly civility' see Bhabha 1994b [1985].

13 This archive is freely available in a documentary sourcebook, such as Thomas Karis and Gwendolen M. Carter's four volumes entitled *From Protest to Challenge* (1972).

14 This is also the drift of revisionism in history and religious studies, in which it is disputed that the African colonial subject was invariably overdetermined. The Gambian missiologist Lamin Sanneh (1989),

for example, relies on a notion of 'translation' to argue that a process of cultural 'translation' reinvigorated Christianity. The historian Richard Elphick (1995), following Sanneh, adopts the translation argument as well. See de Kock 1996:12–15 for a summary of positions that take issue with historical schemata of colonial 'overdetermination from without.' The positions include those of Terence Ranger (1986), Richard Gray (1990), Jean Comaroff and John Comaroff (1991), Paul Landau (1992), Norman Etherington (1994), and Elizabeth Elbourne (1996). Attwell's (1997: 562) idea of the 'transvaluation' of Enlightenment ideals also is instructive.

15   Jameson derived this distinction from the work of Edmond Ortigues in *Le Discours et le Symbole* (1962).

16   Marks (1986: 47–48) writes: 'For the prosperous peasantry settled on the Protestant mission stations of the Cape and Natal, as for the petty bourgeoisie that derived from it and that in the last third of the nineteenth century was forged out of a diverse set of regionally and ethnically defined local groupings into a self-conscious and coherent national bourgeoisie in the new cities of Kimberley and Johannesburg, the mid-Victorian "code-words" *progress* and *improvement* had a material reality. It was out of the mid-Victorian vision of a progressive world order, based on the virtues of free labour, secure property rights linked to a free market in land and individual tenure, equality before the law, and some notion of "no taxation without representation" that African Christians in the nineteenth century constructed their world.' Marks (1986: 70) remarks also on the powerful missionary symbolism of 'Christ the King'.

17   Marks (1986: 70) remarks on the 'enormous strength in nineteenth-century South Africa' of 'The Great White Queen' as the symbol of imperial hegemony.

18   For an elaboration of this argument see de Kock (1996: 116-40).

19   Marks continues: 'This was . . . because the demands of monopoly capital, first on the diamond fields of Kimberley, then in the gold mines of the Witwatersrand, for vast quantities of unskilled, cheap labour, and the speed with which that labour had to be conjured up, conquered, and coerced left little room in the long run for an enfranchised black peasantry and artisan class. At the same time, the African elite was rendered more vulnerable by the growing insecurity that underpinned late nineteenth-century imperial expansion, and by the parallel changes in ideology shaped by social Darwinism, 'Anglo-Saxon race pride', and notions of national efficiency on the one hand, together with the rise of Afrikaner nationalism and the consolidation of settler society in South Africa on the other' (57).

20   Cobley (1990: 230) comments on the fact that African nationalism, as moulded by the black 'petty bourgeoisie' from the 1920s onward, and especially in the 1930s, was an 'inclusive' form of African nationalism; this inclusivity encompassed 'back-to-Africa' Garveyites, unitary 'African nationalism', and even variants of 'ethno-nationalism'. The 'inclusive' brand of African nationalism emerged in the 1940s, a key period in the development of African nationalism, 'as the dominant ideology in black nationalist politics'. Marks (1986: 60–61) writes of the formation of the South African Native National Congress in 1912 that 'the black elite saw their way forward through an inclusive, liberal-democratic nationalism. This was itself in part a challenge to the exclusive nationalism being forged by the Afrikaner petty bourgeoisie at this time.'

References

Anderson, Benedict
    1983 *Imagined Communities: Reflections on the Origin and Spread of Nationalism*, rev. ed. (London: Verso).
Ashcroft, Bill, Gareth Griffiths, and Helen Tiffin
    1989 *The Empire Writes Back: Theory and Practice in Post-Colonial Literatures* (New York: Routledge).
Attwell, David
    1993 *J.M. Coetzee: South Africa and the Politics of Writing* (Berkeley: University of California Press; Cape Town: David Philip).
    1997 'Intimate Enmity in the Journal of Tiyo Soga', *Critical Inquiry* 23(3): 557–77.

Bhabha, Homi K.

    1986 'Foreword: Remembering Fanon', in *Black Skin, White Masks*, vii–xxvi (London: Pluto).

    1994a *The Location of Culture* (London: Routledge).

    1994b [1985] 'Sly Civility,' in Bhabha 1994a: 93– 101.

Bonner, Philip

    1982 'The Transvaal Native Congress, 1917–1920: The Radicalisation of the Black Petty Bourgeoisie on the Rand', in *Industrialisation and Social change in South Africa: African Class Formation, Culture, and Consciousness, 1870–1930*, edited by Shula Marks and Richard Rathbone, 270–313 (London: Longman).

Chakrabarty, Dipesh

    1992 'Postcoloniality and the Artifice of History', *Representations* 32: 1–26.

Cobley, Alan Gregor

    1990 *Class and Consciousness: The Black Petty Bourgeoisie in South Africa, 1924 to 1950* (New York: Greenwood Press).

Coetzee, J. M.

    1986 *Foe* (Johannesburg: Ravan).

Comaroff, Jean, and John Comaroff

    1991 *Of Revelation and Revolution: Christianity, Colonialism, and Consciousness in South Africa*, vol. 1 (Chicago: University of Chicago Press).

Coplan, David

    1982 'The Emergence of an African Working-Class Culture', in *Industrialisation and Social Change in South Africa: African Class Formation, Culture, and Consciousness, 1870–1930*, edited by Shula Marks and Richard Rathbone, 358–75 (London: Longman).

De Kock, Leon

    1996 *Civilising Barbarians: Missionary Narrative and African Textual Response in Nineteenth-Century South Africa* (Johannesburg: Witwatersrand University Press).

Dubow, Saul

    1989 *Racial Segregation and the Origins of Apartheid in Modern South Africa* (London: Macmillan).

    1995 *Scientific Racism in Modern South Africa* (Cambridge: Cambridge University Press).

During, Simon

    1990 'Literature – Nationalism's Other? The Case for Revision', in *Nation and Narration*, edited by Homi K. Bhabha, 139–53 (London: Routledge).

Elbourne, Elizabeth

    1996 'Early Khoisan Uses of Mission Christianity', in *Missions and Christianity in South African History*, edited by Henry Bredekamp and Richard Ross, 65–95 (Johannesburg: Witwatersrand University Press).

Elphick, Richard

    1995 'Writing Religion into History: The Case of South African Christianity', in *Missions and Christianity in South African History*, edited by Henry Bredekamp and Richard Ross, 11–26 (Johannesburg: Witwatersrand University Press).

Etherington, Norman

    1994 'Recent Trends in the Historiography of Christianity in Southern Africa'. Paper presented at the Journal of Southern African Studies Twentieth Anniversary Conference, York, September.

Fanon, Frantz

    1986 [1952] *Black Skin, White Masks*, translated by Charles Lam Markham (London: Pluto).

Fletcher, Kate

    1996 'Liberalism, Education and 'Unification' in the Cape Colony 1902–1908'. Paper presented at South Africa 1895–1921: Test of Empire Conference, Oxford, March.

Gerhart, Gail M.

    1978 *Black Power in South Africa: The Evolution of an Ideology* (Berkeley: University of California Press).

Gray, Richard
    1990 *Black Christians and White Missionaries* (London: Yale University Press).
Guetti, James L.
    1993 *Wittgenstein and the Grammar of Literary Experience* (Athens: University of Georgia Press).
Harries, Patrick
    1989 'Exclusion, Classification and Internal Colonialism: The Emergence of Ethnicity among the Tsonga-Speakers of South Africa', in *The Creation of Tribalism in Southern Africa*, edited by Leroy Vail, 82–117 (London: James Currey).
Jabavu, D. D. T.
    1935 *The Findings of the All African Convention* (Alice: Lovedale Press).
Jameson, Fredric
    1977 'Imaginary and Symbolic in Lacan', *Yale French Studies* 55/56: 338-95.
Karis, Thomas, and Gwendolen M. Carter, eds.
    1972 *From Protest to Challenges Documentary History of African Politics in South Africa 1882–1964*, 4 vols. (Stanford: Hoover Institution Press).
Kistner, Ulrike
    1989 'Literature and the National Question', *South African Society for General Literary Studies* 9: 26–44.
Kuper, Leo
    1965 *An African Bourgeoisie: Race, Class and Politics in South Africa* (New Haven: Yale University Press).
Landau, Paul Stuart
    1992 'The Making of Christianity in a Southern African Kingdom: Gammangwato, circa 1870–1940.' Ph.D. diss., University of Wisconsin.
Lodge, Tom
    1983 *Black Politics in South Africa since 1945* (Johannesburg: Ravan).
    1990 'Charters from the Past: The African National Congress and Its Historiographical Traditions', *Radical History Review* 46/47: 161–88.
Low, Gail Ching-Liang
    1996 *White Skins/Black Masks: Representation and Colonialism* (London: Routledge).
Marks, Shula
    1986 *The Ambiguities of Dependence in South Africa: Class, Nationalism, and the State in Twentieth-Century Natal* (Johannesburg: Ravan).
Mudimbe, V. Y
    1994 *The Idea of Africa* (Bloomington: Indiana University Press).
Ndebele, Njabulo
    1984 'Actors and Interpreters: Popular Culture and Progressive Formalism. Sol Plaatje Memorial Lecture'. University of Bophuthatswana, Mmabatho, September.
Peires, Jeffrey
    1979 'The Lovedale Press: Literature for the Bantu Revisited', *History in Africa: A Journal of Method* 6: 155–75.
Plaatje, Sol
    1976 [1915] 'The Late Allan King' (obituary), *African World Annual*, December 1915; printed in *English in Africa* 3(2): 27.
Prinsloo, Mastin
    1998 'Behind the Back of a Declarative History: Acts of Erasure in Leon de Kock's Civilising Barbarians: Missionary Narrative and African Textual Response in Nineteenth-Century South Africa,' *English Academy Review*, 15: 32–41.
Ranger, Terence
    1986 'Religious Movements and Politics in Sub-Saharan Africa', *African Studies Review* 29 (2) 1–69.

Said, Edward W.
    1978 *Orientalism* (London: Routledge and Kegan Paul).
Sanneh, Lamin
    1989 *Translating the Message: The Missionary Impact on Culture* (New York: Orbis).
Shepherd, R. H. W.
    1945 *Lovedale and Literature for the Bantu* (Alice: Lovedale Press).
Spivak, Gayatri Chakravorty
    1988 'Can the Subaltern Speak', in *Marxism and the Interpretation of Culture*, edited by Cary Nelson and Lawrence Grossberg, 271–313 (London: Macmillan).
Vail, Leroy, ed.
    1989 *The Creation of Tribalism in Southern Africa* (London: James Currey).
Walshe, Peter
    1987 [1970] *The Rise of African Nationalism in South Africa: The African National Congress, 1912–1952* (Johannesburg: Ad. Donker).
Westermann, Diedrich
    1934 *The African To-Day* (London: Humphrey Milford for the Oxford University Press and the International Institute for African Languages and Cultures).
Willan, Brian
    1996 'Sol Plaatje and Empire: Three Moments'. Paper presented at South Africa 1895–1921: Test of Empire Conference, Oxford, March.
Worden, Nigel
    1995 *The Making of Modern South Africa* (Oxford: Blackwell).

SIX

Black Hamlet:
Psychoanalysis on Trial in South Africa

Jonathan Crewe

The main title of this essay, *Black Hamlet,* directly repeats the title of a book by Wulf Sachs first published in 1937. The author was a Lithuanian Jew who, like many of his compatriots, settled in South Africa.[1] A physician and psychoanalyst who received training in St. Petersburg, Cologne, and London, Sachs introduced psychoanalysis into South Africa and set up the first training institute in Johannesburg. As psychoanalytic pioneer and authoritative expositor, he also published a book, to which Freud gave a prefatory stamp of approval, entitled *Psychoanalysis: Its Meaning and Practical Application* (1934). *Black Hamlet* was republished in the United States in 1947 in a widely read version titled *Black Anger.*[2] It was subsequently forgotten, however, until its republication in 1996 by the Johns Hopkins University Press in its Parallax series, devoted to 're-visions of culture and society' (Sachs 1996). The Hopkins edition is introduced and extensively contextualised by Saul Dubow, an African historian, and by Jacqueline Rose, the well-known psychoanalytic theorist and literary critic who has also written about the South African novelist Bessie Head.

Both the nature of *Black Hamlet* and the reasons for its republication by Johns Hopkins are explained on the dust jacket:

> A Jewish physician and pioneering psychiatrist, Wulf Sachs first met the man he calls 'John Chavafambira' in a Johannesburg slum. The year was 1933, and Sachs wanted to learn whether psychoanalysis was applicable across different cultures. John, as he is called throughout, was a Manyika healer-diviner eager to learn the methods of European medicine. For the next two and a half years Sachs psychoanalysed John by means of free association. The result is *Black Hamlet* – a narrative, even novelistic, reconstruction of one black South African's life set against the background of two worlds in collision.

The worlds said to be in collision are those of European urban modernity and African traditional life.

I shall add at once, for future reference, that both Sachs and Chavafambira feature in an interesting travel journal compiled in 1937–1938, after the publication of *Black Hamlet,* by an African American visitor, Ralph Bunche. Bunche, at that time still a radical political scientist from Howard University, became a more conservative diplomat after World War II and won the Nobel Peace Prize in 1950 as a negotiator of the Arab-Israeli conflict (Edgar 1992). We learn from Bunche's journal that Sachs nervously entertained him on several occasions in segregated white restaurants, that he met Sachs's wife as well, and that Sachs gave him access to an asylum for black mental patients in which he worked.[3] Bunche's travel notes supply a useful cross-reference for some of Sachs's claims and representations.

The current revival of interest in *Black Hamlet* is further explained in the dust jacket blurb: 'Some sixty years after its publication, the text still reads with remarkable urgency. It has much to offer a modern readership with interests in the construction of social identity, the relationship between knowledge and power, and the interconnections between psychoanalytic, literary, and historical thought.' Rose and Dubow sketch out, in their introductions, many of the political, historical, epistemological and ethnographic issues that the book raises. Rose elaborates further in the chapter entitled 'Black Hamlet' in her book *States of Fantasy* (1996: 38–55). I will note, again for future reference, that this chapter concerns Sachs's self-conscious inability to become African and his corresponding, highly reluctant Zionism, professed in a letter to Freud.[4]

From all this contemporary interest it is rightly inferred that *Black Hamlet* is a rich cultural text. For what it is worth, the book possesses the additional commendation of being artfully written and grippingly readable.[5] It also provides a memorably vivid image of 1930s Johannesburg as a crowded, rapidly expanding, multiethnic city, in which formal apartheid was rapidly taking shape on the basis of an endemic, brutal, yet still relatively unsystematic – one might say 'untheorised' – white racism. What Sachs called 'black anger' is pervasively voiced by black speakers in the book, subjected to poverty, uprooting, overcrowding, squalor, injustice, insult, and almost continuous police harassment. The literally maddening effects of this treatment become apparent in the book's account of the black insane, who are warehoused rather than treated in the state's racially segregated institutions. In these institutions Sachs must always confront certain limits – both the therapeutic insufficiency and the social unavailability of psychoanalysis. The explicit, angry connections the chronic patients make between their mental states and their socio-political abuses constitute a scandal for apolitical Western psychotherapy, represented by Sachs in his double guise as a medically trained psychiatrist and a psychoanalyst. Bunche notes that one patient 'seemed to delight in being insolent and impudent to Sachs as he questioned him' (Edgar 1992: 188).

Moreover the function of psychoanalysis as the analyst's means of distancing and defending himself from an unmanageable reality is intimated when Bunche reports that two women patients who have been domestic workers spend all their days washing floors. Overriding the obvious connection Bunche makes between the patients' madness and their former employment, Sachs assimilates this compulsive floor washing to Lady Macbeth's compulsive hand washing, canonically discussed by Freud (ibid.: 189).

These stark obstacles to credible psychoanalytic functioning in South Africa might seem sufficient to forestall any substantive consideration of psychoanalysis either in

Sachs's text or in our reading of it. Moreover *Black Hamlet* reveals a situation in which Western psychotherapy is not merely compromised by political forces but is always on the verge of being overwhelmed and displaced by them. In this respect *Black Hamlet*, written shortly after the introduction of psychoanalysis into South Africa, can be read as prophetic, and not only with respect to South Africa. Yet more than simple failure remains at issue, both in Sachs's text and for contemporary reading. Sachs notably does not include in his own account the two black Ladies Macbeth along with the black Hamlet. Nor does he just attempt to map psychoanalysis – or Shakespeare for that matter – over the entire world he views. Nor is he only on the defensive. Something more like an extended *in situ* trial of psychoanalysis is undertaken in *Black Hamlet*, as a result of which Sachs's own priorities appear to shift, as noted by Rose and Dubow. Right at the end of the book, for example, Sachs (320) says of his black interlocutors:

> So they continued to come to me with their grievances and their difficulties, showing amazing confidence in me. It was as if, laying their tragedy bare to me, they hoped I would reveal it to the conscience of the world. (And maybe their entreaties were in the end responsible for my writing this book.)

Setting aside the issue of white liberal patronage in Sachs's declaration, let us simply note that appealing to 'the conscience of the world' comes to take precedence as a motive over the book's formally announced intention to demonstrate the universality of psychoanalysis. Sachs's renaming the book *Black Anger* and his updating of John's life history in it seem consistent with this shift in priorities.[6] Rather than simply vindicating psychoanalysis in his encounter with the man he calls John, Sachs appears to have undergone as much of a South African political education as he can receive. It is only one of the novelistic ironies of *Black Hamlet* that it recounts the education of its analyst-narrator even more than that of its protagonist as a young man from the provinces. (The provinces are represented by Manyikaland in what was then Rhodesia, from which John had immigrated.)

Sachs's apparent shift in perspective notwithstanding, I want to consider the fortunes not only of psychoanalysis but also of the self-consciously pioneering psychoanalyst in this book. *Black Hamlet* is a text in which a universalising psychoanalysis puts itself to the test methodologically and epistemologically, but it inescapably does so politically and morally as well. It is also, perhaps unexpectedly, on trial at all these levels, as is the analyst, in a setting conceived as alien.[7] Sachs's consciousness of being on trial becomes increasingly explicit and troubling to him as the book proceeds. His inability to live up to the responsibilities he has hubristically assumed, or is regarded by the black community as having assumed, makes him fear the judgement of that community. On one occasion a group of annoyed black visitors composes itself in his own mind into a general tribunal on his conduct. When Sachs cries out 'Didn't I myself, a Jew, belong to a people ceaselessly driven from pillar to post?' (286), the question remains rhetorical only; since Sachs believes that he cannot make this shared history perspicuous to his imagined black judges. In other words, he finds himself in the helpless position of the black accused in a white courtroom.

Reversals like this enable Rose to situate *Black Hamlet* in a still-growing body of texts that represents psychoanalysis on trial in colonial or postcolonial settings, for example, in Zaire and Haiti. These trials can, of course, be taken to include the still-expanding critique of a universalising, Western psychoanalysis initiated by Frantz Fanon's 'The Negro and Psychopathology' (1952: 141–69), a critique he subsumed in his more general proposition that colonialism itself should be placed on trial. In *Black Hamlet* psychoanalysis is on trial as therapy and as epistemology but also as a privileged Western discourse of good intentions historically implicated in Western racism and colonialism. The professional role does not shield the well-meaning analyst from social scrutiny, nor does the white colonial monopoly on judicial institutions shield the analyst from judgement.

To put this differently, we could say that Sachs tries to inscribe the South African native subject in the colonial global imaginary of 1930s psychoanalysis. At the site of colonial encounter, however, the attempt increasingly seems like one in which an ill-fitting template is imposed on political and cultural realities it cannot encompass. In that sense the text becomes both self-problematising and assimilable to postcolonial critiques of a colonising psychoanalysis.

For psychoanalysis to be on trial in *Black Hamlet,* then, is for it to be subject to judgement, yet the nature of the proceeding is more accurately conveyed by the German term *Prozess* than the English term *trial*. More readily than the English term, the German one can signify both a judicial proceeding culminating in a verdict and a process without closure. Neither trial nor judgement is precluded, but the ambiguous term can also signify a complex cultural process subsuming and exceeding the judicial one. It can further imply the involvement of all parties to the trial in an ongoing drama of cultural conflict, interaction, and transformation.[8]

Two disclaimers are necessary, however, if psychoanalysis is to be seen as meaningfully on trial in any sense in *Black Hamlet*. First, what is staged in Sachs's book cannot be construed as a fair trial of psychoanalysis or of the analyst. Imagined tribunals notwithstanding, Sachs is always in the self-claimed 'European' position, which is in fact the alien one, of racial and economic domination. Sachs also represents himself and his interlocutor within European conventions of fictional and biographical narrative, dialogue, and characterisation along with those of comparative ethnography. The dust jacket description of *Black Hamlet* as 'novelistic' is not only accurate but draws attention to fictional components of *Black Hamlet* that are no more extraneous than they are in Freud's texts. Moreover Sachs's Standard English is the normative language of the text, into which John's limited English as a second language is absorbed while being marked as grammatically irregular. Bunche comments as well on John's limited command of English (Edgar 1992: 166).

Sachs additionally has the power to name 'John Chavafambira' in his text under the necessity or pretext of protecting his identity. Sachs's assignment of a 'white' name to an African man who may be differently named follows standard colonial practice. Moreover Sachs's conjunction of a European 'Christian' name, as it would have been regarded in South Africa, with a fictitious African surname aligns him as a scientific missionary with his Christian-missionary predecessors. It doesn't help that the name *John* was often employed by whites in South Africa as an insultingly generic one for addressing any black man.

Furthermore, even when trying hardest to be impartial, Sachs often translates practices of African healing into the terms of archaic European witchcraft: the traditional healer-diviner is always presumptively a witch doctor, even though Sachs periodically uses the Manyika term *nganga*. Both dialogue and cultural translation thus remain more than problematic throughout *Black Hamlet;* the cultural residues of European witchcraft are projected into the supposedly primitive black community. In fact Sachs's vindication of white medicine in Africa requires the demystification of a racially coded black magic. Sachs (72) writes at the beginning of the book:

> The fact that John was a witch doctor added interest to my study. At that time, a witch-doctor was to me a romantically mysterious figure. I thought of witches, witchcraft, and witch-doctors in the confused manner of all Europeans, who imagine witch-doctors to possess supernatural powers of good and evil, but actually this was by no means the case, as will be apparent from the story of this man's life.

When a somewhat chastened Sachs later attempts an even-handed comparison between what he calls 'White and Black Medicine', the comparison is still compromised by an uneradicated European distinction between white and black magic.

My second caveat is that, notwithstanding the dust jacket billing, *Black Hamlet* is not a psychoanalytic case history. The man who Sachs calls John has not put himself forward as a patient, and Sachs himself disclaims analysis, preferring to characterise their prolonged encounter, disingenuously or otherwise, as a professional dialogue. Nor does money change hands. The interlocutor cannot afford to pay and would hardly choose to do so if he could, given his rooted disbelief in Western psychotherapy. (Sachs asserts, on the other hand, that paid native informants merely tell the investigator what they think he or she wishes to hear.) Finally and to his credit, Sachs does not claim to affect a psychoanalytic cure of John's neuroses. Although Sachs concludes the book by observing that John's conflicts have been resolved and that he has thereby gained a measure of optimism (largely invested in the future of his son), that change has occurred wholly within the frame of John's Manyika beliefs. It is only as a supporter and interlocutor, not as a Freudian psychotherapist, that Sachs has been able to assist John.

Even if psychoanalysis as a therapy is neither subject to a fair trial nor technically on trial in *Black Hamlet*, however, the cross-cultural and epistemological credentials of psychoanalysis are indeed put to the test, and explicitly so. In fact Sachs tries to have it both ways, at once proclaiming and disclaiming analysis. His disclaimer of therapy does, however, give his book the default status of powerful cultural interpretation. That is never disclaimed. In keeping, the 1937 edition is subtitled 'The Mind of an African Negro Revealed by Psychoanalysis'. The entire book falls under this rubric, even if psychoanalysis is not explicitly on trial at every single moment in it. In revealing the mind of a Negro, Sachs at once proclaims the universal validity of psychoanalysis and confers full human recognition on his subject.[9] He also confidently resorts to free association, competitive and comparative dream interpretation, and somewhat imperious diagnosis. He even periodically claims victories, as when, for example, John's usually prophetic mode of dream interpretation comes into line with his psychoanalytic one or when he believes he has elicited from John an acknowledgement of aggressive feelings toward himself. Apparently oblivious of his own aggressivity in forcing the acknowledgement, Sachs writes, with presumably unintended irony: 'So I talked to him day after day, until I won. And the months that followed were the most successful of the whole period of our relationship' (215).

Overall Sachs can never relinquish his belief in the superiority of Western scientific medicine. At most he credits John with sincerity in holding his own groundless beliefs and with an authentic impulse to heal. According to Sachs, John is at least no charlatan, unlike many of his black and white counterparts.[10] Yet the certain danger and dubious benefits of even the best-intentioned native practice are confirmed for Sachs when one of John's divinations leads his client to murder an innocent man, whom he has mistaken for an evil spirit. The haplessly deluded killer will probably be executed, while John fails to step forward in court and admit his part, even though the killer is counting on him. Sachs must then become John's saviour by spiriting him over the border into what was then Rhodesia, now Zimbabwe, until the trouble has blown over.

In short then, Sachs starts off positioned on the psychoanalytic high ground and never fully yields that ground. Yet that presumption steadily erodes in the course of the book, as does the presumptive authority of the analyst. As a result the figure of the European analyst who knows best generally functions more heuristically and ironically than dogmatically in *Black Hamlet*. The increasing self-consciousness of the analyst under pressure results in many disturbing recognitions of a kind that have subsequently become a staple of cultural criticism.

To take only one example, the recognition of a convergence between ethnographic and police interrogation results from one of the book's most painful episodes. John is temporarily alienated from Sachs after he has been brutally interrogated by two policemen, who suspect him, as a known African healer, of murdering infant twins (whom whites believe are regularly killed at birth in black cultures). Sachs's own interrogation of John on this touchy subject becomes indistinguishable in John's mind from the police interrogation, especially as Sachs is teamed throughout the book with the anthropologist Ellen Goodman in his inquiries into African beliefs.[11] Both psychoanalytic and anthropological inquiry come under increasing suspicion in the black community as the book proceeds, as does any distinction between well-meaning, liberal whites who can be trusted, and malignant, oppressive ones who cannot. Indeed the good whites are increasingly seen as the infiltrating agents of the bad when the residents of the particular shanty settlement are threatened with eviction. A black speaker at a public meeting says: 'The liberal Englishman is no better than the Dutchman . . . and the Jew is just as bad as either. They all want to squeeze the last penny out of us and give us as little in return as possible' (226).

In case Sachs should miss the point, John says to him in an undertone: 'Listen! He is speaking of Swartyard' – that is, of the place in which he lives and is visited by Sachs and Goodman.

Such as it can be, then, Sachs (71) announces his trial of psychoanalysis as follows:

> In the year 1928 I began studying natives at an African Mental Hospital. My research there was primarily on the Vegetative Nervous System, though I also made use of the opportunity for psychological observation. And it was not long before I made what was to me a startling discovery. I discovered that the manifestations of insanity, in its form, content, origin, and causation are identical in both natives and Europeans [Bunche reports this claim by Sachs (Edgar 1992:189)]. There is perhaps a slight difference in the nature of the delusions and complexes of the native as compared with the European; but the difference is no greater than that found in comparing an insane Englishman with the mentally deranged Frenchman or German. This discovery made me inquisitive to know if the working fundamental principles of the mind in its normal state were not also the same. I had difficulties in approaching this problem for many reasons. To begin with, it was difficult to find a native who would be willing to become the object [sic] of a deep and protracted psychoanalytical study.

It appears that in affirming the universality of psychoanalysis, Sachs will additionally affirm the full humanity of the native through an aetiology of madness he is discovered to share with whites.[12] The native subject is thus qualified for humanity – the implicit defining norm being a European one – on psychopathological grounds before he qualifies on what Sachs will call normal grounds. This always problematic move to educe the normal by starting from the pathological rather than vice versa follows Freud, as does Sachs's elated and self-authorising rhetoric of discovery. Sachs's discovery having been made and the truth of psychoanalysis having been put at stake, the way is open for Sachs to identify John as the black Hamlet.

Let us briefly recall the set-up in which that identification can take place. The psychoanalytic reading of *Hamlet*, in which the disclosure of a repressed Oedipus complex becomes the key that unlocks Hamlet's character, was one to which both Freud and Ernest Jones laid claim (Freud 1965; Jones 1910, 1949). This interpretation was not simply an instance of applied psychoanalysis but rather a formative moment in psychoanalytic discourse. Freud relied on the text of Shakespeare's *Hamlet* rather than on Sophocles's *Oedipus Rex* for indispensable confirmation of repressed oedipal desire, the fact of repression being explained in terms of historical change between the unrepressed transparency of archaic Greek culture and the repressed opacity of modern European culture (see Lupton and Reinhard 1993). In effect, the text of *Hamlet* functioned as an important prop in the development both of psychoanalytic thinking and of its metapsychological ambitions. If it is something of a critical maxim now that Shakespeare is so Freudian because Freud is so Shakespearean, that is because the foundational status of *Hamlet* and other Shakespearean texts in psychoanalysis has become increasingly apparent.

Furthermore Shakespeare's play lent its enormous prestige, not least in the German-speaking world, to the psychoanalytic enterprise. At the same time the psychoanalytic claim to have solved the eternal enigma of Hamlet was practically equivalent – certainly in Sachs's view – to Oedipus's own solution to the Sphinx's riddle. Finally, Shakespeare's *Hamlet* powerfully underwrote the psychoanalytic logic of educing the universal norm from pathological symptoms, since the character Hamlet famously had been established as a baffling melancholic by a succession of Shakespeare critics up to and including A. C. Bradley in *Shakespearean Tragedy* (1991 [1903]). For the psychoanalytic critic, the singular puzzle of Hamlet's character was solved by the demonstration that his inaction symptomatically revealed a universal structure of repression. Hamlet's inaction stood exposed in the Freud-Jones interpretation as the neurotic form of action, all Hamlet's vital energies being consumed in the activity of repression.

When Sachs recognises John as the black Hamlet, he closely follows the language and logic of the Freud-Jones interpretation, in effect rediscovering the Oedipus complex in his African interlocutor. For Sachs the Hamlet parallel is clinched by some circumstances of John's life. Like Hamlet's, John's father died while John was young; John is intensely fixated on his mother, who has married an uncle John believes has usurped his rightful succession to his father's place as an admired healer. Obligingly John goes so far as to relate a dream of incest with his mother. Sachs even deplores John's 'Hamletism' – his repeatedly alleged irresolution – with some of the same testiness Jones displays toward Shakespeare's Hamlet.[13] In fact Jones virtually replaces the inadequate Hamlet as tragic hero with the figure of the analyst as intellectual hero. As Jones (1949: 103) concludes, '[Hamlet's] paralysis arises, however, not from physical or moral cowardice, but from that intellectual cowardice, that reluctance to dare the exploration of his inmost soul, which Hamlet shares with the rest of the human race.' The implied exception to this general rule is, of course, the analyst, who dares just that exploration. Let us, however, note the specular relation of the analyst to his subject that sets the stage for this aggressive displacement; let us also note Jones's apparent need to negotiate his role as analyst through Hamlet. This unheralded process of negotiation will be repeated throughout Sachs's text, though in even more complex terms since Sachs is simultaneously negotiating his own deracinated subjectivity in relation to that of the deracinated other.

Comparably to Jones, Sachs finds a vocation in his text in trying to inspire a neurotic John into constructive or even heroic action. Yet his representation of John is critically and betrayingly contradictory on this point, since John often seems to deserve and even to get credit for acting as forcefully as he can within the limits of a racist society. What helps explain this fundamental contradiction is that John's Hamletism, described in one sentence as his 'personal tragedy' and in the very next sentence as a 'universal phenomenon' (236) must, in its universal dimension, logically implicate and even threaten Sachs as well. To speak of delay or irresolution, as Sachs does, unavoidably raises the question of problematic or compromised agency in general.

When Sachs feels overwhelmed by his own self-assumed responsibilities, he cries out, perhaps unwittingly echoing Shakespeare's Hamlet, 'How could I, one small individual, root up the curse of humanity?' (286). Thus when, late in the book, Sachs begins to see John as Odysseus rather than as Hamlet, we learn something about what he desires for John but perhaps even more about what he desires for himself in John's place. John as Hamlet becomes at once the mirror of Sachs's felt incapacity and the agent of his epic aspiration. In short, although Sachs began the book by assuming the heroic intellectual agency already asserted by Jones, that agency has become severely compromised in the represented milieu of South Africa by the time Sachs identifies John as the black Hamlet. The fact that this key identification is delayed until almost two-thirds of the way through the book gives point to the question 'Whose Hamletism is this?'

One may speculate about why Sachs delays the moment of full identification, possible explanations being that he wishes to stage an interpretative coup or to give the appearance of induction to a foregone conclusion. Yet the effect of delay makes his psychoanalytic interpretation of John seem belated, non-contextual, intrusive, and practically redundant when it finally arrives. So explanatory has the socio-cultural matrix become by then that little seems left for psychoanalysis to explain, at least about John.[14] The compromised agency at once figured and negotiated through John's alleged Hamletism is implicitly that of the pioneering psychoanalyst. Sachs's anxieties regarding his own agency do not necessarily end with his analytic agency either.

All commentators have noted that Sachs's commitments as a Lithuanian Jewish socialist make him an anomalous figure in white Anglo-Boer South Africa. Sachs's European-socialist view of the police and the law courts is closer to that of blacks than whites in South Africa. Without question Sachs's entry into the black community and his attempt to maintain inter-subjective relations with black people were daringly out of line with white communal norms; one result was Sachs's eviction on a pretext from his offices in downtown Johannesburg. Yet Sachs's political agency as a European Jewish radical is hardly less circumscribed than John's.[15] The thwarting of radical political agency in South Africa during the 1930s is broadly confirmed by Bunche's travel notes. Even the displaced agency of writing is compromised for Sachs. A European-educated black speaker has warned John against associating with him, and implicitly with Goodman, by describing Sachs as 'another busybody who will write about [you]' (198). Sachs adds, 'The reader will see he was not far from the truth.'

Therefore little mystery seems to exist about whose Hamletism – or rather whose anxiety regarding agency – the book principally represents. Sachs proves no exception to the rule that (male) Shakespeare critics find themselves reflected in 'their' Hamlets. Yet Sachs's projection of his own Hamletism rebounds on his own most fundamental claims and assumptions as a European analyst. One of these, let us recall, is that psychoanalysis will demonstrate the native's full participation in humanity.

Although this is the claim with which the book begins, Sachs (237) belatedly confesses that he in fact began by regarding John as a convenient anthropological specimen. His full acknowledgement of John as a human interlocutor thus also is delayed in the book. Not only has Sachs's agency been compromised by then, but he has come to feel himself objectified by the reverse-anthropological gaze of his black interlocutors. The human recognition he confers on John concurrently with the Hamlet identification is thus increasingly the recognition he seeks as the alien.[16]

Along with psychoanalysis the early modern humanism and European Enlightenment in which it is packaged enable Sachs to reclaim a common humanity in which he as well as John can participate. Yet while resorting, conventionally enough, to Shakespeare as the implicit guarantor of this universality, Sachs effects a transfer of European normativeness to the African by blackening Hamlet. That is to say, in the act of invoking a Eurocentric, universalising psychoanalysis, to which Fanon later objected for its erasure of cultural and political differences, Sachs subjects the universal to powers of cultural contingency, mobility, and even locality.[17] Despite or because of this contradiction, it becomes possible for Sachs to continue yoking psychoanalytic discourse to his own desire, however ambivalent, to become African.

What it would actually have meant for Sachs to become African is defined by Rose as having 'crossed over', a possibility arising from, among other things, the racially indeterminate positioning of Jews in orientalist Western representation.[18] It must be emphasised that Sachs never professes this desire in *Black Hamlet*, however, nor does he make any claim to 'identify' with the African as opposed to the European. It is not clear that any such claim would have made sense in the psychological and political idioms of Sachs's time. Sachs certainly never claims to have been received as African by the black community. Yet the life story he tells about John glosses both his desire to belong as African and the actual or self-imposed limits to it.

John's life story, as recounted to and relayed by Sachs, includes a good deal of ethnographic lore, family history, and novelistic representation of a man 'caught between two worlds in collision', as the dust jacket has it. It also includes such typical experiences of the black South African man as arrest under the race laws and a rape accusation by an elderly white woman. Although not even the whites believe that accusation, John has to abandon his job as a waiter and flee the town where he lives since the accusation will be enough to bring down the full force of police reprisal.[19]

In telling the story of John's life, Sachs has more on his mind, however, than typifying black experience in racist South African society. He also tells how he seeks to verify the accuracy of John's memories and perceptions by retracing the entire course of John's life. He visits all the places and meets all the people still living of whom John has spoken, ultimately returning to John's place of origin in Manyikaland. Violating all psychotherapeutic protocols, he freely embroils himself in John's political and personal life. He eventually certifies the fullness and accuracy of John's memories. Yet Sachs's commitment to verification may go beyond the call of scientific inquiry. It is as if retracing John's steps becomes Sachs's way of inserting himself into John's life and inhabiting his subjectivity. This possibility gains support from Sachs's use of free indirect speech, noted by Rose, a device marking an unstable threshold between self and other. It gains support as well from Sachs's shifts into John's eyewitnessing position. These shifts depend in turn on Sachs's claim, confirmed to a degree by Bunche (Edgar 1992: 166), that '[John] had a remarkable gift for observing and noting details, and reproducing them long afterwards with exceptional vividness' (Sachs 1996: 140). The book's novelistic realism and effects of vivid immediacy remain grounded in the power of undistorted recall Sachs attributes to John.[20]

Recounting John's arrival in Johannesburg for the first time, Sachs begins by saying, 'I can clearly visualise John's arrival at Johannesburg Station, for I have many times witnessed the arrival of the natives' train myself' (140). Yet the first-person narrator soon merges his witnessing into John's:

> John had time to study the life around him . . . On his right was a small, wizened, yellow-skinned Hottentot, clad in a ragged miscellany, clutching his tall shepherd's staff and swearing softly but competently in Afrikaans. In front of him was a huge, copper-skinned Zulu, in crimson and black blanket worn with an insolent air as he made his way through the throng . . . John attempted to follow in the wake of this Zulu, but was held up by a compact group of half a dozen women, their hair dressed fantastically, their bodies draped with brown woollen garments, bead embroidered, a dozen copper necklets sheathing their throats.

So the virtuoso passage continues, noting the babel of languages spoken as well as the exotic ethnic spectrum. No doubt the foreignness of Johannesburg to an immigrant Lithuanian accounts for the fluidity with which Sachs can merge his viewing into that of John as an immigrant Manyika. Although it is far from clear that Sachs's exoticising gaze is shared by John – that gaze betrays the presence of the European – Sachs's merging with John is quite enough to prompt the question 'Whose life is this?' in addition to my earlier question 'Whose Hamletism is this?' The question of whose life it is becomes especially pressing whenever Sachs's narrative moves beyond the frame of a putatively shared immigrant identity to engage questions of desire and sexuality in John's life.

Sachs's warrant for broaching these questions is at once psychoanalytic and ethnographic. Sachs is on his own professional ground, so to speak, as a psychoanalyst posing questions of sexuality as fundamental, yet his professional interrogation is rendered somewhat ironic by the fact that both the urbanised John and the African asylum attendant reveal a more worldly, tolerant consciousness of sexual variety than does the pathologising 1930s psychoanalyst. Sachs remains singularly reticent throughout concerning his own sexuality, or for that matter his marriage, of which we learn only from Bunche. Although John supposedly understands non-traditional sexualities as effects of modern urban breakdown in sexual mores, it is not clear whose provincialism is really being corrected by the encounter with foreign city life. John, at any rate, takes transvestism and male homosexuality in his stride. Moreover one of the few African terms quoted directly in the book is *nyatsi,* which Sachs translates as 'back-door husband,' referring to the lovers, apparently accepted as a matter of course, of married women in the African community. John's reported or ventriloquised indifference to the violation of sexual taboos opens up more an unregulated field of desire and practice in the book than that typically allowed by 1930s Freudian psychopathology. Insofar as Sachs repositions himself in the narrative of John's life, thereby inhabiting the desire of the 'other', he is, perhaps above all, reconfiguring his own trajectories of desire and imaginary identification. That, at all events, seems strikingly borne out by his highly participatory 'commentary' on John's concluding sexual adventure in the book.

For John, the one binding taboo remains that against relationships, defined as incestuous, between members of the same clan. That taboo, and the romantic transgression it incites, enter the narrative of John's life at an early stage. Shortly after John first leaves home as a young immigrant, he comes upon a supposedly bewitched village. Although John does not yet feel entitled by maturity to practice as a diviner, he is so moved by the plight of the people that he agrees to smell out the witch. Before he has done so, a beautiful young woman of his own Manyika people, to whom he feels strongly attracted, confesses that she is the alien witch in the village and inevitably will be smelled out and put to death. John decamps after sleeping with her, leaving the village to its fate. He subsequently marries a woman with whom he is not in love and continues to be haunted by the memory of the beautiful witch.

Toward the end of the book Sachs approves John's choice of a new love object in place of the nagging wife, over whose alleged misdeeds the two men have hitherto been able to bond. (Bunche too notes with some scorn that John seems henpecked [Edgar 1992:166]). The new object of romance is like a reincarnation of the bewitching woman, alien yet familial, whom John had encountered on his first journey to Johannesburg. About the new development in John's love life, Sachs (314) writes:

> He became completely infatuated with a young girl, a stranger to the kraal. She was of exceptional beauty, judged even by European standards – what the anthropologists would describe as a hamitic type[21]. . . . I was sincere in my approval, for it pleased me to discover John's new criterion of beauty to be no longer that of a primitive kraal man but of a Europeanised black man.

The fact that Sachs immediately brings this stranger under European aesthetic and anthropological review strongly implies his own participation in the desire attributed to John. This participation is confirmed when Sachs follows his appreciative account of the hamitic woman with a horrifically negative, racist picture of the so-called negroid woman. Sachs represents the negroid woman, as distinct from the so-called hamitic one, as aesthetically repellent and therefore erotically undesirable. Sachs is thus evidently trying to negotiate the simultaneous appeal and dread of the exotic Other by deploying contemporary categories of racial science (hamitic, negroid). Not only is John's woman thereby made safe for 'white' consumption, but also John is abruptly 'Europeanised', thereby legitimising the desire in which Sachs so enthusiastically participates.

My next question practically asks itself: 'Whose romance is this?' Both Sachs's appropriation of John's love story and a highly ironic rebound of his earlier attempt to demystify African witchcraft answer that question: Sachs is the one bewitched. Moreover Sachs's tale turns out to be one of incest, of a taboo at once maintained and violated. After he has slept with the new woman, John is horrified to discover that she belongs to his clan. Having implicated himself Sachs remains implicated even in this highly charged phase of the story. Sachs offers no psychoanalytic observation on the fact that John had 'forgotten' to ask the woman to which clan she belongs. This moment of strategic forgetting cries out for psychoanalytic recognition, yet no such recognition is forthcoming from Sachs, immersed as he apparently is in the romance of the 'other'.

It can hardly be doubted that this story transcribes some of the complex desires and continuing taboos bound up with Sachs's impulse to cross over. While seeking to inhabit the desire and subjectivity of the other, thus in effect 'becoming African', he also, at this critical moment, defensively reinscribes the taboos. He assimilates the derogatory Afrikaans term *kraal* for a rural African settlement into his standard English and tellingly romanticises only the black woman who is not one. Moreover Sachs enjoys John's moment of infatuation as his own moment of triumph: John has learned to desire what is formally constituted as desirable by the white man. John thus becomes the assimilated or 'Europeanised' other. It is surely to the fantasies of a white readership rather than to 'the conscience of the world' that this romance makes its appeal. Africanisation of the white man – or white transculturation – seems to have discovered its own limits here.

Yet even that isn't quite the end of the matter. The providential arrival of this 'hamitic' woman alters the homosocial configuration in which Sachs and John have bonded through the nagging wife. The presence of the new woman, conspicuously an object of Sachs's fantasy as well as desire, prompts reflection on the relations between men that she facilitates, at least for Sachs. Not merely object but relay between men, the projected bewitching woman may serve at once to precipitate and buffer a homoerotic attraction to be suspected – or inevitably present? – in Sachs's tireless pursuit of John. That particular form of attraction, the repression of which Fanon identified as a prime cause of what he called negrophobia, is not necessarily absent, even if Sachs never articulates it. Sachs's disconcerting outburst of negrophobia as soon as the 'hamitic' woman comes into the picture is not necessarily prompted by heterosexual anxieties alone. The possible crossing of different trajectories or objects of desire is facilitated by the phonological proximity of the hamitic to the hamletic; as near-homonyms, they can stand in for each other. That John's relationship to his new love interest turns out to violate clan taboos and is therefore 'impossible' conserves Sachs's intimate bonding relationship with John while also practically forestalling any homoerotic potential. Perhaps this is as close as Sachs can ever get to 'becoming African' within the prevailing norms and genres of self-inscription.

If the claims of psychoanalysis remain at issue through all this, their vindication has become strikingly ironic: the unconscious lavishly on display seems to be that of the analyst, not the subject, who merely undergoes an oedipal implant.[22] Sachs even sets himself up for an ironic denouement since he has asked John whether the African diviner can divine his own condition. John candidly admits that he cannot. In Sachs's implied contrast, the European analyst can: Freud's self-analysis exemplifies the power of the analyst to attain self-understanding. Yet if self-understanding seems ever more remote from Sachs as the book progresses, a fact that exposes him increasingly to irony at his expense, his psychoanalytic framing of the narrative nevertheless provides the reader with a context for reading him against himself, so to speak, even if not necessarily for reading John.

Despite or because of these ironies, it might seem that enough evidence has been mustered by now to warrant a negative verdict on psychoanalysis in this particular South African trial. Both its functioning and its failure to function can be faulted repeatedly, and it does little to change pre-apartheid South African society. Sachs's own apparent shift in priorities could be brought in evidence against the discipline he advocates. Instead of pronouncing a concluding negative verdict, however, I will end by remarking that the historical and cultural functioning of psychoanalysis could not be terminated by any such a verdict. Responsibility both for and to psychoanalysis – and to the European literary traditions it subsumes – continues to be assumed in current global discourse. Moreover the language of psychoanalysis continues to supply terms for negotiating between what Rose calls phantasmagoric identifications and the shifting realpolitik of political and cultural identity. Without its universalising problematic, psychoanalysis would be nothing, yet only in submitting itself to the mediation, reflection, and self-alienation on which Fanon insisted can it negotiate its own transition from a colonised to a postcolonial world. Sachs's *Black Hamlet* does not effect the transition, yet it makes a beginning, leaving much of the work still to be done.

Notes

1   See Robert R. Edgar 1992: 349 for a capsule biography, expanded by Jacqueline Rose (1996). For a slightly revised version of Rose's introduction to this volume see Rose 1998.

2   Thus this possibly indicates a broader trend. The African American psychiatrists William H. Grier and Price M. Cobbs produced an influential book titled *Black Rage* in 1968. The work of Richard Wright, especially *Native Son* (1940), may also have helped reveal the 'black rage' underlying any appearance of black acquiescence in racist oppression.

3   In general Bunche's deadpan journal entries and snapshots of South Africa corroborate Sachs, yet Bunche's account of John, lacking the affective and transferential involvements of Sachs's narrative, is brief and unflattering (Edgar 1992: 166–67). Bunche reports on John's practices as a diviner only with scorn, and he adopts the local white term *witch-doctor* rather than *nyanga* to characterise the African healer.

4   As regards this Zionism, and Sachs's consciousness of a Mosaic vocation to deliver the oppressed, the relevant Freudian text is *Moses and Monotheism*. I will focus on Sachs only in the South African context, however, without further reference to his Zionism and its implications. In this general connection, see

Caruth 1996. Rose (1996) notes some increasingly salient parallels between present-day Israel and apartheid-era South Africa.

5   It should be said that Sachs's narrative of John's life, opinions, and subjectivity has a poignancy and evidentiary value that can by no means be discounted. In other words, Sachs's narrative is not an act of pure ventriloquism but of attempted subjective recognition and representation that is far from common in South African or any other 'white writing'.

6   According to Sachs (1947), John is left looking toward America for hope, his own vocation for political leadership having failed. Edgar (1992: 22–25) reports that other black South Africans do so, too, and describes Bunche's increasing involvement in the emancipatory projects of black South Africans. Edgar (ibid.: 2–3) further notes that black South African consciousness of America comes partly from the little-known history of post-Civil War African American immigration and missionary ventures into South Africa.

7   The 1987 special issue of *Critical Inquiry* titled 'Trials of Psychoanalysis' implies that psychoanalysis must withstand examination on all these levels. Psychoanalysis has also been politically and methodologically on trial in a great deal of recent work in criticism and cultural studies. See, for example, Sander Gilman 1993, Anne McClintock 1995, Juliet MacCannell 1996, Claudia Tate 1996, Patricia Elliot 1996, Willy Apollon 1996, and Andreas Bertholdi 1998. Reflecting a provisional consensus regarding the methodological situation, Rose (1985:95) wrote in her capacity as a Shakespeare critic: 'Rather than apply psychoanalysis to literature, as if psychoanalysis were a method to be mapped on to the literary text, I will try to show how psychoanalysis and literary criticism share with the literature they address a terrain of language, fantasy and sexuality.' The pertinence of this observation to *Black Hamlet* could hardly be exaggerated.

8   Perhaps the South African Truth and Reconciliation Commission, as distinct, for example, from the Nuremberg Tribunal after World War II, constitutes a difficult and problematic trial in this extended sense. Although not bargained for in the parliamentary act that established the Truth Commission, psychoanalytic notions of trauma and healing have been implicated in these proceedings and even more strongly in critiques of their deficiencies as proceedings.

9   In his professional life Sachs reintroduced a cultural differential between white and black in making his best-known independent psychoanalytic claim, namely the counter-political one that the long duration of breast-feeding in African cultures makes Africans dependent and needy throughout their lives. The claim is noted without comment by Bunche (Edgar 1992: 186); the dependency also asserted by Octave Mannoni was decisively rejected by Fanon (1952).

10   Consistently with the gender discourse of the book, which is very much that of its time, John is also a more dignified figure than the huge, grotesque African woman who practices divination for a mixed black and white clientele in the Johannesburg slums. That she drops dead in a spectacular fit of vatic hysteria seems like a judgement.

11   Although almost as many different attitudes toward twins exist as different African cultures, John confirms twin killing amongst the Manyika, though he claims that it is performed by midwives. The issue is touchy because the alleged African killing of twins functioned as one differential, in South Africa and elsewhere, between 'civilised' and 'savage'.

12   Sachs's claim, condescending as it may seem now, has a polemical context sketched in Dubow's introduction to *Black Hamlet* and is certainly 'progressive' in relation to prevailing colonial discourses of African psychology and psychopathology in the context of so-called detribalisation. See also Bertholdi 1998.

13   Sachs's overwhelming desire to make the interpretation stick has to overcome the predictable resistance of white readers, but no doubt it also has to overcome his own resistance as an analyst steeped in the racially infused conventional literary criticism of his time: 'John's tragedy, at first glance, may seem far beneath Hamlet's, and one is justified in ridiculing at the start any comparison between John the witch-doctor and the Danish prince' (Sachs 1996: 237). Sachs presents a more detailed psychoanalytic reading of *Hamlet* in *Psychoanalysis* (1934: 197–212), explicitly invoking 'Mourning and Melancholia' (Freud 1953–1974) as well as the Oedipus complex.

14   Moreover as Rose (1996: 40–41), citing Robert Weimann 1978, points out, the insertion of *Hamlet* into this African context threatens both the terms of the psychoanalytic interpretation and Shakespeare's European modernity by reflexively bringing into view the 'archaic' features of Shakespeare's play: '*Hamlet* is at least partly a prenaturalistic, prerepresentational text, one in which Hamlet's oddity as a character (prince, madman, buffoon in a seeming rotation of roles) serves as a reminder of the more collective, publicly shared forms of identity which, at the time Shakespeare was writing, were historically on the wane.'

15   See Rose 1996: 49–51 for a more extensive discussion of Sachs's political agency and aspirations.

16   Many of these reversals could be read as classic Lacanian ones between analyst and analysand and yet it might be productive now to examine Sachs's writings and Jacques Lacan's theorising as roughly concurrent initiatives in a shared time frame.

17   If poststructuralist psychoanalysis renegotiates the universalising claims of psychoanalysis, in effect substituting oedipal 'structure' for 'content', it does not thereby escape Fanon's anticolonialist critique.

18   Perhaps the phrase 'crossing over', with its Mosaic inflection, underestimates the difficulties of any crossing Sachs might have wished to make, since the vectors of political and psychic mobility are multiple. Both Bunche's presence on the scene and Sachs's readdressing his book to American readers in 1947 attest to fluidities of identity, role, and positioning not fully bargained for by Sachs, as does Bunche's subsequent role as negotiator between Arabs and Israelis. Moreover Jews had not always found themselves situated in the white or European position Sachs occupies in Africa vis-à-vis his black interlocutor. It could be thus debated whether or not Jewish 'whiteness' is primarily at stake in Sachs's self-constructions. In this connection see Brian Cheyette 1996, 1997.

19   The untouchability of the white woman was a taboo ferociously enforced in South Africa as elsewhere without regard to legal niceties or to any actual desire or behaviour of black men. Bunche, who is curious on this point, mentions that Sachs's white nurse seems to elicit no sexual interest from the male asylum inmates (Edgar 1992: 189). Ironically, Goodman is 'protected' by this taboo in pursuing her career as anthropologist.

20   Without discounting the testimony corroborated by Bunche, we can hardly doubt that Sachs is attributing to John the uncompromised memory and testimonial veracity mythically associated in the West with preliterate mentalities.

21   While the force of the term *hamitic* at the time Sachs was writing was probably more linguistic than anthropological, it nevertheless functioned as a late-nineteenth-century racist term still astonishingly deployed, for example, by the African historians Roland Anthony Oliver and. D. Fage as late as 1963. In this 'history' hamitic people are light-skinned, alien bringers of culture to West Africa. The term designates North African 'races' such as the Egyptians and Barber as distinct from yet akin to the 'Semitic' ones in which Sachs as Jew is placed.

22   I don't say this altogether facetiously, since Rose's chapter on *Black Hamlet* in the Hopkins edition begins with a discussion of black-white organ transplants. If Sachs's unwitting vindication of his discipline can only be ironic, however, the irony necessarily implicates my own reading as well, which retains the Freudian category of the unconscious without necessarily binding it to any particular structure or content.

References

Apollon, Willy
    1996 'Postcolonialism and Psychoanalysis: The Example of Haiti', *Journal for the Psychoanalysis of Culture and Society* 1(1): 43–52.
Bertholdi, Andreas
    1998 'Shakespeare, Psychoanalysis, and the Colonial Encounter: The Case of Wolf Sachs's *Black Hamlet*', in *Post-Colonial Shakespeare*, edited by Ania Loomba and Martin Orkin 235-58 (London: Routledge).

Bradley, A. C.

1991 [1903] *Shakespearean Tragedy: Lectures on 'Hamlet', 'Othello', 'King Lear', and 'Macbeth'* (Harmondsworth: Penguin Books).

Caruth, Cathy

1996 *Unclaimed Experience: Trauma, Narrative and History* (Baltimore: Johns Hopkins University Press).

Cheyette, Bryan

1996 *Constructions of 'The Jew' in English Literature and Society: Racial Representations, 1875–1945* (Cambridge: Cambridge University Press).

1997 'White Skin, Black Masks: Jews and Jewishness in the Writings of George Eliot and Frantz Fanon', in *Cultural Readings of Imperialism: Edward Said and the Gravity of History,* edited by Keith Ansell-Pearson, Benita Parry, and Judith Squires, 106–26 (New York: St. Martin's Press).

Cobbs, Price M., and William H. Grier

1968 *Black Rage* (New York: Basic Books).

Edgar, Robert R., ed.

1992 *An African American in South Africa: The Travel Notes of Ralph Bunche, 28 September 1937–1 January 1938* (Johannesburg: Witwatersrand University Press).

Elliot, Patricia

1996 'Working through Racism: Confronting the Strangely Familiar', *Journal for the Psychoanalysis of Culture and Society* 1(1): 63–72.

Fanon, Frantz

1952 *Black Skin, White Masks,* translated by Charles Lam Markmann (New York: Grove Press).

Freud, Sigmund

1953–1974 'Mourning and Melancholia', in *The Standard Edition of the Complete Psychological Works*, vol. 14, translated by James Strachey (London: Hogarth Press).

1958 *Moses and Monotheism,* translated by Katherine Jones (New York: Vintage).

1965 *The Interpretation of Dreams,* translated by James Strachey (New York: Avon Books).

Gilman, Sander

1993 *Freud, Race and Gender* (Princeton: Princeton University Press).

Jones, Ernest

1910 'The Oedipus Complex as an Explanation of Hamlet's "Mystery"', *American Journal of Psychology* (21).

1949 *Hamlet and Oedipus* (Garden City: Doubleday).

Lupton, Julia Reinhard, and Kenneth Reinhard

1993 *After Oedipus: Shakespeare in Psychoanalysis.* (Ithaca: Cornell University Press).

MacCannell, Juliet Flower

1996 'The Post-Colonial Unconscious, or, the White Man's Thing', *Journal for the Psychoanalysis of Culture and Society* 1(1): 27–42.

McClintock, Anne

1995 *Imperial Leather: Race, Gender and Sexuality in the Colonial Context* (New York: Routledge).

Oliver, Roland Anthony, and J. D. Fage

1963 *A Short History of Africa* (New York: New York University Press).

Rose, Jacqueline

1985 'Sexuality in the Reading of Shakespeare: *Hamlet* and *Measure for Measure*', in *Alternative Shakespeares,* edited by John Drakakis, 95–118 (New York: Methuen).

1996 *States of Fantasy* (Oxford: Clarendon Press).

1998 'Wulf Sachs' *Black Hamlet',* in *The Psychoanalysis of Race,* edited by Christopher Lane, 333–52 (New York: Columbia University Press).

Sachs, Wulf

    1934 *Psychoanalysis: Its Meaning and Practical Applications* (London: Cassell).

    1937 *Black Hamlet: The Mind of an African Negro Revealed by Psychoanalysis* (London: Geoffrey Bles).

    1947 *Black Anger* (New York: Grove Press).

    1996 *Black Hamlet,* introduction by Saul Dubow and Jacqueline Rose (Baltimore: Johns Hopkins University Press).

Tate, Claudia

    1996 'Psychoanalysis as Enemy and Ally of African Americans', *Journal for the Psychoanalysis of Culture and Society* 1(1): 53–62.

Weimann, Robert

    1978 *Shakespeare and the Popular Tradition in the Theater,* translated by Robert Schwartz (Baltimore: Johns Hopkins University Press).

Wright, Richard

    1940 *Native Son* (New York: Harper and Brothers).

SEVEN

The Experimental Turn in Black South African Fiction

David Attwell

Our survival depends on a tactical cosmopolitanism.

Njabulo Ndebele, *Africa Talks Back*[1]

1

Since the late 1960s, a truism in discussions of black South African writing – fiction in particular – has been that conditions have militated against the development of a fully-fledged experimentalism. The predominant mode, it is said, is the literature of witness, documentary, and protest – varieties of realism, although with the exception of Alex La Guma, local practices of realism are not easily described in terms of their European counterparts such as naturalism, or social and critical realism. So axiomatic has this position been, indeed, that it seems naive to propose a critical archaeology in pursuit of anything resembling a local black modernism or postmodernism.

The reasons for this tendency are not hard to find. Lewis Nkosi, who represents something of a lone voice in his consistently trenchant interventions in this field, once suggested that what is generally expected from South Africans is 'not so much art as confidential reports about the condition of society, its health or lack of it, its ability to survive' (1981: 76). What is exceptional about this remark is its tone: it is seldom that anyone treats the subject ironically; on the contrary, more often than not with respect to black writing the claim is that realism of a direct and polemical kind is the most logical and principled of modes of representation and of responses to apartheid and apartheid conditions. In her contribution to this volume on the question of the 'rhetoric of urgency' in South African literary culture, Louise Bethlehem rightly speaks of a tendency to conflate a 'trope-of-truth' with the 'trope-as-truth'; in other words, Bethlehem discerns a narrowly instrumental view of language in South African literary culture, where the mediations inherent in language as a semiotic system are wished away simply because it seems ethically desirable to do so.

Nadine Gordimer's reflections on this subject are instructive in revealing how consequential this position has been for South African authorship. She distinguishes between her own self-chosen immersion in the novelistic tradition, and the kinds of demands that are appropriately made of black writers. The latter, she says, who have responded not so much to an orthodoxy but to a genuine impulse, reached a point where they decided 'to discard the lantern of artistic truth that reveals human worth through human ambiguity, and to see by the flames of burning vehicles only the strong, thick lines that draw heroes' (1989: 293). She qualifies this by referring to work of the early 1980s by Njabulo Ndebele, Es'kia Mphahlele and Ahmed Essop, which reserves the right to interpret, 'for the post-revolutionary future', 'that nobility in ordinary men and women to be found only among their doubts, culpabilities, shortcomings: their courage-in-spite-of' (ibid.: 293). Even here, Gordimer's acknowledgement does not speak of formal or literary or experimental self-consciousness in black writing, merely a more complex realism. For the most part, her sense of a neighbouring black tradition whose aesthetics she generally finds inimical to her own, despite being drawn to it in a spirit of comradeship, has helped to define her own, rather different course, one which has been, in some respects, the much lonelier one of struggling, as she represents it, to reconcile social responsibility with art. The ideal of the writer, she once poignantly remarked, lay in Walter Benjamin's storyteller, who 'could let the wick of his life be consumed completely by the gentle flame of his story' (ibid.: 300). The tendency to polarise white and black in terms of their relationship with experimental traditions therefore runs deep, entering the self-construction of as prominent an *oeuvre* as Gordimer's.

Like Gordimer, Nkosi accepts that the polarisation is a historical reality, but in his essay 'Postmodernism and Black Writing in South Africa', he says candidly that the black tendency to avoid experimentalism is the result not of a principled abjuration (the way Gordimer and others credit it) but simply of the deprivation and isolation of the black writer. Indeed, Nkosi goes so far as to argue with a kind of spade-calling relish that the 'breadline asceticism', 'prim disapproval of irony', and 'petty realism' of much black writing gives it an essentially 'colonial status' (1998: 77–80). Despite this forthrightness, Nkosi's purpose is actually benign: it is to open a more complex debate about how we might recognise and theorise black literary experimentalism when we see it. He makes the obvious but necessary point that if a black experimentalism is to emerge, it will do so under its own animating conditions and along its own paths of development, not those that have obtained for Western and white South African writers (ibid.: 84). The distinction marks a departure from an earlier version of the argument, which first appeared in 1967, involving the often-cited statement that black fiction was filled with 'journalistic fact parading outrageously as imaginative literature' (1979: 222). That intervention led, at the time, to a productive exchange with J. M. Coetzee (well before the appearance of his first novel, *Dusklands*) who responded by asking, 'What value does the experimental line hold for Africa? . . . Does not the experimental line assume *and perpetuate* a rift between the writer and society at large which is a fact of life in the West but need not become a fact of life in Africa?' (1973: 6). Coetzee's question later led him to examine Alex La Guma's critical realism, which he treats as a form of experimentalism which does *not* fall into the conservatism which haunts Nkosi's argument (cf. Attwell 1993: 12). We now know, of course, that when his own novelistic career got under way, Coetzee did not pursue the idea of weaving critical or any other realism into his own experimental practice, except by way of parody. In Nkosi's more recent essay, the questions he raises are essentially about the origins and development of South African epistemologies and forms of subjectivity, rather than the fate of European modernism in the country. Indeed, in insisting that if a local experimentalism is to develop it should not be understood in linear terms with Western practice at the high point, Nkosi's position is rather close to the question Coetzee put to him. The dangers of the linear, Eurocentric construction of black experimentalism, says Nkosi (1998: 87), are evident in the cautionary tale of B. W. Vilakazi, who in the 1930s attempted to write poetry in isiZulu using prosody and rhyme derived from English verse forms. The implication is that if one demands certain kinds of experimentalism on cue, one would have to expect aesthetic Frankensteins.

The awkward response to Nkosi must be, however, that black writing is indeed replete with instances of aesthetic self-consciousness, not excluding the very kinds of experimentalism that one associates with modernism. This assertion may seem remarkable in the face of so much commentary to the contrary, not only of an academic kind but also statements of cultural activism (dating especially from the 1980s) in which affirmations of the transparent political message are to be found in prominent manifestos, such as those of the Congress of South African Writers (Cosaw), the cultural desks of the African National Congress (ANC), United Democratic Front (UDF) and Congress of South African Trade Unions (Cosatu), as well as in arguments reiterated in festivals such as 'Towards a People's Culture' and 'Culture in Another South Africa', which celebrated the culture of resistance (cf. Parry 1994: 12). It is worth observing that a great deal of this kind of statement, however, is circular and self-perpetuating; that is to say, assertions about the overwhelming prevalence of documentary realism all too frequently involve generalisations based on other critical statements with little or no discussion of the literature's actual qualities: its range, its idiosyncracies, its very unfinishedness – sadly, also its high points. In an unguarded moment, Coetzee once remarked on what he saw as a 'programmatic refusal' in the fiction of Serote and Sipho Sepamla 'to create a structure in which there is some centre of intelligence, a refusal, that is, to recognise that making sense of life inside a book is different from making sense of real life – not more or less difficult, just different' (undated: 4). The appropriate way to read this statement is to see in it *Coetzee's* determination to carve out a space for himself and for the possibility of a late-modernist or postmodern or broadly self-reflexive metafictional enterprise in South Africa, in the unwelcoming climate described by Bethlehem; indeed, if we are to speak of a lonely poetics in South Africa, Coetzee's of the 1970s and 1980s was perhaps the loneliest of all. But Coetzee himself would probably agree that we should not mistake this reaction for a general description of black writing, from which we can quickly cull enough anecdotal evidence to suggest a widespread and even at times a surprisingly orthodox interest in modernist experimentalism.

What does it mean, for instance, that Njabulo Ndebele confesses that while reading for the English Tripos at Cambridge in the early 1970s (with an undergraduate degree in English already behind him) he experimented with Joycean internal monologue in isiZulu (Lindfors: 226). And perhaps we should take seriously the fact that despite the aggression of his language, Muthobi Mutloatse is going down the well-trodden road of the modernist manifesto when he declares, in his notorious introduction to the collection of short fiction of the Black Consciousness period, *Forced Landing*:

> We are involved in and consumed by an exciting experimental art form that I can only call, to coin a phrase, 'proemdra': Prose, Poem and Drama in one!
>
> We will have to *donder* conventional literature: old-fashioned critic and reader alike. We are going to pee, spit and shit on literary convention before we are through; we are going to kick and pull and push and drag literature into the form we prefer.
>
> (1980: 5)

As Nkosi points out, readers familiar with the twentieth century's long history of aesthetic revolutionising will look on this as 'defiant insouciance' (1998: 77); nevertheless, it declares an experimental horizon, one which, furthermore, is more than apparent in several of the contributions to Mutloatse's collection itself, which does not include much 'proemdra' but which does include samples of allegory, political fable and even science fiction. For an earlier example, we might turn to the 'Interludes' in Es'kia Mphahlele's autobiography, *Down Second Avenue* (1959). The following passage – which deals with a child's insomnia in a crowded township home and his identification with fugitives from the curfew outside – is typical:

> Saturday night and it's ten to ten, I can hear the big curfew bell at the police station peal 'ten to ten, ten to ten, ten to ten' for the black man to be out of the streets to be home to be out of the policeman's reach. Year after year every night the sound of the bell floats in the air at ten minutes to ten and the Black man must run home and the Black man must sleep or have a night special permit. The whistle is very near now and the hunted man must be in Second Avenue but the bell goes on peeling lustily and so Black man you must run wherever you are, run.
>
> (ibid.: 50)

The passage is experimental in a number of ways: its visceral pacing, and its fusion of the boy's consciousness with that of the imagined fugitive, a fusion which seems to stand for a collective self, the speech of which is captured in an imagined black (diasporic) argot. In Nkosi's own *Mating Birds* (1987) one finds a different kind of inventiveness: the novel crafts a dispassionate, self-ironising introspection on the causes and consequences of inter-racial sexual violence, in a voice that keeps company with Albert Camus's *The Outsider* and Richard Wright's *Bigger Thomas*. Yet another example might be Dugmore Boetie's *Familiarity is the Kingdom of the Lost* (1969) – the very title suggests an experimental impulse – which blurs the distinction between artist and con-man. One could go on, but for the moment it is enough to name what these examples represent: black South African writing *has* been touched by what Coetzee calls the 'experimental line'. If garden variety forms of realism do abound, it is not true to say that they have crowded out the more adventurous flowerings of experimentalism. One should add that the phenomenon we are observing (inchoate, perhaps, but objectively present) goes well beyond the improvisational bricolage of an earlier generation, that of the 'new Africans' such as Sol Plaatje and Herbert Dhlomo, who patched oral modes of narration to Shakespearean generic patterns and Romantic diction, producing something like a *faux* or *naïf* modernism, but without the self-conscious avant-gardism which is evident in the examples I have given (cf. Attwell 1999).

Definitional dangers could beset us at this point. The simple procedure of defining what modernism or postmodernism are, and applying these crude categories to local black writing – thus ignoring Nkosi's cautionary note – is not available to us. Coetzee's phrase, 'the experimental line', is useful precisely because it recognises that attempts to be categorical can be artificial and distracting. Nevertheless, since the reader would have noticed that I prefer the term experimentalism to the more overdetermined categories of modernism or postmodernism, it seems necessary to offer a working definition of what I mean by experimentalism. In *Sources of the Self* (1989), Charles Taylor refers to twentieth century modernisms collectively as 'epiphanic art,' meaning self-consciously aesthetic practices of the late nineteenth and twentieth centuries which try to initiate an epistemological renewal in response to conditions we associate with modernity. This is close enough (because it is general enough) to what I mean by experimentalism, although at certain points in the argument I shall have to refine or qualify it. Something I do wish to emphasise as a general assumption in my argument, since it is so relevant to black writing, is that as Taylor also points out, all the modernist revolutions (like their Romantic precursors) may detach themselves from various kinds of worldliness or from prior cultural monoliths or institutions, but what they share is a desire to affirm the *agency* in terms of which the new subject or practice they are heralding would like to be understood (1989: 456-493). This emphasis on the agency which is carried in projects of epistemological renewal is fundamental to the writing under discussion.

In order to understand this phenomenon properly we need to add other terms: shortly, I shall speak of 'reflexivity' and of 'cultural struggle'. Before doing so, though, I shall pick up once again Nkosi's insistence that the black South African context imposes its own caveats. Nkosi argues that certain features of modernism and postmodernism which we may think of as definitive – for example, the break-up of the Cartesian, rational self, and the veneration of the decentred subject – are inherent in *traditional* culture. The example he gives is the celebrated one of Nonqawuse, the Xhosa prophet whose role in the disastrous Cattle-Killing of 1856 was to provide a millenarian symbolic language. That language was not entirely autochthonous since it was already informed by missionary teaching; therefore, the kind of splitting Nkosi is referring to may equally be a function of the syncretic epistemologies emerging from the colonial encounter. A different example might be that of the initiate who feels the call to become an *isangoma* or diviner as a disruption of the rational self, as the ancestors badger and irritate him or her into service. Indeed, in his poem 'uMamina' in *Amal'ezulu* (1945) Vilakazi uses this as a metaphor for poetic inspiration, in order to ground the concept of the muse in a local field of reference. Whilst Vilakazi's experiments with English rhyme might have been doomed, as I mentioned earlier, this aspect of his experimentalism is decidedly an African modernism, one which draws on the pre-modern in a manner not procedurally different from European primitivism.

Nkosi's argument therefore points to ways in which the temporal axes of modernism and postmodernism may need to be revised in the local context. The same could be said for the spatial. To take an obvious example: when European modernism registers spatial dislocations, it frequently does so in terms of the expatriate or exile (Conrad in Africa, Hemingway in Paris, Lawrence in Mexico, etc.). This pattern is not absent from black South African writing – one thinks of Mphahlele's reflections on a man in a glass house, in this case the places of exile being Denver and Philadelphia (Manganyi 1983: 288-289). Equally and more powerfully, though, black South African writing can reflect a sense of dislocation *at home*. The force of this can be gauged from the fact that before the term *township* became the standard descriptor of the black dormitory suburb, the common term was *location*. Ironically, the location names a place of permanent unease or unsettlement, a place where one experiences one's *dislocation* from rural life, economic independence, political representation, and citizenship. The boy's consciousness in the passage from *Down Second Avenue* cited earlier develops precisely around this disorientation. This is where modernist decentring speaks to the spectral nightmare which was apartheid itself, the disempowering effects of which Ndebele will try to resist in his theory of the 'ordinary' – I shall come back to this question.

Thus far then, I have collected examples of black experimentalism which must complicate the critical orthodoxy with which I began, and I have begun to suggest (following Nkosi's leads) that what is required is a more contextual theorising about what we are looking for and what the phenomenon might mean when we find it. Let me now come to the nub of my argument, in which I would like to focus on a particular, recent moment in the history of black fiction in South Africa. I wish to argue that in the work of Ndebele and Zakes Mda we have an experimentalism in which a process of epistemological recovery and revision is fully under way. Far from being partial or inchoate, the experimentalism of their practice is self-conscious and programmatic (to refer to Coetzee's 'programmatic refusal', mentioned earlier). Their practice is also, I suggest, reflexive (to pick up that term now), in the sense in which John Noyes speaks of a reflexive theorising, by which he means a practice which is concerned both with identity and how its 'conceptualisation relates to the moment of its performance', that is to say, 'how in the act of theorisation, a specific constellation of ideas comes together to define and delimit the individual's position in a particular social and historical order' (2000: 49). For Graham Pechey, this is the deeper meaning of the term 'cultural struggle', one which is not fully registered in the instrumental senses given to it in debates about resistance. 'To emphasise "culture" as struggle,' says Pechey, 'is to speak of that struggle's subjects, the birth and growth of its forms of subjectivity, the complex socially symbolic acts whereby it makes it makers' (1994: 25). What we are concerned with here, then, is how this reflexivity and sense of cultural struggle have come to be encoded in black fiction. For what we find in Ndebele and Mda is indeed an attempt to develop a transformative fictional practice answering to the specific situation of black South African subjectivity under the conditions of modernity defined by the apartheid city.

This description begs the question of other modes of experimentalism in black writing: Bessie Head, for instance, or more recently, Zoë Wicomb. Undoubtedly, their work is both modernist and postmodern in specific ways, some of which have to do with gendered modes of representation and their implied subject-positions. But I argue that the case I am making can be made all too easily with respect to Head and Wicomb, whose gender-positions and whose exilic relation to their material weighs more heavily than it does with writers like Ndebele and Mda. What I am pursuing, in other words, in terms of the larger dimensions of the argument, is the meaning of a fictional practice informed by a desire to articulate a black, urban South African epistemology. Ndebele and Mda offer the most sustained examples of this project in recent fiction. It is quite possible, as Anthony O'Brien (2001: 59) has suggested, that Head, in her efforts to reconstitute a 'private sphere' in the context of a Botswana village, is an influence on Ndebele. This may be so, but it is a different question.

A final, brief word of theory before turning to the writing. Debates around Theodor Adorno and Georg Lukács's positions on the political agency of modernism might be useful as further points of reference. In the mid-1980s, Neil Lazarus published a pathbreaking essay in which he explored the relevance of Adorno's thinking on modernism to South Africa. Adorno's defence of modernism affirms the value of the insider's 'immanent critique', a critique associated with the power of difficult language to resist reification. Lazarus (1986: 134) argues that this position, which sees modernism as an attempt to refashion a world sunk in the torpor of the administered society and demoralised by fascism, applies *mutatis mutandis* to the work of Breyten Breytenbach, André Brink and J. M. Coetzee in the context of apartheid in the 1970s. By definition, however, surely this account of modernism cannot apply in any straightforward way to black writers, whose relationship to social conditions is such as to position them not inside the headgear of apartheid – to use a mining metaphor – but *outside* it? In other words, we would expect black writing to establish a certain distance from the apartheid insider's consciousness, locating itself in a different subject-position altogether. Adorno's argument, of course, comes to us as an alternative to Lukács's rather stringent critique of the 'ideology' of modernism, a critique of the kind of self-consciousness which paralyses living connections between the subject and society. It was this principle that Gordimer (1984: 6) invoked in her critical review of Coetzee's *Life & Times of Michael K* when it first appeared, a position that would in all likelihood have been informed by Gordimer's sense of what black readers might make of the novel's quietist hero. The Lukácsian position would be common cause for black South African writers, who have sought to protect their connectedness with their readerships; as Mutloatse (1980: 1) puts it, 'no black writer can afford the luxury of isolation from his immediate audience'. As we have seen, however, from Mutloatse's own concerns and those of others, it would be inaccurate to say that black writing is untouched by modernism.

What we are trying to understand, then, is an experimentalism which is both socially connected and aesthetically reflexive, a practice which, in Nkosi's terms, is both 'task' and 'mask', one which enables the critique and subject-construction that we might associate with realism, but which also announces the epistemological invigoration that we associate with the modern movement.

2

In his critique of *Fools and Other Stories* (1983), which he reads in the light of Ndebele's essays in *The Rediscovery of the Ordinary* (1991; 1994), Michael Vaughan (followed later by Benita Parry) points out that despite the claims Ndebele makes for a mode of fiction which is close to the orality of black communities, a mode which in some ways echoes the storytelling traditions of rural life, in his own fiction Ndebele does little to disturb the traditions of Western realism (Vaughan 1990: 191; Parry 1994: 17). One could endorse this to a degree by pointing out that certain features of Ndebele's theory of fiction – for example, that part of it which contrasts psychological depth with the mere repetition of stereotypes – are part of realism's stock-in-trade, adding little to what E. M. Forster said about character in *Aspects of the Novel*. What deserves more careful consideration, though, is the fact that Ndebele dramatises a process of epistemological recovery in his stories.

The stories seem straightforwardly representational in the way they lay out certain dynamics of South African society, such as tensions between the generations, class divisions and aspirations, political alliances, clashing accounts of tradition, etc. But this is not where the emphasis falls; instead, it falls on the growth of consciousness and its connection to the data of daily life in a black community. The stories are profoundly about language, knowledge and cultural agency, and how *these* instruments of power are to be understood, acquired, and developed. The formal properties of the stories serve this inquiry, and in a sense I shall shortly explain, their overarching project is to make 'form' their 'content'.

Ndebele's fiction and essays would not have been possible without the Black Consciousness movement, which was founded on a theory of the self. That is to say, against apartheid's denigration of blackness, its relegation of black agency to minor (rural, and underclass) regimes of labour, political representation and citizenship, Steve Biko and his associates claimed a modern identity on behalf of black South Africans, an identity defined eclectically with reference to third-world and African-American intellectual currents, but one which participates nevertheless in post-enlightenment, modern assumptions about selfhood: namely, its autonomy and agency. Ndebele's fictional project brings aspects of realism into this social movement, its particular contribution being to stage an epistemological recovery. In doing so, it implicitly critiques the legacies of Bantu and missionary education, both of which disrupted the continuities there might have been between the black subject and the practices of literate culture. Such continuities have had to be re-created ever since, by writers' re-appropriating the instruments of culture, using and developing them on their own terms. Indeed it is possible, as A. C. Jordan and his successors in black literary history have done, to read the history of black writing in South Africa on precisely these lines. This process of self-recovery is staged in *Fools* in terms of an implicit *Bildungsroman* which underlies and links all of the stories in the narrative of a boy who comes to develop the kind of social imagination out of which an appropriately subject-centred activism is possible. It would be wrong to suggest that *Fools* is typical of the literature of Black Consciousness, which was decidedly a literature of advocacy. Rather, Ndebele explores the conditions of possibility – epistemological, primarily, but also ethical – under which programmes of advocacy might either thrive or die.

One way to approach Ndebele's recovery of a self-directed epistemology would be, once again, via the work of Charles Taylor. Taylor is relevant not only in the general terms of his inquiry into what he calls the 'sources of the self' in modernity, but more specifically in terms of his suggestion that the modern concern with selfhood starts with an affirmation, in early modern society, of ordinary life. This affirmation, says Taylor, is theological in origin, indeed it is inaugurated by the Reformation, and what we have come to think of as later, fundamental shifts of culture, including the Enlightenment and Romanticism, really secularise and deepen this original moment (1989: 211–233). Arguments involving aesthetic revolutions are really arguments over the appropriate 'symbolic goods' which will serve this affirmation at given moments of history. 'Affirming ordinary life,' says Taylor, 'has meant valuing the efficacious control of things by which it is preserved and enhanced' (ibid.: 232).

Seen from this longer perspective, in his call for 'the rediscovery of the ordinary' (the coincidence of terms with Taylor is felicitous but non-essential) Ndebele is laying claim to what Taylor is naming, that is to say, the symbolic goods of modern selfhood, on behalf of black South Africans. When Vaughan says that Ndebele is, despite himself, writing within the Western tradition of realism, he misses the reason for Ndebele's doing so, which is that Ndebele wishes to access one of the historical forms by which a self-conscious expansion and affirmation of selfhood has been achieved. The progress of the self in the context of what Ian Watt famously called 'a full and authentic report of human experience' (1957: 35) is in these stories being placed at the feet of a social and intellectual community which is still working out the terms of its historical actualisation. The underlying purpose of all life-writing, including autobiography and the *Bildungsroman*, says Taylor, is to distinguish 'the life-shape from the events', and these forms provide the intellectual spine of *Fools*.

Following Vaughan, Benita Parry (1994: 17) suggests that Ndebele's interest in formal experiment is limited. Her view is that Ndebele treats form as 'the handmaiden of the new content, enabling the assumed reader to recognise an authentic version of a familiar world, and not as the means of representation, which can reveal that what is being offered is a fabrication, thereby interrupting expectations, defamiliarising "the real", and resituating the reader as interrogator rather than recipient'. This critique seems to me to undervalue the degree to which the issues Parry is raising are implicit in the stories' own concerns, for the formal inventiveness Parry wishes from Ndebele would principally serve the recovery of epistemological agency, something which is at the heart of Ndebele's project. Moreover, it is not strictly true to say that Ndebele wants his reader simply 'to recognise an authentic version of a familiar world' because what he is doing, in fact, is instantiating a world and more especially a subject-position which, in a crucial sense, has not been fully present to literary representation at all.

The reader would have noticed that I speak of experimentalism in Ndebele while acknowledging his realism, thus tempting contradiction. Indeed, I *am* arguing that Ndebele brings these things together, that is, his realism ought to be understood as participating in the afterlife of modernism. In his own time and place, after all, Ndebele is drawing on the symbolic goods of realism long after the effects of modernism have been widely felt; moreover, the history of realism's emergence in Europe is being reprised under critical conditions, such that the social intensity and historical telescoping inherent in the project give it the force of an intervention, a revisionism which is more characteristic of twentieth than nineteenth century aesthetic history. One could argue, in fact, that Ndebele's project recovers some of the epistemological freshness that once adhered to realism itself.

At the centre of *Fools* lies an experiment in projecting a contextually nuanced subjectivity. The trick the reader is required to catch in the opening paragraphs of the first of the stories, 'The Test', is to recognise the historical weight that supports this apparently ingenuous project as it is rendered in free indirect discourse: 'As he felt the first drops of rain on his bare arms, Thoba wondered if he should run home quickly before there was a downpour. He shivered briefly, and his teeth chattered for a moment as a cold breeze blew and then stopped' (1983: 1). Self-consciousness and timidity are matched by a certain aesthetic sensuousness: 'He looked down at his arms. There they were: tiny drops of rain, some sitting on goose pimples, others between them. Fly's spit, he thought' (ibid.: 2). As it does in *The Portrait of the Artist as a Young Man*, of which this image-making is surely an echo, the child's sensitivity isolates him to a degree from his peers and from the soccer game in which he is, and is not, a participant.

To open his collection this way, Ndebele takes palpable risks, not least the accusation of fiddling while the townships burn; of distracting readers from the mature resistance which had become a reality in the Black Consciousness movement and the Soweto Revolt which it had inspired five years before the stories were written. That 'The Test' unfolds around a group of boys – carefully delineated in class terms, revealing the proximity of the middle-class black child to his impoverished peers – reflects the irruption of June 1976. 'The Test' is an archetypal tale of self-actualisation, encoded in the events of the story as a challenge by the boys to withstand the elements of a high-veld storm on one's bare torso, 'like a horse in the rain'. The simple drama of the story tracks a moment in Thoba's emergence as he runs home in the falling rain and cold, through familiar but now unhomely streets, mindful of a folkloric beast of who might swallow him, past the A. M. E. and Dutch Reformed Churches, and especially, past the humiliating women who are known to his mother. When he reaches home, he curls up in bed and contemplates his soreness and humiliation as badges of honour.

What is important here is simply the fact of focalisation, which collects together a sweeping historical legacy. The subject-position is an act of epistemological leverage on Ndebele's part. The very boundedness of the child's world, in which he cannot recognise the apartheid social engineering which has shaped Charterston township, is an affirmation of this experiential reality and perspective; it is from this consciousness, and no other, that maturity and autonomy must develop. The gesture here is not substantially different from that of J. M. Coetzee's in *Waiting for the Barbarians*: it is a difference of scale, not of kind, for where Coetzee uses a deliberately non-South African and to a degree ahistorical milieu in order to challenge the comprehensive capturing of space and consciousness which was under way in late apartheid, Ndebele, too, clears a space, in this context one in which a mode of consciousness and agency can begin to extend itself, independent of the political discourses that swirl around him.

I have intimated that the subjectivity at the centre of Ndebele's stories is provisional and unfinished. Its dynamic and, as we shall see, dialectical attributes are intimately connected with questions of language. This emerges most forcefully in 'The Prophetess', where the boy – perhaps the same boy – visits a prophetess from an independent church to have water blessed for use by his ailing mother. As she sings and prays, the boy is in awe, and while it is clear that her creed has no particular meaning for him – his middle-class background seems to preclude him from uncomplicated belief in what she represents – what he takes away is her potency, simply her power to speak and symbolise. On the way home, the bottle breaks in a street encounter, whereupon the boy fills it with unblessed tap water which he gives to his mother, who drinks it and feels revived. This turn of events confirms our impression that the boy is a child of calculation, indeed of modernity, but the absence of guilt on his part, and the rush of pride and affection with which the story ends, imply continuity between the generations; more importantly, they imply a compacting of the prophetess's powers into the boy's subject-position, his feelings and familial relationships (ibid.: 51–52). What heals the mother, obviously, is love – fuelled by the boy's experience of poetic elevation. Ndebele's subject, who is on his way to claiming the rights and powers of a secular democratic order, achieves expansion through contact with a tradition of indigenous spiritualism. It is not the content of this spiritualism that matters, but its epiphanic charge.

This pattern is developed further in 'Uncle', in which Ndebele places the same developing consciousness in contact with a cultural order we have come to associate with the 1950s. The itinerant uncle, Lovington, who takes the boy under his wing for the duration of his visit to the family, is a jazz musician and to some degree a proponent of cultural pan-Africanism. He teaches the boy how to turn a clichéd school exercise on 'places I have visited' into a lesson on reclaiming a personal and communal geography, providing instruction, *inter alia*, on the pride and antiquity of Egypt. Most memorably, he turns evening bathing into a ritual activity in which the boy, having cleansed himself

– his awakening to sexual potency is very much in the background – is encouraged to imagine himself a volcano.

Steadily, Lovington's catechism links the child's developing masculinity to the idea of revolution, as he imagines himself a member of a throng moving through history, undaunted by the oppressive armoury of the alien modernity that confronts them – the factories, towns and jets in the sky 'like hundreds of vultures' (ibid.: 107). It is an induction into the unashamedly masculine culture of the epic (qualifications to this troubling virilism arrive in the subsequent story, which foregrounds the moral authority of women over the men) with, once again, a telescoping effect in which the energies of Africa's mid-twentieth century moment of decolonisation become the personalised heritage of the child of apartheid.

In the most complex of the stories, however, the novella *Fools*, Ndebele resists suggesting that an achieved, much less a revolutionary consciousness is easy to hand. Indeed, the subject-position is split at this point between two characters, the older, corrupted and cynical schoolteacher Zamani, and his young antagonist, the idealist Zani. It is here that agency becomes dialectical, something which is reinforced by careful historical contextualisation. The story is set in 1966, a moment falling precisely between the demoralisation following the Sharpeville massacre, and the utopianism of Black Consciousness, a moment when resistance has to reinvent itself, with the exiled movement beginning to organise for armed propaganda and the internal movement caught between generations. These are the historical coordinates of what Zani calls Charterston's 'stagnant isolation' (ibid.: 170).

As their complementary names suggest, Zamani and Zani are elements of a composite dilemma. Indeed, the plotting suggests their connectedness: when the story opens with their encounter on the platform of Springs Station, they are both in the midst of compromising love affairs, Zamani with a mistress, Candu, and Zani with a girlfriend who may be pregnant, Ntozakhe; later, Zamani turns out to be the rapist of Zani's younger sister, Busi, an event from which a child is born whom Zamani refuses to acknowledge; Zani becomes the supportive friend to Zamani's injured wife, Nosipho, and so on. The point is, Zani is really Zamani's younger self, and they represent complementary positions on the issues the story confronts. Ndebele adopts a similar view of historical agency in his well-cited poem, 'The Revolution of the Aged', which stages a debate about acts of resistance needing to be correctly timed. The poem suggests that such acts must await the arrival of actors who can understand, with due historical weight, the implications of their actions: 'now is the time / pluck the apple / and feed the future with its ripeness' (ibid.: 388).

The tension between the protagonists comes to a head when Zamani, at the risk of losing his job since he is at the mercy of an intellectually colonised headmaster, agrees to Zani's visiting his classroom to proselytise the children over a demeaning national holiday, the Day of the Covenant. Zani addresses the ten-year-olds as Ladies and Gentlemen, haranguing them with the historical events of Blood River and its consequences, when the Boers defeated the Zulu king Dingane's troops and vowed afterwards to keep the day in religious memory. Zamani's reflections on Zani's performance follow:

> That they heard, I was sure; but that they understood, was impossible . . . and it struck me at that moment how evenly serious Zani's language was. He had become his books, and when he moved out of them, he came out without a social language. He spoke to me in the same way he spoke to those children. Is that how he had spoken in the bar, and then got stabbed? I wondered if he was not another instance of disembodiment: the obscenity of high seriousness.
>
> (ibid.: 217)

'Disembodied', 'obscene' high seriousness has just shown itself in another form in the classroom, in the uncomprehending recitation by a child of an epic poem on one of the Zulu kings. These examples of discourse drained of subject-centredness are linked with another kind of disembodiment: a piece of amateurish pornography showing locked genitalia, which Zamani discovers being passed around, drawn (significantly) on the back of a poster calling for resistance to the national holiday. These connections are harsh indeed: autochthonous tradition, black history, and pornography. The point of the connections is to insist that revolutionary language must be 'social', that is to say, it must speak to and elicit the consciousness of those who are to be its agents. The larger context for this, what amounts to a critique from within of resistance culture, is not difficult to map: it lies in the legacy of Bantu Education and in the structural constraints on black intellectual life which has had to rely on what Ndebele elsewhere (1991: 24–27) describes as an implicit information order which has been fashioned by others, notably liberal and radical historians, universities, and publishers. Seen in this light, Ndebele's project is about *reconnection*: linking subjects as agents-of-meaning with the resistance culture which is their proper heritage.

Zani and Zamani's failures and achievements are again juxtaposed at the end of the story. Zani's attempts to mobilise the community end in disarray when he flees the whip of an outraged 'Boer' who attacks black picnickers on the disputed national holiday. His tortured reflections ring with the story's title:

> 'What have I found anywhere? Everything seems so small. Am I that small too? Tell me. Have there been many years in which this smallness has turned into a tradition; many years of this crushing sleep of smallness? What is there to be done? It is so easy to make plans, and then everything comes crashing down because the proper act seems so rare. So many acts get done, and so few of them are proper . . . But I ran too. And the wind that blew against my face as I ran sounded like the very sound of shame. The sound of victims laughing at victims. Feeding on their victimness, until it becomes an obscene virtue. Is there ever an excuse for ignorance? And when victims spit upon victims, should they not be called fools? Fools of darkness? Should they not be trampled upon?'
>
> (Ndebele 1983: 278)

Given that Zani's despair is one position among others that the story offers, and that it is the predictable result of his *hubris*, it is curious that Ndebele should emphasise this outburst in his title. But I suggest that the importance Ndebele attaches to the notion of 'fools' here – victims feeding on their victimage – is related to the principle of sub-ject-centredness and the ownership of agency. Auto-critique, the argument would run, is a necessary condition for a thoroughgoing autonomy. Where the prize to be won by collective action – nothing less than a democratic revolution – is of such magnitude, it is of signal importance that an over-reaching immaturity such as Zani's be expunged. Zani's chastening self-discovery, in other words, in which he confronts his weaknesses and gauges the extent to which they represent a common condition, is a crucial step on the road to individual and collective empowerment. His discovery is very like that of the artist Mandla's in the story, 'Uncle', who finds the recognition he achieves in Johan-nesburg's elite galleries demeaning, and who later carves a figure, 'The Hunchback', which he explains in part by saying that in the township of Orlando East, 'I do not have to pretend. I am nothing, and that is where I begin, rather than from an imagined somethingness. My mind can never rot here because I've learnt to humble myself before the people, beginning from the somethingness that has always sustained them' (ibid.: 80).

Zani's humiliation is matched by a moment of triumphant rehabilitation in Za-mani. Instead of fleeing the white man with the whip, he stands and takes the blows in a moment of what O'Brien (2001: 49) calls 'a Ghandian parable of the truth-force of African presence':

> The blows stopped; and I knew I had crushed him. I had crushed him with the sheer force of my presence. I was there, and would be there to the end of time: a perpetual symbol of his failure to have a world without me. And he walked away to his car, a man without a shadow, the sun couldn't see him. And the sound of his car when he drove away seemed so irrelevant. There he went: a member of a people whose sole gift to the world has been the perfection of hate. And because there was nothing much more in them, they will forever destroy, consuming us and themselves in a great fire. But the people of the north will come down and settle the land again, as they have done for thousands of years.
>
> (Ndebele 1983: 276)

This quietism is not offered as a general solution, because of what it represents in *Zamani's* development: it represents his victory over self-hatred, his overcoming of the very kind of debilitating consciousness of one's failures that Zani has expressed and which has turned Zamani into a cynic. Nor does the passage have to be seen as a moment of Africanist essentialism, for Zamani's image of the Africans who will come down from the north to re-settle a land destroyed by whites is his grasping at metaphor in the resolution of a personal drama. However, whilst it cannot be taken as a last word, it does resonate with the assurance of Black Consciousness. At the Hector Peterson Museum in Soweto one is able to view video footage of Biko explaining that blacks will never oppress whites when they are in power since their sheer numbers will preclude them from having to protect their ascendancy.

O'Brien points to another moment in which Ndebele articulates a principled autonomy, about the same time as the completion of *Fools*. This involved his intervention in the naming of an anthology of black poetry to be published by Ravan Press, the publishers of *Staffrider* magazine. Before it became *The Return of the Amasi Bird*, the title was to be *Ask Any Black Man*, to which Ndebele responded, 'who should ask any black man? Surely not another African.' He goes on to argue that the time for implicit appeals for dialogue with whites is over: 'I have gone *far beyond* begging to be "heard". I am not even demanding. It is the pure force of my people's inevitable presence that I want to consolidate.' As O'Brien (2001: 49) points out, Zamani's moment of truth-force matches Ndebele's own.

In his discussion of Ndebele's essays, O'Brien (ibid.: 40) shows the degree to which their core project is indeed a developmental analysis of black intellectual agency. They conduct 'an inquiry into rethinking and remaking power/knowledge – "breaking down closed epistemological structures", freeing the entire social imagination of the oppressed – on the basis of an actual historical emergence of . . . a new hegemony, borne by the historically new subjects of the mass movement'. One has to agree with this emphasis and add that the project is intrinsic to the fiction as well; what the fiction, especially the title story, enables us to gauge, however, is the extent to which this project in subject-formation represents a putative ideal; it is, in the best sense, an inquiry: the *bildungsroman* is never rounded-off.

We might develop O'Brien's observation that there is some autobiographical pressure behind the project. In some of Ndebele's writing as a student, such as his contribution on 'Black Development' to Biko's collection, *Black Viewpoint* (1972), two things stand out. Firstly, his precociousness, in judgments such as the following: 'The peasants on the white farms have almost no political consciousness' (1972: 16); 'The urban blacks are the most socio-politically aware among the black groups' (ibid.: 17–18); 'The black middle class is also characterised by a general lack of creative imagination' (ibid.: 22); and

> the black must set about destroying the old and static customs and traditions that have . . . made Africa the world's human zoo and museum of human evolution. When customs no longer cater for the proper development of adequate human expression, they should be removed. Almost all the so-called tribal customs must be destroyed, because they cannot even do so little as to help the black man get food for the day.
>
> (ibid.: 26)

This is the kind of Zani-speak which falls under the scrutiny of *Fools*. The second observation, however, is the consistency of his most deeply held views:

> The blacks must ignore the frustrated black journalist who says that South African blacks must win the political kingdom first before they begin to create artistic works of any meaning and merit. Indeed, it is the great artworks that inspire a bondaged people towards seeking freedom. An imaginative exploration of the miserable human conditions in which people live, touches

the fibre of revolt in them; the fibre that seeks to reassert human dignity. Indeed, an intellectual awakening is a vital pre-requisite to any significant social change.

(ibid.: 27)

It is now for the black man to begin to work. It is work that involves a whole human re-orienta-tion. The blacks must awaken intellectually, spiritually, socially, morally, culturally and in many other ways that make life worth living. If the whites do not want to change their attitudes, let the blacks advance and leave them behind . . . The blacks must know what they want when they cry for freedom. They should not be put in the situation whereby when they get this freedom they do not know what to do with it. The struggle is more than a racial one; it is also a human one; a human struggle involves development in all human activities that are the marks of true civilisation.

(ibid.: 28)

The over-arching thesis of 1972 is much the same as it is in 1994, which marks the pub-lication of the collected, re-authorised version of *The Rediscovery of the Ordinary*. What is different in that interim, however, is the degree of reflexivity with which the project is conducted, Ndebele's study in fiction of the conditions under which the emergence of the 'social imagination' is possible.

3

If Ndebele re-deploys realism's resources in an experimental intervention, Zakes Mda takes us further down the same road. Let us begin with Toloki in his first novel, *Ways of Dying*. Toloki is theatrical – his signature outfit of top hat and cloak is acquired in a costume-hire shop – and his diet and personal habits (Swiss roll and green onions; a re-fusal to wash) set him apart. He has an eclectic mysticism which has nothing to do with oral culture, nor has his role as Professional Mourner, which is self-invented. Part ring-master, part shaman, his practice is, however, empty of explicit metaphysical comfort, since his mourning takes the form of incomprehensible grunts. Toloki has no message other than to teach people that they must grieve. Later, through his companion Noria, he learns 'how to live,' but this knowledge does not translate into a programme. When the children of the township view Toloki's drawings, or his and Noria's shack which they have turned into a place of intimacy by the appropriation and transformation of imagery torn from the pages of *Home and Garden*, 'they cannot say what the meaning is. It is not even necessary to say, or even to know, what the meaning is. It is enough only to know that there is a meaning, and it is a profound one' (Mda 1995b: 187).

My claim here is that Mda is toying with modernism's characteristic position of non- or anti-instrumentalism. The notion that one can re-fashion the world by style, that complex language is in itself a mode of resistance (to refer again to Adorno) is given a new, anthropomorphic embodiment in the figure of Toloki. If I may be allowed to draw on the author's own account of Toloki's genesis, the decisive influence on Mda was the figure of Vercueil in Coetzee's *Age of Iron*. Vercueil, of course, is a tramp with a history of seafaring, a wanderer who smells of fatality; for this among other reasons, Elizabeth Curren, Coetzee's protagonist who is suffering from terminal cancer, constructs him as her Angel of Death. The connection with Toloki is obvious, in the a-social behaviour and the association with death. More importantly, Vercueil is the key figure of alterity in Coetzee's text and as such, the agent of that novel's estrangement from the real. The intertextuality between *Age of Iron* and *Ways of Dying* is an explicit instance of the movement of modernist practice across the racial divide of authorship in South Africa. Indeed, Mda has mentioned to me another instance of his indebtedness to Coetzee: the arms-length treatment of the historical period to which his novel refers was developed under the influence of *Waiting for the Barbarians*. It is interesting and telling that Mda has come in for some of the same criticism that Coetzee faced in the 1970s and 1980s, for displacing the social landscape of apartheid onto a symbolic or allegorical plane (cf. Farred 2000).

Toloki embodies, then, a certain experimental practice of the South African township. His empty showmanship derives, via Coetzee it seems, from that feature of late modernism which is apparent in Beckett's defence of Joyce's *Work in Progress*, where he argues that 'form is content, content is form . . . [Joyce's] writing is not *about* something; *it is that something itself*' (1998: 451). However, we will not find in Mda Beckett's scorn for the philistinism which insists on finding a core of rationality in the literary text: 'the rapid skimming and absorption of the scant cream of sense is made possible by what I may simply call a continuous process of copious intellectual salivation' (ibid.: 450). (Let me note in passing, though, that this tone is similar to Coetzee's (1988: 4) in 'The Novel Today', where he says that stories are not messages plus a covering of art: 'On the keyboard on which stories are written, the plus key does not work' [4].) Mda would not deride instrumental modes of thought to this extent. If I may put it so awkwardly, Mda reinstrumentalises modernism's anti-instrumentalism, bringing it into an effective relationship with a given context and history. This contextualisation precludes the delivering of messages, the flattening out of performance or its reduction to simple meaning, but what Mda dramatises is the power of non-instrumental art to awaken listeners to their precariousness, to stir up affective capacities, and to remind them that despite the brutalisation which is their daily lot, they are still agents of culture – which makes Mda's writing a development from Ndebele's. The historical context of Toloki's performance is the wasteland of city and township in that narrow interregnum of South Africa between 1990 and 1994, that is, between the unbanning of the liberation movements and the first democratic election, when death has become a way of life, with Third Force killings engineered by security agents, the massacre of squatters by vigilantes, and the necklacing of child activists accused by being collaborators. To the African subjects who inhabit this space, Toloki offers not words of consolation but a symbolic presence whose function it is to symbolise. What Mda places before his readers is a performance which stands for the symbolic function, the point being to restore the image of the man-of-ritual, and the maker-of-culture.

The pattern is not restricted to Toloki in Mda's fiction. One finds it in Dikosha in *She Plays with the Darkness*, whose dancing is a peculiarly celebratory mourning, and to some degree also in Camagu in *The Heart of Redness*, who is drawn to the mysterious NomaRussia at a wake on the roof of a Hillbrow building. In these examples, modernity seems endemically linked to death, something also apparent in the actions of the unbelievers in *The Heart of Redness*, the non-traditionalists who need bouts of public grieving to cope with the consequences of their abandonment of their cultural past. The point is, Mda renders history – colonialism, apartheid – as a process of creeping death which necessitates modes of aesthetic production – the professional mourner, the dancer, *ritual*, in general – which are offered as sources of hope. Mda pits stylised aesthetic humanism against historically-induced death and by so doing, he participates in Coetzee's 'experimental line', but on his own terms.

The Heart of Redness, Mda's most ambitious work to date, is filled with a rather different aesthetic self-consciousness. The title echoes *Heart of Darkness*, as does the character, Sir Harry Smith, Mda's version of the historical colonial governor, who leads his troops into battle against the Xhosa with 'Extermination!' emblazoned on their hats (2000: 20). But the novel also locates itself in other traditions: Xhosa narratives such as S. E. K. Mqhayi's *Ityala Lamawele* ('The Trial of the Twins') and A. C. Jordan's *Ingqumbo Yeminyanya* ('The Wrath of the Ancestors'), which in their own ways are texts which deal with the Xhosa encounter with modernity. It also refers to Chinua Achebe's early fiction. There are a number of strong allusions to *Things Fall Apart*, including a memorable linking of the governor of the Cape Colony, Sir George Grey, with the district commissioner of Achebe's novel who writes Okonkwo's story as an episode in the history of 'pacification'. But Mda's aesthetics in this novel also go beyond the literary: he uses the Xhosa principle of twinning, and as Johan Jacobs has shown, the tradition of split-tone or overtone singing, *umngqokolo*, as a structural device: both in a generalised use of diglossia (unitalicised terms from isiXhosa used extensively alongside English) and in the arrangement of the narrative itself. The text is organised around two historical moments as well as two opposed social tendencies, one involving *ubuqaba* (conservatism, traditionalism, the 'Believers', their 'redness', from the red ochre with which the women adorn themselves and colour their skirts), the other involving *ubugqobokha* (literally 'piercedness', or enlightenment, the 'Unbelievers', with their faith in schooling and modernity). In addition to the gnomic traditions of isiXhosa and traditional music, Mda uses the set-piece debates that are typical of theatre-for-development, another arm of his expressive practice. All told, the novel is multi-voiced and multi-disciplinary, an elaborately colourful, allegorical, historiographic mural, infused with the freeing of representational energy which the post-apartheid moment seems to promise. If black fiction comprises a unified tradition, then the effect of *The Heart of Redness* will be to put an end to the generalisation this essay has sought to confront, that it has not risen above elementary forms of realism.

But this is perhaps not even the most significant of the novel's innovations. Instead of focusing on racial conflict, or apartheid and its counter-histories, *The Heart of Redness* foregrounds the encounter with modernity, not as completed event, but as unfinished business, over which the amaXhosa – and through figures like Dalton and Camagu, South Africans in general – must take charge. The decisive depriviledging of the apartheid years and their struggles comes in the form of their relegation to the relatively unexplored 'Middle Generations'. Mda's larger canvas serves his mapping of the Xhosa response to modernity at a number of levels, beginning with the shock of its intrusion in the form of the demise of Xikixa, who becomes the 'headless ancestor' when during the war of Mlanjeni, in a moment of iconographic reversal, he is decapitated and the flesh is boiled off his skull to preserve it for future studies in phrenology. The psychic disturbance of this moment, which is witnessed by the old man's sons and which robs them of the means to lay him to rest, produces the splitting referred to earlier, with Twin and Twin-Twin falling into the rivalling camps of Believers and Unbelievers, answering respectively the call of indigenous and exogenous allegiances. The contemporary heirs of Twin and Twin-Twin, Zim and Bhonco, and their homesteads, are similarly caught in this division. With the apartheid years in the background, two historical moments encapsulate the ongoing struggle over modernity: in the first, around 1856, it is the prophetic movement started by Nonqawuse and sustained by her uncle, Mhlakaza, that provides the point of reference; in the second, it is the emergence of democracy in 1994, and more especially the period immediately after the elections when political freedom needs to be translated into autonomous social development. In choosing these moments as narrative *foci*, Mda, like Ndebele, implicitly places in question the problem of agency.

In the mid-nineteenth century, 'belief' takes the form of the millenarian Cattle-Killing movement; 'unbelief' a readiness to cast in one's lot with what calls itself civilisation. Both positions bring degrees of catastrophe: to the believers, it brings famine, loss of land and power; to the unbelievers, loss of self. The believers resent their neighbours' charge of backwardness; the unbelievers engage in their bouts of mourning. The contemporary version of this crisis takes place in the same rural, seaside village of the nineteenth century story, Qolorha, whose residents must now decide how to take possession of their freedom. To a degree, the novel resembles a *roman a thèse* as it stages the debates in the community over appropriate modes of development: do they welcome the developers who will turn the village into a casino and hotel resort, cashing in on globalisation with all its dangers, or do they try to manage eco- and cultural tourism on their own terms?

The subject-position in terms of which these choices become personal, affective, and ethical, is principally that of Camagu, a PhD graduate in communications who returns from exile to vote, only to find himself marginalised by the new elite and its nepotism which has already proved to be the forte of the 'Aristocrats of the Revolution'. Camagu is about to abandon his country and return abroad when he discovers the true meaning of his presence, indeed his quest, at a rooftop wake which he stumbles upon in Hillbrow. She is the mysterious NomaRussia, whose singing stirs in him an irrepressible longing, and whom he pursues to Qolorha, her name suggesting the Cattle-Killing, with its allusion to the Xhosa belief of 1856 that since the Russians had recently finished off Sir George Cathcart in the Crimean War, the very man who had given them so much trouble in Mlanjeni's war of 1852, they would assist the ancestors on their return to drive the settlers into the sea. NomaRussia dies before Camagu finds her, but his romantic life takes on other forms, centrally an allegorical love-triangle in which he must choose between Qukezwa, who is mystically in touch with indigenous natural life, and Xoliswa, the school teacher who wears smart suits and shoes and who imagines that the America which is represented by Eddie Murphy and Dolly Parton is the apogee of everything desirable and sophisticated.

Camagu's quest reverses that trope of South Africa's literature of modernisation, the 'Jim-goes-to-Jo'burg' theme which we find in Alan Paton and an earlier generation of black writers (notably R. R. R. Dhlomo in *An African Tragedy*). The reversal is telling: instead of narrating the emergence of the African as modern subject – the end of innocence – the novel attempts a *reintegration* of the already-modern subject into the dilemmas of Southern Africa's postcoloniality. Like Soyinka's figure of the interpreter, Camagu is a returnee who needs to discover who he is, in the professional sense, but more importantly in cultural terms, and the choices before him are modelled by Qukezwa and Xoliswa. In the final analysis, it is the side of belief that receives Mda's endorsement, with Qukezwa becoming the chosen one and the believers winning the strategic battle over the village's development. The decision is affirmed in the conception and birth of Heitsi, Qukezwa's daughter by Camagu, who is conceived by a kind of immaculate conception as the lovers are out horseriding.

As the resolution of Camagu's quest suggests, Mda is not content to allow the central choice imposed by modernity – return to the source, or, as it were, cash in – to remain unanswered. Camagu, and therefore the novel, offer a modernised Africanism as the inevitable path into the future. But of particular interest to the concerns of this essay are the tropological moves Mda makes to nudge his text towards resolutions at the deeper symbolic levels. Undoubtedly, modernity introduces splitting, a splitting of political allegiances and subjectivities, but against this, Mda asserts the metaphorical and ontological power of twinning. In Mqhayi's *Ityala Lamawele*, conflict over inheritance and patriarchal authority between twins is resolved by the court's insistence that they are to rule jointly and wisely. This is in keeping with a traditional position which interprets twinship as a *single* identity. In Mda's hands, splitting and twinning comprise a warp and woof, a weaving of pattern and tension which gives definition to South African postcolonial modernity.

Mda's closing paragraphs are enigmatic. One of the reasons for this is that he brings together different registers which we may loosely call the politico-economic and the prophetic. Here is the politico-economic:

> As [Camagu] drives back home he sees wattle trees along the road. Qukezwa taught him that these are enemy trees. All along the way he cannot see any of the indigenous trees that grow in abundance in Qolorha. Just the wattle and other imported trees. He feels fortunate that he lives in Qolorha. Those who want to preserve indigenous plants and birds have won the day there. At least for now. But for how long? The whole country is ruled by greed. Everyone wants to

have his or her snout in the trough. Sooner or later the powers that be may decide, in the name of the people, that it is good for the people to have a gambling complex at Qolorha-by-Sea. And the gambling complex shall come into being. And of course the powers that be or their proxies – in the form of wives, sons, daughters, cousins – shall be given equity. And so the people shall be empowered.

(Mda 200: 319)

The powers that be – the State, no doubt, and those who drive the economy – are mistaken, even treasonous in siding with unbelief, which is what capitulating to globalisation and material acquisitiveness amounts to. The bitterness of that final phrase – 'and so the people shall be empowered' – is made more deeply ironic by its echo of the Freedom Charter, which has been debased in its association with 'equity' in the financial sense. This register offers critique, therefore, the passage's implication being that freedom will never mean freedom from having to make hard ethical decisions in relation to development – to that extent, tradition cannot supply ready answers either. But then there is the prophetic register, such as we find in the novel's final paragraph:

Oh, this Heitsi! He is afraid of the sea. How will he survive without the sea? How will he carry out the business of saving his people? Qukezwa grabs him by his hand and drags him into the water. He is screaming and kicking wildly. Wild waves come and cover them for a while, then rush back again. Qukezwa laughs excitedly. Heitsi screams even louder, pulling away from her grip, 'No, mama! No! This boy does not belong in the sea! This boy belongs in the man village!'

(ibid.: 319-320)

At this point, Mda has conflated the two narratives, bringing about a deliberate merging of identities such that the Heitsi of this passage, the child of Qukezwa and Camagu, carries within himself the identity of Heitsi, the child of Twin and his wife Qukezwa of the nineteenth century, and behind both stands the figure of Heitsi Eibib, 'the earliest prophet of the Khoikhoi' (ibid.: 24), a touchstone of indigenous symbolic power. Similarly, the early and later Qukezwas have merged, and prior to this passage, somewhat disturbingly, John Dalton, the white man who sides with the believers and whose 'heart is an umXhosa heart' (ibid.: 7), has nearly been murdered by the unbelieving Bhonco for the part the historical Dalton, John Dalton's predecessor, played in the humiliation of the 'headless ancestor'. In this general merging of identities, one asks, is Mda trying to impose a cyclic, pre-modern conception of history – the eternal return – on his tale?

Possibly, but the conclusion is not quite that straightforward. In the passage, Qukezwa wants Heitsi to learn to be comfortable in the sea, water being the element from which the shades will return; it is the element of prophecy, of millenarianism, of salvation. But the story is too multifaceted, the tensions of Xhosa symbolic life are too contradictory, for Qukezwa to have the final word. It is given to Heitsi, who chooses not the sea but the village, therefore people over prophecy, and the future over the past.

There is nothing in this resolution to qualify Mda's overarching thesis that the future must entail the working-out of an African modernity, but the emphasis is tilted, finally, towards open-endedness. The position is Fanonist, in the sense of these famous lines from the essay on national culture:

> It is not enough to try to get back to the people in that past out of which they have already emerged; rather, we must join them in that fluctuating movement which they are just giving shape to, and which, as soon as it has started, will be the signal for everything to be called into question. Let there be no mistake about it; it is to this zone of occult instability where the people dwell that we must come . . .
>
> (1963: 227)

National cultures are not to be discovered, pre-formed, Fanon is saying, by returning to icons of indigenous purity forgotten in the wake of colonialism; they are to be made from the all the resources at a people's disposal, in acts of appeasement not to the past, but to the future, for at the end of the quest to make peace with the past, there is still the question of living in time.

4

This essay has turned on two conceptual axes: the first is realism and experimentalism, the second is the real and the subject's relation to it. My contention is that the positions circulating in the critical literature about black South African fiction are the result of privileging the first set of terms over the second, that is to say, realism and the real predominate over experimentalism and the subject. I began by saying that the reasons for this privileging are not hard to find: the climate of expectation around the literature has appeared to necessitate it. The trouble with this emphasis is that it comes at a heavy price: unwittingly, it has always suggested that black fiction is epistemologically naive, indeed wide-eyed in its confrontation with history, like a rabbit caught in the headlights.

Why does it seem so important to be able to claim an 'experimental line' for black South African writing? The simple answer is that *not* to do so is demeaning and in any case, inaccurate. But behind the question of whether laying claim to a tradition of experimentalism is necessary or not, lies the trickier, political problem – one the reader would have anticipated – of whether black writing repeats the subject-construction of European literature, or whether it offers something distinctive and original. At the heart of *that* question lies the vexed issue of humanism, and the problem of whether the subject-construction I have described in Ndebele and Mda repeats Europe's – or liberal South Africa's – desire to perpetuate a reactionary subjectivity which has proved itself to be politically evasive and socially exclusive.

This, essentially, is the argument offered by Kelwyn Sole in his critique of Ndebele. Ndebele may be a radical humanist, says Sole, but he is still a humanist (1993: 91).

Presumably, in his more flaunted aesthetics and his construction of symbolic rituals to oppose apartheid's deathliness, Mda would come in for similar criticism. Sole argues that Ndebele's conceptual framework bears the hallmarks of intellectual humanism: moral abstractions, binary oppositions, and a tendency to wish 'for a certain type of human nature to prevail in South Africa' (ibid.: 96). Ndebele also overrates the role of literature in providing instruction, its capacity 'to form certain types of human experience and perception' and install 'reason and knowledge into citizens' (ibid.: 97). The price of this tendency is 'the absence of any concentrated attention given . . . to those social forces which divide human beings and position them in antagonistic groups within the nation' (ibid.).

The skeleton that Sole sees lurking in Ndebele's theory cupboard is Matthew Arnold and his successors with their efforts to position literary humanism at the centre of public education and civil society. Accordingly, the debate in which Sole positions Ndebele is the one that dominated South African literary-critical politics in the 1970s and 1980s between liberal humanism and Marxism. Is this appropriate? To entertain Sole's critique, one would have to accept that the Ndebele of the 1980s shares in some equivalent way Arnold's defensiveness and concern for literature to acquire a middle-class social mission. Surely, even if one were to concede that Ndebele's protagonists are middle-class, the historical project defining their endeavours is politically emergent rather than reactive. The critique would also imply that the tendency of liberal-humanism to seal its preferred modes of subjectivity off from history and the influence of ideology is repeated in Ndebele. This would certainly traduce Ndebele's writing, its particular formation and its sensitivity to the class-positions of its protagonists. In fact, Ndebele's concerns are generally coded not in terms of humanist ethics but in terms of the social conditions of agency against a particular historical background. Sole's conclusion, indeed, to the effect that 'when all is said and done, aspiring writers have to trust their own judgment, and the direction in which their own particular priorities and vision are taking them' ('it is the writers themselves, as they struggle to develop identity, direction and technique, who will have to choose how best to express their chosen concerns' [ibid.: 98]) is an entirely apt summary of Ndebele's project. It precisely defines Zani's development and as we have seen, in certain respects Ndebele's own.

My claim, then, is that the subject-construction in this writing carries a post-humanist historicity. But perhaps a full and final answer to the question of whether this writing represents repetition or renewal is not really possible, since the question itself is opened to the future as a utopian gesture. As Graham Pechey puts it, '[h]aving helped to worst its foes under the old order, [post-apartheid reason] now has the challenge of reminding its friends under the new that democracy is a hypothetical point in socio-political infinity rather than an accomplished fact in the gift of a sect' (1998: 14). It falls to this reason 'to ensure that the (modern) tragedy of the country's earlier efforts at hitching a lift into the future . . . does not repeat itself as (postmodern) farce' (ibid.: 14). John Noyes (2000: 60) also offers valuable counsel. To apply his more general theory to the context: Ndebele's dialectical account of agency, and Mda's imaging of the tensions arising from Xhosa responses to modernity, may reveal the 'collapse of a [prior] discourse of truth', but equally, they could lead us to 'what enables the enactment of human rights in practice'.

Note

1   In Bernth Lindfors, *Africa Talks Back: Interviews with Anglophone African Authors* (2002: 245).

References

Attwell, David
1993 *J. M. Coetzee: South Africa and the Politics of Writing* (Berkeley and London: University of California Press).
1999 'Reprisals of Modernity in Black South African "Mission" Writing'. *Journal of Southern African Studies* 25, 2 (June): 267–285.

Beckett, Samuel
1998 'From "Dante . . . Bruno . . . Vico . . . Joyce" 1929'. Vassiliki Kolocotroni, Jane Goodman and Olga Taxidou, eds. *Modernism: An Anthology of Sources and Documents.* (Chicago: University of Chicago Press: 449–451).

Bethlehem, Louise
2001 '"A Primary Need as Strong as Hunger": The Rhetoric of Urgency in South African Literary Culture under Apartheid'. *Poetics Today* 22, 2 (Summer): 365–389.

Boetie, Dugmore
1969 *Familiarity is the Kingdom of the Lost* (London: Arena).

Coetzee, J. M.
1973 'Alex La Guma and the Responsibility of the South African Writer'. *New African Literature and the Arts.* Vol. 3: 116–124 Joseph Okpaku, ed (New York: Third World).
1988 'The Novel Today'. *Upstream* 6 (1): 2–5.
Undated 'Grubbing for the Ideological Implications: A Clash (More or Less) with J. M. Coetzee' (interview), in *Sjambok*, edited by Alan Thorold and Richard Wicksteed. (University of Cape Town).

Dhlomo, R. R. R.
1930 *An African Tragedy* (Alice: Lovedale).

Fanon, Frantz
1963 'On National Culture'. *The Wretched of the Earth* (New York:Grove Press): 206–248.

Farred, Grant
2000 'Mourning the Post-Apartheid State Already? The Poetics of Loss in Zakes Mda's Ways of Dying' *Modern Fiction Studies* 46, 1 (Spring): 183–206.

Gordimer, Nadine
1984 'The Idea of Gardening'. *New York Review of Books* 2 Feb 1984: 3, 6.
1989 *The Essential Gesture: Writing, Politics and Places.* Stephen Clingman, ed. (London: Penguin).

Jordan, A. C.
1940 *Ingqumbo yeminyana* (Alice: Lovedale).
1973 *Towards an African Literature: The Emergence of Literary Form in Xhosa* (Berkeley, CA: University of California Press).

Lazarus, Neil
1986 'Modernism and Modernity: T. W. Adorno and Contemporary White South African Literature'. *Cultural Critique* 5: 131–155.

Lindfors, Bernth
>   2002 [1986] Interview with Njabulo Ndebele. In *African Talks Back: Interviews with Anglophone African Authors* (Trenton, NJ: Africa World Press): 226–248.

Manganyi, N. Chabani
>   1983 *Exiles and Homecomings: A biography of Es'kia Mphahlele* (Johannesburg: Ravan Press).

Mda, Zakes
>   1995a *She Plays with the Darkness* (Florida Hills: Vivlia).
>   1995b *Ways of Dying* (Cape Town: Oxford University Press).
>   2000 *The Heart of Redness* (Cape Town: Oxford University Press).

Mphahlele, Esk'ia
>   1959 *Down Second Avenue* (London: Faber).

Mqhayi, S. E. K.
>   1914 *Ityala lamawele* (Alice: Lovedale).

Mutloatse, Mothobi, ed.
>   1980 *Forced Landing: Africa South: Contemporary Writings* (Johannesburg: Ravan Press).

Ndebele, Njabulo
>   1972 'Black Development' in B. S. Biko, ed. *Black Viewpoint* Durban (Spro-Cas): 13–28.
>   1980 'The Revolution of the Aged'. *Staffrider* 3, 4: 2.
>   1983 *Fools and Other Stories.* Johannesburg: Ravan Press.
>   1994 *South African Literature and Culture: The Rediscovery of the Ordinary*. With an introduction by Graham Pechey (Manchester and New York: Manchester University Press).

Nkosi, Lewis.
>   1979 [1967] 'Fiction by Black South Africans: Richard Rive, Bloke Modisane, Ezekiel Mphahlele, Alex La Guma'. Ulli Beier, ed. *Introduction to African Literature: An Anthology of Critical Writing* (Harlow: London): 221–227.
>   1981 *Tasks and Masks: Themes and Styles of African Literature* (Harlow: Longman).
>   1979 Mating Birds (Johannesburg: Ravan Press).
>   1998 'Postmodernism and Black Writing in South Africa'. In Derek Attridge and Rosemary Jolly, eds. *Writing South Africa: Literature, Apartheid and Democracy 1948–1995* (Cambridge University Press): 75–90.

Noyes, John
>   2000 'The Place of the Human'. In Sarah Nuttall and Cheryl-Ann Michael, eds. *Senses of Culture: South African Culture Studies* (Cape Town: Oxford University Press): 49–60.

O'Brien, Anthony
>   2001 *Against Normalisation: Writing Radical Democracy in South Africa* (Durham, NC: Duke University Press).

Parry, Benita
>   1994 'Some Provisional Speculations on the Critique of "Resistance" Literature'. In Elle Boehmer, Laura Chrisman and Kenneth Parker, eds. *Altered State? Writing and South Africa* (Sydney: Dangaroo Press): 11–24.

Pechey, Graham
>   1994 '"Cultural Struggle" and the Narratives of South African Freedom'. In Elleke Boehmer, Laura Chrisman and Kenneth Parker, eds. *Altered State? Writing and South Africa* (Sydney: Dangaroo Press): 25-35.
>   1998 'Post-Apartheid Reason: Critical Theory in South Africa' *Current Writing* (10, 2): 3-18.

Sole, Kelwyn
>   1993 'The Role of the Writer in a Time of Transition' *Staffrider* 11, 1-4: 90-98.

Taylor, Charles
>   1989 *Sources of the Self: The Making of the Modern Identity* (Cambridge University Press).

Vaughan, Michael

    1990 'Storytelling and Politics in Fiction.' *Rendering Things Visible: Essays on South African Literary Culture* (Johannesburg: Ravan Press): 186-204.

Vilakazi, B. W.

    1945 *Amal'ezulu* Bantu Treasury Series No. 8. (Johannesburg: University of the Witwatersrand Press).

Watt, Ian

    1957 *The Rise of the Novel: Studies in Defoe, Richardson and Fielding* (Harmondsworth: Penguin).

EIGHT

Tradurre e Tradire:
The Treason and Translation of Breyten Breytenbach

Simon Lewis

The point of the Italian proverb *tradurre e tradire* is that exact translation is never possible and that any translation therefore implies some 'betrayal' of the original. My purpose in this essay, however, is not to look at the possibility or impossibility of translation but rather to reverse the identity statement *tradurre e tradire* to examine to what extent betrayal is an act of translation. In particular, I wish to revisit the case of Breyten Breytenbach, especially through analysis of his *The True Confessions of an Albino Terrorist* (1994 [1984]) to suggest that the abandonment by establishment Afrikaans authors of notions of linguistic purity seriously undermined mainstream Afrikaner notions of racial purity. Thus, while Breytenbach's formal treason may have been politically inconsequential, his self-translation away from establishment Afrikaans – whether in the 'imitative Euro-modernism' (Chapman 1996: 248) of the Sestiger ('Sixties') group or the English of *Confessions* – did serious, though not necessarily intentional, political work.[1] Furthermore Breytenbach's treason/translation leaves the door open for still further political work by showing the possibility of Afrikaans as a genuinely local, thoroughly hybrid language. Under the new dispensation after 1994, Afrikaans does not need to be thought of in racial terms – whether as some Herderian *Sprachgeist* of the Volk or as the language of the oppressor – but might be conceived of as the language of local and national dissent (neither black nor white, neither traditionally African nor Europeanly modern) pitted against global and international systems of an Anglophone world order.

Even in an English version of the Italian proverb *tradurre e tradire*, say, 'translation is treason', survives a trace of the etymological similarity on which the Italian depends, an etymological similarity intriguing not only in its own right but in possible elaborations to such modern English words as *trade* and *tradition*. All these words have their sources in the Latin verbs *trado* (I betray – literally, I give across) or *traduco* (literally, I lead across), with *trade* and *traduce* the modern English words (though not necessarily the meanings of those words) most directly derived from them. Modern English *translation*, in form, derives from Latin *transfero* (supine form *translatum*) with its implications of *carrying* across rather than giving or leading. In the Romance languages the concept of linguistic translation thus is expressed in metaphorical terms (*metaphor* itself etymologically conveys the idea of carrying across, of course), not in terms of language itself as in the Afrikaans *vertaling*: approximately, 'languaging over' or 're-languaging'.

The connection between language, or putting into language, or putting into another language, and betrayal is thus present etymologically in Romance languages, less obvious in English, and absent in Afrikaans. However, the conceptual link between language, specifically translation, and betrayal is nowhere more apparent than in Afrikaans, where notions of linguistic and national identity have been fiercely contested right from the first concerted attempts by the Genootskap van Regte Afrikaners (GRA) to translate this (ironically creole) vernacular into regularized form in the newspaper first published in Paarl in 1875, the *Patriot*.[2] Ever since, the notion of the *regte* or *ware* Afrikaner ('true Afrikaner') has involved a complex set of identities with regard to birth land, nation, language, family, religion, race, and politics. Recent language historians, such as Achmat Davids, have emphasised the deliberate 'dutchification' of Afrikaans involved in the process of limiting the establishment variety of the language to whites and creating a racially exclusive subgroup of the Afrikaans speakers who identified themselves as Afrikaners.[3] In what follows, although I am aware of considerable problems arising from the simplification, I will be using the term *Afrikaner* to refer to white Afrikaans speakers.

From the last quarter of the nineteenth century through the Anglo-Boer War (1899–1902), the Second Language movement (ca. 1905–1925), the forming of the National Party, and the establishment of apartheid from 1948 until probably the sixties, Afrikaner identities were tightly bound up with patriarchal, authoritarian institutions of family, the Dutch Reformed Church, the National Party, and state education as well as military, industrial, and infrastructural institutions. Under apartheid it became habitual to talk of the 'laager' mentality of the Afrikaners, referring to the wagon circles used by the Voortrekkers to defend themselves as they trekked away from British control and into black South Africa. The Great Trek (ca. 1838 on) itself became the equivalent of the Exodus from Egypt, with Voortrekker leaders such as Piet Retief cast as Moses and the Volk as God's chosen people. Over time even outsiders came to adopt such similarly monolithic terms, describing the Afrikaners as the 'white tribe' of South Africa – although with negative connotations of the 'primitive' attached. By the time of the formation of the Republic of South Africa (1961) such stereotypes of the Afrikaner, whether with positive or negative connotations of Afrikanerdom, appeared as solid as the Voortrekker monument near Pretoria, his (because Afrikanerdom was intensely patriarchal) mind illuminated no less fleetingly or infrequently.[4] Of course the appearance was a constructed one, even a managed one, used in the ruling National Party's interest. Afrikaans was deployed rhetorically as defining the spirit of the Afrikaners, and appeals to this *Sprachgeist* worked remarkably successfully to unify this small group of people ('no more than the population of an average-sized American or European city' [de Klerk 1975: xiii]) into a reliable electorate united against the rest of the world. When P. W. Botha, for instance, presented to that electorate the notion that South Africa was faced with a 'total onslaught' from the rest of the world, his racially exclusive rhetoric might be seen as a 1980s extension of the linguistic self-fashioning of the Afrikaner

Volk. In particular it harked back to the post-Boer War period, when the movers and shakers of the Second Language movement turned anger against British attempts to eradicate Afrikaans to their own benefit. On that occasion, as Michael Chapman (1996: 117) has it, High Commissioner Alfred Milner's restrictive legislation 'so provoked Boer reaction that the survival of Afrikanerdom was ensured'.[5] Building the nation from words in the first few decades of the century involved a 'translation' of Afrikaans from the kitchen to the salon, the purification of a 'low', bastardised language into a high literary language. And in the same way that poets, such as C. J. Langenhoven and 'Totius' (J. D. du Toit), played a crucial role in this transformation, creating a unified Volk, so the poet Breytenbach has played a crucial role in dismantling the monolithic state apparatus that the creation of the Volk made possible. Indeed the process whereby this nation built from words undid itself and finally abandoned apartheid, the political system that had become what Jacques Derrida called 'Racism's last word,' seems to me to involve a new 'translation' of Afrikaans-ness, shifting the meaning of *Sprachgeist* and Volk once again.[6]

We are all familiar now with the ceremonial markers of this process as history – Nelson Mandela's walk to freedom after twenty-seven years of incarceration on February 11, 1990, and his subsequent inauguration in May 1994 as South Africa's first democratically elected president. Various factors are commonly held to have prompted the process, including South Africa's economic decline, itself variously the result of international sanctions and disinvestment, internal strikes, boycotts and stayaways, and the sheer cost of running apartheid.[7] On the political front the National Party was under pressure from all sides nationally and internationally, not least because the years from 1989 on had seen the collapse of communism in the Soviet Union and its East European satellites. Rob Nixon sees this latter factor – 'the collapse of the Communist/anti-Communist condominium' – as crucial because in the apparent discrediting of communism, the anticommunist rhetoric on which apartheid depended was no longer viable (Nixon 1994). Certainly the euphoria at the general election, genuine though it may have been, ought to have been tempered by the thought that apartheid's 'demise will not be credited only to the account of moral standards' (Derrida 1986a: 335). And Albie Sachs's warning that the denial of revolutionary change to South Africa's resistance movements might represent apartheid's last victory has, in many respects, been prophetic.[8] Whatever the case, one factor that has not received much attention is what I am calling the 'translation' of the Afrikaner mind, a process that allowed formerly heretical views to become unexceptional and former heretics to become heroes.

In defence of that totalising term *the Afrikaner mind*, I would draw attention again to the construction of a peculiarly monolithic social identity over the last 120 years or so, but I would also point out that that construction has not just been a case of self-definition. As my earlier reference to Lord Milner has suggested, the urgency for and success of Afrikaner self-definition was in reaction to external forces – not least to the racial and ethnic categorization of the English. Consequently, one factor that got in the way of 'translation' before 1990 was that an Afrikaner's sense of himself or herself as an individual could not be expressed in any other social grouping, that is, non-white, non-Calvinist, non-Afrikaans speaking, non-National Party supporting, anti-patriarchal. Johan Louw-Potgieter's 1988 social-psychological study of 'dissident Afrikaners' bears this out: only one of his small sample of twenty-one 'dissidents' *never* thought of himself as an Afrikaner or dissident Afrikaner; he could only replace that lost sense of social identity by thinking of himself rather optimistically as a 'world citizen' or else negatively as 'stateless' (Louw-Potgieter 1988: 59). Language remained the chief criterion of those who still defined themselves as Afrikaners, and Louw-Potgieter was surprised to 'find little evidence for one of the most obvious strategies of identity maintenance of disaffected group members, namely rejection of the in-group language' (ibid.: 66).

Although the power relations are different, it seems as though the reluctance to abandon the mother tongue arises from a sense of betrayal and guilt similar to that felt by African writers who wrote in English, French, or Portuguese. Ngugi wa Thiong'o (1986: 7) cites a speech by Chinua Achebe in 1964 in which Achebe asks: 'Is it right that a man should abandon his mother tongue for someone else's? It looks like a dreadful betrayal and produces a guilty feeling.' But whereas African writers writing in English at least had the consolation (Ngugi would see it perhaps as temptation) that their 'betrayal' rendered them able to use an international language, one whose specifically local, national *Sprachgeist* had been watered down, dissident Afrikaans writers in South Africa who *did not* betray their mother tongue aligned themselves with the language of the specifically local and national oppressor.[9] In this context Breytenbach's decision to recount his prison experience in English represents a deliberate attempt to distance himself from a language that by the 1970s no longer represented a formerly victimised imagined community but instead represented a brutal state apparatus. It also, as Louw-Potgieter's study indicates, suggests a psychological wrench no less massive than the intellectual wrench that drove Breytenbach to terrorism.

Indeed the case of Breytenbach illustrates the dissident Afrikaner problem perfectly, and Jack Cope is surely correct in his 1982 study to treat him as exemplary of the 'adversary within' Afrikanerdom. Recently turned sixty years old, Breytenbach is the grand old *enfant terrible* of Afrikaans letters, his career marked at all stages by a tension characteristic of late twentieth-century South African literature between the desire for aesthetic sophistication and political impact.[10] In the 1960s, when Breytenbach first came to prominence as a member of the avant-gardist Sestiger movement, local critics, while recognising his stature as the leading poet of his generation, objected to his 'imitative Euro-modernism' (Chapman 1996: 248), apparently wanting him to play the role of bard of the Volk assumed by earlier nationalist Afrikaans poets, such as J. D. du Toit ('Totius') and C. J. Langenhoven (author of the old national anthem 'Die Stem van Suid Afrika' ['The Voice of South Africa']). Breytenbach, however, would not be straitjacketed in that way. Not only did he refuse to stay within the fold by moving to Paris in the early 1960s, he further scandalised Afrikaner nationalist opinion by marrying a Vietnamese woman there. The marriage was, of course, illegal under South African law – even though it had taken place abroad – and Breyten and Yolande Breytenbach were not allowed to return to South Africa as husband and wife.

Breytenbach at this point still continued to write in Afrikaans and even from exile achieved a growing reputation in South Africa as one of the most significant and original Afrikaans poets. At the same time living in France also gave him unparalleled access to international literary circles. To this day he is easily the best-known Afrikaans poet outside South Africa, indeed one of the few whose work exists in translation. He is thus uniquely placed among Afrikaans writers: to put it crudely, while Afrikaner nationalists might have wanted to claim him as torchbearer for the language and its expressive capabilities, the international literary community (as represented by organisations such as PEN International) expected him to fulfil the role of the dissident, disowning the politics associated with Afrikanerdom. How Breytenbach used Afrikaans, and whether or not he used it, became important in a way not experienced by any other writer, even those fellow Sestigers André Brink and Etienne Leroux, whose provocatively anti-nationalist novels *Kennis van die Aand* (published in English as *Looking on Darkness*) and *Magersfontein, O Magersfontein* were banned in the 1970s.

Intellectually opposed to apartheid and personally victimised by it, Breytenbach's status as white Afrikaner, however, prevented him from feeling fully a part of the liberation struggle. When he was granted special dispensation to visit South Africa with Yolande in 1973, he was 'greeted by a fanfare of publicity, friendliness and overwhelming hospitality, unexpected and even overwhelming to the poet' (Cope 1982: 176). His fellow writers and friends told him that 'as a writer he had no alternative but to write, and leave politics and combat to those with the essential practical ability' (ibid.:177). While Breytenbach could make no such clear separation between writing and politics, the feeling that he was once more being sucked into white Afrikanerdom, that he'd merely been a slightly prodigal son, was impressed on him. (This was about the time Prime Minister B. J. Vorster responded to Brink's 'flaunting of religion and sex [by telling] the author to have his hair cut!' [Chapman 1996: 250]). For Breytenbach, the fact that he could not claim a South African identity outside his race was most forcibly impressed on him by the Coloured Afrikaans writer Adam Small, whose two-line poem – 'My wife is not a golden lotus / not even an ordinary flower' – drew attention to the way in which Breyten and Yolande's celebrity status removed them from the day-to-day sufferings of the majority of South Africans under apartheid (Cope 1982: 190).

Looking back on that time in *Confessions*, Breytenbach (1994 [1984]: 74) expressed the problem: 'How could I as a White man, express my opposition to the system, which means to the exploitation and the degradation, effectively, whilst identifying myself with the cause of the Black majority? How could I relate to them?' His response was to become an 'albino terrorist', setting up an organisation called Okhela specifically geared to 'creating forms of aid to militant White opposition to the Apartheid regime in the country, of establishing these points of aid abroad, of helping the White militants in obtaining a basic training when abroad, permitting them to carry on the struggle clandestinely upon their return to the country' (ibid.: 77).[11] His subsequent career as a terrorist was a spectacular failure. On returning to South Africa in 1975 under a false passport, sporting a beard and a phoney French accent, 'M. Galaska' was followed from the moment he landed, allowed to wander the country and incriminate friends and accomplices before being arrested at Jan Smuts Airport in August 1975. The friendly attention of a South African Airways hostess on his flight into South Africa seems to suggest that his cover was blown long before he left Europe.[12] Whatever the case, in Breytenbach we have the Afrikaner traitor par excellence. He was by no means the first or only dissident – Bram Fischer is an obvious earlier example,[13] and one whose impact is less indirect – but as an innovative user of Afrikaans in poetry, Breytenbach was the first whose betrayal could affect the *Sprachgeist*.

In her essay 'Acting Bits/Identity Talk,' Gayatri Spivak (1992: 785) talks about the 'cultural productivity' that arises as the result of the stripping of 'identity'. She is uneasy about being bound by notions of 'speaking as', for as soon as one 'speaks as' one is in danger of being neutralised (what one says is explained away in terms of an association made other by being known from the outside and from the outset). We might see Breytenbach's resort to 'terrorism' therefore as an attempt to break out of the neutralising hold of being seen as – whatever else he may have been – a white Afrikaner. Unable to see much 'cultural productivity' in 1973 arising from his exile in Paris, he strips himself of his identity and recasts himself as an albino terrorist. While the terrorism proved an ineffective act, however, his description *in English* of that experience and his subsequent seven and a half years in jail drove a treacherous wedge into the once monolithic linguistic construct of Afrikanerdom.

One factor that compounded the difficulty of this treacherous self-translation was that Breytenbach's identity with Afrikanerdom was of a particularly intimate, familial nature.[14] The figure of Jan Breytenbach, Breyten's military bigwig brother, is a formidable presence in *Confessions*, someone whom Breyten has to define himself against and with. At one point Breyten Breytenbach (1994 [1984]: 311) recounts that his father received a letter from South African prime minister Vorster rejecting a plea for Breyten's early release and consoling his father that at least he had one heroic son (Jan) to balance out the betrayal of Breyten. Literary father figures also took a keen interest in Breytenbach's experience. D. J. Opperman, Breytenbach's former mentor at the University of Cape Town, attended his second trial and visited him in jail despite being severely weakened by illness. On his visit to Breytenbach in jail, Opperman assured his former pupil that he 'was still alive as a poet, that there was interest for [his] work among the students, and . . . that it would be fatal for [him] to break entirely with the Afrikaners' (ibid.: 302).

With such pressure on him to stay within the fold of expressive literary Afrikaans, it is easy to see why Breytenbach might sound defeatist about his role as a writer. After all, the state was apparently so untroubled by what he was doing with words that they allowed the publication of the memoir of his 1973 visit (published in English as *A Season in Paradise* [1980]) and of a new collection of poems *Blomskryf* (1977). What the state did with words, by contrast, was brutally effective: the language of the law, in branding Breytenbach a traitor, sentenced him to nine years in jail. Faced with such disparity between the ineffectiveness of his own words and actions and the words and actions of the state, it is not surprising that Breytenbach (ibid.: 355) derided the earlier attention paid to his literary language as merely having 'helped entrench the reactionary forces in the country.'

While Breytenbach's scorn at his own literary effects appears to buy into standard divisions between the literary and the political, the polite and the brutal, the style and themes of *The True Confessions of an Albino Terrorist*, not least Breytenbach's use of the mirror in which one does not see oneself but sees one's other, deconstruct such divisions with suitably Derridean complexity. In 1982, when he was composing the book and recomposing himself after his jail term, Breytenbach seemed overwhelmed by the apparent futility of his writing as contrasted with the brutal reality of apartheid South Africa. He underestimated, however, the potential agency of his own words.

Before I attempt to demonstrate what *Confessions* does or comes to do politically, let me first give some analysis of it in literary terms. The book is written mainly in the form of a first-person meditation or address to 'Mr I', the Mr Interrogator/Investigator who is simultaneously Breytenbach's own 'I', his actual investigators and interrogators, and the inquisitive eye of the reader. To say it is written at all, though, is to be slightly misleading, as Breytenbach in a note on his composition of the book tells us that he had first of all talked the book into a tape and then edited from the transcripts drawn up by Yolande. 'Therefore, I was,' he writes, 'in the first instance, in all intimacy, talking to her; telling her all which I'd had to hold back over the years' (ibid.: 338). While such auto-referentiality calls into question the neat boundaries of speaking and writing, of single and joint authorship, of authenticity, completeness and accuracy, the use of the composite addressee within the main body of the text produces a radically unsettled speaking subject: first person, second person, and third person pronouns become virtually interchangeable. Quite early on in the book, for instance, in a three-page 'recapitulation', the speaker *becomes* Mr I., the interrogator/investigator who calls Breytenbach (now in the second person) 'the sheep that strayed,' who insists on their mutual knowledge, and who claims that their obsession to find out everything stems from 'lov[ing] you so'. This insidious voice says that 'it has been like this from the beginning of time – you and I entwined and related, parasite and prey. Image and mirror-image.' 'You are my book,' the voice says; 'I create your past' (ibid.: 57) Finally, the investigator's confidence and aggression disappear, to be replaced by a plea: 'Don't leave me alone! I am the Afrikaner. Why dost thou not love me?' (ibid.: 59).

Such slippages between grammatical subject positions occur throughout the text, blurring boundaries of identity and power and insisting on the unstable linguistic constructions both of Breytenbach's individual identity and of the Afrikaner's social identity. At one level is the rather ridiculous example of the police trying to get Breytenbach to give them the whereabouts of a certain fictional character called Panus, whom Breytenbach had created in 1971 in a prose piece called *Om te Vlieg* [In order to fly] (ibid.: 49). Such literary denial of stable, essential identities – whether individual or social, biographical or fictional – clearly repudiates the racial boundaries drawn by apartheid. Breytenbach's (ibid.: 74) serious play goes further, however, leading him to reject the kind of liberalism that, while apparently opposing apartheid, does so by still drawing boundaries between us and them: 'My revulsion of Apartheid could not only be because of what it is doing to all the "un-whites", could not be really resilient if moti-vated by a "do-good" approach, but because of how it was affecting *me*. The corruption of the elite is the corruption of privilege and ease and power and paternalism.'

In prison Breytenbach found all sorts of other boundaries collapsing, too. As an 'albino in a white land' (Breytenbach 1994 [1984]: 260), he was exposed to and exposes the horrendous brutality of prison life in apartheid South Africa, stressing over and over that that brutality was not freakish but 'typical of that mirror which the South African penal universe holds up to the Apartheid society' (ibid.: 273). Using the fable in which a frog reluctantly agrees to ferry a scorpion across a river only to be stung to death halfway across – the drowning scorpion claims he could not help himself being made that way – Breytenbach shows how the Afrikaner has destroyed himself by destroying others, that 'the Afrikaner is a product of the system which he has produced' (ibid.: 284).

That system allowed Breytenbach to continue writing while in prison (although under severe restrictions) 'for the sake of Afrikaans literature' (ibid.: 159). Remarkably enough given the stringent censorship laws, a number of Breytenbach's books appeared in Afrikaans and in translation while he was still in jail: collections of poems called *Voetskrif* (1976) and *Blomskryf* (1977) and the memoir of his 1973 visit *'n Seisoen in die Paradys* ('A Season in Paradise') (1980). Apparently some members of the Afrikaner establishment found it harder to stifle the expression of a fellow Afrikaner than they did the expression of non-Afrikaners. Breytenbach (ibid.) wonders if that decision was not 'a way of theirs to establish in their own minds their fairness', but nonetheless it il-lustrates again his significance to Afrikaans and hence to Afrikanerdom. Whatever the content of his words, the use of Afrikaans in itself and by a poet makes Breytenbach capable still of bearing the language forward. An extraordinary circularity here both brands him traitor to Afrikanerdom and simultaneously establishes him as representa-tive of Afrikanerdom's new tradition. Even after Breytenbach's second trial (when he was acquitted on a range of trumped up charges of attempted escape and continued subversion), he was allowed to continue writing as a result of 'persistent pressure by the literary establishment' (ibid.: 162).

Writing in prison though, under severe restrictions, and with the legal identity of traitor slapped on you, necessarily makes your writing change; as Spivak has it, the stripping of identity becomes culturally productive. At the most obvious level, this cul-tural productivity took the form of Breytenbach's writing for others, whether letters of appeal to the authorities or personal letters to loved ones. He even composed letters on behalf of some of his warders (ibid.: 169). That experience led Breytenbach to the con-clusion that 'a letter in prison is public property' (ibid.: 163) and that the value put on originality might be 'just a bourgeois vice' (ibid.: 168).[15]

It is the cultural productivity at the national level, though, that interests me. Breytenbach's experiences, resulting from his being legally defined as a traitor, helped him change the language and hence the culture of which he, as poet, was an exemplar. This despite Breytenbach's apparent repudiation of Afrikaans and Afrikanerdom in *Confessions*. For even though *The True Confessions of an Albino Terrorist* is written in English and shows greater affection for French than any other language, it still strikes me as a work of Afrikanerdom, albeit of a new kind of hybrid Afrikanerdom.[16] Given his treatment by other Afrikaners, it is not surprising that Breytenbach (ibid.: 280) wants to disidentify with them and declares, 'I do not consider myself an Afrikaner.' However, he is caught between his disavowal of himself as an Afrikaner as a 'political definition' and his awareness that 'Afrikaans is a means of communication intimately interacting with the specific characteristics of South African life and history, and enriching the land in a dialectic of mutual shaping' (ibid.: 354). It seems to me that Breytenbach's temporary refusal of Afrikaans – though understandable – was a pessimistic undervaluation of his cultural productivity.

Confessions remains an Afrikaans text in a number of ways. First, it still uses a number of Afrikaans phrases, especially those that are least translatable, such as slang phrases and direct translations into English of Afrikaans idioms. In both of these cases it might be argued that Breytenbach is merely bent on deriding Afrikaans and those proponents of the language who insist on the language's purity: the slang phrases, for instance, include such impure prison inventions as *holpond*, translating literally as 'arse pound' (ibid.: 227) to describe the anus when used as a hiding place, or *kakkebale* to describe hang gliders, whom the prisoners optimistically called on to *kak 'n baal* ('shit a bale') of *dagga* ('marijuana') into the prison as they flew overhead (ibid.: 178). Frequently, almost habitually, when Breytenbach records the language of insults, he does so by recording the Afrikaans term, for example, *Geduldige Poessoekers* ('patient cunt hunters') for GD-PS, the letters standing for *Gevangenisdiens* ('prison service') (ibid.: 224). Elsewhere Breytenbach (ibid.: 208) mocks the splenetic anger of one of his warders (the so-called Captain Sodom) by skilfully using free indirect speech: 'He's no fool, he assured me. He knows what goes for what. He's no doll and he wasn't born under a turkey either.' That last phrase, a direct translation from Afrikaans idiom, makes Sodom sound a good deal more ridiculous than an English equivalent phrase (say, 'he wasn't born yesterday') would have. Such cross-linguistic mockery was a staple of anti-Afrikaner ridicule in South Africa that assumed the makers of the jokes were much cleverer than 'the "hairybacks" and the "rock spiders"' (ibid.: 344).

These apparently derogatory traces of Afrikaans words in the text should not, however, be understood as representing Breytenbach's spite against the language itself. Quite the contrary, he writes in a three-page afterword, 'A Position on the Struggle for the *Taal* (being Afrikaans)': while 'official Afrikaans is the tool of the racist' (hence mocked and rejected), it is actually 'spoken by more so-called Coloureds, and in one form or another by a larger number of Blacks than there are Whites in the country,' and has 'escaped entirely from the control of the Afrikaners. In that shape it is a virile medium, ever being renewed, which so far finds but little reflection in the writing' (ibid.: 354). Breytenbach's emphasis on the impurity of the language, therefore, represents a position on language entirely consistent with his political position – rejecting linguistic and political ideologues who wish to categorise and control. Those impure prison neologisms are part and parcel of the Afrikaans that Breytenbach wants to speak – that 'means of communication intimately interacting with the specific characteristics of South African life and history' (ibid.) – even if they do not appear to belong in the vocabulary of those who 'pretend that Afrikaans is the youngest in the family of Germanic languages' (ibid.: 353).

More importantly than rejecting Afrikaans therefore, *Confessions* takes Afrikaans on in two ways: it tackles Afrikaans, and it advances it. It most explicitly tackles Afrikaans by squarely labelling the language as a Creole, as African as its name implies. Breytenbach thus undermines one of the fundamental myths of the Afrikaners as God's Chosen People, pure in every way. 'To be African is to be a bastard,' he writes. 'The heart of Africa is metamorphosis' (ibid.). Writing nearly a decade later, Rian Malan hammered Breytenbach's wedge further into the edifice of Afrikanerdom. The opening chapter of *My Traitor's Heart* (1991 [1990]) starkly repudiates notions of racial purity by describing the cross-racial nature of Malan's ancestry, a repudiation all the more powerful since Malan is the grandson of D. F. Malan, South Africa's first National Party prime minister.[17] In the same way that Malan's text finishes by providing a model of a new white African-ness – one without guarantees but a positive model nonetheless – Breytenbach's text with all its impurities forces a recognition that Afrikaans is not a European language with local variants (such as Small's 'Kaaps') but, as its name claims, an African one. At the time of writing *Confessions* Breytenbach was scathing about the 'charade' that *Sestiger* dissidence or contemporary white dissident writing 'could translate the South African reality.' He saw 'white writers – of the "liberal" kind – . . . getting a – personal – kick out of flouting some tribal taboos' (Breytenbach 1994 [1984]: 355). I would argue that while he may be right about the immediate effect, the longer view has shown that *Sestiger* betrayal *was* culturally productive, becoming a 'formation,' as Ampie Coetzee (1996: 108) has it, 'within which Afrikaner intellectuals could gradually develop their careful academic criticism of the system'. It wasn't a purely personal 'kick' but part of the extension of Afrikaans in democratic ways.

The extension is one similar to the extension and diffusion of all the languages of South Africa at the time. In thoroughly Foucauldian manner, the repressions of South African apartheid could not prevent the hybridising of all languages, and in fact, as Breytenbach's and other prison writers' work shows, the very repressions led to new forms of expression. Jeremy Cronin, whose multi-punning *Inside* (1983) recasts imprisonment into poetry, showed, as did Breytenbach, that even under scrutiny, even in solitary confinement, people find ways to communicate. Cronin's celebrated poem 'To learn how to speak' is a manifesto urging the use of a new language not limited to old orthodoxies and orthographies but open to the 'voices of this land', whether those use Afrikaans (words ending in '-kuil, -pan, -fontein'), Zulu ('songololo'), or township English ('the 5:15 ikwata bust fife / Chwannisberg train') (Bunn and Taylor 1987: 81–82).[18]

All of this might sound too glib, putting too fine a gloss on what was a vicious struggle in which 'treason' had a material definition and the likely outcome that one would be 'translated,' if not from life to death (with the possibility of further 'translation' to the pantheon of heroes), then at least from full health to a maimed state.[19] Breytenbach repeatedly stresses, for instance, that one does not 'survive' an incarceration such as his, and his text is full of references to those with him who went to the gallows or were otherwise tortured. However, culture is a weapon of struggle, and Breytenbach's traitorous self-translation can be reclaimed by progressive forces in the new South Africa who want to resist both the separatism of old-style Afrikaner nationalism and the neo-colonial dependency that would privilege English. Now more than ever the polyglot South Africa needs to remain in a perpetual state of treason and translation; let the eleven 'official' languages of the new state remain official, but let there also arise a hybridised, unofficial, unfixed, ever-changing South African language through which a new national sense can be created that avoids the racial exclusivity of the old nationalism.

As a first gesture to honour this new hybrid, may I suggest that the Afrikaans Taalmonument (which Breytenbach describes as an 'abomination' and 'insult') be spray-painted in rainbow colours and opened to the public for writing on in the same way that a prison wall can become a palimpsest of subversive and personal graffiti.[20] One of the first lines might be a quotation from Walter Benjamin (1969: 80): 'For the sake of pure language he breaks through decayed barriers of his own language.'

Notes

1   The Sestigers were a group of young Afrikaans writers, including Breyten Breytenbach and André Brink, who published together from 1963 on in a magazine, first called *Sestig* and later renamed *Sestiger*. As Jack Cope (1982: 100) sees it, 'The younger and more radical followers of the group wished to rid themselves of authority, to speak in their own authentic voice. Their theorising was influenced by French existentialism and their style by surrealism.'

2   One of the founders of the GRA, S. J. du Toit, saw the translation of the Bible as a primary requirement in the building of a civilised Afrikaans identity. It should also be noted that Afrikaans newspapers from the *Patriot* on have frequently insisted on the subjective affiliation of their readership with the land or social group. The first recognised poet to use Afrikaans as a medium for his verse, Eugene N. Marais, pushed for the use and recognition of Afrikaans through his newspaper *Land en Volk* [Land and people], while another of the leaders of the Second Afrikaans Language Movement, Gustav S. Preller, called his newspaper *De Volkstem* ['The People's Voice'] (Chapman 1996: 120). While modern South Africa's leading Cape Town Afrikaans-medium newspaper remains *Die Burger* ['The Citizen'], English-medium papers are *Mails, Timeses, Arguses, Despatches, Mercuries*, etc., all connoting objective observation and communication.

3   See Davids 1996. In that same issue of *Mutatu*, Vernon February also talks of the need to correct 'the distorted history of Afrikaans' (83).

4   In Breytenbach's (1994: 41) words the Voortrekker monument features a 'barbaric altar in the crypt upon which it is said a single shaft of light is calculated to fall on a certain day of the year to light up the chiselled words: "Ons vir jou Suid-Afrika"' ('We are yours, South Africa').

5   In attempting to ensure the dominance of the British element, politically and culturally, Milner proscribed Dutch as a medium of instruction in government schools (Davenport 1977:151). Pressure from Gustav Preller and other leaders of the Second Language Movement led to the eventual recognition of Afrikaans in 1925 as one of South Africa's official languages.

6   I am referring to the debate originally conducted in *Critical Inquiry* 12, no. 1, and 13, no. 1, between Jacques Derrida and (jointly) Anne McClintock and Rob Nixon, which deals with the National Party government's attempts to avoid using the word *apartheid* to describe its policies. Derrida insists that 'whether or not the term is pronounced by South African officials, *apartheid* remains the *effective* watchword of power in South Africa' (Derrida 1986b: 361).

7   See the McClintock-Nixon-Derrida debate for an analysis of the cost of running apartheid, with particu-
     lar reference to the possibility that those costs may actually have supported capitalism in South Africa (see
     esp. McClintock and Nixon 1986: 346–52).

8   Many commentators have remarked that in averting revolution in South Africa the ruling elite in fact
     salvaged their power, a claim backed up, for instance, by the fact that 90 percent of the capital, 95 percent
     of industry, and four-fifths of the farms in South Africa are still white owned. For a poetic expression of
     disappointment in the lack of change in the new South Africa, see Jeremy Cronin's (1996: 11) recent poem
     'Even the Dead', which among other things brilliantly juxtaposes extracts from South African newspapers
     with a quotation from Walter Benjamin: 'Only that historian will have the gift of fanning some sparks of
     hope in the past who is firmly convinced that even the dead will not be safe from the enemy if he wins.
     And this enemy has not ceased to be victorious.'

9   This dilemma was even more awkward for black Afrikaans writers, whose social identity, due to the nature
     of apartheid, was defined more obviously by race than by language. In 1987 Hein Willemse recorded that
     'since 1944 only fourteen black Afrikaans writers, mostly poets, have published their work' (Bunn and
     Taylor 1987: 241).

10   In the post-apartheid period Breytenbach has continued to be a major player in South African letters, criti-
     cal both of the current government and of residual Afrikaner uptightness. In a remarkably productive peri-
     od he has, among other things, been one of the prime movers of the annual Durban Poetry Festival, which
     attracts poets from around the world, and has continued to scandalise conservative opinion through his
     work. As Charl Blignaut (1998) says in a review of *Boklied*, staged at the Klein Karoo Kunstefees in 1998,
     'Love him or hate him, Breytenbach has furthered the cause of Afrikaans literature, that even his critics
     can't deny.'

11   The designation *albino* appears to be an attempt by Breytenbach to reconceive his whiteness as freakish
     rather than normative. Okhela presumably took its name from the Zulu term *ukokhela*, which means to
     start a fire or to bring fire-starting materials on behalf of someone else. (I am grateful to Anthony O'Brien
     of Queen's College, City University of New York, for this information.)

12   Evidence presented to the Truth and Reconciliation Commission indicates that 'air hostesses of the state
     carrier, South African Airways, were required or put under pressure to eavesdrop on passengers' conversa-
     tions and to report those of a suspicious nature to the security police' (Truth and Reconciliation Commis-
     sion 1999, 5: 220).

13   Brilliant scion of a prominent Afrikaner family from the Orange Free State, Fischer became a Communist
     in the 1930s and acted as lead counsel in defending Nelson Mandela and his co-accused in the lengthy
     Treason Trial at the end of the 1950s. Fischer himself was subsequently tried under the Suppression of
     Communism Act, was sentenced to life imprisonment in May 1966, and died of cancer in 1975. His life,
     recently the subject of a biography by Stephen Clingman (2000), provided the model for Lionel Burger in
     Nadine Gordimer's novel *Burger's Daughter* (1979).

14   In some ways this would be a commonplace remark, given the smallness and insularity of the Afrikaner
     population. All three historians of Afrikaner identity (Rian Malan, W. A. de Klerk, and Marq de Villiers)
     whose work I have consulted for this essay have family connections with Afrikaner heroes and leaders.
     The name of the clique that ran apartheid South Africa, the *Broederbond* (band of brothers), may not be
     entirely literal but is certainly more than metaphorical.

15   Breytenbach's breakdown of the notions of public/private, written/oral seems in keeping with other trends
     in South African literature over the last twenty years or so, not least the collaboration in *Die Swerfjare van
     Poppie Nongena* (1987 [1978]) where the white Afrikaans author Elsa Joubert published in novel form the
     life story of her black Afrikaans-speaking maid Poppie Nongena. The two women struck a deal whereby
     Joubert claimed the literary credit, but Nongena got R2 000 to build a house. At the same time (from the
     late 1970s on) interest in oral poetry increased, especially in the opportunities for adapting local tradi-
     tions of praise singing to trade unionism, protest, and so on. The polyglot, multi-viewpoint narration of

Marlene van Niekerk's award-winning *Triomf* (1994) also depends on the irregularity of spoken language in all its scatological richness. Such trends in literary expression also seem to me to be in keeping with the trend of South African historians to distrust documentary evidence (almost exclusively European) or at least to amend it with oral records, and the compilation of transcripts from the hours of testimony to the Truth and Reconciliation Commission represents a very significant shift toward granting value to the demotic. I am also reminded of the determination of Zoë Wicomb, author of *You Can't Get Lost in Cape Town* (2000 [1987]), to move away from Western notions of 'elevated writing' and to concentrate on promoting literacy rather than literature in the new South Africa (quoted in Raiskin 1996: 231).

16   For example, Breytenbach records that in jail reading French, any French, was like being back home (Breytenbach 1994 [1984]: 168), and he recalls the annual experience of talking to Red Cross officials in French as one of great 'joy' (ibid.: 206).

17   Following Breytenbach, a kind of subgenre of Afrikaans confessional works has developed, including the African National Congress (ANC) activist Carl Niehaus *Om te Veg vir Hoop* ['Fighting for hope'] (1993) and the poet/broadcaster Antjie Krog's *Country of My Skull* (1998).

18   While this essay has concentrated exclusively on male writers, it is worth noting that women writers have also been influential in translating/betraying Afrikaans. Hein Willemse and Christell Stander trace a counter-patriarchal tradition in women's writing back to the 1920s and 1930s through trade union journals, such as that of the garment workers' union. Such class- and gender-based writing involved affiliations that were not solely intra-Volk. Jack Cope (1982: 80–81) describes how Ingrid Jonker's work in the fifties resisted Afrikaner patriarchy and identified her with the dispossessed. More recently Antjie Krog betrayed Afrikaner sexual decorum by producing 'explicit and erotic verse', betrayed Afrikaner linguistic purity by utilising Sotho verse forms, myths, and vocabulary (Bunn and Taylor 1987: 33), and defiantly used 'her talents in the service of underprivileged but culturally hungry and creatively hopeful members of the black community' (van der Merwe 1996: 121). Krog's work as a reporter on the Truth and Reconciliation Commission and her subsequent book *Country of My Skull* (1998) also provoked the ire of old-style white Afrikaner nationalists. Joan Hambidge is the first out lesbian Afrikaner woman poet. The boundaries have been tumbling.

19   Cronin (1998: 40), for instance, remains resolutely materialist, sceptical about Breytenbach's current work in South Africa. He credits Breytenbach as 'our most accomplished lyricist able to invest landscape and sexuality with a great anarchic surge of libidinal energy,' but considers such 'libidinal subversion' too erratic to transform and democratise South Africa.

20   Breytenbach's (1994 [1984]: 242) full description of the monument is: 'The granite penis erected against the flank of the mountain above Paarl, that finger in the eye, is an abomination, and not only an insult to anybody's aesthetic feelings but also an incredibly obtuse and insensitive and arrogant insult to the non-Afrikaner people of South Africa.' The monument was inaugurated on October 10, 1975, to mark the centenary of the first Afrikaans language movement. Its architect, Jan van Wyk, claimed that it stood for a 'language not a race' and imagined its iconography would indicate the Creole nature of Afrikaans, with a small wall in the middle that was 'neither magical Africa nor enlightened West . . . that's the Malayan language and culture from the East' (Goldblatt 1998: 247). Breytenbach's comments indicate that van Wyk's message did not come across clearly.

References

Benjamin, Walter
    1969 *Illuminations* (New York: Schocken).
Blignaut, Charl
    1998 'Time of the Signs', *Mail and Guardian*, April 16 (available online at http://www. mg.co.za/mg/art/theatre/p804/f/980416-boklied.html).

Breytenbach, Breyten
　　1971 *Om te Vlieg* (Cape Town: Buren).
　　1976 *Voetskrif* (Doornfontein: Perskor).
　　1977 *Blomskryf* (Johannesburg: Taurus).
　　1980 *A Season in Paradise* (New York: Persea).
　　1994 [1984] *The True Confessions of an Albino Terrorist* (San Diego: Harcourt Brace).
Brink, André
　　1974 *Looking on Darkness* (London: W. H. Allen).
Bunn, David, and Jane Taylor, eds.
　　1987 *From South Africa: New Writing, Photographs, and Art* (Evanston: Northwestern University Press).
Chapman, Michael
　　1996 *Southern African Literatures* (London: Longman).
Clingman, Stephen
　　2000 *Bram Fischer: Afrikaner Revolutionary* (Amherst: University of Massachusetts Press). Coetzee, Ampie
　　1996 'Afrikaans Literature in the Service of Ethnic Politics?' *Matatu* 15/16: 117–140.
Cope, Jack
　　1982 *The Adversary Within: Dissident Writers in Afrikaans* (Cape Town: David Philip).
Cronin, Jeremy
　　1996 'Even the Dead', *New Coin* 32(2): 5–11.
　　1998 'Interview', *New Coin* 34 (2): 33–41.
Davenport, T. R. H.
　　1977 *South Africa: A Modern History* (Johannesburg: Macmillan).
Davids, Achmat
　　1996 'Laying the Lie of the 'Boer' Language: An Alternative View of the Genesis of Afrikaans,' *Matatu* 15/16: 13–58.
De Klerk, W. A.
　　1975 *The Puritan in Africa* (Harmondsworth: Penguin).
Derrida, Jacques
　　1986a 'Racism's Last Word', in *Race, Writing and Difference*, edited by Henry Louis Gates, Jr., 329–38 (Chicago: University of Chicago Press).
　　1986b 'But, beyond ... (Open Letter to Anne McClintock and Rob Nixon)', in *Race, Writing and Difference*, edited by Henry Louis Gates, Jr., 354-69 (Chicago: University of Chicago Press).
De Villiers, Marq
　　1988 *White Tribe Dreaming: Apartheid's Bitter Roots as Witnessed by Eight Generations of an Afrikaner Family* (New York: Viking).
February, Vernon
　　1996 'The Many Voices of the Land', *Matatu* 15/16: 73–90.
Goldblatt, David
　　1998 *South Africa: The Structure of Things Then* (New York: Monacelli).
Gordimer, Nadine
　　1979 *Burger's Daughter* (London: Jonathan Cape).
Joubert, Elsa
　　1987 [1978] *Poppie Nongena* (New York: Henry Holt).
Krog, Antjie
　　1998 *Country of My Skull: Guilt, Sorrow and the Limits of Forgiveness in the New South Africa* (New York: Random House).
Leroux, Etienne
　　1983 [1976] *Magersfontein, O Magersfontein* (Wynberg: Hutchinson).

Louw-Potgieter, Johan
    1988 *Afrikaner Dissidents: A Social Psychological Study of Identity and Dessent* (Bristol: Multilingual Matters).
Malan, Rian
    1991 [1990] *My Traitor's Heart: A South African Exile Returns Home to Face His Country, His Tribe, and His Conscience* (New York: Vintage).
McClintock, Anne, and Rob Nixon
    1986 'No Names Apart: The Separation of Word and History in Derrida's "Le Dernier Mot du Racisme"', in *'Race', Writing and Difference*, edited by Henry Louis Gates Jr., 339–53 (Chicago: University of Chicago Press).
Ngugi wa Thiong'o
    1986 *Decolonising the Mind: The Politics of Language in African Literature* (London: James Currey).
Niehaus, Carl
    1993 *Om te Veg vir Hoop* (Cape Town: Human and Rousseau).
Nixon, Rob
    1994 *Homelands, Harlem and Hollywood: South African Culture and the World Beyond* (New York: Routledge).
Raiskin, Judith
    1996 *Snow on the Cane Fields: Women's Writing and Creole Subjectivity* (Minneapolis: University of Minnesota Press).
Sachs, Albie
    1990 *Soft Vengeance of a Freedom Fighter* (London: Grafton).
Spivak, Gayatri Chakravorty
    1992 'Acting Bits/Identity Talk', *Critical Inquiry* 18: 770–803.
Truth and Reconciliation Commission
    1999 *Truth and Reconciliation Commission of South Africa Report*, International Ed., 5 vols. (London: Macmillan).
Van der Merwe, Philip
    1996 'What the Canon Saw: Socio-Political History, Afrikaans Poetry and its Great Tradition', *Matatu* 15/16: 117–140.
Van Niekerk, Marlene
    1999 [1994] *Triomf* (London: Little, Brown).
Wicomb, Zoë
    2000 [1987] *You Can't Get Lost in Cape Town* (New York: Feminist Press).
Willemse, Hein, and Christell Stander
    1992 'Winding through Nationalism, Patriarchy, Privilege and Concern: A Selected Overview of Afrikaans Women Writers', *Research in African Literatures* 23 (3): 5–24.

NINE

Narrative Time and the Space of the Image: The Truth of the Lie in Winnie Madikizela-Mandela's Testimony before the Truth and Reconciliation Commission

Dirk Klopper

1

> When the past speaks it always speaks as an oracle.
>
> Friedrich Nietzsche, *Beyond Good and Evil*

South Africa's Interim Constitution, adopted in 1993 as the basis for a new democratic order, made provision in its final clause for the establishment of a mechanism whereby amnesty would be granted to those guilty of committing human rights violations associated with political objectives. The cutoff date was determined as 'after 8 October 1990 and before 6 December 1993'. The motivation for this provision was 'that there is a need for understanding but not for vengeance, a need for reparation but not for retaliation, a need for *ubuntu* (the African philosophy of humanism) but not for victimisation' (Krog 1998: vi). A year later parliament's Justice Portfolio Committee drafted legislation establishing a Truth and Reconciliation Commission.

The TRC, as it came to be called, was given several interlocking tasks. It was to conduct investigations and hold hearings into the causes, nature, and extent of human rights violations committed between March 1, 1960, and the cutoff date, the purpose being to gain as complete a picture as possible of the recent past under apartheid rule. It was to grant amnesty to persons who had committed acts of human rights violations in the specified period, provided these acts had been politically motivated and applicants made full disclosure of the relevant facts. It was to recommend appropriate reparation to apartheid victims. Finally, the TRC was to compile a report of its findings and recommend measures to prevent future human rights violations. It had at its disposal an investigative unit and a research unit and was granted the power to subpoena persons to appear before special hearings.

It was before such a special hearing that Winnie Madikizela-Mandela appeared to account for the activities of the Mandela United Football Club, a group of township youngsters closely associated with her in the late 1980s and early 1990s. The 'football club' acted as Madikizela-Mandela's personal bodyguard. Members of the club lived at the Mandela house and embarked on a reign of terror in the area and beyond, imposing their own form of revolutionary praxis on township residents and punishing so-called 'informers' and 'collaborators'. Several children subsequently went missing or were discovered dead. The TRC asked Madikizela-Mandela to explain. Although she made her appearance in an event broadcast live on SABC TV3 over three days, she failed to disclose any new information or to reveal her role in the events. Instead, she engaged doggedly in an elaborate hoax of deferral, evasion, displacement, and denial, finally apologising reluctantly and vaguely for whatever it was that had 'gone wrong'.

The present article seeks to analyse the rhetoric of the lie and to ask whether or not the lie paradoxically reveals some order of truth in the way that the psychoanalytic symptom, for example, may be said both to conceal and to reveal the truth, albeit a structural and relational truth rather than an empirical and objective truth. Formulation of the problem in terms of paradox is intended to draw attention to a division that characterises both the TRC function, as the next section will demonstrate, as well as TRC studies. Antithetical views exist around such issues as the objectives, composition, and methodology of the TRC and the implications these have for the delivery of truth. Such differences of perspective are evident in two published works on the TRC, Antjie Krog's *Country of My Skull* (1998) and Anthea Jeffery's *The Truth About the Truth Commission* (1999).

For two years Krog served as special reporter on TRC activities for SABC radio as well as the *Mail and Guardian* newspaper, spending months on end in intimate contact with the TRC's proceedings countrywide, sleeping fitfully in anonymous hotel rooms, and sitting through hours of harrowing testimony in remote halls. *Country of My Skull* offers a subjective account of the significance of these TRC hearings. Employing postmodern techniques of self-remembering, reflexivity, fragmentation, pastiche, and metanarrative, it is itself testimony of the author's own implication in the reality the work seeks to convey. When, after offering an account of a session with radio staff who were 'breaking down,' the narrator is accused of distorting the truth of what happened, she replies:

> 'Yes, I know, it's a new story that I constructed from all the other information I picked up over the months about people's reactions and psychologists' advice. I'm not reporting or keeping minutes. I'm telling. If I have to say every time that so-and-so said this, and then at another time so-and-so said that, it gets boring. I cut and paste the upper layer, in order to get the second layer told, which is actually the story I want to tell. I change some people's names when I think they might be annoyed or might not understand the distortions.'

> 'But then you're not busy with the truth!'

> 'I am busy with the truth . . . my truth. Of course, it's quilted together from hundreds of stories that we've experienced or heard about in the past two years. Seen from my perspective, shaped by my state of mind at the time and now also by the audience I'm telling the story to. In every story there is hearsay, there is a grouping together of things that didn't necessarily happen

together, there are assumptions, there are exaggerations to bring home the enormities of situations, there is downplaying to confirm innocence. So also the lies. And the stories that date from earlier times.'

(Krog 1998: 170–171)

Distortions, lies, and narrative interference. In terms of presentation and intent, Jeffery's work could not differ more decisively from Krog's project. While commending the TRC for exposing apartheid atrocities and for providing victims with relief in allowing them to tell their own stories, *The Truth About the Truth Commission* employs an incisive analytical style to criticise the inadequacy of the TRC procedures and conclusions, showing how the TRC failed to observe basic legal principles of impartiality and admissible evidence and drawing attention to its irregularities and contradictions. It adopts a sceptical attitude toward the TRC's differentiation of truth into four orders. To the conventional legal requirement of 'factual and objective truth', the TRC had, according to Jeffery 1999, added 'social or dialogue truth' (arrived at through 'interaction, discussion and debate') and 'narrative truth' (perceptions, stories and the meaning and of facts 'within the context of human relations'). *The Truth About the Truth Commission* suggests that allowance for such forms of untested assertion leads ultimately to obfuscation and bias.

Attempting to determine the truth of the lie could be construed, from Jeffercy's perspective, as simply adding to the confusion. Yet a kind of creative confusion may define the nature of the subject under consideration. The *Truth About the Truth Commission* reveals that, in the cases of many important instances of human rights violations that appeared before the TRC, judicial investigations had already done more thorough investigation than TRC could hope to achieve. If the objective truth of events could be, and in many instances had been, arrived at through more rigorous legal processes, why hold the TRC proceedings in the first place? The TRC would always have a symbolic value over and the beyond its legalistic functions. What perhaps had not been foreseen is the way in which the TRC would allow its confessional and therapeutic functions to dictate the kind of truth it was to discover. In a sense the TRC proceedings were hijacked from the legal sphere. This was bound to occur if the TRC was to become a vehicle of reconciliation rather than a bureaucracy of information processing. It came to play its own role outside the control of the politician and managed in the process to offend those of opposing political persuasions, from F. W. de Klerk to Thabo Mbeki.

No doubt exists as to the extent to which Archbishop Desmond Tutu's influence, as chairperson, prevailed on the functioning and tone of the TRC. Krog's account makes explicit reference to his incisive presence. But the role of the media in shaping the TRC process cannot be excluded. Apart from the evening news bulletins on television and the daily newspaper reports, SABC TV3 also ran an hour-long TRC Special Report on Sunday nights. The public was saturated with images of victims and perpetrators as the past was displayed and dissected. Tutu's style, his restrained flamboyance, fitted well with media requirements, especially the visual media, and he featured prominently, dressed in scarlet robes, showing an expressive demeanour, calling on the rainbow nation to embrace the healing processes of disclosure and forgiveness, and offering tough love as an alternative to secrecy, pain, and guilt. Given that the TRC proceedings became a public spectacle, it is not difficult to see that its orders of social, narrative, and healing truth were a necessary response to an actual situation. The circumstances called for a flexible system employing situational criteria responsive to the complex interplay of a range of psychic factors and social needs.

When Jacques Lacan (1977c) invokes truth, it is as an appeal to the subject's own truth, the truth that confers upon the subject the capacity for 'full speech' and that results from his or her having 'assumed' his or her history. The term *assumes* carries echoes of a miraculous 'assumption,' and indeed Lacan's text is shot through with such redemptive terms as *grace* and *love*. Lacan shows how the history of the subject is recoverable through metaphor, in such forms as bodily symptoms, archival images, communal myths, and personal linguistic turns. In contrast with what Lacan calls 'empty speech' associated with the formal system of language, in which the subject is merely objectified, 'full speech' implicates the subject by providing him or her with a space from which he or she is able to speak as himself or herself.

A noteworthy correspondence exists between Lacan's notions of 'empty speech' versus 'full speech' and Walter Benjamin's 'empty time' versus the 'time of the now'. Benjamin's essay 'Theses on the Philosophy of History' (1968: 256) employs a similar vocabulary of redemption in describing a liberatory act in which mankind 'receives the fullness of its past'. The correspondence is more significant, however, than a mere convergence of terms. It resides also in Benjamin's structural view of the 'time of the now' and his characterisation of 'empty time' as 'homogeneous' and formally 'recitative', like the sequential telling of 'the beads of a rosary' (255). As in Lacan, liberation occurs through a reconfiguration of the past from the point of view of the present.

Benjamin argues that the past cannot be apprehended 'the way it really was'. Instead, memory is seized 'as it flashes up at a moment of danger'. Such access to memory is mediated by the image, which occurs 'at an instant when it can be recognised and is never seen again' (257). Recognition of the image momentarily arrests the temporal flow of thought and replaces the progression of time with a static configuration. Arrested in this way by the force of the image, the thought process crystallises into a 'structure' in which it is possible, says Benjamin, to recognise the sign of 'a Messianic cessation of happening' (265). To paraphrase Benjamin, one might say that by way of the image the past is recognised in the present, and this recognition leads to an apocalyptic end of linear time.

Tutu has projected the TRC as potentially ushering in a similarly redeemed mankind. In this context strict legal procedure becomes superfluous if not obstructive. But if the legal procedure is jettisoned, everything rests on the efficacy of the project of social redemption. Did the TRC deliver a redemptive history? Lacan's vocabulary of redemption is partly ironic, and he is careful to maintain a distinction between the imaginary event, conceived of as plenitude, and the symbolic event, which presupposes difference and loss. This is not true, however, of Benjamin's vocabulary of redemption, which is ambiguous rather than ironic. In fact his image of redemption comes perilously close at times to Lacan's imaginary captivation. The characteristic indeterminacy of Benjamin's style is evident in his celebrated description of the 'angel of history':

> His face is turned toward the past. Where we perceive a chain of events, he sees one single catastrophe, which keeps piling wreckage upon wreckage and hurls it in front of his feet. The angel would like to stay, awaken the dead, and make whole what has been smashed. But a storm is blowing from Paradise; it has got caught in his wings with such violence that the angel can no longer close them. This storm irresistibly propels him into the future to which his back is turned, while the pile of debris before him grows skyward. This storm is what we call progress.
>
> (Ibid.: 259–60)

Claudia Braude (1996) suggests that Benjamin's image of the angel of history should be interpreted as a psychoanalytic figure and that this figure may be employed to represent the workings of the TRC. She describes the angel as confronting 'a traumatic past in order to heal the associated traumas' (43), and identifies the angel with the historical materialist, arguing that 'the historical materialist's production of a redeemed history, citable in all its moments, and the angel of history's recognition of the need to treat the wreckage of the past before moving into the future are concerned with the same thing: creating a redeemed, intact society, free from the baggage and lies of the past' (ibid.). The TRC is similarly concerned with creating such a redeemed society.

But the angel of history is described in more equivocal terms than allowed for by Braude. Why, in Benjamin's description, is the angel ineffectual? Why is he unable 'to stay, awaken the dead, and make whole what has been smashed'? Benjamin attributes the angel's failure to the inexorable progression of linear time, a storm that blows from 'Paradise' and 'propels him into the future to which his back is turned'. If the storm propels him into the future, it must be blowing from the past, which is where paradise is therefore located, right in the midst of the catastrophe that transfixes the angel and renders him impotent. Braude's identification of the angel of history with the historical materialist ironically incapacitates the latter. First, as the qualifying 'But a storm' indicates, the angel is impotent in the face of disaster. Second, the reference of the pronoun *we* in 'Where we perceive a chain of events, he sees one single catastrophe' is unclear, rendering ambiguous the identity of the angel himself, who is defined precisely in relation to the *we*. Third, the angel has his back to the future. In this he is only partially like Benjamin's (1968: 256) 'redeemed mankind' who, although it has received 'the fullness of its past,' is oriented not toward the past but toward 'Judgement Day', a future end of time.

This much is true also of Lacan's (1977c: 48) psychoanalytic subject, for whom 'conjectures about the past are balanced against promises of the future'. The angel of history has been transfixed by a catastrophe located in the past and, as he is blown into the future backwards, keeps piling wreckage at his feet. He is indeed a psychoanalytic figure but not in the sense intended by Braude. The catastrophe that produces the debris of broken images before which he stiffens suggests loss rather than 'fullness', the absence of phallic plenitude. The storm emanates from a lost paradise, and loss of phallic plenitude is what constitutes the catastrophe, one marked by broken images that spellbind the angel. Lacan speaks of these images of the fragmented body as invested with a magical, captivating effect. The angel is fixated on a primal catastrophe that is reiterated in the present and extends indefinitely into the future. He desires to gather the fragments and make them whole again but is riveted by the horror to which he is witness. Thus he is engaged not in an act of reconstruction but in an act resembling that of pathological mourning. It may be that the TRC is also a kind of 'angel of history' and that a similarly incapacitating melancholia characterises its dream of a recoverable unity, a redeemed humankind.

With its unconscious loss, its ambivalent structure of narcissistic self-absorption and self-depletion, its avolition, and its impotence (Freud 1953a), melancholia characterises in a clinically precise manner the cataleptic posture assumed by the angel of history. The angel at once invokes and punishes his desire for imaginary plenitude, endlessly reiterating the catastrophic event that severs him from paradise. He appears to be assaulted repeatedly by an event that propels him backward into the future, rendering him unable to close his wings against the force of the storm. It could be that the TRC hearings have delivered just the kind of wreckage that traumatises the angel of history. Krog's account of the TRC hearings reveals the danger of inner fragmentation that intense exposure to the testimonies may bring about. As a symptom of inner fragmentation, she cites loss of speech: 'Naturally and unnaturally without words. Stunned by the knowledge of the price people have paid for their words' (Krog 1998: 49).

Psychoanalysis holds out the hope that such loss of speech is recoverable through analysis of the symptom, that analysis of the symptom will yield the truth of the lie and thereby restore the 'full word'. That the truth in question is not a positivist concern with 'the way it really was' is evident in Lacan's (1977e: 48) remark that 'in psychoanalytic anamnesis, it is not a question of reality, but of truth'. In terms of this truth, the subject 'brings back into present time the origins of his own person' (ibid.: 47) and in thus assuming his or her history is said to 'reorder past contingencies by conferring on them the sense of necessities to come' (ibid.: 48). Lacan draws attention here to synchronicity rather than to succession. The subject assumes his or her history not through the adoption of a temporal narrative but through a structural reordering of experience and life. In this he or she is like Benjamin's 'redeemed mankind', who has assimilated the past into the present, rather than like the ineffectual angel, who remains traumatised by the past.

The question arises as to the kind of knowledge appropriate to the analytical subject. Lacan (1977a: 17) proposes the notion of paranoiac knowledge, saying it corresponds 'to certain critical moments that mark the history of man's mental genesis, each representing a stage in objectifying identification'. Being that which 'constitutes the ego and its objects with attributes of permanence, identity and substantiality' (ibid.), paranoiac knowledge arises when the subject 'fixes upon himself an image that alienates him from himself' (ibid.: 19). It is this paradoxical knowledge of plenitude and loss that a psychoanalytic perspective on Winnie Madikizela-Mandela's evasive appearance before the TRC would seek to deliver, showing what the significance is of the structure of the lie.

Lacan says the subject of analysis is given 'one more opportunity to alienate himself' (Lacan 1977c: 71) so, paradoxically, he or she may find himself or herself: 'I identify myself in language, but only by losing myself in it like an object. What is realised in my history is not the past definite of what was, since it is no more, or even the present perfect of what has been in what I am, but the future anterior of what I shall have been or what I am in the process of becoming' (ibid.: 86). To envisage this future anterior, one must imagine not the melancholic figure of an angel of history, for whom no future exists, but a voice speaking from the void of the past, a past that, as Benjamin (1968: 256) says, has 'become citable in all its moments.' Such a citation is clearly not to be found in the law report, for it is not a matter of what really happened but of how what has happened has been construed by the TRC to form the basis of a new social order. It concerns, that is, the kind of social order the TRC seeks to create.

2

> There is a strong impulse in the country, supported and sustained by the media, for a grand concluding narrative.
>
> Ingrid de Kok, 'Cracked Heirlooms: Memory on Exhibition'

Summing up the findings of the conference at which the principles underlying the TRC were established, Alex Boraine makes reconciliation contingent on truth:

> Reconciliation begins when people deal with the past rather than simply ignoring it or trying to conceal it . . . An act of remembrance is not necessarily morbid; it could be liberating for the victims of injustice as well as for the perpetrators . . . To know the truth is to counter the deceit, the cover-ups, which characterised much of oppression in South Africa. In this sense, truth is the beginning of reconciliation . . . The search for truth is much more a matter of caring for the victims than even the pursuit of justice. To ignore what happened to thousands of people who were victims of abuse under apartheid is to deny them their basic dignity. It is to condemn them to live as nameless victims with little or no chance to begin their lives over again.
>
> (Boraine, Levy, and Scheffer 1994: 152–53)

For Boraine the conjunction *and* linking the nouns *truth* and *reconciliation* marks a temporal-causal relation. In this conception truth precedes and is a precondition for reconciliation. How the truth is understood and may be accessed is only partly addressed by Boraine. He refers to the testimony of human rights victims and abusers, evidence from security files, which may be incomplete and full of deceit, and information supplied by human rights organisations. The truth is regarded as that which actually happened, as 'the way it really was'. The process of truth and reconciliation is conceived in terms of a linear logic: in the act of apprehending truth, reason yields understanding; understanding is a reconciliatory activity as it synthesises diverse information into conceptual wholes. Thus truth leads to understanding, and understanding leads to reconciliation.

From the outset then the TRC was conceived as a legal commission that uses juridical conceptions of evidence and inference to arrive at justice. As in a court of law, legitimate evidence is that which can be established as verifiable, noncontradictory, and coherent fact. From such evidence alone, may inferences be made about the truth of events? But, as Jeffery has shown, the juridical function of the TRC proved inherently limited. Boraine seems to recognise in advance its inherent juridical limitation when he slides from the notion of 'justice' to that of 'caring' as definitional of the 'search for truth'. The notion of 'caring' for victims, of 'healing' victims and perpetrators, as Boraine (ibid.: xv) also puts it, alludes to a level of functioning of the TRC that is not legal but psychological. At this level the TRC functions as a therapeutic commission that uses the practice of cathartic disclosure to uncover the truth and to exorcise the pain. Here the truth is conceived as emotional and inward, as a subjective experience rather than an objective fact. This kind of truth brings regeneration, giving victims a 'chance to begin their lives over again'. The rhetoric verges on the religious, and the subtext contains implications of confession, absolution, and spiritual rebirth. Ingrid de Kok (1998: 60) observes that the TRC is saturated with the symbolic enactment of healing in its 'semi-religious staging, its confessional syntax, and its many clerical commissioners'. Max du Preez (1997b) calls the TRC chairperson, Archbishop Desmond Tutu, the 'priest of the nation'. Krog (1998: 259) adopts an openly reverential attitude toward Tutu and at one point is stirred by him to exclaim: 'Ah, the Commission! The deepest heart of my heart.'

As evidenced in the commentary on the works of Krog and Jeffery respectively, the juridical and the therapeutic functions of the TRC are uneasily combined. Each has its own separate logic or temporality, and when brought together they create a disjunction rather than a conjunction. The desire to have truth and reconciliation represent a causal sequence of events, such that would satisfy the twin demands of the juridical and the therapeutic, fractures truth into the objective and the subjective and splits reconciliation into justice and what may be called an inner release from suffering. But if, as Jeffery argues, the TRC does not deliver justice, neither, argues Anthony Holiday (1998), does it satisfy the conditions for an inner release which he names forgiveness. Holiday (1998: 45) differentiates between contractual formulas and the formulas of forgiveness, arguing that 'since public utterances provide no cast-iron warrant that the sincerity conditions have been met, forgiveness is not something we can expect to happen as if it were an entitlement flowing from a contract, but only something for which we may hope'. Drawing a further distinction between the therapeutic and the truly remorseful, Holiday (ibid: 45) says that sincere forgiveness consists of a release from remorse made possible by 'a distinctive attitude towards one another in respect of each other's inwardness'. Holiday thus sees true remorse as requiring a discourse of inter-subjectivity, one that, because of the format of the TRC, is excluded from the relations between victims and perpetrators.

The overwhelming need to explain the connection between truth and reconcili-ation by means of a causal narrative, whether conceived of as a narrative of external justice or one of internal remorse and forgiveness, issues from the Enlightenment ideal of a liberating reason that is able to discern the truth and act appropriately upon it. This ideal of emancipation and progress informs South Africa's constitution, its courts, and its commissions. But when someone refuses to make an appearance before the TRC or, having made an appearance, refuses to divulge the truth, the event cannot be narrativ-ised, as it defies the rational causal principle on which narrative rests. In such cases the conjunction *and* may be seen to serve an iterative rather than a temporal function. As such it constitutes repetition without change, analogous to a trauma that is replayed in fantasy but not resolved.

If the temporal gives rise to narrative, then the iterative gives rise to the image, which is organised structurally and spatially. Steven Robins claims that apartheid abuses emanating from the TRC 'will be written . . . into official histories of the new na-tion' (Robins 1998: 120) and argues that the rewriting of personal memory as national narrative 'reconfigures and erases the fragmented character and silences of embodied experiences of violence' (ibid.: 123). In Robins's view the 'embodied experience' is not amenable to national narrativisation. Such an experience may be seen as correspond-ing to Benjamin's redemptive recognition of the event as mediated by the image, as the image is precisely an experience that has been given a body, a sensation. As image, redemption cannot but speak the archaic language of the body. It is on the basis of the image that the body is first apprehended and that relations between bodies are subse-quently postulated.

The form of redemption offered by the image is, nevertheless, ambiguous. The basis of the image is repetition, as the image constitutes the doubling of an object for a subject. The exemplary instance of such a doubling is the subject's recognition of his or her own reflection in a mirror. Lacan (1997d: 4) suggests that the relation between the subject and his or her external, objectified image, described as an imaginary iden-tification by which the subject is captivated, illustrates the way in which the subject, in his or her infantile narcissistic phase, relates to his or her reality. These early imaginary identifications are repeated in the captivating images of the subject's subsequent experi-ences.

Freud's (1953b) investigations into the repetition compulsion had led him to the image of the double as herald of what he called the 'uncanny', which he associated with the disclosure of repressed material. Homi Bhabha (1994a) takes up the idea of the uncanny in the distinction he draws between history as narrative structure and history as repetition. He speaks of the national narrative as surmounting 'the ghostly time of repetition' (143) and suggests that 'such an apprehension of the "double and split" time of national representation . . . leads us to question the homogeneous and horizontal view associated with the nation's imagined community' (144). Repetition is seen as destabilising linear certainty. As in Benjamin, the image, in the process of doubling, exercises an uncanny power of disruption over the linear certainties of the narrative. Bhabha argues that 'the demand for a holistic, representative vision of society could only be represented in a discourse that was at the same time obsessively fixed upon, and uncertain of, the boundaries of society, and the margins of the text' (ibid.). The TRC attempts to fix such a boundary, a margin. But the nation is split at the very moment of narration between what Bhabha calls 'the continuist, accumulative temporality of the pedagogical, and the repetitious, recursive strategy of the performative' (145).

Bhabha speaks of the 'liminality of the people – their double-inscription as pedagogical objects and performative subjects' (151). Such inner contradiction is masked by the hegemonic social order until a spectacular event, like Madikizela-Mandela's TRC hearing, displays the duplicity in dramatic fashion. The effect of an event such as this is to provide the shock whereby, as Benjamin says, the flow of empty time crystallises into a significant structure.

3

Are we concerned here with an adequate response to indescribable atrocity or are we rather concerned with the implications of such atrocity for the law, which would found a different social order?

Nicholas Dawes, 'Constituting Nationality: South Africa in the Fold of the "Interim"'

Holiday and Robins each argue that the TRC hearings constitute a grand narrative of reconciliation and that this narrative, like all grand narratives, perpetrates a falsehood. If this is the case, Madikizela-Mandela's evasive appearance before the special hearing may be construed, as lie, as a doubling by which the narrative assurances of the TRC proceedings are uncannily destabilised. Given Madikizela-Mandela's high media profile over a long period of time, it is unavoidable that she has been constructed in terms of popular images. Each of these images articulates a doubling, of which the TRC appearance is simply the most recent. Evident in these images is a structure of repetition that at every point subverts the narrative of liberation serving as its facade. In the 1970s Madikizela-Mandela emerged as the spectral double of Nelson Mandela himself and used this space, supported by international media coverage, to voice the aspirations of the oppressed. In the full glare of the world media she liberated herself and symbolically all those shackled to apartheid law by defying her banning order. This had the important effect of shifting and dividing the power of the African National Congress (ANC) in exile by proclaiming a new locus of struggle within the borders of the state. In the 1980s she appeared in the townships with raised fist, icon of a revolution that, at street level, with the advent of the Self Defence Units (SDUs), frequently employed terror to combat terror, thus constituting a double of the inhumanity the revolution sought to oppose. In the 1990s she was ostracised by the ANC leadership but continued to command popular support, especially among the voiceless poor. As icon of a marginal community that was once the *raison d'être* and driving force of the revolution, she compels the ANC to confront not an enemy but itself, its other self, those who, as John Pilger (1998) reveals, continue to be as peripheral to centres of political and economic power as before.

The Madikizela-Mandela hearing, with its lurid cast of what she herself calls 'lunatic' characters (du Preez 1997c), offers for contemplation a grotesque parody of the aims and methods of the liberation movement. Evidence centres on the activity of the Mandela United Football Club, whose coach, Jerry Richardson, appears in court with a small football that he places on the table in front of him. The coach is accused of being a police informer and a murderer. The players are accused of being a gang of political criminals, whose reign of intimidation, abduction, torture, and murder eventually galvanised members of the community into setting fire to the Mandela house. The liberation struggle appears, in the testimony, as a game, the rules of which are determined by the Football Club itself. Bearing in his manner the spurious dignity of his office as coach and oblivious to the sinister irony of his revelations, Richardson describes in his evidence how Stompie Seipei had been 'kicked around like a football' (ibid.). He goes on to state that later Seipei was 'slaughtered like a goat' (ibid.). The semantics of football merge oddly with the semantics of the tribal family, a conjunction evident in the name Mandela United Football Club. The Football Club is given a family name, but the name has an ambiguous reference. In the absence of the father, the traditional family head, the mother assumes the name and stands in for the absent male. She is mother of the nation, the phallic mother. Madikizela-Mandela herself enacted a fantasy of agent of castration when she accused Paul Verryn, a Methodist minister, of sodomising Seipei and others, instigated the boy's abduction, initiated the assault on Seipei under the pretext that he was a police informer, and according to the evidence of Katize Cebekhulu, murdered Seipei.

Madikizela-Mandela did not apply for amnesty for her alleged part in the deaths of eight individuals at the hands of the Football Club. Summoned to appear before a Section 29 closed hearing, she requested a public appearance and was granted a special hearing before the TRC. Given her controversial role in the liberation struggle in the late 1980s, this hearing confounded the roles of victim and perpetrator, destabilising the TRC's narrative oppositions.

Notwithstanding the view expressed by Justice Minister Dullah Omar that a 'fundamental difference' exists between the violations allegedly committed by Madikizela-Mandela and those committed by agents of the apartheid state (du Preez 1997a), the hearing reveals the uncanny resemblance between the ethos of the liberation struggle as practised by the Football Club and the ethos of the apartheid regime as practised, for example, by the Civil Co-operation Bureau (CCB), a notorious hit squad housed at Vlakplaas. Semantics again are revealing. While Richardson speaks of Seipei being slaughtered like a goat, the TRC also hears how Sizwe Kondile was incinerated on an open fire as CCB operatives were having a barbecue close by, leading Charity Kondile,

Sizwe's mother, to exclaim that Dirk Coetzee, commander of Vlakplaas, had *braai*ed ('barbecued') her son (Krog 1998: 234). Through a range of rhetorical devices, African custom and Afrikaner custom are unexpectedly associated within what emerges as a highly ambiguous and unstable political framework, in which militant opponents speak an interrelated rather than a different language. If the TRC acts as midwife of a commonality, it may be that, in the nation's imaginary, it is the commonality of a shared pathology, of a common duplicity, rather than of a unifying humanity. Jacques Pauw (1991) uses the phrase 'heart of the whore' to describe the CCB. This characterisation is apt also with regard to the football 'family' and its oedipal 'mother'. Says Richardson: 'Only myself could touch Mommy – not anyone else. I loved her' (Krog 1998: 249). The Madikizela-Mandela hearing reveals, as it were, the heart of the whore of liberty. It is the heart not as essence but as representation, repetition, pulsation.

The Football Club is no more the essence of the liberation movement than the CCB is the essence of the apartheid regime. Both represent a splitting and a doubling that, from a psychoanalytic perspective, signify the emergence of the unconscious by which the subject has been constituted as divided.

The external division between the apartheid regime and the liberation movement is repeated, then, as an internal division within both. This ambivalence of external and internal, this momentary doubling of the one in relation to the other, recalls Bhabha's (1994: 11) description of the 'unhomely moment' as one that 'relates the traumatic ambivalences of a personal, psychic history to the wider disjunctions of political existence.' The 'unhomely moment' arises from what Bhabha calls 'disavowal' (10). Disavowal is precisely what characterises, most obviously, Madikizela-Mandela's testimony but also, through a lack of emotional and moral involvement, the testimony of someone like Coetzee. As defensive reaction, disavowal constitutes resistance, and through such resistance the unconscious is made manifest. In relation to Madikizela-Mandela, the term 'resistance' acquires a peculiar ambiguity through the convergence of its political and psychological dimensions of meaning. While Madikizela-Mandela does not speak the past, she does repeat it. In this repetition lies her truth. What she repeats is the silencing of political resistance, the way she herself was silenced by the apartheid state when she was subjected to a banning order confining her to the small town of Brandfort and prohibiting her from making public pronouncements. By repeating this silencing of the voice of resistance, by depriving her acts of resistance of a voice, she assumes the role of her own oppressor. In so doing, through such negation, she performs an act of psychological resistance. Of interest is the interplay between opposing levels of meaning within the term *resistance,* which results in resistance denoting antithetical events on the one hand and the inner division of events on the other. A splitting, a doubling, and an inversion occur.

By virtue of repeating rather than verbalising her past, Madikizela-Mandela displays an enthralment with the performative. But this does not mean that her hearing is not assimilated into the pedagogical. Exposing the contradictions and filling the silences of her discourse, the summation provided by TRC commissioner Dumisa Ntsebeza (in du Preez 1997c) shows how, through the apparatus of a body such as the TRC, charged with arriving at a national truth, the 'homogeneous and horizontal view associated with the nation's imagined community' (Bhabha 1994a: 144) imposes itself. In the absence of Madikizela-Mandela's voice, in the fractures opened up by her non-disclosures, Ntsebeza's voice, and through his voice the voice of the TRC as contained in its final report, will stand as an inferential record of what transpired at the Mandela house during Christmas and New Year's of 1987–1988. The 'homogeneous and horizontal' knowledge provided by the pedagogical, which seeks to piece together the fragments of evidence into a consistent narrative, thus prevails as 'official' knowledge. Excluded is a negative knowledge yielded by the repetitious structure of the performative. Such knowledge reveals not a given real, truth as identified by empirical evidence, but the fantasy relations of an imaginary identification, that ghostly double that emerges as the 'uncanny.' The ghost that haunts the TRC narrative of truth and reconciliation is that of the tribe, an exclusive group whose affiliation is familial rather than national, based on the solidarity of the group rather than on the mutual responsibilities of legal individuals. The TRC narrative seeks precisely to repress tribal affiliation and to bring into existence a social contract founded on personal responsibility, what Tutu and others call a new 'moral order' (du Preez 1997c). The new order inscribed in the structures, processes, and final report of the TRC is one in which the individual is bound to the group not through narcissistic but through legal relations.

By refusing the discourse of truth and reconciliation, Madikizela-Mandela clings to an imaginary characterised by conflation of the tribal and the revolutionary. In the register of the imaginary, which comprises the most archaic structures of identity, revolution promises a return to Africa, to the idealised tribal past, a return, that is, to the undifferentiated relation with the mother, with mother Africa. Madikizela-Mandela embodies this archaic fantasy and its narcissistic appeal. Nevertheless, does integrity not exist in this adherence to an ecstatic truth, one that capitulation to the TRC's narrative would belie? Does Madikizela-Mandela not thereby validate rather than betray those revolutionary 'others' who do not occupy positions of power and prestige in the new regime, who were not properly demobilised and 'rehabilitated' for civilian life after the 1994 elections, and who, some of them, have now turned to professional crime as a kind of reductio ad absurdum of the liberation struggle? Is she not a dark angel of history? Krog (1998: 260) broaches the issue by describing Madikizela-Mandela as representing an ideal of clan honour: 'Winnie is the monarch of the people for whom the new system does not work. She symbolises their collective honour. She personifies their aspirations and their right to status. She has to cling to that honour. If she admits to wrongdoing, she dishonours them all.' Krog speaks of the TRC as attempting to eradicate a culture of shame and honour, which is rooted in the group, and to replace it with a culture of guilt and responsibility, which is rooted in the individual (260, 262–63) In her account the Madikizela-Mandela hearing represents a struggle over how the new nation conceives of itself. She maintains, 'The essence of this hearing was the collision of two cultures alive in the black community' (260). She takes Madikizela-Mandela as capitulating to the new order in her apology to Tutu. Yet the phrasing is ambiguous, evident in the slippage between *honour* and *honourable*. 'By admitting that things went wrong, she herself wiped out her whole culture of honour . . . A space was created for the first time for both her and her followers to admit in an honourable way that things went wrong' (ibid.). Krog sees Tutu's appeal to Madikizela-Mandela, 'You are a great person and you will enhance your greatness if you say, "I am sorry,"' as making it possible for her simultaneously to retain her honour and to lose it by admitting that 'things' 'went wrong' (ibid.).

Krog's analysis rests on the assumption that Madikizela-Mandela does assume personal responsibility in her apology. But a close reading of her actual words suggests otherwise. First, Madikizela-Mandela reaffirms a traditional familial and tribal framework when she replies to Tutu, 'You are the father I have always known . . . and I hope you will continue to be' (du Preez 1997c). Her appeal to the solidarity of a mythical blood relationship persists in the face of Tutu's emotional appeal to the individual conscience. Second, in her awkward, faltering apology, she implies that events were determined by things beyond her control: 'For that part of . . . we are aware that there are factors that led to that . . . for this I am sorry' (ibid.). The fragmentary qualifications render the apology incoherent, perpetuating rather than retracting the denial that characterised her testimony from the start. In effect she offers an apology only for that over which she had no control, for those impersonal and external 'factors' responsible for 'things' going 'wrong'. Rather than undergo a change of heart, Madikizela-Mandela allows the evasions to repeat themselves. Her defences are shaken but not abandoned. She remains, to the last, a defiant figure of resistance.

The modern subject is the narrative subject, the subject of history, of linear causal processes and rational-empirical understanding. It is to the creation of this subject that the TRC is dedicated. Its structures are designed to facilitate public disclosure of the self as subject of a narrative. Where fragmentation has occurred, a unitary order will arise through the intervention of the TRC. This intervention is partly legal, partly theological, and partly psychological. That it is also partly political, or perhaps primarily political, is clear in Tutu's extended statement at the conclusion of what was to have been the last TRC Special Report on SABC TV. He speaks of truth and reconciliation as a political imperative: 'To seek to have reconciliation on the basis of a lie is to look for a . . . spurious reconciliation. We are going to try and understand why people took particular positions, what we hope will be a common understanding of what happened. And it is important if you are seeking to become one that you begin to have a common history, a common perspective on what took place' (du Preez 1997b). Through the medium of the TRC, through its rhetoric and practice, the justice system, God, self, and the nation-state are all enlisted in the creation of a common identity in the place of such segregation of identity as existed previously under the divisive apartheid state.

The success of apartheid rested not only on the division between white and black but also on the division between modernising and traditionalist tendencies within the white and the black communities respectively. The exploitation of such internal communal divisions to sustain the external racial division goes back to the eastern frontier of the early nineteenth century, where imperial authority coexisted with both tribal authority and colonial authority. Just how tentatively poised between traditionalism and modernism South Africa continues to be is evident in Thabo Mbeki's notion of an 'African Renaissance'. The phrase is split between two frames of reference. On the one hand it alludes to an Africanist philosophy, which keeps alive the ideal of familial/ tribal/ethnic plenitude. In this respect the phrase registers the rebirth, after colonialism, of an African identity, what Chabani Manganyi (1973) calls 'being-black-in-the-world', an identity seen as rooted in African communalism, in ubuntu. On the other hand the phrase makes reference to a distinct epoch in Western history associated with the birth of the modern subject and its pursuit of self-realisation. The faultline exposed by the Madikizela-Mandela hearing, the split between a modern discourse of the self and an imaginary identification with the tribal family, is evident at many levels of South Africa's sociopolitical existence.

The imaginary self is an archaic double whose uncanny manifestation shadows the modern self as narrativised by the TRC. The imaginary is aligned with the body, with the body's drives and its representations. What Benjamin describes as the redemptive image is at the same time the captivating image. The angel of history, that equivocal figure who renders Benjamin's ecstatic embrace of the image unsure, is redeemed humankind's familiar spirit, its narcissistic other. In this relation no change exists, no miraculous transfiguration, only a doubling and redoubling of mirror images in which the subject seeks its unity and permanence but finds instead in repetition its fragmentation. Revolutionary discourse, being narcissistic, evokes a phallic plenitude even as it attests, in its failure to return history to the past and thereby attain closure, to a castrative, catastrophic loss. Julia Kristeva (1987: 120) describes revolutionary discourse as the affirmation of an absolute, God-like subjectivity and sees in the pursuit of ultimate freedom a form of terror against externality, difference, and absence.

The narrative of the self, by which the TRC seeks to exclude the imaginary, comprises a temporal succession of events in which past, present, and future constitute a linear progression leading from disunity and conflict to unity and harmony. Rather than offering simultaneity of fragmentation and wholeness, as in the case of the imaginary, narrative offers a progression from fragmentation to wholeness, from what one might, in the context of the TRC, call disclosure to closure. However, in its pursuit of a telos of closure, the TRC narrative risks foreclosure. It risks imposing a predetermined meaning on the heterogeneity of what Robins calls 'embodied experience'. By virtue of its linear teleology, the TRC narrative seeks to bring about a transcendence of the fragmented body of the South African body politic and, as a logical consequence, the attainment of a unified humanity, conceived of as both the individual made whole and the nation reconciled in unity. The denouement is implicit in the plot. The characters have set roles to play, and their experience is deemed relevant only in as far as it fits with the overall structure of the TRC. They are objectified by the TRC discourse.

This does not mean that the TRC is at fault or that the Promotion of National Unity and Reconciliation Act of 1995, which created the TRC, is spurious. Given its function as an institution of the new nation-state as well as the constraints of time and resources under which it was forced to operate, the TRC could not have been a different kind of entity. It could not have provided the intensive psychic resolution aimed at by psychotherapy. It could not have offered the spiritual absolution promised by the religious confessional. It could not have offered the juridical pronouncement of a court of law without becoming punitive and thereby undermining its stated aim of reconciliation. It could not have granted full restitution for the deprivations suffered by the black population at the hands of the colonial system. The dream of a TRC that would miraculously heal the individual subject and the nation is as much a product of fantasy as the dream of Madikizela-Mandela as the mother of us all. Such dreams are a function of what Lacan (1977b: 141) calls 'imaginary reminiscence', which he opposes to 'symbolic recollection'.

It is not a question of what the TRC achieves or fails to achieve. It is a question of how it is read, of what its narrative is interpreted as signifying beyond its explicit pronouncements, how its silences are reconstructed and its ambiguities are resolved. In terms of its own logic, the TRC cannot but narrativise Madikizela-Mandela's testimony as deceptive. The present reading sees in this testimony the spectre of a double that haunts and unsettles the TRC narrative of truth and reconciliation. The TRC narrative both conceals and, through the mechanisms of the disguise, reveals the double in opposition to which it has come into being. In struggling with Madikizela-Mandela's testimony, the TRC can be seen to be struggling with itself.

Unlike Benjamin's 'angel of history', Lacan's (1977c: 88) subject of 'full speech' is not captivated by a fragmented past in which he or she seeks an originary wholeness but has brought about the 'realisation . . . of his history in his relation to a future'. This subject of a 'future anterior' is neither self nor other but a 'process of becoming', a process constituted by the primordial splitting of the subject without which there would be no change and therefore no process (ibid.: 86). Kristeva speaks in this regard of the 'thetic', which, she says, originates in the imaginary (Kristeva 1986: 113) and makes possible the constitution of the symbolic as an order of 'propositions' and 'positions' (ibid.: 98). She claims that all signification is thetic in that it requires an identification that enables the subject to separate 'from and through his image, from and through his objects' (ibid.). Signification as thesis, as the positing of a discursive position, is inaugurated by a sacrificial break that, in the case of traditional society, takes the form of a literal killing of an appropriate material body: 'In all known archaic societies, this founding break of the symbolic order is represented by murder – the killing of a man, a slave, a prisoner, an animal' (ibid: 119).

Murder and meaning. A core concern that emerged during the TRC hearings is the distinction between legitimate and illegitimate, meaningful and meaningless, acts of murder. At one point the ANC felt compelled to defend its former actions by stating that violations committed by members of the liberation movement were not comparable to those committed by members of the apartheid forces (du Preez 1997a). Indeed it is generally accepted that sacrifices had to be made to advance the cause of freedom and progress. Madikizela-Mandela herself sacrificed much for the liberation struggle, thereby earning a right, as it were, to speak out, to make categorical pronouncements. But something went horribly wrong, and when called to account for herself, she remained silent. What she actually wanted to say at the TRC hearing had nothing to do with the deaths of Seipei and others. She wanted to use the TRC hearing as a forum for positioning herself in relation to the ANC National Congress with which the hearing coincided. This was to be the moment that inaugurated her political future. Throughout her testimony Madikizela-Mandela deferred giving specific responses to questions until her summation at the end, when, she said, she would deal globally with the issues raised. But when the moment arrived, when she stood up to deliver her concluding statement, she ignored the past and began to speak about the upcoming National Congress. She was cut short by Tutu, who, annoyed by the blatant political opportunism and its effects on her supporters in the audience, admonished the latter, accusing them of reducing the hearing to a 'show' and to 'parliament', to a political spectacle. He pleaded: 'Please, no clapping. We are not at a show . . . Clapping can be intimidatory. It influences all kinds of things.' Then he asserted his authority: 'I am the chairperson. I will not have heckling. This is not parliament' (SABC TV3 1997).

In an interview at the time of the Madikizela-Mandela hearing, Mbeki spoke of a tension within the ANC between individualism, allied with subjectivity and the cult of the personality, and communalism, associated with objectivity and the supremacy of organisational structures. In terms of this construction, Madikizela-Mandela is a renegade narcissist who has followed her pleasure principle into a political wilderness. Attempting to use the ANC to launch her political career in the new South Africa, she was instead crucified by it. The ANC founds its truth on her lie, creates in her silence its own speech. It emerges from the hearing and the congress that followed divided from its other, creating itself anew from the rupture. In terms of this process of self-definition, no question of reconciliation exists. Madikizela-Mandela is a sacrifice the ANC had to perform, but the double does not thereby disappear. History repeats itself doubling the past even as it seeks to transcend it.

Those for whom the epic of the conquering self lacks the truth of the negative and for whom narcissistic captivation is an oppression, those who endeavour to apprehend phenomena in their dialectical turn, may, as de Kok (1998: 61–62) suggests, find in the elegy an appropriate form for the implication of death in life. The elegiac holds out the promise of transforming melancholia into mourning, so one may grieve for the dead and have done with grief. But if one does not know who the dead are or what happened to them, how can one grieve? And what if the sense of loss exceeds any attempt at its verbalisation? Lolo Sono was one of the boys who allegedly died at Madikizela-Mandela's hands. During the hearing his mother said: 'I'm having . . . dreams . . . When I'm sleeping I can see him flying from the sky, coming home, saying that, mum, I am back home. Then I open my arms and try to hug him, and say, welcome home' (du Preez 1997c). After the hearing she cried out in anguish to journalists: 'Let me take it out of my chest . . . Help me to find Lolo's remains' (du Preez 1997c). This is the gaping heart exposed, raw, and inconsolable, outside narrative and image, a pain to which no elegy can give voice or body. Its subject is irrecoverable, has not been returned. The remains, the remainder, slips away between the heart's demand and its signification of desire, leaving what Derrida (1991: 21), referring to the sense of loss experienced by Holocaust survivors, describes as 'an incinerating blaze where nothingness appears.' We cannot speak this horror, he says.

References

Benjamin, Walter
> 1968 'Theses on the Philosophy of History', in *Illuminations*, edited and introduced by Hannah Arendt, 255–66 (Glasgow: Collins).

Bhabha, Homi
> 1994a 'Dissemination', in *The Location of Culture*, 139–170 (London and New York: Routledge).
> 1994b 'Introduction: Locations of Culture', in *The Location of Culture,* 1–18 (London and New York: Routledge).

Boraine, Alex, Janet Levy, and Ronel Scheffer, eds.
> 1994 *Dealing with the Past: Truth and Reconciliation in South Africa* (Cape Town: IDASA).

Braude, Claudia
> 1996 'The Archbishop, the Private Detective and the Angel of History: The Production of South African Public Memory and the Truth and Reconciliation Commission', *Current Writing* 8 (2) 39–65.

Dawes, Nicholas
> 1997 'Constituting Nationality: South Africa in the Fold of the "Interim"', *Jouvert: A Journal of Postcolonial Studies* 1(2). Available online at <http://social.chass.ncsu.edu/jouvert/vii2/Dawes.htm>

De Kok, Ingrid
> 1998 'Cracked Heirlooms: Memory on Exhibition', in *Negotiating the Past: The making of Memory in South Africa*, edited by Sarah Nuttall and Carli Coetzee, 57–71(Cape Town: Oxford University Press).

Derrida, Jacques
> 1991 *Cinders,* edited by Ned Luckache (Lincoln: University of Nebraska Press).

Du Preez, Max
> 1997a TRC Special Report, SABC TV3, November 23.
> 1997b TRC Special Report, SABC TV3, November 30.
> 1997c TRC Special Report, SABC TV3, December 7.

Freud, Sigmund
> 1953a 'Mourning and Melancholia', in *Collected Papers IV,* edited by Ernest Jones, 152–170 (London: Hogarth Press and The Institute of Psychoanalysis).
> 1953b 'The "Uncanny"'; in *Collected Papers IV*, edited by Ernest Jones, 368–407 (London: Hogarth Press and Institute of Psychoanalysis).

Holiday, Anthony
> 1998 'Forgiving and Forgetting: The Truth and Reconciliation Commission', in *Negotiating the Past,* edited by Sarah Nuttall and Carli Coetzee, 43–56 (Cape Town: Oxford University Press).

Jeffery, Anthea
> 1999 *The Truth about the Truth Commission* (Johannesburg: South African Institute of Race Relations).

Kristeva, Julia

1986 'Revolution in Poetic Language', in *The Kristeva Reader,* edited by Toril Moi, 89–136 (New York: Columbia University Press).

1987 'On the Melancholic Imaginary', in *Discourse in Psychoanalysis and Literature*, edited by Shlomith Rimmon-Kenan, 104–23 (London and New York: Methuen).

Krog, Antjie

1998 *Country of My Skull* (Johannesburg: Random House).

Lacan, Jacques

1977a 'Aggressivity in Psychoanalysis', in *Ecrits: A Selection,* 8–29 (London: Routledge).

1977b 'The Freudian Thing, or the Meaning of the Return to Freud in Psychoanalysis', in *Ecrits: A Selection,* 114–45 (London: Routledge).

1977c 'The Function and Field of Speech and Language in Psychoanalysis,' in *Ecrits: A Selection,* 30–113 (London: Routledge).

1997d 'The Mirror Stage as Formative of the Function of the I', in *Ecrits: A Selection,* 1–7 (London: Routledge).

Manganyi, N. Chabani

1973 *Being-Back-in-the-World* (Johannesburg: SPRO-CAS/Ravan).

Nietzsche, Friedrich

1968 *Beyond Good and Evil* (Harmondsworth: Penguin Books).

Pauw, Jacques

1991 *In the Heart of the Whore: The Story of Apartheid's Death Squads* (Johannesburg: Southern Book Publishers).

Pilger, John

1998 *Apartheid Did Not Die* (21 April Carlton TV for Broadcast ITV).

Robins, Steven

1998 'Silence in My Father's House: Memory, Nationalism, and Narratives of the Body', in *Negotiating the Past: The Making of Memory in South Africa*, edited by Sarah Nuttall and Carli Coetzee, 120–40 (Cape Town: Oxford University Press).

SABC TV3

1997 'Live Coverage of Winnie Madikizela-Mandela's Appearance before a Special Hearing of the TRC', December 5.

TEN

'Shoo – This Book Makes Me to Think!' Education, Entertainment, and 'Life Skills' Comics in South Africa

Loren Kruger
Patricia Watson Shariff[1]

In South Africa today, the clear-cut opposition between the state and the people, which sustained the anti-apartheid struggle, has been replaced by many local skirmishes, whose participants, from the state to the neighbourhood, compete for the designation of 'the people'. This proliferation of cultural definitions and debates challenges the once unassailable image of *people's culture* defined as 'cultural weapon' (Masakela 1989), which was a normative paradigm for mobilisation against apartheid and for a 'people's government'.[2] This normative paradigm has given way to competing popular cultures – forms, practices, and habits of consumption – in contradictory relation to on-going grassroots struggles, regional, mass media, and formal, non-formal, and informal education.[3] Although this sense of uncertainty has left cultural practitioners and critics searching for points of reference as the paradigm dissolves, it has also provided South Africans with an opportunity to redefine the popular dimension of education and entertainment, not only at home or in multiple regional and international contexts abroad but also in relation to ongoing debates in anthropology, media studies, and education about how, what, and why different cultural practices are locally understood as global, metropolitan, or modern.

In not quite post-apartheid South Africa, formal education is anything but popular. The Department of Education continues to struggle with the legacy of apartheid – a bloated administrative infrastructure that included the parallel operations of white, Coloured, Indian, urban black, and ten bantustan education systems – gross disparities in the distribution of resources under apartheid, and the sluggish reform of curricula since then (Hartshorne 1992). This legacy has led to the social and economic dislocation of the so-called lost generation of youth, especially young men who followed the call in the 1980s for 'liberation now, education later'.[4] This educational and social crisis has been exacerbated as nongovernmental organisations (NGOs), such as the South African Council on Higher Education (Sached) and Pro-Matriculation (Promat), which had responded to the implosion of the school system after the Soweto uprising of 1976 by creating non-formal institutions for educating blacks, have been closing due to the loss of funds from international organisations that once supported anti-apartheid activity.[5] These non-formal educational institutions, together with university extensions, such as the Departments of Education and Applied English Language Studies (AELS) at the University of the Witwatersrand (Wits), had taken up the task of educating urban and urbanising youth in anticipation of a post-apartheid South Africa in which they might act as free, modern agents rather than subjects of a repressive state.[6] To engage secondary school and other students not merely as objects of schooling but rather as agents of their own education and self-creation by informal as well as formal means, these institutions had used media not conventionally associated with schooling, such as comics or graphic fiction, in educational publications, such as Sached's *Upbeat* and *Learn and Teach,* which targeted youth and newly literate adults respectively.

More recently, while the formal system remains bogged down in debates about post-apartheid education policy, independent publishing companies, such as the Story Circle and the Storyteller Group, and NGOs, like the Soul City project of the Institute for Urban Primary Health Care (IUPHC), have produced 'life skills' comics that dramatise the challenges that urbanising youth face in the realms of health, socialisation, sex, and schooling in the form of graphic stories.[7] As a medium that traverses the boundaries between formal and informal communication, pleasure and instruction, fiction and daily life, the 'life skills' comic is an exemplary site for mapping this in-between territory. Produced in collaboration with target readers and not merely tested *on* them, graphic stories have engaged readers not just as objects of instruction or as consumers but as potential producers of popular cultural artefacts, materials, and discourses that could articulate, represent, and shape their negotiation of the promise and pitfalls of modernity in South Africa.

Modernity, for many South Africans as for other denizens of the South, means the desired, anticipated, and deferred good life after liberation. This desire may focus directly on immediate needs – housing, health, employment – but also engages with the contradictions unresolved by liberation – the promise of abundance and the persistence of scarcity, the aspiration of autonomy and the reality of dependence, or the thrills and threats of city life, especially in the Johannesburg metropolis. For the urbanising youth readers of *Upbeat* in the 1970s and of more recent graphic stories like the Storyteller Group's *Heart to Heart* (first published in 1994) and the Soul City project's *Body and Soul* (1997), aspiring to modernity includes an unsettled but compelling mixture of formal education; consumption of clothing, music, and other goods identified with urban life; economic uncertainty; and a precarious autonomy from the constraints of kinship and other 'traditional' obligations.

The 'life skills' comics live up to their name by engaging directly with the gaps between young people's lifestyle aspirations and the life skills that might help achieve them. Not only do the stories deal with young people struggling to succeed in an urban environment that can be exhilarating and dangerous but the accompanying workbooks also encourage readers to develop alternative solutions to sexual, social, or economic crises faced by the characters and to enter competitions on these questions, for which the prizes are desired consumer goods. In particular the Storyteller Group's *Heart to*

Heart project (1991–1998) produced two versions of a graphic romance and a graphic account of workshops that staged and documented student authorship and went on to produce a facilitator's guide, a student workbook, a board game, and writing competitions to encourage further use of the comic in formal, informal, and non-formal education.[8] Competitions range from submitting responses to questions about moments in the story to short stories or radio scenarios based on the plot and characters. Prizes range from T-shirts to cassette players. This model was appropriated by the Soul City project, a multimedia enterprise, supplementing radio and television dramas with 'life-skills' comics (along with student workbooks that call for responses to alternative scenarios). Purchased by the Education Department in 1998 and marketed in Africa and the Caribbean alongside videotapes of its popular television serial, Soul City's 'life-skills' packet has a potential audience of over ten million students.[9] Although subsidised by donors and distributed below cost rather than sold retail for profit, the 'life skills' comics nonetheless encourage readers to link the acquisition of new life skills with the appropriation of modern lifestyles and, in this respect, recall the for-profit commercial magazines that have appealed to urbanising black consumers, from *Drum* (since the 1950s) to *Bona* (1960s) and *Tribute* (1980s) (Laden 1997), even though *edutaining* (educational and entertaining) comics do not endorse wholesale absorption into a life of acquisitive consumption as *the* way to modernity, African or otherwise.

This article does not presume to investigate all institutions rethinking education in South Africa or to provide a definitive account of a distinctively South African modernity. Instead, we propose a preliminary examination of graphic stories as instruments of education in areas from literacy to health education to socialisation as well as instances of performance and textual production that resist complete instrumentalisation by retaining some artistic autonomy and interpretive play. We hope to illuminate the specificity of local comics and their similarities and differences with texts and practices localised in comparable third world sites, such as Kenya or India, or the minority communities of so-called First World societies, such as the United States, and thus to show how these texts work on cultural practices and institutions by operating at the intersections of art and instruction, development and leisure, literacy and visual. The *Heart to Heart* project occupies a prominent place in our discussion because the series of texts, especially the linking *Students' Story*, represents the process of its own production and thus highlights the students' difficult but necessary negotiation in structured enactments and improvisations, friendly and unfriendly, of the tension between what Raymond Williams (1981) calls the 'subjunctive mood' of socially critical fictions (here the re-enactment and revision of the romance in performance) and the indicative mood of social norms and actions that the performance attempts to transform.[10]

By explicitly juxtaposing (but not equating) reading texts with enacting scenarios and both of these modes of interpretation with the consumption of goods, 'life skills' comics also provide readers of *this* text with an opportunity for examining the intersection of mass-market media (including print) and material cultural studies, the world of verbal and visual texts and the world of goods. As Daniel Miller (1998a: 9), on examining goods, and David Morley (1995: 308–13) on reading readers and viewers of mass media have argued, texts and goods are neither merely signs nor merely artefacts. The appropriation of texts by readers and learners involves interpretation as well as consumption, and this interpretation is reflexive in that it affects the multiple social roles and subjectivities of readers as well as their evaluations of the contexts of reading and social action (Fairclough 1996). While our focus is on the structure, meaning, and interpretation of 'life skills' comics and our points of reference primarily the critical discourses of literary, educational, and performance studies, our discussion acknowledges consumption (to quote Miller 1995): it thus links, between the instruction of 'life skills' through reading and enactment, structured or improvised, and the appropriation of 'life styles' as well as *habiti* (Bourdieu's *habitus* in plural), the combination of 'habitual inclinations', 'regulated improvisations', and the 'system of durable dispositions' that sustains them (Bourdieu 1977: 74–83).

We would also suggest that attending to specific local reappropriations of mass-cultural forms should complicate generalised characterisations of 'global culture' and globalisation as the standardised dissemination of metropolitan (often American) habits of mass-culture consumption. This suggestion is not in and of itself new, since studies of the recontextualisation of British, French, American, or other metropolitan goods, texts, or practices, from Coca-Cola to *haute couture* (Miller 1998b; Friedman 1994) in locations from Trinidad to Cameroon, demonstrate how metropolitan artefacts may signify locality as well as globality. Noteworthy in this context is the investment of readers and consumers in a local but nonetheless metropolitan rather than a global prestige culture. Unlike earlier generations of South Africans (in, say, the Sophiatown era of the 1950s or even the Black Consciousness Movement era of the 1970s), who turned to black diaspora culture (especially in the United States) for inspiration, this generation has, in part due to South Africa's enforced isolation from global cultures in the 1980s, tended to focus on Johannesburg (or *Egoli,* place of gold, in its vernacular name). This localism has also affected critical and academic discourse about South Africa, which has tended to be particularist if not parochial (Bozzoli and Delius 1990). Opening up to the world of academic exchange as well as other cultural traffic offers an opportunity to investigate the exemplarity of South Africa as a society in which first and third worlds, North and South, globalised consumer culture and localised deprivations, and popular appropriations of that culture persist in uneasy coexistence; but it also calls for caution in the face of glib assertions of 'global cultural studies'. As the Australian critic Meaghan Morris (1992: 456–57) writes, the legitimation of local debates as globally significant or as generalisable 'theory' all too often depends on decontextualising local practices and diluting their specific relevance with 'liberally employed metonyms of wider debates,' such as 'difference' or 'subversion'. While we would not go so far as to assert the 'impossibility' of 'global cultural studies' (Stratton and Ang 1996), we would suggest that studies of 'South Africa in the Global Imaginary' should take cognisance of the ways the manifestations of this Imaginary eclipse the 'global' or 'theoretical' implications of the merely 'local' or 'empirical'. Although we use the local/global pair as a heuristic tool, we prefer to think of these terms as processes of localisation and globalisation in environments, whether urban and evidently metropolitan or rural and apparently not metropolitan, that contextualise and complicate claims to theoretical stability or authority.

Modernity, Urbanity, and Literacy in English

In a society such as South Africa, first and third worlds, North and South, globalised consumer culture and localised deprivations, and popular appropriations of the arte-facts of the culture persist side by side or on top of each other in uneasy coexistence. The perception of the city – and by extension the metropolitan world – as crucible of modernity pervades rural and urban communities and is reflected not only in accelerat-ing migration to the cities but in the penetration of urban cultural artefacts and habits into the rural areas: advertisement billboards, clothing, language, listening to the radio, hanging out in discos or shebeens.[11]

If the city is the exemplary site of the dialectic of modernity, English – or the Eng-lishes in current use – is its medium.[12] In uneasy relation to local Englishes, the local version of metropolitan English still functions – not least for those who lack it – as the means to master the modern world. The association of English with modernity has a long but not unambiguous history in South Africa. In colonial and neo-colonial times, up to and including the 1930s and 1940s, when English speakers dominated the social and economic spheres, English was the medium of instruction for the mission schools that provided the sole opportunity for formal education for Africans (Hartshorne 1992: 186–217). Although this education reached only a tiny elite, its graduates, such as the dramatist and essayist Herbert Dhlomo (now canonised as the 'father of black South African drama') and more recently the writer and academic Es'kia Mphahlele, vocifer-ously defended access to English alongside the franchise as the key to agency in the modern world.[13] Even when the Nationalist government attempted after 1950 to en-force primary education in the ethnic vernaculars, English continued to promise eman-cipation (Mphahlele 1984). The government's attempt to force Afrikaans on secondary school students provoked the Soweto uprising in 1976, and while students' defence of the right to learn in English was only one item among many others on the agenda, from the improvement of the schools through the cessation of the apartheid government's interference in Soweto governance to the abolition of that government altogether, it functioned as a trigger for further revolt (Christie 1985).

Today, as debate on the institutionalisation of South Africa's eleven official lan-guages continues, English retains its prestige. This is true despite reminders by influ-ential endoglossic ('indigenous') language advocates, such as the Kenyan-born Ngugi wa Thiong'o, who lives in exile in the United States and writes fiction in Gikuyu and non-fiction in English and Gikuyu, that English schooling played a key role in the production of colonised subjects (Ngugi 1986, 1997) and despite the eloquence of the Final Report of the Language Planning Task Action Group (Langtag), which argues for the promotion of languages other than English and Afrikaans not merely in schools and on signs and official forms but in other 'higher-status functions', including parliamentary speeches and scientific papers (Alexander 1996). English nevertheless remains the language of choice of African parents who struggle to get their children into English-medium schools (McKenzie 1994, 1998), largely because it is synonymous with access to material and symbolic resources. Moreover local and localised intellectuals continue to argue – in English – the relative merits of English as a 'pan-African' 'unifying force' (Mphahlele 1984: 103), a powerful medium for subverting the colonial inheritance (Omotoso 1991: 34), or a language reduced to a functional tool of corporate or instructional communication (Ndebele 1987: 13–15).

Current arguments about English recognise the need to negotiate the symbolic and material capital of the most powerful exoglossic ('foreign') language in the world against the claims of local endoglossic languages. Since lack of access to English had previously disfranchised the majority (Granville et al. 1998), current popular demands for greater provision of English are understandable even though these demands increase the capital of English in the linguistic marketplace (Janks 1995) at the expense of endoglossic languages. The tension between Langtag's advocacy for multilingualism and for the parity of endoglossic and exoglossic languages on the one hand and the ongoing hegemony of English on the other has yet to be resolved. Yet actual English usage challenges that hegemony from within. South African English has lost some of its exoglossic character in a sociolinguistic environment shaped by regional endoglossic usage and by the pressures and opportunities of invention and improvisation characteristic of a powerful language appropriated by diverse social and ethnic groups (Mesthrie 1995). If it has not yet become practicable to separate the 'acquisition of knowledge from the acquisition of English' (Ndebele 1987: 14) through the systematic elevation of the other official endoglossic languages, it is everywhere evident that the Englishes in ordinary use in commerce and in leisure and in artistic, as it were *extraordinary,* use in poetry, theatre, and to a lesser degree in published fiction have responded to the pressures and opportunities of life in South Africa.

If literacy is to empower learners in this environment, it ought to be approached ethnographically (Fabian 1993: 82–83). As anthropologists studying literacy elsewhere in Africa (Bhola 1990; Smith 1990; Fabian 1993) have argued, learners believe that economic rewards and social status should accrue directly from the acquisition of new skills (Smith 1990: 264). For the learners as well as the teachers literacy should be understood not merely in terms of the acquisition of skills by those allegedly empty of education, a prejudice that Paolo Freire famously denounced as 'banking education'. Freire argued instead for the merits of 'problem-posing education' (or 'conscientisation') (Freire 1972: 45–59), in which teachers and students participate in a process of immersion and mutual absorption that addresses the aspirations and skill of those seeking literacy as well as those imparting it and takes into account apparently external issues, such as the social status and economic rewards believed by both parties to accrue from the acquisition of new skills. In a city like Johannesburg, which offers youth the spectacle of success in representations of new black elites without necessarily offering them the means to that success, literacy is not an abstract development goal, but neither can it be a magic passport to success. Conscientisation should empower students to recognise not only formally acquired skills but also informal strategies for survival, such as local literacies marginalised by formal literacy training (Street 1994), and thus to understand literacy as a broad social and cultural competence pointing to modernity, autonomy, and reinvention of identity (Bhola 1990: 18). But it should also prepare them to recognise the constraints on self-reinvention in an economy of scarcity.

Recontextualising Pulp Fiction: Comics and Critical Education

Acknowledging that literacy operates in different linguistic and cultural registers and requires the ability to traverse the boundaries between registers and therefore to perform different, even incompatible roles, the producers of 'life skills' comics have steered their texts toward an intersection with but not capitulation to the mass-marketed comics of the global leisure industry. The anti-apartheid didactic strips that appeared in NGO-funded periodicals, such as *Learn and Teach* and *Upbeat,* as well as 'classic comic' versions of literary texts, such as Bessie Head's *The Collector of Treasures,* Can Themba's *The Suit,* and Alex La Guma's *A Glass of Wine,* published together as *Deep Cuts* (Storyteller Group 1993), dealt gingerly with the taint of melodrama and romance associated with photonovella or photocomic romances, whose plots favour adventure and marriage drama and whose titles – like *Kyk* or *See* – encourage voracious but passive consumption. The photocomic, like the chapbooks sold in Nigerian markets in the 1950s and 1960s or the comics in *Joe,* 'Africa's Entertainment Fortnightly', a magazine directed at the urbanising classes in 1970s Kenya, captured the attention of readers whose own precarious circumstances prompted consumption of fantasies about fame and fortune in the city. While these romances usually rest on a conservative worldview, in which tricksters get their comeuppance and women stand by their men, their language and format and the profiles of their authors as self-made or self-making men suggest popular resilience under difficult circumstances (Barber 1987; Fredericksen 1995).

More recent writers and producers, such as Peter Esterhuysen and Neil Napper of the Storyteller Group, have been quicker to acknowledge the popularity of these media and thus the potential of a popular comic form that might combine the accessibility of the chapbook with the critical instruction of *Learn and Teach*.[14] The difficulty has been in acknowledging and attempting to transform the contradictory expectations of their target readers, many of whom desire success framed in terms of access to globalised material and cultural goods while remaining sceptical about their own chances of survival in the ferocious but unevenly developed capitalism of the local postcolonial city.

Even the photocomic, a narrative form noted for its rough newsprint pages between glossy and sometimes lurid covers and for its sentimentally prurient visual and verbal text, can be appropriated for critical education.[15] For instance, Story Circle's *Roxy*

(Story Circle 1993), subtitled *Life, Love, and Sex in the Nineties,* portrays the lives of coloured and to a lesser extent African teenagers in Cape Town. The comic features young locals introduced with head shots as though they were stars, and the story deals directly with sexual and social dilemmas faced by young people, who might be Christian or Muslim, heterosexual or homosexual, men or women.[16] The text incorporates debates on issues like the roles of women, gay identity and the pressures of 'traditional' custom as well as pointed advice on drugs, alcohol, and safer sex through condom use by embedding these topics within scenes of family gossip or peer-group teasing and a narrative framework borrowed from the melodrama and romance conventions of the photocomic.[17] The photocomic provides a familiar format, a generic framework, and an appeal to sentiment more immediately engaging than overt instruction, but *Roxy's* images escape the awkward prurience of the mass-market romances. It opts instead for a visual style that combines the verisimilitude of photographs of young locals with the affective appeal of exaggerated gestures and facial expressions, occasionally off-kilter framing, and printed sound effects. The result is explicitly didactic and emotionally engaging (Figure 1).[18]

Roxy's strategic combination of sentiment and instruction seeks not only to grant legitimate space to taboo topics but to *naturalise* them as part of everyday life and so to make dealing with them part of the pleasure of recognising the everyday and the local as 'storied' (Esterhuysen 1991: 276), as legitimate material for representation. Its characters and images also expand the realm of the local and the familiar. Whereas commercial photocomics until recently featured exclusively white or exclusively coloured characters and still appear to target primarily the white or coloured population, predominantly in the Western Cape, *Roxy* both acknowledges and explodes this inherited regionalism and its associated history of segregation. It introduces African and white characters to a setting (in this case Woodstock in Cape Town) that is historically associated with a distinctly hybrid identity marked by the coloured community's English/Afrikaans code switching as well as by the historical attachment to the city. But it does not go so far as to incorporate the isiXhosa/English/Afrikaans code switching characteristic of African youth (but not unheard among coloured youth) in the region. The cover reinforces this change (Figure 2). It follows photocomic convention in displaying a young, sexy heroine, Roxy, whose warmly tinted image dwarfs the background, and in framing her with the melodramatic subtitle 'picture thriller'. But it recontextualises that convention by matching Roxy's image in size and dominance with that of Mzamo, her African boyfriend, and by superimposing both on a street at dusk in Woodstock. The story also shifts locale and local authority by moving the climax of their story from the streets and kitchens of Woodstock, an established inner-city and relatively racially integrated – or at least culturally assimilated – settlement for more than a century, to a shebeen and backyard room in a peri-urban township created for black 'temporary inhabitants' by apartheid architects in the 1960s.

This integration of environment and inhabitants as much as the candid messages about sexuality and socialisation has appealed to young readers not only in the Western

Figure 1 *Roxy* (Story Circle 1993: 11). Reprinted with permission from Macmillan, South Africa.

Figure 2   *Roxy* (Story Circle 1993: cover). Reprinted with permission from Macmillan, South Africa.

Cape but as far away as rural KwaZulu-Natal on the other side of the country. This appeal is all the more noteworthy in a region characterised by relative ethnic and linguistic homogeneity as well as a political class (led by the Zulu-identified Inkatha Freedom Party) dedicated to enforcing that homogeneity through the symbolic construction of cultural and ethnic difference between the mutually intelligible Nguni speech communities (isiZulu and isiXhosa, isiNdebele and siSwati [Swazi]). As Helene Schneider (1994), director of the Centre for Health Policy, argues, the rural reception of an evidently urban text suggests that urban and rural readers' sense of affiliation with the place and their (self-)recognition in the story cannot be inserted into a split between urban and rural, modern and 'traditional' affiliation that conventional modernisation theory presumes.[19] While rural readers' avid response to this photocomic confirms its impact on their socialisation if not on their formal education, the fact that the avid interest of rural readers escaped the initial attention of the producers suggests a moment of unpredictability that challenges the presumption that identification depends always on localisation.

Despite the complexity of rural readers' responses to urban stories that they perceive as different from themselves but nonetheless authoritative by virtue of their urbanity, the production of 'life skills' comics has remained largely in thrall to the city, either as the location and theme of the edutaining graphic story or as the site of its production. The most influential producers, from the Storyteller Group (1990 on) to the Soul City project (1994 on), have been based in Johannesburg in Gauteng, South Africa's most urbanised province, and have focused their stories on the aspirations of city or would-be city youth. One of the first full-length (thirty-two A4 pages) stories, *99 Sharp Street: The River of Our Dreams* (Storyteller Group 1991; storyboard by Peter Esterhuysen), shows the lives of students at Studywell College, a fictional but plausible for-profit school in Hillbrow, South Africa's densest inner-city area. Its more recent successor, *Body and Soul* (Soul City 1997; storyboard by Esterhuysen), uses secondary school students and other characters from the *Soul City* television series (begun in 1994) to depict young people grappling with life in Alexandra, a densely populated but underserviced area of formal and informal dwellings on the edge of Sandton, one of the country's wealthiest suburbs, and problems ranging from sexual coercion to the cost of school to the power of local gangs.

These graphic stories portray the economic, social, and sexual pressures on young people in a turbulent urban environment. Although this is an environment under strain, it is the only one on view. Although many people living in Gauteng metropolitan areas are new arrivals, almost all the characters appear to take the urban environment and urban ways, including fluent English and familiarity with Western medicine, for granted. The stories use verbal and visual language familiar to youth in that environment, including such argots as *tsotsitaal* and its successors – *99 Sharp Street: The River of Our Dreams,* for instance, alludes to 'sharp, sharp,' the usual response to 'Eita Da! Hoezit' or 'Heyta Ngwenya?' (Roughly, 'Yo! What's Happenin'?') – and a concatenation of violent or sentimental images that recalls television, which assumes fluency in comic conventions, including speech and thought bubbles, juxtaposed 'long shots' and close-ups, and general adherence to a left/right narrative progression.

At the same time the stories deploy a graphic style that quotes what might be called the international art or alternative comic. According to Esterhuysen (1991: 275). The clear-line style of *99 Sharp Street: The River of Our Dreams* (by the Portuguese South African Carlos Carvalho) draws on the work of Hergé, the creator of *Tintin* who is familiar to educated South Africans, while the vivid colour pictures of powerful women in lush but poor landscapes by Justin Wells for the *Heart to Heart* project (Storyteller Group 1994), a rare *rural* story, recall the frames and especially the covers of Gilbert Hernandez's stories about Chelo and other tough women in Palomar, a fictional Latin American village. The local appropriation of globalised models produces much more interesting results than a generalised reference to some homogenous 'global culture,' however. In the work of American artists like 'Los Bros' Hernandez, for instance, the metropolis is itself subject to contention. Spanish code-switching characters and locales, from powerful peasant women in remote villages to women mechanics in a futuristic version of the inner-city barrio, represent a response to the local and global metropolis from a particular site (East Los Angeles and its Chicanos and other Latin American denizens) that is deemed peripheral by the dominant Anglo culture of the United States.[20] In South Africa 'life skills' comics do not simply import an international 'alternative' culture. For one thing, they steer clear of the elliptical, postmodern irony of the 'art comic' in favour of a thoroughly modern commitment to the enlightenment project and a narrative and visual format that can instruct as well as amuse.[21] At the same time they use the visually stylised form of the comic familiar to urban blacks but not always to those for whom the city is still new.[22]

The dominance of urban patterns of interpretation and consumption also tends to be reinforced by distribution. Produced in 1990 with only limited NGO funding, a short series of *99 Sharp Street* episodes on urban youth initially circulated as 'free' inserts in the mail-order catalogue sent to 700,000 subscribers of Sales House, a Johannesburg retailer selling clothing – and urban lifestyles – to white-collar black workers and students (ibid.: 274), at high interest, before its full-length version was made available for literacy education. *Body and Soul*, on the other hand, has profited from the *Soul City* television series' impressive ratings and a subsidy from the Health Department. Along with the facilitator's handbook and student workbooks, the comic has been bought by the Education Department for use in schools nation-wide, a potential readership of more than ten million. This dramatic expansion, however, has not always been accompanied by an acknowledgement of the impact of urban stories, lifestyles, and modes of interpretation on rural readers without immediate access to them. Both *99 Sharp Street* and the *Soul City Life-Skills Packet* presume the normative authority of the city and its agents.[23]

From Spect-action to Social Action: Performance, *Reformance*, and Changing Social Roles

By shifting the location of the story and its production to a village school in Gazankulu Bantustan, the *Heart to Heart* project contested the naturalised hegemony of the city while highlighting the layers of social and theatrical enactment embedded in young readers' responses to and identification with characters and situations in the stories. For this reason, before we can analyse the project, we ought to acknowledge not only education and literacy discourses but also the performative extension and transformation of Freirean conscientisation. Performance provides a way to enact and therefore to test theoretical claims about literacy, consumption, and the potential for self-reinvention; it also provides crucial links between the discourses and practices of critical literacy and theatre for development.

The term *theatre for development* has been used to describe related but not always identical practices. At one extreme it refers to the use of theatre techniques (actors presenting a script for an audience) to communicate the development policy of national or international agencies or to implement technical solutions to immediate problems (such as the use of condoms by people at risk of AIDS). At the other extreme it includes performances devised by locals and visitors intended to facilitate analysis of long-term causes and thus to develop the social agency and the dramatic skills of the performers. This opposition, often summarised as that between a 'domesticating top-down' and a 'participatory bottom-up' approach (Kerr 1995:149), draws on the work of Freire and his student Augusto Boal, peripatetic Brazilian theatre and political activist. Freire's image of the teacher who gives up the role of expert for that of collaborator engaged in a collective struggle has inspired educators to use their training to articulate the aspirations of oppressed communities, and Boal's (1992: 2) call to transform spectators into spect-actors has motivated theatre for development workers, such as the South African playwright Zakes Mda working in Lesotho with the Maratholi Travelling Theatre, to encourage dramatic actors to move to social action – from changing the structure of agricultural aid to debating the role of the South African National Union of Mineworkers *vis-à-vis* the families of the miners in Lesotho (Mda 1993: 22). This exhortation to action nonetheless leaves unresolved the practical tensions between visiting experts and local participants. In some cases locally trained experts identifying with the technical solutions of modernisation regard the recalcitrance of rural clients as mere backwardness. As David Kerr (1995:159) documents in Botswana, *Laedza Banani* (roughly, The sun is up, let us work together), for instance, was shaped less by the populist aspirations of participants or the explicitly Boalian projections of activists like Kerr or Mda than by the 'large contingent of government health staff on the . . . board'.

In South Africa, before the introduction of Boal's methods, these tensions manifested themselves in Health Education (HE) theatre projects, from Barney Simon's work under Ford Foundation auspices with black nurses at mission hospitals in the Transkei and KwaZulu in 1973 to more recent projects, such as current theatre against

AIDS. Whereas the hospital report identified theatre in technical terms, as a 'means of conveying HE messages' (Simon 1974: 80), Simon and the nurse-performers came to evaluate their performances in the communities as a process of education through self-education. Nurse-performers educated themselves off an attachment to hard-won expertise toward an understanding of the 'ends of a person', as one nurse put it, the impact of apartheid on physical and psychic health, and the value of traditional medicine and other 'non-scientific' practices for their patients (ibid.). In 1987 Clive Evian, a doctor specialising in community medicine and associated with the nongovernmental Progressive Primary Care Network, established health education role-playing for nurses, patients, and lay people in the community at the Wits Rural Facility (WRF) in the Mhala-Mhala District. Set up with the initial purpose of educating *nurses* away from absolute reliance on their expertise and associated social status, which tended to be expressed in impatience if not outright hostility toward rural patients, this theatrical activity eventually included lay as well as professional health and community workers. It served not only to convey HE messages but also to provide occasions for broader interaction between the WRF, its clients, and other community members and to encourage lay people, through role-playing, to become educators themselves. As head of the AIDS prevention programme at the Johannesburg Health Department from 1989 to 1994, Evian developed a skit designed to dramatise, in conflicts between individual men and women, immediate controversies about condom use, safe sex, and long-term conflicts around gender socialisation. The dramatic groups mixed lay health workers and student actors, thus further narrowing the expertise gap (Evian 1992, 1994; Ngwenya 1994; Schneider 1994, 1998).

Workers in health education theatre remain cautious about claiming that theatre skits can eliminate risky behaviour, particularly in the middle of the nation-wide AIDS epidemic. Yet several of them, including Evian and the Puppets against AIDS director Gary Friedman, have noted that young spectators, such as students in Soweto schools, in response to the skits comment on the behaviour of characters in the skits but also take on the role of lay educators themselves (Evian 1992: 35–37; Friedman 1992: 39; Kruger 1999a: 207–9).[24] The reaction of the Soweto student audience reflected, on the one hand, anxieties about AIDS and rapidly changing gender norms, often expressed as advice to the characters, and on the other hand, a willingness to explore social agency, expressed as interest in performance and health education training. The tentative character of the response also suggests that conscientisation is less likely to happen suddenly than in fits and starts provoked by the performance and subsequent experiences of the participants. At the same time the intersection of attempts on the part of producers to reform social and personal behaviour with explorations of social and performance roles on the part of spectators (and potential actors), like the Soweto students, suggests the potential power of the synthesis – or syncresis – of reform and performance, of what the performance scholar Shannon Jackson (1996: 339) has called *reformance*: the attempt to re-create individuals by reforming behaviours and environments along alternative lines.[25]

Although Boal's name and method reached beyond university circles to theatre education in South Africa (as opposed to Lesotho or Botswana) only in 1996 by way of the Tsogang Theatre Education Development Trust, which brought Boal himself to South Africa in 1997, these earlier experiments with spectator interaction clearly grapple with the same fundamental challenge of transforming both formal role-players and audiences into social actors. Performance, or the transformation of spect-action or role-playing in performance into social action, is no simple matter. But the performative and social enactments it encompasses provide an illuminating frame for examining the evolution of *Heart to Heart* from the initial programme of reading 99 *Sharp Street* to the creation and re-creation of new comics by means of performance.

Grassroots under Egoli City: Location and Agency in *Heart to Heart*

The *Heart to Heart* project (1991–1998) combined workshops with students around fourteen to twenty-four years old with the production of a graphic story that expressed and also shaped student concerns about sexuality, the influence of gender socialisation, educational and economic imperatives, and the links and gaps between urban and rural youth. The project was organised by Patricia Watson Shariff, initially as a teacher and researcher based at AELS and later as a scriptwriter and art director for the Storyteller Group. That group was persuaded to support her efforts with funding from AELS. The project involved students at Magwagwaza High School in Timbavati village in the Mhala-Mhala region, a densely populated rural area near the Kruger National Park, whose poverty and marginalisation under apartheid and the Gazankulu Bantustan had been offset somewhat by services and employment offered by the Wits Rural Facility and the associated Tintswalo Hospital.[26]

Published in 1994 by the Storyteller Group and revised in 1996 and 1998, *Heart to Heart* has several original features that distinguish it from earlier comics:

1   The workshops combined the following methodologies: Freirean principles of literacy development, critical feminist pedagogy, and dialogue and performance forms modelled on Boal's forum theatre but modified by new theatre in education strategies designed to develop critical awareness of gender bias in the participants.

2   It complicated the conventional hegemony of the city and the one-way dissemination of professional expertise from city to country. Students reading 99 *Sharp Street: The River of Our Dreams,* produced in and for Johannesburg, in turn produced *Heart to Heart,* a rural love story for local and, in time, international readers also.

3   Not only does the published graphic text *Heart to Heart* include two versions of a romance about love and marriage (the sentimental *Dream Love* produced through the first workshop in 1991) and its revision in *True Love* (produced through the second cycle of workshops with the same students in 1993); it also has the linking *Students' Story,* which represents the students' words and actions in dialogue based

on workshops. The workshops were designed to test changes to the *Dream Love* script, and the resulting *Students' Story* captured the contribution of the performance process to the production of the revised love story, *True Love*.

4   The project combined the immediate production with longer-term exploration of and challenges to entrenched habits of gender socialisation. So it raised important if unresolved questions about the effects not only of apartheid but also of practices identified as 'traditional' culture.

Latent in the project were questions about the tensions in contemporary xiTsonga society between patriarchal social authority and the growing economic autonomy of women, between individual rights and the demands of community cohesion, or between local legitimacy and institutions like the Wits Rural Facility (WRF), the rural extension of a metropolitan university placed uneasily between its liberal promoters and, until 1994, the subservient Bantustan administration. Such questions underlay the workshops even if participants were not always willing to tackle them directly.[27]

The popularity of urban stories such as *99 Sharp Street* among rural students provided the occasion for *Heart to Heart* as well as the point of departure for investigating – by means of performance – the ways in which rural youth negotiate popular culture and social scripts that they perceive as urban. The students' evident enjoyment of *99 Sharp Street* was coloured by their sense of its association with *Egoli* (Johannesburg's vernacular name more aptly captures its association with gold, glamour, and other metropolitan attractions).[28] Could their own environment – one of rural poverty with pockets of wealth, represented either by remote-controlled institutions like WRF or by a few local big-wigs associated with the Bantustan administration or local black businesses – be 'storied' or their own lives 'performed'? It was in response to the students' scepticism that Watson Shariff proposed organising workshops to produce a local story. To a degree the logistical constraints on the workshop held in 1991 reproduced this asymmetrical relationship between urban centre and rural periphery. Though staged in the rural periphery, the project necessarily depended on the centre, from the Storyteller Group's sponsorship to the use of the WRF. The WRF functioned as a local *Egoli* by virtue of its institutional prestige, employment prospects, and literal and figurative connections to Johannesburg but required transporting students from Timbavati on the other side of the 'border' in 'independent' Gazankulu.

Student reactions to this occasion suggest an awareness of the dialectic between agency and dependence as well as an emerging understanding of the effect of performance (an apparently extra-daily event) on their everyday lives. While they responded enthusiastically to the prospect of creating a story of their own, many suspected that the researcher from *Egoli* or WRF, *Egoli's* surrogate, would not fully acknowledge their role in the process. To combat this suspicion, the second workshop cycle was held in a school hall in the village. Additional compensation, such as food, free study guides, English teaching during a local teachers' strike (with their permission), and assurance that their names would appear in the final publication, helped establish the legitimacy of the project in a community where many receive little from metropolitan capital – financial or cultural. As these negotiations demonstrate, the project laboured under economic and social pressures, from the need for subsidised meals to the community's fraught relationship with the Bantustan administration to family concerns about their daughters' exposure to inappropriate activity. An outsider might regard these pressures external to the workshops, but they turn out to be fundamental. Negotiations with teachers, students, and members of the community had the potential to alter the conditions of performance (the workshops and associated discussions) and thus alter the conditions of social action and the balance between agency and dependence, or modernisation and traditionalisation, while problematising neat parallels between them.

The first version of this story, *Dream Love,* was 'driven by the youth' in that the student participants generated the romance plot, in which a young woman (Tintswalo) is swept off her feet by an older, wealthier businessman (Magezi). The conclusion – the birth of a baby followed by a spectacular wedding – endorses Tintswalo's willingness to abandon school for marriage but leaves unresolved the tension between the young wife and her mother-in-law and Magezi's relationship with another girlfriend (Mafresh), whose name represents a more ambiguous kind of 'free agency'. This plot reflects the local importance of (relative) wealth in a 'good match' as well as generalisable tensions between the 'traditional' family structure, exemplified by the mother-in-law's suspicion of the *xitlakati* (discardable rag: by implication, used goods) daughter-in-law, and 'modernity', exemplified by her daughter-in-law's aspirations to formal education and autonomy.

While *Dream Love* certainly is situated in Timbavati and the pictured environment of half-built schools and improvised dwellings does depict the reality of rural poverty, Justin Wells's graphic style crafts a localised vocabulary of romance, if not through conspicuous consumption of global commodities then through glamorous portraits in close-up with everyday village detail in the background (Storyteller Group 1994: 1) as well as the wedding party at the end (ibid.: 9) (Figure 3). In this way it appears to respond to the local consumption of a transnational cultural product: the soap opera romances, such as *Days of Our Lives* and *Santa Barbara*, aired in South African since the 1980s.[29] However, the lavish weddings featured on soap operas in the United States are modest affairs in comparison with the wedding in *Dream Love*; what the latter lacks in first world prestige it makes up for in an equivalently spectacular emphasis on conspicuous consumption. An African wedding usually runs three or four days, with each family trying to outdo the other. The bride and groom have several outfits, which they wear for different rituals or occasions associated with the wedding. Cows are slaughtered, and invited and uninvited guests are fed and entertained. At the same time the graphic images replace the glossy studio shots of imported soap operas with representations of rural environments that capture the syncretic character of the African wedding: in the contrastive dress of Magezi ('Western suit') and Tintswalo ('traditional garb'), the combination of religious and musical forms, and in the use of bright colours, which signify wealth and abundance for rural readers.[30]

* Ndza ku rhandza - I love you

Figure 3   The wedding party at the end of 'Dream Love' *(Heart to Heart* 1994: 9)

The gender politics of the romance, even in this sentimental version, also suggest a departure from soap opera but not immediately in favour of strong female agents. Soap opera's primary audience is generally thought to be women, who, like the fans of *The Bold and the Beautiful* in *So What's New?* (1991), a play about four feisty, independent Soweto women by Fatima Dike, a veteran playwright in South Africa, derive pleasure from its focus on emotion and interpersonal relationships as well as on glamorous protagonists' manipulation of their rivals.[31] Yet the romance plot of *Dream Love* articulates the preferences of the male participants, who appeared to take pleasure not only in the image of an alluring but passive female but also in the action of a male protagonist whose economic and sexual power contrasted sharply with their own bleak prospects. Even though they faced a situation in which masculine authority was undermined by the drying up of jobs in mining and manufacture and by the growing autonomy of working women, the male students constructed Magezi as financially well off and resisted proposals to make his status more closely resemble their own.[32] In other words, their subjunctive enactment in this case reinforced rather than challenged entrenched patriarchal habits.

Although they prepared a storyboard based on the *Dream Love* romance scenario, the Storyteller Group resisted the story's reproduction of sexist stereotyping. This outcome highlighted a conflict of interests common to 'life skills' stories that attempt to be both popular (sustained through the story's idealisation of reality, which reflects the dominant values and aspirations of its readers) and educational (aiming to critique and transform everyday reality by resisting that idealisation). The Storyteller Group faced the dilemma of rejecting the students' input in the first workshop or attempting to change it. More forceful guidance of student responses and more interventional workshop methods would enable both the male and the female students to challenge the received representations of patriarchal stereotypes that had threatened to foreclose the conscientising potential of the workshops (Watson Shariff 1998: chaps. 7 and 8).

Nonetheless, the occasion of this foreclosure, the performance of the male participants that silenced the women in the group, was also the site where conscientisation might take place. It offered a chance to work with the tension between the popular and educational dimensions of the story, between the participants' idealisation of their reality through the story and the beginning of a critical transformation of that reality. Before working on role-playing and dramatising alternative scenarios to key moments of *Dream Love* in the second set of workshops in 1992, Watson Shariff reconfigured the place and thus the occasion of the performance. By moving the venue from WRF to Timbavati village and by offering services and compensation for the students' work, she made it easier for the students to see the project as their own. Separating the workshops from the constraints of the classroom allowed students to be less formal and to speak xiTsonga as well as English, and it allowed Watson Shariff to mitigate against the authoritarian instruction prevalent in South African schools (Watson Shariff 1998: 58–61).

To this reconfiguration of place and occasion Watson Shariff added the reorganisa-
tion of the immediate space of the forum theatre so participants might find it easier to
review and revise the conventions and conditions of subjunctive and indicative enactment that had marginalised the women in the 1991 workshops that produced *Dream
Love*. To this end Watson Shariff took on a more interventionist role than Boal's forum
theatre implies:

1   She seated the women apart from the men to provide the former with physical as
     well as moral support to speak up individually or in chorus.
2   She used her authority to withhold from the men the privilege of speaking sponta-
     neously as a group, requiring instead that each speak from a 'hot seat' unaided by
     his peers.
3   She broke the convention of the facilitator as an apparently disinterested 'joker'
     (Boal 1992: 21) at moments of deadlocked conflict. She posed instead questions
     that highlighted her position of authority and the feminist critique of patriarchy
     underlying her procedure.

All three procedures were intended to facilitate the process of 'rupturing the homogenisation of the male and female students' positions on gender and . . . assumptions about
dating, teenage sexual practices, and male violence against women' (Watson Shariff
1998: 365). As the linking *Students' Story* shows, revising the space and the action did
not automatically transform the gender imbalance of the performance or that of the student's general interaction, but it did produce new alignments. The women as a group
gained the space to voice challenges to the prevailing view of female subordination,
which they had previously tolerated. Further, some male participants turned away from
the adamant defence of patriarchal prerogatives to acknowledge the claims of women,
as citizens of a 'new' South Africa, to fair and equal treatment in the domestic as well
as the public sphere and to grant that this accommodation would involve relinquishing
automatic privilege.

The result of the second set of workshops was not only *True Love* but also the representation of the workshops themselves in the linking *Students' Story* and in 1994
in text that frames all three graphic stories: an introduction in the front inside cover
of all editions explains the rationale and the process of revision, and a photograph of
the workshop and a complete list of participants and sponsors in the back inside cover
legitimates their authorship. But *True Love*, the second version of the romance depicted
in the same lush images as *Dream Love*, captured the eye of student readers in the focus
groups, many of whom looked only later at the linking *Students' Story* (Watson Shariff
1994).[33] The seductive images enabled the writers to draw their readers in by repeating
the apparently familiar scenario only to surprise them with pointed alteration of image
as well as text. *True Love* begins with the same first page and apparent preparations for
the wedding, only to deconstruct this idyll as a daydream (Storyteller Group 1994: 20).
Thereafter it continually juxtaposes elements of the 'dream' script and romantic images
with Tintswalo's scepticism, where previously she had been swept away. It culminates
in her indignant reaction to discovering her lover Magezi, with Mafresh at the Club

Mauritius, where she had previously been ready to be reassured (Storyteller Group 1996: 29) (Figure 4). Instead of a conclusion, the end leaves Tintswalo and her friend Lindi debating the relative merits of sex, marriage and education. Finally, in a virtuoso display of the disjunction between romantic expectations and uncertain outcome, it has the angular figures from the students' linking *Students' Story* literally roll up the lush landscape as the creators inspect their handiwork (Storyteller Group 1994: 228) (Figure 5).

Although many readers came only afterward to *Students' Story*, its stylised images of the workshops capture on paper the multidimensional relationality of performance, the clash of forms, places, and occasions of social as well as dramatic representation, and the multiple discourses that frame and mark the liminal space between them.[34] It also traces the process of creating meaning and thus provides opportunities for critical evaluation through the representation of the students' re-enactments, revision of, and interventions in *Dream Love*. When asked to re-enact the discovery in Club Mauritius, however, 'most . . . acted [it] . . . as it is in the *Dream Love* story' (Storyteller Group 1994: 15). One couple departed from the pattern by reversing the roles: Magezi finds Tintswalo with another boyfriend (16). Where the conventional re-enactment endorsed the double standard that allowed Magezi's promiscuity, and thus reinforced the characters' and the actors' pragmatic acceptance that his money and social prestige granted him access to several women, the revision provoked arguments that ranged from (stereo-) typical reactions, such as 'Beat her' and 'A man needs more than one woman', to more critical responses, such as 'It's unfair of you to expect your girlfriend to be faithful when

Figure 4 Anguish versus anger in Tintswalo's reaction to Magezi and Mafresh
('From Dream Love to True Love', *Heart to Heart* 1996: 29)

* Shayile! - Work is over!

Figure 5 The creators literally roll up their handiwork *(Heart to Heart* 1994: 28)

you're not' (16). In addition to articulating a gender gap, the graphic also highlights the age range of the students in the workshop. While younger boys, who were more likely to be subject to beatings themselves, especially from teachers (17), strongly defended Magezi's authority as 'head of the family' (16), older students argued for reasonable conflict resolution (16) (Figure 6).

The re-enactment and revision of this scene presents an instance and a critique of the strategy of 'simultaneous dramaturgy' (Boal 1979: 132). Boal argues that participants' grasp of the conflict is sharpened if they change only the decision, not the agents, at the moment of crisis and so maintain the social reality of the conflict between the protagonist (usually a member of an oppressed class) and the antagonist (usually a member of a dominant class). Watson Shariff's (1998: 368) procedure allowed for the possibility that the antagonist (here the conservative male student) might identify with the struggle of the protagonist (here the rebellious version of Tintswalo). This particular scene undoes the authority of the already existing script (an authority otherwise reinforced by the presence of its author/workshop facilitator) and thus goes further toward transforming the student spectator/readers of that script into creators (Boal 1992: 2) of their own script, even if this process cannot ensure that they will translate it into social action beyond the liminal space of the workshop. The re-enactment of this scene and the workshop as a whole also highlight the unresolved ambiguity of the facilitator's role. Although Watson Shariff did not give instruction or expert advice in the manner of some of the more programmatic kinds of theatre for development, such as the AIDS skit mentioned earlier, she did ask leading questions, such as 'Which girls would like their boyfriends to love them without having sex?' At the same time, she stresses the necessity and the difficulty of ongoing revision by drawing the reader into the crisis of the *Students' Story*: 'After the workshops, we were all very tired' (Storyteller Group 1994: 7). In addition she invites comment from future readers: 'This publication shows that there is no one story that can speak for everyone' (ii).

The reactions of target readers – students and young people in urban, peri-urban, and rural areas – suggest that the producers' work on foregrounding the process of production and on the multiplicity of potential stories made available to these readers tools for invention and reflection that had not been readily accessible to them before. To a degree, participants in focus groups read *Dream Love* and *True Love* literally or indicatively in that they interpreted these stories as indications of actual behaviour patterns, as well as normatively, as instructions for better modes of behaviour (Watson Shariff 1994: 4, 6, 8). The responses registered conflict along gender lines but also suggested that male participants identified with the story: 'It doesn't have advice only for women but also for me' (4). In addition they suggested that both male and female students saw in the 'students'' story an opportunity for re-enactment and revision, for subjunctive as well as indicative action: 'It's got more ideas in it'; 'I think we can do a continuation of the *Students' Story*'; 'The actors saw their mistakes and changed them' (8). This attention to process as well as to the ways a story about a particular rural place might

Figure 6 The student performance and debate (*Heart to Heart* 1994: 16)

nonetheless resonate in other places – urban or rural – suggests the development of creative agency in shaping the story (11) rather than merely obeying its instructions.

What sets *Heart to Heart* apart from many rural culture-for-development projects elsewhere in southern Africa, particularly those in theatre for development, is firstly its acknowledgement of the local impact of transnational cultural forms and the appeal of texts and artefacts that represent urban success to local readers, and secondly, its effective appropriation of formal and affective features from mass-cultural forms like soap operas and comics for educational purposes. Student and teacher responses confirmed the importance of negotiating students' ambivalent responses to the appeal of mass culture (Watson Shariff 1994: 7). The mixture of seduction and instruction is reflected in, for instance: 'The Dream Love is so nice. That's how I dream . . . but after I read *True Love* I was really confused. I went back and finished the *Students' Story* . . . Shoo, this book makes me [to] think' (ibid.: 1). It is also acknowledged in the revised format of the 1996 and 1988 editions. These editions reinforce the discourse of instruction through 'The Choice Game,' a board game plotting the consequences of life choices as well as through illustrated questions that focus on key moments of decision or revision in both romances. It concludes, however, not with the record of participants provided in the first edition but with a competition, sponsored by the Department of Health, a for-profit company; Lovers Plus Condoms; and the non-profit Society for Family Health. The competition invites readers to write or draw a story or poster along the lines of *Heart to Heart;* the prizes include a SONY CD player, a wind-up radio, T-shirts, and other items advertising condoms. The practice of promising participants consumer goods otherwise out of reach and status symbols like the CD player, like the glamorous and sexy images in the stories, has not been universally applauded. Indeed some Africanist cultural practitioners, such as the theatre director Jerry Mofokeng, who has protested the commercialisation of African culture in such products as *Sarafina* (1996), argued that *Heart to Heart's* images were too overtly sexy to reflect African rural mores. This charge has some merit, but it underestimates the complex relationship between urban and rural habits and aspirations in young people in both environments and the value of the analytic moment in student responses to the story over and above the evident appeal of the images and the status associated with the prizes offered. As recognised in a recent collection of research projects at the intersection of global and local practices of consumption and the invention of personal and social roles (Miller 1995), acknowledging consumption has enabled the project to encourage young South Africans to read and to 'make to think', in the words of our title, as they aspire to reinvent themselves through consumption as well as education.

The edutaining graphic story as a genre in South Africa, including the work of the Soul City project, the Storyteller Group, and the Story Circle, is remarkable in general: it draws on modes of oral transmission and live performance but stresses the value of appropriating mass mediation from print to video. These groups recognise the ambiguous impact of national and international capital – Liberty Life Insurance in the case of the Storyteller Group, British Petroleum and Nestlé in the case of Soul City –

alongside state subsidies from the Department of Health and foreign aid, especially from the European Union, while demonstrating how this capital may be put to use.[35] These stories acknowledge, moreover, that the lives of their audiences and interlocutors, even in marginalised areas like the former Bantustans, are shaped in positive as well as negative ways by the pleasures of mass-mediated cultural consumption. The achievements of these local projects are grounded in their capacity to *entertain* these pleasures in dialogue with but not in subservience to the pressure of immediate need.

The *Heart to Heart* project is exemplary because its producers respect the specific concerns of rural and urban communities while showing their necessary and productive interaction. *Heart to Heart's* significance for culture and development lies in the way the graphic story and the different accounts of its creation make visible the tension between manipulation and communication, critical intervention and outside imposition. This tension troubles and animates not only this particular project but the staging of conscientisation more generally, which, as Mda's (1993: 186) dissection of theatre for development reminds us, is not an automatic product of certain forms or practices. What it can do is provide a stage for enacting the dialectic between fiction and daily practice or, in Raymond Williams's words, between 'subjunctive' and 'indicative' action. The project highlights the process of conscientisation through performance and the contribution of performance in general and structured role-playing in particular to the work of literacy, gender, and ethnic – such as xiTsonga – identification, socialisation, and self-representation. This stage occupies a small space in an education system that still relies heavily on rote learning and corporal punishment to discipline overflowing classes of unevenly prepared students. It nonetheless offers room for alternative scenarios, whose constituent elements are local but whose resonance, as in the cases of *Heart to Heart* and the *Soul City Life-Skills Packet*, are national and international in scope. *Heart to Heart* has been translated into French for African countries that retain French-language education and into isiZulu and Sesotho for the local market, while the *Soul City Life-Skills Packet* has been distributed in southern Africa in English and Portuguese (in Mozambique).[36] The production and distribution of these texts/goods helps as much as their consumption to redirect the flow of cultural capital in ways that challenge the binary opposition between centre and periphery to produce a more differentiated understanding of modernity.

Notes

1   This is a jointly written article. The order in which the authors' names appear should not be construed as a hierarchy.

2   When Barbara Masakela, then African National Congress (ANC) secretary for culture, used the terms *people's culture* and *cultural weapon* as synonyms at the Conference for Another South Africa in Amsterdam in 1989, this normative collocation of culture and agitprop was ANC policy as well as the practice of anti-apartheid cultural workers in South Africa. Later that same year, however, Albie Sachs, also of the ANC, delivered a speech in Lusaka that challenged the authority and the effectiveness of agitprop. The

debates unleashed by this speech continue. For Sachs's speech and a sample of immediate responses, see Ingrid de Kok and Karen Press, 1990.

3   By non-formal education we mean education that is organised and systematic (hence not *in*formal) while operating at one remove from formal, that is, certified education.

4   The dysfunctional state of the Department of Education and the school system in general provides the occasion for but not the subject of this argument. The 1997 *White Paper on Population Policy* estimates that 36 per cent of the national population of forty million people have a primary education (grades one through seven) and 36 per cent a secondary education as well (grades eight through twelve) but notes that only 8 per cent of the African population has the matric (secondary school) certificate while the figure for whites is 61 per cent. It also acknowledges that at least 11 per cent of African children aged seven to eleven are not in school. The same document estimates adult mother-tongue literacy at 82 per cent (76 per cent African, 99,5 per cent white) but leaves the reader to infer the unsaid: a quarter of the adult population (more than ten million people) remains illiterate, and those reading their home languages would not necessarily be able to read signs and documents in urban areas, such as Gauteng, South Africa's most metropolitan area, where official – as against commercial – signs in languages other than English or Afrikaans are still rare.

5   After the installation of the Mandela government in 1994, international funding that had deliberately bypassed the apartheid government to support anti-apartheid NGOs began to flow into government coffers. This change has deprived NGOs that challenge inadequacies in government delivery, especially in the area of education, of the capital to supplement and to criticise government operations. More lucrative government employment has also discouraged black professionals from working for NGOs. See the comments of ex-Promat director Helmut Bertelsman (1996) and of Nicole Turner (1998).

6   We use the term *urbanising* rather than *urban* to emphasise the dynamic character of the accelerating migration to South African cities as well as the precarious position of new arrivals.

7   We use the term 'graphic story' to identify hand-drawn and printed picture stories from the photonovella or photocomic, which have been common in South Africa since the 1960s. *Life skills comic* has become the standard term in use by health and social workers, while black target readers tend to refer to the texts as *stories* or simply *books*. These readers are literate enough to recognise the format even if they are not completely at home with its conventions. This urbanising readership should therefore be distinguished from rural non-readers, whose lack of exposure to printed media and graphic stories have led to misinterpretation of educational materials elsewhere in Africa. See Kees Epskamp 1992.

8   Independent publishers in post-apartheid South Africa remain restricted by production costs and distribution difficulties. Confronting a public unwilling to pay more than R2 for a comic that costs R10 to produce and a distribution system dominated by monopolies like the Central News Agency (CNA), non-formal entities like the Storyteller Group can attain mass distribution and consumption ironically by relying on formal institutions for the dissemination of comics. Their ability to enter the marketplace is thus constrained by the priorities of donors and formal institutions, including schools.

9   Although television is outside the purview of this paper, the educational soap opera *Soul City* (which began in 1994) deserves passing attention here because of its successful combination of a mass-cultural entertainment form and 'life skill' education. Capitalising on the popularity of American soap operas, *Soul City* became one of the top three shows on SATV. It combines the emotional register and cliff-hanger dramaturgy of soap opera with the pedagogic directness of theatre for development; responses suggest that the target audience of urbanising women are more likely to take note of the instruction within the drama if they are absorbed in and by the fate of key characters in the drama. For a more detailed discussion of the dramaturgy of *Soul City* and the cultural politics of broadcasting in South Africa see Loren Kruger 1999b.

10   This articulation of the subjunctive action of socially critical fictions and the indicative action that its producers hope to provoke in actual practice draws on Williams's analysis of critical theatre and media in 'Brecht and Beyond' 1981: 219, 224.

11   The 1997 *White Paper on Population Policy* notes that between 1991 and 1996 the population shifted from 49 per cent to 51 per cent urban but does not take account of urban-bound migration from outside South Africa.

12   On the distinction between normative English and local Englishes see Bill Ashcroft *et al*. 1989: 41-44.

13   For a historical investigation of the paradoxes facing African intellectuals using English in the colonial and neo-colonial periods, see Leon de Kock's article on the making of a civil imaginary in colonial South Africa, also in this volume.

14   Esterhuysen (1995: 274) refers briefly to the Nigerian chapbooks and to the mass distribution of photono-vellas in Mexico to highlight the popular *aspirations* of the Storyteller Group but does not mention the comics in *Joe,* which bear more resemblance to the Storyteller project, since they attempted to combine comic stories with social commentary, or to other projects under way in southern Africa (see Epskamp 1992).

15   In their embrace, albeit cautious, of literary forms still dismissed by educational authorities as 'trashy' or 'trivial,' these projects differ markedly from those that attempt to use graphic forms to promote the instruction of indigenous 'high' or 'classical' texts against imported 'trash,' such as the Amar Chitra Katha series of 'classic comics' versions of classical Indian epics, including the *Mahabharatha* (Pai 1995).

16   Usage acknowledges the ongoing relevance of ethnic difference in an officially non-racial polity: 'African' refers to people who have historically spoken Bantu languages, whether or not they identify themselves as members of a tribe or practitioners of animism; 'coloured' refers to people of mixed descent, who have historically spoken Afrikaans and, more recently, English and whose religious affiliation tends to be Chris-tian or Muslim. Coloured inhabitants of the Western Cape ports, especially Cape Town, have for various reasons – among them cosmopolitan contact and the disassociation from Afrikaner or African patriarchal nationalism – tended to be more tolerant of homosexuality than other sectors of South African society (Gevisser 1994: 28), a tendency reflected in *Roxy.*

17   *Roxy* was initiated by the Medical Research Council's National AIDS Research Program (since absorbed into the current Department of Health) in collaboration with an NGO, the Progressive Primary Health Care Network (PPHCN) based in the coloured township of Athlone, and was produced by the Story Circle from workshops with young people at Vista High School and the Ulwazi Centre. A print run of seventy thousand was financed by the AIDS Foundation of South Africa and what was then the Depart-ment of National Health and was distributed free through PPHCN, Planned Parenthood (South Africa), and clinics and NGO social service centres, including Catholic Welfare and Development (Story Circle 1993: ii). Story Circle has since ceased operations. Further information from the former Story Circle co-ordinator Grant Schreiber is available at grantschreiber@hotmail.com.

18   Didactic explicitness may put off Western readers trained to privilege the aesthetic indirection of the 'liter-ary work of art'. Nonetheless, the combination of explicit argument and sentimental narrative responds more directly to conventions followed by black spectators and readers, as the varied vocal responses of black theatre audiences attest. See Zakes Mda 1993 and Kruger 1999a.

19   This legitimation strategy is not the exclusive province of developing countries. Beginning in 1990 the New York City subway system featured a graphic serial in English and Spanish that tracked the fortunes of a group of friends beset by love, betrayal, and AIDS. Using a medium popular with Caribbean and Latin American migrants (and their American-born children), the series attempted to alert heterosexual people of colour, whose rate of AIDS infection was by 1990 much higher than that of white gay men. This model was reproduced elsewhere in the United States by NGOs and university extensions, such as that at

Washington University, which also targeted young Latinos and which directly influenced Story Circle's work, as noted by Grant Schreiber (1999), formerly of Story Circle.

20   Gilbert Hernandez's designs for the Palomar stories, such as 'Chelo's Burden' (1986), 'La sopa de gran pena' (Heartbreak soup, 1987), and 'A Little Story' (1985), draw on various sources: the high-contrast frames of George Herriman (*Krazy Kat*), the rounded figures in tropical settings of Walt Kelly (*Pogo*) and Jesse Marsh (*Tarzan*), the voluptuous figures of R. Crumb (*Fritz the Cat*), as well as the cinematic treatments of third world survivors and victims in Luis Buñuel's *Los Olvidados* and Hector Babenco's *Pixote*.

21   Our distinction between modern(ity) and postmodern(ity) here, as elsewhere in the essay, follows the broad historical and philosophical tradition of the European Enlightenment and its discontents, including Theodor Wiesengrund Adorno, Jürgen Habermas, and their successors, rather than the narrower aesthetic term *modernism* which, in the Anglo-American context, tends to refer to modernists who are hostile to modernity, such as T. S. Eliot.

22   Both *99 Sharp Street* and *Body and Soul* mix varieties of street slang with local standard English (at about tenth-grade level) but presume familiarity with the graphic fiction form. *Nonceba's Story* (1996), a story based on the Soul City series published before *Body and Soul*, acknowledges older, less-fluent readers than the *Body and Soul* audience in that it includes instructions for deciphering the conventions of graphic fiction, including the relationships among the images, the speech and thought bubbles, and the narrative text (Institute for Urban Primary Health Care 1996a: ii), but even this advice presumes that readers either are able to read the instructions or to get help close at hand from literate family members; in other words, that they have access to literacy if not complete mastery.

23   Potential readership figures are based on the school-going population, about fourteen million. In her presentation to the Department of Education, Education Manager Lebo Ramafoko (1998) argued that children as young as ten would benefit from reading and discussing stories about sex, drugs, and gang activity.

24   These comments are based on observations of the Johannesburg Health Department's skit performed in Orlando High School and other venues and interviews with Evian and the AIDS theatre director Mhlalahesi Vundla, at the Johannesburg Health Department in 1994. The public image of theatre against AIDS and of the government's AIDS policy in general have been tarnished by the scandal surrounding *Sarafina II* (1996), a very expensive 'AIDS musical' by Mbongeni Ngema, creator of *Sarafina* (1986), the 'liberation musical' loosely based on the Soweto uprising of 1976. *Sarafina II*, funded by the Department of Health at over R14 million, propagated myths rather than facts about the aetiology of AIDS and played only twice in Soweto. Small-scale projects continue to engage with the concerns of local communities. For *Sarafina II's* mismanagement of funds and misleading representation of AIDS see the Public Protector's Report (Baqwa 1996). For a description of the performance see Mda (1997: 295–99). Those interested in the aetiology of the scandal can consult articles in the *Mail and Guardian*, available online at http://www.mg.co.za.

25   Jackson (1996) discusses the role of performance in social reform in turn-of-the-century Chicago, where social workers used drama and social role-playing in the Americanisation of recent immigrant women. Our point here is to introduce the term *performance* as useful for this and other discussions of spect-action and social action.

26   During the 1980s the official designation of Gazankulu was that of 'self-governing homeland' as opposed to the 'independent states' of Transkei and Bophuthatswana, whose 'independence' was recognised only by the apartheid state. Most South Africans saw this 'independence' for the fraud it was and continued to call all these territories bantustans to emphasise their dependence on the central state. The Mhala-Mhala region is now on the disputed border between the Mpumalanga and Northern Provinces. For a discussion of the administration of Gazankulu and the impact of Bantu Education policy on the region see Patricia Watson Shariff 1998: chapter 2.

27 The 1996 thirty-two-page comic is supplemented by a four-page pullout with activity sheets and a board game as well as a separate facilitator's guide. Observations here draw on the published text *Heart to Heart* (Storyteller Group 1994); the revisions (1996, 1998); the documentation of its impact (Watson Shariff 1994); the facilitator's guide that emerged from the focus groups (Croucamp and Watson Shariff 1996); and interviews with Shirley Ngwenya of WRF's Health Services Development Unit (HSDU), Judith McKenzie, formerly of HSDU, and Helene Schneider of the Centre for Health Policy. *Heart to Heart* is available from Storyteller Group, PO Box 617, Melville 2109, and Johannesburg; or from Neil Velasquez Napper at storyteller@icon.co.za. For a step-by-step analysis of the workshops in the overall context of educational strategy, see Watson Shariff 1998.

28 *Egoli* (or *eGoli*) means place of gold. This isiNguni (isiZulu/isiXhosa) name for Johannesburg is also used in xiTsonga, the community language of the area and now one of South Africa's official languages. It also signifies, in more general terms, a site that defines prestige for those far away from it.

29 On the conspicuous consumption of soap opera weddings see Lauren Rabinowitz 1992. While South African audiences are for the most part not in a financial or geographical position to participate in 'soap opera bridal fantasies' marketed in *Soap Opera Digest* and *Modern Bride,* they have avidly watched these and other series, which outnumber local television series and whose popularity inspired *Soul City.*

30 Epskamp (1992: 90) argues that new readers targeted by educational comics in rural Swaziland in the 1980s preferred graphic images, whose colours were naturalistic in relation to the objects represented (brown skin, green grass, etc.) but 'sparkling' and brighter than a photograph, highlighting the well-being of the characters pictured.

31 Although this argument has been popular among metropolitan feminists, it has been critiqued recently. Lauren Rabinowitz (1992: 276–77) argues that 30 per cent of the American soap opera audience is male.

32 Apartheid political economy favoured a migrant male workforce, dislocated from both Bantustan and labour markets. Although the structural asymmetry between white city and black rural slums left most women and children in desperate poverty, the Bantustan bureaucracies employed educated women (almost all as teachers, nurses, or clerks) rather than men, many of whom regarded this as 'women's work', preferring work as miners or, failing that, as security guards. Comments by WRF officers, such as Shirley Ngwenya, corroborate our own observations about local perceptions of gendered labour, as do the desires expressed by community men and women in response to questions posed by visiting experts from the International Development Trust at public meetings in surrounding villages. In a community that still expects *ilobola* (the bride-wealth owed by a suitor to his wife's male relatives), the underemployment of young men makes formal marriage and the attendant prestige more remote (Stadler 1993).

33 This text contains citations of students in focus groups in other rural, peri-urban, and metropolitan schools.

34 We use *liminal* to mark the place of this workshop on the threshold between social and theatrical action. We thus follow Victor Turner's (1982: 53–56) larger sense of the term to mark the threshold between social and theatrical drama, rather than his narrower use of *liminal* to mean 'traditional', ritual, holistic performance, as against 'liminoid' performances in modern societies.

35 Capital can be capricious. AELS got permission to release some money from Liberty Life, its principal donor, to continue research, but the limited sum of R20 000 forced the Storyteller Group to invest another R80 000 in the second phase.

36 *Heart to Heart* has been translated into French for *La Planète jeune* (a youth magazine distributed in Francophone Africa), and a million comics in English, isiZulu, and Sesotho have been bought by the Health and Education Departments for dissemination in clinics, AIDS agencies, and schools in South Africa. The *Soul City* television series has been marketed to all the countries surrounding South Africa as well as in the Anglophone Caribbean.

References

Alexander, Neville

1996 *Final Report of the Language Task Action Group* (Pretoria: Department of Arts, Culture, Science, and Technology).

Ashcroft, Bill, Gareth Griffiths, and Helen Tiffin

1989 *The Empire Writes Back: Theory and Practice in Post-colonial Literatures* (London:Routledge).

Baqwa, Selby

1996 *Investigation of The Play Sarafina II': Public Protector's Report* (Pretoria: Office of the Public Protector). Online at http://www.gov.za/reports/1996/sarafina.htm.

Barber, Karen

1987 'Popular Arts in Africa,' *African Studies Review* 30(3): 1–78.

Bertelsman, Helmut

1996 'NGOs Walk Where Others Fear to Tread', *Mail and Guardian,* electronic ed., April 12. Online at http://web.sn.org/wmail/issues/960412/AFRICA30.html

Bhola, H. S.

1990 'Overview of Literacy in sub-Saharan Africa'. Special issue, *African Studies Review* 33 (3) 5–20.

Boal, Augusto

1979 *Theatre of the Oppressed,* translated by Charles McBride and Maria-Odilia Leal McBride (New York: Urizen).

1992 *Games for Actors and non-Actors,* translated by Adrian Jackson (London: Routledge).

Bourdieu, Pierre

1977 *Outline of a Theory of Practice,* translated by Richard Nice (Cambridge: Cambridge University Press).

Bozzoli, Belinda, and Peter Delius

1990 'Radical History and South African Society', *Radical History Review* 46/47: 13-35.

Christie, Pam

1985 *The Right to Learn: The Struggle for Education in South Africa* (Johannesburg: Sached Trust and Ravan).

Croucamp, Andre, and Patricia Watson Shariff

1996 *Heart to Heart: Facilitator's Guide* (Johannesburg: Storyteller's Group).

De Kok, Ingrid, and Karen Press, eds.

1990 *Spring is Rebellious: Arguments about Cultural Freedom by Albie Sachs and Respondents* (CapeTown: Buchu Books).

Epskamp, Kees

1992 'Cross-Cultural Interpretations of Cartoons and Drawings', in *The Empowerment of Culture: Development Communication and the Popular Media,* edited by Ad Boeren and Kees Epskamp, 79–94 (The Hague: Center for the Study of Education in Developing Countries).

Esterhuysen, Peter

1991 '"Heyta Ngwenya". "Sharp, Sharp". Popular Visual Literature and a New Pedagogy', in *Media Matters in South Africa,* edited by Bob Ferguson, 274–79 (Durban: University of Natal).

Evian, Clive

1992 'Community Theatre and AIDS Education in South Africa', *Progress,* Spring/ Summer, 34-37.

1994 Interview with Loren Kruger, November 4.

Fabian, Johannes

1993 'Keep Listening: Ethnography and Reading', in *The Ethnography of Reading,* edited by Jonathan Boyarim, 80–97 (Berkeley: University of California Press).

Fairclough, Norman

1996 'Global Capitalism and Critical Awareness of Language', *Language Awareness* 8 (2): 71–83.

Fredericksen, Bodil Folke
1991 'Joe: The Sweetest Reading in Africa', *African Languages and Cultures* 4(2): 135–55.
Freire, Paolo
1972 *Pedagogy of the Oppressed,* translated by M. B. Ramos (Harmondsworth: Penguin).
Friedman, Gary
1992 'Puppetry and AIDS Education', *Progress,* Spring/Summer, 38-40.
Friedman, Jonathan
1994 'The Political Economy of Elegance: An African Cult of Beauty', in *Consumption and Identity,* edited by Jonathan Friedman, 167–88 (Chur: Harwood Academic Publishers).
Gevisser, Mark
1994 'A Different Fight for Freedom: A History of Gay and Lesbian Lives in South Africa,' in *Defiant Desire,* edited by Mark Gevisser and Edwin Cameron, 14–56 (Johannesburg: Ravan).
Granville, Stella, Hilary Janks, Michael Joseph, Maganta Mphahlele, Esther Ramani, Yvonne Reed, and Patricia Watson Shariff
1998 'English with or Without G(u)ilt: A Position Paper on Language in Education Policy for South Africa', *Language and Education* 12(4): 254–74.
Hartshorne, Ken
1992 *Crisis and Challenge: Black Education 1910–1990* (Cape Town: Oxford University Press).
Hernandez, Gilbert
1994 [1985] 'A Little Story', in *Music for Mechanics* (Love and Rockets No. 1) by Los Bros Hernandez (Seattle: Fantagraphics).
1996 [1987] 'La sopa de gran pena', in *Chelo's Burden* (Love and Rockets No. 2) by Los Bros Hernandez (Seattle: Fantagraphics).
Institute for Urban Primary Health Care (IUPHC)
1996a *Nonceba's Story* (Johannesburg: IUPHC).
1996b *'Let the Sky To Be the Limit'*: *Soul City Evaluation Report* (Johannesburg: IUPHC).
1997 *Soul City: Life-Skills Packet* (Johannesburg: IUPHC).
Jackson, Shannon
1996 'Civic Play-Housekeeping: Gender, Theatre, and American Reform', *Theatre Journal* 48: 337-61.
Janks, Hilary
1995 'The Research and Development of Critical Language Awareness Materials for Use in South African Secondary Schools.' Ph.D. diss., Lancaster University.
Kerr, David
1995 *African Popular Theatre* (Portsmouth: Heinemann).
Kruger, Loren
1999a *The Drama of South Africa: Plays, Pageants, and Publics since 1910* (London: Routledge).
1999b 'Theater for Development and TV Nation: Notes on Educational Soap Opera in South Africa', *Research in African Literatures* 30 (4): 105-6.
Laden, Sonja
1997 'Middle-Class Matters; or, How to Keep Whites Whiter, Colours Brighter, and Blacks Beautiful', Special issue, *Critical Arts,* 11 (1–2): 120–41.
Maingard, Jacqueline
1997 'Transforming Television Broadcasting in a Democratic South Africa', *Screen* 38: 260–74.
Masakela, Barbara
1989 'Keynote Address', in *Culture in Another South Africa,* edited by Willem Campschreur and Joost Divendal (New York: Olive Branch Press).

McKenzie, Judith
> 1994 Interview with Loren Kruger, November 15.
> 1998 Telephone conversation with Loren Kruger, March 10.

Mda, Zakes
> 1993 *When People Play People: Development Communication through Theatre* (Johannesburg: Witwatersrand University Press).
> 1997 'When People Play People in Post-Apartheid South Africa' (interview by Denis Salter), *Brecht Yearbook* 22: 283-303.

Mesthrie, Rajend ed.
> 1995 *Language and Social History: Studies in South African Sociolinguistics* (Cape Town: David Philip).

Miller, Daniel
> 1998a 'Why Some Things Matter', in *Material Culture: Why Some Things Matter,* edited by Daniel Miller; 3-23 (London: Routledge).
> 1998b 'Coca-Cola: A Black Sweet Drink from Trinidad', *Material Culture: Why Some Things Matter,* edited by Daniel Miller, 169–88 (London: Routledge), ed.
> 1995 *Acknowledging Consumption: A Review of New Studies* (London: Routledge).

Ministry for Welfare and Population Development
> 1997 *White Paper on Population Development* (Pretoria: Government Publications). Online at http://www.gov.za/whitepaper/1997/popdraft.htm.

Mofokeng, Jerry
> 1996 'Theatre for Export: The Commercialization of the Black People's Struggle in South African Export Musicals', in *Theatre and Change in South Africa,* edited by Geoffrey Davis and Anne Fuchs, 84–89 (Amsterdam: Overseas Publishers Association).

Morley, David
> 1995 'Theories of Consumption in Media Studies', in Miller 1995: 296-328.

Morris, Meaghan
> 1992 'On the Beach', in *Cultural Studies,* edited by Lawrence Grossberg, Gary Nelson, and Paula Treichler, 451–71 (New York: Routledge).

Mphahlele, Es'kia
> 1984 'Prometheus in Chains: The Fate of English in South Africa', *English Academy Review* 2: 89–104.

Ndebele, Njabulo
> 1987 'The English Language and Social Change in South Africa', *English Academy Review* 4:1-16.

Ngugi wa Thiong'o
> 1986 *Decolonising the Mind: The Politics of Language in African Literature* (London: James Curry).
> 1997 'Africa and Its Interpreters.' Keynote address at English Teachers Connect: A Conference on Local Diversity and Global Connections, AELS, University of the Witwatersrand. An abridged version is in the *Mail and Guardian,* electronic ed., July 18. Online at http://web.sn.apc.org/wmail/issues/970718/NEWS24.html.

Ngwenya, Shirley
> 1994 Interview with Loren Kruger, November 15.

Omotoso, Kole
> 1991 *Seasons of Migration to the South: African Crises Reconsidered* (Cape Town: Tafelberg).

Pai, Anant
> 1995 'Comics as a Vehicle of Education and Culture', *Indian Horizons* 44(2): 106– 15.

Rabinowitz, Lauren
> 1992 'Soap Opera Bridal Fantasies', *Screen* 33: 274–83.

Ramafoko, Lebo
> 1998 Interview with Loren Kruger, March 6.

Schneider, Helene
  1994 Conversation with Loren Kruger, November 1.
  1998 Conversation with Loren Kruger, March 10.
Schreiber, Grant
  1999 Telephone conversation with Patricia Watson Shariff, July 30.
Simon, Barney
  1974 'Education through Respect', *The Leech* 44 (2): 84–85.
Smith, David
  1990 'The Anthropology of Literacy Acquisition', in *The Acquisition of Literacy: Ethnographic Perspectives,* edited by Bambi Shiffelin and Perry Gilmore, 260–75 (Norwood, NJ: Ablex).
Stadler, Jonathan
  1993 'Bridewealth and the Deferral of Marriage: Towards an Understanding of Marriage Payments in Timbavati, Gazankulu', *Africa Perspectives* 1 (1) 1–31.
Story Circle
  1993 *Roxy: Life Love, and Sex in the Nineties* (Cape Town: Medical Research Council).
Storyteller Group
  1994 *Heart to Heart* (Johannesburg: Storyteller Group).
  1996 *Heart to Heart: From Dream Love to True Love* (Johannesburg: Storyteller Group).
Stratton, Jon, and Ien Ang
  1996 'On the Impossibility of a Global Cultural Studies: "British" Cultural Studies in an "International" Frame', in *Stuart Hall: Critical Dialogues in Cultural Studies,* edited by David Morley and Kuan-Hsing Chen, 361-91 (London: Routledge).
Street, Brian
  1994 'What Is Meant by Local Literacies', Special issue, *Language and Education* 8 (1–2): 9–17.
Turner, Nicole
  1998 'NGOs Fight for Survival as Funding Dies', *Mail and Guardian,* electronic ed., March 6. Online at http://web.sn.org/wmail/issues/98o3o6/NEWS28.html.
Turner, Victor
  1982 *From Ritual to Theatre* (New York: PAJ Publications).
Usdin, Shereen
  1998 Interview with Loren Kruger, March 6.
Vundla, Mhlalabesi
  1994 Interview with Loren Kruger, September 7.
Watson Shariff, Patricia
  1994 *Does 'Heart to Heart' Work as an Effective Resource in Sexuality Education? A Preliminary Research Report* (Johannesburg: Storyteller Group).
  1998 'Dialogue, Gender, and Performance: Producing a Rural South African Comic beyond the Learner Paradox.' Ph.D. diss., University of Witwatersrand.
Williams, Raymond
  1981 'Brecht and Beyond', in *Politics and Letters: Interviews with New Left Review,* 214–34 (London: New Left Books).

ELEVEN

'Making the Paper Speak Well', or, the Pace of Change in Consumer Magazines for Black South Africans[1]

Sonja Laden

Men and women, old and young, diligently applied themselves to learning to read, by means of spelling-exercises and a little catechism, that we had had printed in the colony. These good people at first set to work with extreme reluctance, protesting that it was ridiculous to hope that a black man would ever be clever enough *to make the paper speak well*. But our entreaties prevailed, and they resolved to try: a slight improvement soon became visible, in spite of all that had been said to the contrary, and each meeting gave promise of still greater success.

Eugene Casalis, *The Basutos; or, Twenty-three years in South Africa*

1 Magazines as Cultural Tools: From *Kgotla* Auriture/ Orality to Uses of Print

The magazine form is typically presumed to mark the emergence of modern social formations that are recognisably literate and bourgeois and inherently grounded in eighteenth-century notions that harness Western capitalist economy to the articulation of social mobility, the rise of consumer culture, and transformations in lifestyle choices and sociocultural tastes. How then does the magazine form come to be a viable print commodity for black South Africans, whose access to the workings of Western capitalist economy; literacy and literate culture; universal suffrage and civil rights; regulated patterns of production, consumption, and urbanisation; ownership of property; status; and urban 'middle-class' dispositions has been severely curbed? Why, moreover, should consumer magazines be culturally relevant or meaningful to them, given the high rates of illiteracy in South Africa, the high cost of the magazines relative to the earnings of many black South Africans, and the fact that consumer magazines are typically held to promote a range of lifestyle options and commodities that for all intents and purposes seems to lie well beyond the reach of most of their target readership? In particular, why should magazines published specifically for black South Africans be produced primarily in English?

These and related questions are considered here in an attempt to assess some of the ways consumer magazines for black South Africans function seminally as 'cultural tools' (see Swidler 1986; Even-Zohar 1994, 1997) through which specifically urban, middle-class repertoires are codified, disseminated, and legitimised for and by black South Africans living in urban(ising) environments. This essay draws on a broader examination of seven consumer magazines published primarily though not exclusively in English, intended for and consumed largely by black South Africans. These include *Drum* (first issued 1951), *Bona* (first issued 1956), *Pace* (first issued 1978), *True Love* (first issued 1975), *Thandi* (first issued 1985, merged with *Bona* 1999, withdrawn soon after), *Tribute* (first issued 1986), and *Ebony South Africa* (November 1995-July 2000).

These magazines are themselves stratified and can be ranked in terms of their codifying strategies: linguistic register, verbal and visual sophistication, print technology, quality of paper and correlative cost, and content, which ranges from routine domestic practices to refined and trendy lifestyle choices and addresses private and collective interests in both apolitical, non-partisan topics and conspicuously political issues. With the exception of *Drum,* which in 1995 became a bimonthly publication and has since become a weekly magazine, all these magazines are monthlies. In what follows I will describe some of the strategies manifest in these magazines, especially in *Pace,* where language seems to be most consciously deployed as a vector for strategising sociocultural identity and change.

On another level, no less striking is the role played by these magazines in consolidating the emergence of a prevailing black middle class in South Africa's urban environments despite or perhaps in direct response to the legislated policies of the apartheid machine.[2] Apartheid sought forcibly to remove black South Africans from urban environments and to impose a rigid segregation on their trading and residential property rights throughout the country. Nonetheless, it is becoming increasingly evident that black South Africans have long been more than passive subscribers to and casualties of colonialist legacies and the apartheid regime. In this sense, against arguments that would reduce the magazine form among black South Africans to a mechanism of cultural imperialism, I maintain that the sociosemiotic work of magazines extends way beyond their immediate or most apparent use value.

Like many other 'things', magazines are both concrete, material objects and embodiments or carriers of meanings and social relations, both commodities in themselves and vehicles for the dissemination of a range of other cultural commodities, practices, and beliefs (Beetham 1996: 2). At the same time, as particularly styled print commodities geared to the changing relations between persons, objects, and ways of mediating the world in modern-day South Africa, it may be assumed that they have more uses than, say, literary texts. For, as I hope to show, magazines render meaningful, without always putting into action, a shared repertoire of everyday experiences, lifestyle options, and social practices best described, from a Western or European standpoint, as typically middle class or bourgeois. As though unconsciously, they make perceptible middle-class ideals and values that have long since become what Clifford Geertz (1983) calls 'local knowledge', that is, tacit knowledge shared by virtually everyone in a given culture whose process of acceptance is no longer recalled. Further, because they enable us to trace practices that are by now part of a social 'unconscious', consumer magazines in the South African conjuncture provide us with greater insight into the dialectical workings of sociocultural entities than, say, overtly subversive political publications. For our purposes precisely their evocative power or potency is important, that is, the ways consumer magazines authorise 'aspired to', not necessarily 'given' states of affairs: they confirm existing cultural repertoires and options and formulate new ones, and as effective modelling apparatuses they inspire cultural reordering and revitalisation (see Even-Zohar 1994, 1997,1999; Sheffy 1997).

In addition, while literate proficiency in English may facilitate and constrain some of the practical uses to which black South Africans actually put consumer magazines, it does not, I suspect, necessarily determine the full range of these uses. In particular the use of English in consumer magazines for black South Africans exemplifies how the English language has been strategically mobilised and (re)activated by black South Africans (1) as part and parcel of the urban, middle-class repertoire of discursive and cultural dispositions initially derived from the nineteenth-century missionary enterprise in southern Africa and (2) as a means of strategically transforming this repertoire 'from below', in keeping with the current needs and interests of many black South Africans. Moreover English provides a discursive resource that facilitates access to 'the knowledge, creativity and entertainment of the entire Western world, as well as participation in global trade and commerce' (Webb and Kembo-Sure 2000: 126). This view is further corroborated by the ways various discourses in consumer magazines, including advertising copy, can be said to function alongside 'other forms of display, [as] symbolic representations of cultural resources used in the construction of social identity' (McEwan and Malan 1996: 205). As discursive resources that are also public forums of display, consumer magazines in general and their use of English especially are seminal means of confirming the (by now) permanent presence of black South Africans in South Africa's urban environments, authorising their urban status and legitimising while constituting the respectability of their readers and their active participation in South Africa's middle class(es).

The distinctive ways magazines combine verbal and visual modes of representation appear to have provided black South Africans with an efficient means for integrating and transforming oral traditions, such as public debate, oral poetry and song, storytelling, and historical narrative, all received sources of African 'cultural capital', into literate modes of print culture and 'urban ways of knowing'. In so doing magazines reinstate their own participatory nature as public forums and modes of urban 'performance' culture enhanced by technologies of print.

Remember, too, that the circulation and consumption of consumer magazines is in no way enforced or imposed on their readers anymore than their layout and subject matter are dictated by the the publishing houses that own them. Moreover, although all the publications in question except one were initially owned by white publishers, the trajectories of their ownerships and the ways their readerships have been constructed, maintained over time, and expanded have been further complicated by recent organisational reshuffling and shifts in corporate holdings and distributions of 'white' and 'black' capital (see Tomaselli 1997; Hawthorne 1997: 31).[3]

Moreover all the magazines in question are mediated by black as well as white editors, journalists, and advertisers. This attests both to the social stratification of black print media officials as cultural agents and to the fact that the magazines themselves are an embodiment of this agency. Many black media personalities are social celebrities and use their cultural prestige to promote their magazines and the images they convey as a means of reinforcing their own status as established members of an elite stratum. Like other social celebrities, they inspire in their reading public individual and collective aspirations by suggesting and endorsing new models for social conduct. This is done both overtly, albeit seemingly by chance, by regularly supplying the public with glimpses of their own lifestyles, experiences, and personalities, and covertly through their strategic decision-making procedures concerning the content and layout of the magazines. As role models they stimulate the reading public's desire for new knowledge, self-perceptions, and glamorous lifestyle practices even as they authorise the marketing of new material commodities, including the magazines themselves.

Pace magazine is a noteworthy case in point. It is owned by Caxton, an English-owned publishing firm that merged with the Afrikaans-owned publisher Perskor in 1998, traded shares with the African-owned corporation Nail, and acquired *Bona* in 1999. Targeting a relatively sophisticated urban readership, *Pace's* editor in chief Force Kashane seems to be particularly attuned to the uses of language as an indicator of and vehicle for social change in South Africa. Unlike most other magazines for black South Africans, Kashane's publication makes a point of representing in written discourse some of the ways spoken vernacular languages have recently been incorporated into newly fashioned urban argots and displays of linguistic diversity. *Pace,* it may be argued, both manifests sociolinguistic change in metropolitan South Africa and functions as a vehicle of this change.

In trying to trace specific correspondences between indigenous traditional social forums, aural/oral modes of performance, and modern contemporary lifestyles, Kashane's role as a multifaceted cultural mediator is especially telling. In a 1992 interview with the present author he recounted that *Pace* was founded in 1978 by Lucas Molete, a jazz musician and journalist, and pointed out that Kashane joined the magazine in 1979 as sports editor. Unlike Molete and the subsequent editor Vusi Khumalo, who both were practising jazz musicians as well as journalists, Kashane had planned to be a professional soccer star but took up journalism when a car accident put paid to his hopes for a sporting career. Interestingly, however, Kashane is at once a practising *sangoma* (traditional healer and diviner), who serves his ancestors in true African tradition, and a preacher at the Lion of Judah's Apostolic Church in Soweto, where practising *sangomas* and *inyangas* (traditional healers who use herbalist remedies) are allowed to hold key positions. Moreover, in keeping with the musical talents of *Pace's* past editors, Kashane recently became a choir leader at the church and in 2000 recorded an album of religious music entitled *Masibambaneni* and dedicated, under the banner of *Ditau*

Tsa Judah ('Lion of Judah'), to the people of KwaZulu-Natal and Gauteng who 'have yet to see peace' *(Pace,* July 2000: 59). Comprising a selection of traditional gospel renditions and 'folk songs-cum-hymns', which 'promote harmony and goodwill and are often sung in praise at ceremonies and funerals', the music is rhythmic and celebratory yet still religious in tone.

While today Kashane claims no contradiction exists between his involvement with the church and received traditions of the African spiritual world (ibid.), in 1992 he insisted that his practice as a traditional healer was a means of bridging the gulf between traces of older indigenous African traditions and modern contemporary lifestyles. It would appear then that, despite his position as the editor of a contemporary consumer magazine published in English for black South Africans, Kashane's attempts to revive and relegitimise indigenous African traditions and vernaculars are by no means accidental. Indeed emblematised, as it were, in his multiple persona, they seem to represent an editorial vision anchored in a broader grasp of historical processes and patterns that may well be shared by other media practitioners and cultural brokers in a wide range of 'South African' idioms. These are currently generated by and through changes in language, performance, literate culture, media, lifestyle and fashion, and the business and corporate sector. Frequently combining autochthonous practices with modern modes of conduct, these modes of self-presentation revalidate, even as they construct and transform, a sense of 'past' rural experiences for today's black urban dwellers. (See Geshiere and Nyamnjoh 1998 for a similar discussion of witchcraft related to 'variations in the evolvement of urban-rural relations' in Cameroon.)

Given the way traditional sources for the production of historical knowledge, such as the chiefdom courtyard, the *kgoro* or *kgotla,* were dislocated under the impacts of colonisation, Christianity, migration, and urbanisation on (southern) Africa's indigenous peoples, the focus of public gatherings and social organisation necessarily changed in both urban and rural social structures, as did the shape of the household. Briefly, in precolonial times the *kgoro* or *kgotla* was the principal and legal forum for public assembly and debate, settling family disputes, negotiation, and participation in shared social agendas, including informal learning (i.e., hunting, obedience, and manly conduct), storytelling, and marriage ceremonies. Significantly, too, 'the advantages of seniority, position and patronage' in the *kgoro* or *kgotla* 'were offset by the authority granted to eloquent disputation in its own right' (Coplan 1994: 38). It must be emphasised, though, that neither the social functions of the *kgotla* nor the rhetorical skills it authorised were accessible to women (see Schapera 1938: 28; Ngcongco 1989; cf. Preston-Whyte 1974: 210; Hofmeyr 1993: 78–102; Coplan 1994: 38).[4]

Given the fact that the emergence of the magazine form for black South Africans dovetails with the consolidation of the apartheid regime in the late 1940s, I would view it, among other things, as a dislocated version of the *kgoro/kgotla* that enables people to forge alternative forms of civil sociability, cooperation, and social collectivity and to select alternative attitudes toward and sources of authority: a means of generating a sense of social order within a prevailing climate of heightened socio-political instability. More specifically correlations may be teased out between the social and discursive function(s) of the *kgoro* or *kgotla* and those ascribed to the magazine form in the sense that both provide a more or less public participatory forum for a collaborative collectivity of people in which literal exchanges take place, whether orally or in writing. They both provide a space to impart information, voice opinions, articulate disapproval and criticism, express humour, offer help and restitution to injured parties, and discuss current issues, political and non-political alike.[5] Thus although the physical space of the *kgoro/kgotla* has disappeared, it may be argued that some of its social functions have been relocated and to some extent continued and transformed in the textual space of the magazine form for black South Africans in urban environments. One way to begin exploring this possibility is by trying to harness the magazine form as 'a repository of miscellaneous information' (*Oxford English Dictionary*, 2d ed.) to the historical unfolding of consumer magazines for black South Africans.

Several decades ago Edward Bok (1921: 292–93), editor of the well-known American magazine *Ladies' Home Journal*, remarked that 'a successful magazine is exactly like a successful store: it must keep its wares constantly fresh and varied to attract the eye and hold the patronage of its customers.' Drawing a direct analogy between the magazine and the nineteenth-century department store, readily traced etymologically in *magazine* and *magasin* (store), Bok's comment suggests a wealth of metaphorical links between differently constructed notions of textual, visual, imaginative, and spatial/geographical spaces (see also Williams 1982: 58–106; Ohmann 1996: 223–48; Garvey 1996: 3–5). No less important is the dictionary denotation of *magazine* as 'a storehouse of information on a specified subject or for a particular class of persons. A periodical publication intended for general rather than learned or professional readers, and consisting of a miscellany of critical and descriptive articles, essays, works of fiction, etc.' (*Oxford English Dictionary*, 2d ed.). All the magazines listed above comprise repositories of miscellaneous information and discourses and, like the *kgoro/kgotla*, fulfil a broad range of social functions.

The magazine page, a very different sort of 'communication paradigm' from the uninterrupted text, requires processing and decoding procedures comparable to those exercised in the *kgotla* and in this sense may be regarded as a site of rhetorical and participationary deliberation. The reader is called on here to process multiple focal points determined by a range of different visual components (textual, graphic, typographic, and pictorial).

I would argue tentatively that the decoding skills applied (and standardised) by a collectivity/community of individual readers in processing the magazine page are both metonymically and metaphorically related to the ways different codificatory strategies and modes of verbal communication are performed (elicited and interrupted) by people in the *kgotla*. As rites of community affiliation, they endorse the social significance of the *kgotla*. As a collaborative forum for and of public deliberation, the *kgotla* may have prefigured processes of communication and social collaboration manifested later both in the magazine as a whole and on the magazine page in particular (cf. Kerr 2000 in its discussion of the *kgotla* as a 'communication paradigm' in its own right).

It should be noted that, although I try to situate the following textual analyses within some of the broader sociohistorical realities and processes of transition in South Africa, I make no attempt to describe the structure of the magazine industry in South Africa, and I provide only partial historical data of some of the individual titles under inquiry. While I do touch on the career of *Pace's* editor in chief Kashane, further ethnographic research is clearly required into the social settings, daily routines, patterns of magazine consumption, and protocols of magazine reading among black South Africans themselves. This kind of sociohistorical data would enable us to begin to determine the relations between alleged and actual uses of the magazines under examination.

2   Seeing Is Believing, or, Toward Magazines of Their Own

From a different historical perspective, consumer magazines for black South Africans can be traced to the onset of the commercial black press in South Africa, whose most significant manifestation, for our purposes, is the first mass-produced photomagazine introduced in the late 1940s, *Zonk!*, the 'African People's Pictorial' (1949–1964). A hitherto ignored yet invaluable historical account of *Zonk!* is provided by Irwin Stanley Manoim (1983), who illuminates the performance-oriented history of *Zonk!* which actually came into being following the staging by *Zonk!*'s founder, Ike Brooks, of a musical by the same name. As an American-style offshoot of the post-war black music industry in South Africa, *Zonk!* foregrounded photojournalism rather than text, focused on entertainment featuring American jazz and movie idols, such as Duke Ellington, Lena Home, Sammy Davis, Jr, and Eartha Kitt, carried editorials by American black intellectuals and authors alongside successful 'unknowns', and promoted successful local sports figures (especially boxers). Manoim also points out that *Zonk!* made a point of downplaying politics and, seeking to promote itself as a new public forum for urban sociability and egalitarianism, encouraged active participation in the magazine by all potential readers, literate, semiliterate, and nonliterate alike, by way of readers' letters, competitions and word puzzles, and individual and group photographs of unknown readers (i.e., noncelebrities). In 1962 *Zonk!* became the first South African publication to feature photo-stories, in which models acted out pre-scripted narrative sequences for the camera. In keeping with the way magazines constantly reconstruct themselves to ensure their ongoing reproduction and durability in the market, these pullout booklets had their own covers and were stitched to the centre of each magazine, and back copies could be purchased from the parent magazine (Manoim 1983).

The impact of *Zonk!* lay in its introduction of visual modes of representation along-side blocks of relatively uninterrupted text. A new kind of grammar, syntax, or underlying logic thus arose, such that visual modes shaped the style rather than the substance of the magazine's representations. *Zonk!*'s mix of verbal and visual information, perceived images, and schemata encompassed a range of cultural models and print technology. It combined strategies for reducing data and relationships from a multitude of domains in the natural world to graphic modes of representation and patterns via the use of contemporary print technologies, pictorial materials (i.e., illustrations, photographs, technical drawings, printed pictures, and comic strips), and colour techniques alongside reproductions of the printed word and blocks of text.

Zonk!'s use of visual representations also exemplifies how representations of products 'map out the social world,' defining not so much what people actually do but what they could conceive of doing (see Williamson 1986: 226). Encountering visual representations enabled readers to become 'virtual witnesses' of sorts in that it became possible for them to experience visually and observe as evidence 'things that they would have seen with their own eyes had they been present' (Olson 1994: 173, 176, paraphrasing Shapin and Shaffer 1985: 500).

Telling in this regard is Manoim's (1983: 115) own reference to the fact that the American heroes featured in *Zonk!* 'didn't have to be real – or even American'. In illustration he notes the American stylisation of a highly popular short story series that recounts the exploits of Ray Malaga, a black South African adventurer modelled on a Peter Cheyney-type hero. Manoim (ibid.) tells us that the Americanised African-sounding pen name of the series writer, a white journalist named Bob Toms, was 'Robert Roro', and he describes Malaga as wearing 'Chicago-inspired clothing' in 'the sketches that accompanied each instalment'. This use of 'virtual' experience ties in with the action-orientedness of African beliefs and perceptions, whereby the force of expressed desire in African cultures is frequently perceived as central to the ways interactions between persons and things are eventually lived out (see Van Beek and Blakely 1994: 17; Kopytoff and Miers 1977: 7–11).

Exemplifying and prefiguring a new model for and of cultural literacy, *Zonk!* and subsequent magazines, such as *Drum* (1951), *Bona* (1956), and *Pace* (1978), provided readers with new tools for accessing and reorganising a variety of cultural dispositions into urban lifestyle patterns or what Bourdieu calls 'habituses' (see Bourdieu 1984: 101–2, 173–225, 372–74, 466–67). Particularly useful to people in various stages of demographic mobility and cultural transition, these magazines also supplied their readers with implied instructions for regulating new modes of social action, which they were likely to internalise and follow 'naturally', consciously or not. These instructions suggested to people new ways to make sense of their changing demographic and material circumstances, and the regularised use of these instructions in a variety of sociocultural practices authorised a new, middle-class repertoire, often organising its users into new urban social networks. In the following section we shall see how the overwhelming use of English in these magazines fulfils similar, supplementary functions.

3 Magazines in English as Manifestations of a Black Middle-Class Repertoire

Inferring a readership's outlook from its reading material is by no means automatic, for people do not necessarily always agree with or promote the values and ideas in the material they read (Davis 1975: 191), nor are the uses to which magazines are put by any means limited to whether or not people have 'real' access to the options evoked (see Lury 1996; Williams 1982). In the South African juncture, especially, the incorporation of magazines into the routines and patterns of people's everyday lives may take place on different levels and may be visible in different ways (see, for instance, Silverstone, Hirsch, and Morely 1992). Like other material objects and forms of technology, magazines may have several different functions, some of which may be far removed from the declared intentions of their producers and marketers, while others may change over time and/or disappear entirely. In other words, the actual purchase of a magazine does not mean that it is necessarily used or even read in the ways we assume: it may be purchased, perused, and studied in various ways (silently by a single individual or read aloud to others) and to different ends (browsed in or paged through for visual rather than verbal gratification), set aside for deferred reading sometime in the future, displayed for show in various social environments (at home or in public places), and more. Moreover magazines for black South Africans have a large 'pass-on' or 'over-the-shoulder' readership, whose ratio is estimated at ten to one, over twice as high than the predicted two-to-one to four-to-one ratio among magazine readers in the West (Cohen 1992, substantiated by the 1998 AMPS-All Media Publishing Survey; for sample figures of British magazine distribution see comparative sales and readership data in Ferguson 1983: 207–8). In other words, vast discrepancies exist between the number of magazine copies circulated and/or disseminated and the number of people who actually buy them. Although their estimated market growth is yet to be conclusively determined, the very durability of the magazines established several decades ago *(Drum* 1951, *Bona* 1956, *True Love* 1975, *Pace* 1978) and the launch and sustained production of newer ones *(Tribute* 1986, *Ebony South Africa* 1995–2000) attest to some measure of their 'success'.

As the main linguistic medium of these magazines and as part of a wider urban middle-class repertoire, English is concretely instrumental on at least two levels. On one level it is functional as a means of literacy teaching/ learning that imparts to readers the literacy skills required to decode the written texts of the magazines themselves. On another level it is often sociosemiotic and/or organisational, its instrumentality related more to the symbolic display of written discourse in English than to the overt functionality of literacy in English among black South Africans today. More generally, in all the magazines we discern two interrelated, at times overlapping sets of dispositions: the one didactic and the other aspirational (addressed in more detail in Laden 1997). Both are pivotal to the dispositions commonly held to be shared by people who aspire to 'middle-class' lives (see note 2). As mentioned in the previous section, these dispositions refer not so much to what people actually do as to what they would be likely to conceive of doing.

Viewed didactically, these magazines serve as an informal educational apparatus targeted on the reading and comprehension skills required to access the knowledge they seek to impart: basic literacy and numeracy skills and basic contextual knowledge. To this end they combine pictorial and visual modes of representation with verbal skills in, say, photo story and comic form, word games, puzzles, advertisements, competitions for both adults and children, and educational supplements. Assuming the combined role of primers and modern-day civility manuals, these magazines also manifest at the level of content a firm didactic stance in many of their features, departments, and advertisements. On the aspirational front, feature articles, readers' letters, advice columns, and short stories are intended to educate and inform by (a) expressing views designed to establish standards of social correctness for a community of readers and (b) promoting role models and celebrities who adhere to these views and associated practices.

Less overtly, soliciting social involvement and collaborative participation by way of these didactic and aspirational drives is another self-promotional strategy. Exemplified in competitions, contests, and word puzzles dispersed throughout the magazines, this mechanism, too, may be historically related to the competitive dimension and operational competence traditionally manifested in oral performances that took place in the *kgotla*, whereby people were united in 'a common excitation over the display of individual prowess in social accomplishment' (Coplan 1994: 204). Advertising goods, brand names, reading practices, the magazines themselves as desirable commodities, and in the South African framework competitions and contests also frequently have mnemonic and educational functions and promote social involvement, reading and writing practices, and self-display. Prizes and awards are offered for winning letters, and individual and group photographs sent in by readers are frequently published. *Drum*, *Pace*, and *Tribute* all offer cash prizes for winning letters. *True Love* awards a R100 prize and a *True Love* T-shirt and cap for the 'letter of the month' and invites readers to send in ideas for stories or personal experiences they would like to share. If these are developed into a feature, the editors promise to pay R250. *Drum* offers R500 to readers for every 'newsworthy true story' that is published and R250 for every published picture or photograph. Competitions abound in all the magazines. An issue of *Pace* (December/January 1998), for instance, features three: the *Pace* Super Bonanza, in which readers are requested to answer a question relating to the number of faces appearing on the 'Mngosi' gossip column page (discussed in detail later), a R1 000 crossword competition, and in the 'Queen' women's section 'competitive', achievement-orientated readers can win free membership in the Ladies Club for Finance Planning and Marketing. The April 1992 issue of *Tribute* offers 'A Week in the Cape for Life' as a means of promoting a time-sharing vacation scheme; the January 1996 edition of *True Love* features a subscription promotion in which sixty readers can each win a watch; *True Love* and Kwela Books have offered ten free copies of *Common Hunger to Sing*, a book paying tribute to South Africa's black women singers who have made significant contributions to urban black culture; a bridal competition sponsored jointly by *True Love* and American Swiss Jewellers offers prizes worth more than R250 000 and *True Love*, Fedics Food Services, and HI Africa (an electrical appliance distributions company) have sponsored a Traditional Recipe Competition offering appliances or cash prizes to three winners. These competitions clearly both exemplify and seek to contribute to a middle-class urban repertoire comprising lifestyles that are both transnational and global (i.e., the bridal, financial planning, and jewellery competitions and the time-share vacation) and locally South African (i.e., the book of South African women singers and the Traditional Recipe Competition). The subscription promotion is, of course, a self-advertising strategy for *True Love*.

At the same time these magazines are instrumental in redefining and relegitimising indigenous customs, values, and beliefs for black South Africans living in urban environments. This is attested by the profusion of debates thrashing out the pros and cons of traditional versus Western, primarily Christian, marriage customs and wedding ceremonies, funeral and burial rites, the social relevance today of bride wealth or *lobola,* the merits of circumcision and other initiation rites, and the advantages of monogamy over polygamy. Of particular interest is the way the inherently African interest in sorcery and witchcraft is being relegitimated for and reworked into the social fabric of metropolitan, middle-class communities. While Western culture has recently experienced a surge of New Age concerns with alchemy, the occult, holistic medicine, and cosmic energies, in African belief systems sorcery and witchcraft have long been central in accounting for unexpected misfortunes (illness, death, accidents) and conspicuous successes (sudden enrichment or a remarkable victory). Relating them by sorcery and witchcraft to the ancestors through human motivations, such as jealousy or ambition, adversity and success are personalised so evil forces can be opposed or fought off (see Geshiere 1997: 69). In this context a growing interest is manifested in *sangomas* and *inyangas,* traditional medicine healers. All the magazines contain information about traditional healing practices and are instrumental in promoting traditional healing services in metropolitan areas. This is noted, for instance, in 'dial-a-*sangoma*' advertisements, where *sangomas* offer to perform by telephone the traditional acts of throwing bones and calling one's ancestors. A number of magazines even feature articles about white *sangomas*, that is, white people who display healing powers that they choose to transmit in 'traditionally African' ways.

Unlike magazines for white readers, many of these magazines do not take for granted their readers' familiarity with the range of cultural products and practices they address and seek to promote. Particularly telling in this regard is the *Bona* 'Word Puzzle', a regular monthly feature that encourages readers to improve their English vocabulary and advises in an intimate, personal tone that, if readers do not know a word, they should ask a friend what it means or look in a dictionary. 'You'll be amazed at how your English will get better and better. And what's more, you could earn lots of MONEY!' (*Bona* 1989b, 1993, 2000b). Correct entries stand to win considerable sums of money: R20 000 in August 1989, R25 000 in October 1993, R30 000 in April 2000.

If no entry is completely correct, entries with the fewest mistakes stand to win R4 000, R5 000 and R6 000 respectively. Strikingly, from 1989 onwards the sentences used in the 'Word Puzzle' have hardly changed, nor have its rules, instructions, or even the promotional text surrounding the competition. A word puzzle is comprised of three or four puzzles, each made up of twenty sentences in which two or three words appear in brackets somewhere in the sentence. Readers are asked to select the most appropriate word for each sentence from the set of brackets and inscribe it into the spaces next to each sentence. Explicit instructions are given to write 'in one letter to each block', and readers are encouraged to fill in multiple entries; this of course costs them more but gives them a better chance of winning.

Both the 'Word Puzzle' itself and the accompanying instructions function as mnemonic devices, repeated verbatim month after month for over a decade. Intended as an exercise in literacy, numeracy, and basic contextual skills, these instructions further illustrate that even the most basic contextual knowledge is not presumed where black readers are concerned. This text, conspicuously printed in larger typeface than other sections of the 'Word Puzzle', reads as follows:

SENDING YOUR ENTRIES

Let's say you have filled out five entries. That means you will have to buy a postal order worth R3. (Remember, 6oc per entry). Now, write your name and address on the coupon at the bottom of the last three entries over the page, and fill in the number of your postal order as well. Now – and this is VERY IMPORTANT

TEAR THE WHOLE PAGE
CAREFULLY OUT OF THE MAGAZINE.
DO NOT CUT OUT ANY OF THE ENTRIES

Now, make your postal order payable to: Bona People's Fund, and put your page from Bona and your postal order into an envelope and send it to: Bona Word Puzzle, Box 32046, Mobeni, 4060. Do not register your entries, rather use that money to fill out extra entries, and make sure you post your entries well before the closing date of this competition.

While the condescending tone of these instructions may well be objectionable to literate readers familiar with such mundane procedures as using a postal service, filling in forms, and addressing coupons and envelopes, such routines are by no means taken for granted here, nor is the literacy they involve. This text exemplifies spoken discourse in written form. The text assumes the immediacy of a performed text being read and experienced simultaneously, in real time as it were. As is often the case in oral narrative situations, the reader is addressed as though she or he were physically present and actually benefiting from the instructive experience.

On another front, medical columns instruct presumably literate readers on the most basic matters of health and hygiene far more explicitly than would a magazine for white readers. For instance, Sister Lindiwe's column entitled 'How to Check Your Newborn Child' *(Bona* 1989a) is intended for women giving birth at home, with or without a midwife, as well as women who have access to a clinic or hospital. Assuming that readers will be able to read it or have it read to them, the text advises mothers of newborn babies to 'check that he's breathing well, that he's a good colour, that his heart is beating strong and fast, and that he can use his muscles' and to make sure the baby is 'wrapped up to keep warm and is properly checked later' *(Bona* 1989a: 114–16). Such basic data is too self-evident to be conveyed to white readers. Moreover white women do not typically give birth at home (except as a deliberate choice) and hence would most likely be under professional care, together with their offspring.

A more recent issue of *Bona* addresses similar points in a less overtly didactic, more indirect fashion in an article entitled 'Checking Up on Mom's Cherub' *(Bona* 2000a). Less informative than confirmational and inspirational, this feature assumes literacy in English and seeks to legitimise child care practices already presumed to prevail among readers, affirming that they are beyond question and should be aspired to. As indicated by the subheading, 'Is my baby developing properly? is a question that mothers often ask themselves – so calm your fears with this quick checklist' *(Bona* 2000a: 124), this article, unlike the one mentioned above, addresses mothers presumed not only to be familiar with health care options (the doctor and clinic) in urban environments but also to know that they are expected to make regular use of them. These implied readers are presumed to know that a paediatrician is a doctor who specialises in children's health and that they need to take their young children for regular health care examinations. The difference in editorial assumptions can be attributed to the presumed (not necessarily factual) predominance of middle-class understandings of the civic and social responsibilities (i.e., medical care and responsible parenting) that go hand in hand with living in metropolitan environments.

Somewhat different aspirational tendencies are manifested in an advertisement featuring a smiling, touched-up, and highlighted portrait of the former Miss South Africa (1995), Basetsana Makgalemele, promoting 'Revlon Realistic Hair Relaxer' *(True Love* 2000: 4). Hair relaxant is frequently used by black South African women to straighten ('relax') their typically curly or frizzy hair. In this advertisement the photographed model's elegantly coifed hair is relaxed and shining, and the copy reads: 'Unsure of the Best Way to Good-looking Hair? Relax' (ibid.). Aspects of being middle class are foregrounded here by the model's celebrity status as a former beauty queen, her acclaimed good looks, and the way the advertised product is denoted not as a hair straightener but euphemistically as a hair *relaxer.* The multiple meanings of the verb *relax* (to make less tense or rigid, to reduce effort for the sake of rest and/or recreation, or to become less tense or anxious) are foregrounded through repetition (in the product's name and in the copy) and, coupled with the visual predominance of the model's identity and appearance, are intended not only to render her overall beauty and hair desirable 'commodities' but to suggest that emulating her esteemed good looks requires minimal effort and can be accomplished with ease.

More overtly didactic are practical advice columns that provide readers with tips regarding efficient housekeeping: home economics and thrifty consumerism, food preparation, entertainment, dressmaking, mending, home decoration, household repairs, as well as parenting and marriage guidance. Pervasive, too, is advice on how to apply elementary first aid, how to ensure safety around the house, and how to go about family planning and securing protection against sexually transmitted diseases. Somewhat surprisingly readers' letters are often blatantly didactic documents, whose social and rhetorical functions seem to be very different from those of readers' letters in the Anglo-American magazine tradition.

Indeed, while readers' letters in Western magazines are intended to simulate oral narrative situations and to this end deploy more sophisticated rhetorical strategies, readers' letters in magazines for black South Africans seem to be more straightforwardly modelled on literate discursive modes. Let us examine the following example. Among the readers' letters to 'Queen', the women's section of *Pace,* is a text containing important basic information about a nation-wide family planning programme in South Africa. Appearing in the letters column and intended to inform female readers about a serious social problem, the segment has clearly been selected and paraphrased from existing professional literature on family planning. It has also been edited, since sentences have been left short, the choice of language is untechnical, and the overall educational message is quite clear (despite the somewhat tedious use of the passive voice at the beginning of the second paragraph). The text of this 'letter', titled 'Family Planning', follows:

> Many people are ignorant about the facts of family planning. All sorts of myths about the different forms of contraception are partly to blame. The family planning programme provides a countrywide service to all the people of South Africa. Its aim is to improve the health of every individual and family, as well as the living standards of all people in the world. It allows them to realise the importance of making decisions when planning families.
>
> The size of the family must be taken into consideration regarding the provision of food, clothing, love, quality time and attention, and education. The postponement of the first pregnancy is also emphasised to help prevent the traumatic and tragic results of teenage pregnancies. Items from the necessity of spacing pregnancies to the advantages of breastfeeding are stressed. Given time, the mother can recuperate emotionally as well as physically after the birth of her child, with the result that she can give enough attention to every child she has.
>
> T. S. Leso, Ba Mokgoko (*Pace* 1990: 69)

Intended to promote Western middle-class ideas of the appropriateness of a manageable nuclear family, this text recommends that forms of contraception among 'all the people of South Africa' will improve the 'living standards of all people' and points out the 'importance of making decisions when planning families' even as it instructs readers on how to base these decisions: on the size of the family; the ability of parents, specifically mothers, to provide tangible (food and clothing) and intangible (love, attention, education) commodities; and ample spacing between births. By contrast, readers' letters published in magazines intended for white South African audiences typically follow discursive conventions standardised in Anglo-American magazines since the beginning of the twentieth century (Ohmann 1996; Beetham 1996). In Anglo-American magazines, letters columns are typically concerned with people and representations of their selves and stances, and letters typically traffic in brief glimpses into states of affairs or social chatter through more personal, written responses by feeling, individual selves (for an insightful analysis of the innuendos of published letters see Spacks 1986: 69–91). Our 'letter' pays no heed to the authorial conventions typically associated with letters published in magazines: it evokes no tone of intimacy or hint of consciousness, implies no relationship or stance, recounts no anecdotal experience, either personal, social, or otherwise; and offers no inside knowledge or interpretation. For our purposes, although it clearly conveys a didactic message and may well be of interest to female readers and/or mothers, this 'letter' adheres to a straightforward literate model of written information, deploying no authorial perspective or rhetorical strategies to enhance its effectiveness. As the editor was sufficiently adept to name the column in which this text appears 'Write of Way', we might infer from this sample that readers' letters are knowingly formulated to convey information that cannot readily be conveyed in traditional oral formats, and to this end they are modelled on literate modes of discourse.

Another reader's letter, in a recent issue of *Drum* (July 23, 1999), bears a somewhat different, more political 'aspirational' stance. This letter reads as though it were sponsored by a government spokesperson and manifests a Victorian ethos of self-help coupled with a Kennedyesque appeal to civic-mindedness ('Ask not what your country can do for you; ask what you can do for your country'). It should be remembered here that the present African National Congress (ANC) government is constantly under fire for not fulfilling promises to improve conditions of employment, housing, education, economic growth, and foreign investment in the new South Africa. Entitled 'Let's Make Our Own Jobs', the letter reads as follows:

> A friend of mine once said: 'South Africans don't suffer from a high unemployment rate, but rather from lack of ideas.' Different people hold different views. However, many people are looking at the option of being self-employed. We as citizens have a role to play in job creation. Every individual is a potential job-creator. It must be clear in our minds the government owes no one a job. The truth is the government isn't responsible for job losses. It's time for us to be responsible for our own lives. We must stop being critical and be constructive. Most people don't look at themselves as contributors but as recipients. It's disappointing that we expect a lot from the government without giving anything. Let's forget the broken promises made by our government and start working.
>
> Thabile Mange, Kagiso

This letter, too, is explicitly modelled on literate discursive modes. Voicing a seemingly apolitical preference for respectable conformity and shared solidarity motivated by liberal, middle-class interests, it illustrates the way views expressed in magazines are often, significantly, carriers of continuity and/or stability, as attested by their fairly conservative, at times even stereotypical representations. From another perspective, this letter goes some way toward attesting that consumer magazines for black South Africans in general are reaffirming, seek to 'make an accepted world for living in' (Davis 1994: 109), and give people a badly needed sense of social stability.

A similar attempt to forge a sense of collective middle-class solidarity is manifested in the following, final example, which stresses similarities between stereotypical beauty concerns among black and white teenagers. Featuring two teenage girls, one black and one white, the advertisement is for a product called 'Clean & Clear, a Shine Control Mattifier' (*True Love* 2000b: 17). Both girls photographed are in their mid-teens, attractive, and lightly made-up, and both have long hair. Although the black model's hair is braided in dreadlocks while the white model's hair is loose and flowing, similarities between them are foregrounded more than differences. The product is that which may be used by people of all skin types and types colours, and the ad appears to be directed at all potential consumers/readers. No allusion is made to the fact that it is featured in a magazine for black South African women, and the copy treats both girls equally stereotypically, as middle-class teenagers, outstanding individuals who 'shine' and are 'self absorbed,' even as they maintain the semblance of being shine-less, that is, perspiration free, respectably under control, and squeaky clean. The lexical composition of this ad is intended less to draw attention to the product itself than to generate a sense of individual yet shared gendered concerns and mutual solidarity among its potential middle-class, teenage consumers and their mothers.

> Even as teenagers, we can't be expected to shine all the time. Okay, so we're not always so great at maths. But where we really never shine is on our faces. Thanks to Clean & Clear's new Shine Control Mattifier. Perfect for use under make-up, the lotion's oil-absorbing particles spread evenly over your skin for 8-hour shine control and a smooth, matt finish that's healthy and beautiful. After all, we're teenagers. We're supposed to be self-absorbed. It's our way of staying Clear & Clean and under control.
>
> (Ibid.)

In many of the examples presented earlier, content takes precedence over rhetoric, and the use of English is no longer marked (i.e., particularly noticeable or unexpected). Precisely as such they all manifest a shared understanding of English as both a social marker and a 'mark of excellence' and an important indication of the ongoing repositioning and successful acceptance of black South Africans, against all odds, into South Africa's urban environments and middle classes.

Most significantly for our purposes, English is typically perceived as 'a middle- and upper-middle-class language' (Webb and Kembo-Sure 2000: 45; Teer-Tomaselli 1996: 415), while Afrikaans is currently held to be distributed among diverse socioeconomic classes, especially in rural and farming areas, and is known to be predominant in certain urban centres (i.e., Pretoria and Bloemfontein). Bantu languages are probably used largely by the working classes (Webb and Kembo-Sure 2000: 45).

It would appear then that English has deliberately been chosen (by magazine producers) and accepted (by their readers/consumers) as the most advantageous linguistic medium since it is considered the language best equipped to serve the variegated interests of all those currently residing in South Africa's urban(ising) environments, especially those aspiring to membership in the middle class(es). Indeed according to the linguist Carol Myers-Scotton (1998: 9), people will generally opt for 'the "best" choice'.

4   Toward a New South African Idiom: Linguistic Diversity in *Pace* and the 'Mngosi' Gossip Column

Against a historical backdrop of pervasive and privileged uses of English, linguistic diversity is becoming increasingly more instrumental in formulating, disseminating, and legitimising a new South African idiom among middle-class black South Africans. Manifested in a variety of public discourses and media, linguistic diversity is gaining ground as a strategic means of negotiating social mobility and, not unlike the use of English, lending respectability to many black urban dwellers, who in this case wish to draw on received indigenous sources of African languages and cultures as part of their 'cultural capital'. Two different kinds of linguistic diversity are used by South African speakers in the culture, although they will not be differentiated below. One relates to the impact of English and Afrikaans on the Bantu languages, that is, 'the interactive mixing of languages which are morphologically and syntactically different' (Finlayson and Slabbert 1997: 1). The second may be described as *mixed language,* a 'characteristic pattern of language use among African township residents in South Africa [that] may well include words or full constituents from several languages' (Finlayson, Calteaux, and MyersScotton 1998: 395). Linguistic diversity of both strains is manifested in various media.

First, a South African magazine, *Y,* intended for the young, up-and-coming yuppie sector in South Africa, was launched in October 1998. Alluding directly to the media organ YFM, a popular South African radio station that targets young listeners, the magazine's use of the letter/logo *Y* as its title is intended to encourage the construction of a 'young' and 'yuppie' readership; this is further testified by the form (layout) and content of the magazine itself. *Y* innovatively deploys a highly informal, South African urban English, heavily seasoned with slang and expletives and embedded with Afrikaans expressions and idioms from a variety of township argots and African vernacular slang. The linguistic diversity flaunted in *Y* signals the expansion and consolidation of a new linguistic idiom that addresses a newly dominant urban sector, namely young black yuppies. As such it manifests and contributes to social mobility and change in

South Africa's urban environments. A similar phenomenon is found in various modes of advertising in different magazines and newspapers and on billboards and television (see Zondi 1995) and is even more pronounced in the lyrics of the reigning popular township dance music form, kwaito, known for its sociocultural relevance and infectious cross-over rhythms drawn from rhythm and blues, reggae, and dance. Linguistic diversity is also conspicuous in several popular South African television soap series, such as *Generations* and *Isidingo,* in which conventional soap-opera techniques are combined with relevant sociopolitical issues, such as reverse discrimination, affirmative action, unemployment, crime, and the influx into South Africa of strongly resented foreign traders and refugees from other African countries, labelled *kwere kwere* ('aliens').

Generally speaking, the effects of linguistic diversity as a marked choice are at least two. In in-group varieties among group members it typically encodes solidarity and unity and so is often used as a means of deliberately playing down and/or neutralising intergroup (both interethnic and interracial) tensions and differences. As noted by David B. Coplan (1985: 208), in South Africa the use of English among black South Africans often symbolises 'urban Africans' desire to overcome ethnic division, local parochialism, and the implications of apartheid'. At the same time using marked (unexpected) linguistic varieties generates social distance between participants and raises the users' own status. More specifically, because English is currently the unmarked (i.e., expected, see Myers-Scotton 1993, 1998) option in many black urban media genres, in the 'Mngosi' column of *Pace* the use of interactive or other linguistic diversity is currently marked (unexpected). As such it presumably generates a sense of solidarity among *Pace* magazine's readers even as it distinguishes them as a singular, socially mobile urban reading community.

In other words, linguistic diversity functions both as a strategy for social solidarity and as a sign of social mobility and professional and cultural distinction, a marker of the unique and specific relationship obtaining between the producers and readers of *Pace.* It enhances the professional status of *Pace's* print-media practitioners, who, by 'utilising their ability to switch from one code to another, show off their linguistic repertoire and therefore show themselves as multidimensional individuals' (Myers-Scotton 1998: 26). It would be interesting to examine to what extent the by now well-established if not canonised position of the 'Mngosi' column has contributed to the increasing standardisation among readers of linguistic diversity as a socially desirable mode of written stylisation to be imitated in spoken and refined in other literate forms.

We now turn to a closer analysis of (written) manifestations of oral narrative traditions and language contact phenomena (i.e., code switching, code mixing, and lexical borrowing) in *Pace's* 'Mngosi' gossip column. I hope to show that the multimodal composition of 'Mngosi', together with the cogent use of gossip laced with linguistic diversity, marks a new urban integration of traditional discursive modes, such as oral storytelling, historical narrative, and praise poetry.

An earlier transposition of spoken language into print occurred in 1951 with the inauguration of *Drum,* which consolidated a new discursive model: colloquial English represented in writing as if in the idiom spoken by black South Africans. Historically the best-known South African magazine for black readers and in its early years identified with a strong political thrust, *Drum,* also marks an important juncture in the evolution of black narrative and discursive forms in South Africa (Sampson 1956; Rabkin 1975; Smith 1985; Chapman 1985; Nicol 1991; and Tyler 1995). Of specific interest to us here is the way *Drum* journalists in the 1950s simulated and authorised a newly stylised 'township slang,' consolidating an Americanised idiom borrowed from adaptations of American popular culture, such as B-rated movies, fashion, cars, and music. This idiom both represented and promoted idealised versions of 'township South Africa of the 1920s. A place of jazz and beauty queens, of gangsters, folk-heroes and witch-doctors, a vibrant, laughing, deadly world' (Nicol 1991: ix). It is well represented by the objections voiced by 'a man with golliwog hair in a floppy American suit, at the Bantu Men's Social Centre' to 'Tribal music! Tribal history! Chiefs! We don't care about chiefs! Give us jazz and film stars, man! We want Duke Ellington, Satchmo, and hot dames! Yes, brother, anything American. You can cut out this junk about kraals and folk-tales and Basutos in blankets – forget it! You're just trying to keep us backward, that's what! Tell us what's happening right here, on the Reef!' (Sampson 1956: 20). For our purposes, *Drum's* significance lies in the discursive model it opened and made available for *Pace*. Through linguistic diversity and code switching, the latter magazine reintroduces into written English discourse African vernaculars intended to simulate township slang 'as it was spoken' in the 1950s and 1960s.

A gossip column regularly featured in *Pace* since 1985, 'Mngosi' is collaboratively written by editor in chief Kashane, assistant editor Joe Khumalo, and a variety of *Pace* journalists and feature editors, some of who have been replaced over time. It resorts to a stylised use of English that is clearly multimodal, that is, it draws on 'more than one semiotic mode of communication simultaneously ... involv[ing] the complex interaction of visual elements and verbal English presented to the eye' (Goodman 1996:39, 69), and is punctuated by linguistic diversity (intended to simulate discursive situations in which actual conversations are in the process of taking place). Thereby, the 'Mngosi' gossip column seeks to revitalise the cultural function of the traditional African storyteller and/or praise poet in a modern-day; urban, journalistic context.

Kashane maintains that initially the 'Mngosi' gossip column was conceived as a means of enabling black magazine journalists to subvert political censorship – in 1983 *Pace* was banned following a report on the funeral of a Pan-Africanist Congress member (Kashane 1992). But how exactly, does gossip serve subversive ends? In her discerning study of gossip, Patricia Ann Meyer Spacks tells us it is seemingly benign. As allegedly frivolous, idle chatter ranging from the malicious to the intimate, gossip typically rehashes 'information or pseudo-information that has already passed through many ears, many mouths, acquiring authority and heightening in the process' (Spacks 1986: 7). Believed to involve little consideration of the issues it addresses, even constituting 'moral avoidance' (ibid.), gossip appears to protect those doing the talking from serious engagement with the world and/or other people. Gossip highlights the awareness of both an 'outside' 'inhabited by those talked about' (ibid.) and an 'inside', the realm of its participant talkers, consolidating a group's sense of itself conveying inside information, heightening self-reflection, enabling the insiders to voice doubt and uncertainty and to try to overcome them. What's more, belonging to the realm of private, '"natural" discourse, gossip often violates "the claims of civility", but it incorporates the possibility that people utterly lacking in public power may affect the views of figures who make things happen in the public sphere' (ibid.: 6–7). In other words, precisely as a function of intimacy, gossip conveniently lends itself to more 'serious' discursive operations that serve public, social purposes, articulating social opinion and determining relations of social power. In this sense gossip may be perceived as a potentially subversive discourse.

By dwelling on 'specific personal particulars', the episodic, anecdotal forms of gossip 'claim other people's experience by interpreting it into story'; in turn, as oral tradition gossip shapes narrative forms and social drama into familiar modes of narrative address and structure, conflict and characterisation, and represents shared values, a worldview, and a reassuring sense of social bonding (ibid.: 11, 14, 15, 22). Historically the reliability of the accounts or anecdotes recounted in 'Mngosi' does not signify: they can be true or not, presented as personal eyewitness accounts or hearsay, or a mixture.

Before we specify how this column operates as a written form of gossip or oral conversation, let us outline some of the concrete, graphological features of 'Mngosi'. To begin with, the column is always placed first in *Pace,* immediately after the table of contents, to catch attention and lure readers into reading the column and then the entire magazine (much like the instrumental opening in a rock song). From 1985 to 1996 the 'Mngosi' column appeared on a full-page spread coloured bright yellow and framed in red, and it consisted of seven or eight printed anecdotal units. Its full title 'Mngosi with the Pace Gang' also bore a Zulu subtitle, *'Sondela Wena Ndabazabantu',* roughly translated as 'Come everyone who wants to hear about everyone else's affairs.' Above the title was a horizontal series of passportlike photographs of the authors themselves, topped by the onomatopoeic 'PSSSSST', an attention-drawing device in the visual medium. The device epitomises the way journalistic gossip trades in the *promise* of private, intimate knowledge even as this is about to be made public, literally in front of the readers' eyes.

Photographs of the 'Mngosi' writers are integral to the column, although the members of the team and their number, like the grouping of their photographs, are open to change. Interestingly, although the 'Mngosi' column has always been a collaborative effort, only since the end of 1999 has this been manifested overtly in a group photograph of its writers; previously the column featured separate photographs of each individual writer.[6] Although the column's changing graphology (i.e., combinations of colour imagery, black and colour typefaces, photography, and use of graphic forms, such as comic strip conventions) is inspired largely by the availability of new image technology in the print media at large, it may also be seen as exemplifying shifting self-perceptions of the 'Mngosi' conjoined persona. As an alliance of commentators, the 'Mngosi' writers

clearly hold 'written forms of observational narrative' in high regard, constantly recon-
firming 'the significance of trivial detail' and the 'imaginative power of specific knowledge about other people' (ibid.: 153), or what might be called 'cultural chatter' even as
they may at times appear not to take seriously their own conversational commentaries
and narrative utterances. The 'Mngosi' gossip column, a collaborative voice often represented in the first-person singular, underscores how gossip re-establishes 'the way in
which small actions define character and comprise experience' (ibid.: 154) and what
Isabel Hofmeyr (1993: 53) calls 'the flexibility of oral storytelling, which continues to
absorb everyday detail and so retain at least a veneer of contemporaneity.'

However, as Ruth Finnegan (1967: 49) has noted, African oral narrative, unlike
Western oral epic narratives, is not 'composed on a grand scale' and hence is not concerned with narrative syntax, heroic characterisation or with large-scale events like wars
and upheavals, though it can indeed convey epic intent (Hofmeyr 1993: 107; Okpewho
1979). In our case epic design is implicit in the large-scale spatial conceptualisation
of the 'Mngosi' narrative units in urban environments and in the picaresque progression of the authors, more than the characters themselves, from one urban situation to
another. If epic typically follows the sociohistorical trajectory of a heroic leader, the
'Mngosi' anecdotes focus on situations that have evolved in urban environments among
members of South Africa's recently emerged black middle class and on the authors' alleged sense of social responsibility toward them.

Narratives are typically modelled on existing forms of folk narrative that seek to
restore social equilibrium and order. Formulated as humorous, often ironical sociohistorical critiques and commentaries, frequently stylised by enacted speech and repetition, and laced with colourful parenthetical interjections, the products of the 'Mngosi'
authors largely engage with a range of situations in which urban persons and states of
affairs seldom, and even so obliquely, allude to the dire circumstances of South Africa's
recent sociocultural and political past. Significantly the critical, ironic tone of 'Mngosi'
yields a correlation between the social function of its producers and that of the *imbongi*
(praise poet). In seeking to promote the principles that those in power ought to rather
than do practice and/or stand for such poets were licensed to use 'ribald language otherwise unacceptable in public' and to 'criticise with impunity persons in positions of
power' while distancing themselves from their subjects of praise/condemnation (Opland 1983: 66–67). Indeed the 'Mngosi' writers seem to model themselves on while
parodying the traditional figure of the praise poet. For example:

> I want to warn adobabes [good-looking girls/babes] who love mingling with amatop shayela
> [big guys, celebrities]. You must be very careful of this TV presenter and deejay that works for
> a popular music station. He has plenty of women who are crazy about his looks and voice.
> Every woman wants to land in his arms but it's unfortunate that the guy happens to be dating
> a woman twice his age and she traps goed for [keeps a strong hold on] her toy boy. So you must
> listen when I warn you about this handsome dude since the Magogo [granny] recently attacked
> a beauty queen who was rumoured to be his girlfriend.
>
> (*Pace* 1997b)

Representing an extended parenthetical interjection rather than a narrative account in its own right, this 'cautionary tale' is firmly anchored in a contemporary urban reality where media celebrities, especially television presenters and deejays, reign supreme, their amorous antics providing their public with the endless fascination of their imminent but not always realised fall into disfavour and disrepute. While the use of language here only mildly engages with the ribald, the moralising, didactic voice of the authors' collaborative persona is at once serious and ironic and foregrounds its own ambiguous stance toward the characters involved. The latter, not identified but presumably well known to the readers, are lampooned as a 'toyboy' who 'happens to be dating a woman twice his age, a handsome dude', and a 'Magogo' (granny) who 'traps goed' (Afrikaans slang for a woman who will not let go of her man).

The deliberate and pervasive (though not absolute) avoidance of naming or overt identification of the characters is conspicuous throughout the columns' anecdotes. On the face of it, this may be attributed to the fact that the 'Mngosi' narratives typically revolve around well-known celebrity figures whose identities are quite obvious to most readers as 'informed observers'. More specifically, I will argue that this stylistic feature derives from the way oral narrative is intended to (1) heighten the mutual relationship between the narrator and his or her audience, (2) obscure the distinction between the real world narrative situation and the represented, fictive world, and (3) adopt a communal approach to characterisation, which tends to favour characters' social dispositions over their individual personalities or traits (Kunene 1989: 199, 237). These objectives have been transposed into the written stylistics of both the column as a whole and its individual manifestations.

While omitting names, the narratives recounted by the 'Mngosi' authorial voices display an abundance of parenthetical intervention, commentary, and response. Directly addressing the reader as though in spoken conversation, parenthetical phrases frequently are positioned at the opening and/or closing segments of 'Mngosi' narrative units yet also may be dispersed elsewhere. Examples include: 'You guys out there had better watch out' *(Pace* 1992); 'Jislaaik! [Afrikaans adaptation of 'Jesus!'] If you ain't heard this one, you ain't heard nuthin', man!'; 'Shh . . . Come hither, lona bondaba ['you with everyone' in Zulu] and get it straight from the gossip factory' *(Pace* 1991/ 1992); 'Hela wena ['hey you' in Zulu], jy praat te veel ['you talk too much' in Afrikaans]'; "Gaa, tshini! ['Go on,' expression of surprise in Xhosa]'; 'Khaloko ['of course' in Zulu]' *(Pace* 1977a); and the following pseudo-epic or extended metaphor: 'Seems to me Zweklakhe Sisulu [son of renowned ANC activist Walter Sisulu, who resigned from the position of director of the South African Broadcasting Authority and is known to have reneged on other leading media posts] has some strong muti ['medicine' in Zulu and Xhosa] that makes people vanish faster than David Copperfield or Houdini ever could!' *(Pace* 1999).

Calling attention to the speakers' position(s) toward their narratives, the characters they focus on, and their readers, these interjections may well be viewed as manifestations of narratorial digression or interruption designed to highlight the emotive function of the authors' attitude(s) and points of view both in the column as a whole and in each separate narrative unit, even as they give the impression of serving a phatic function (Jakobson 1960), that is, merely to confirm the presence of an implied reader/listener by way of repeated address. In both cases these interruptions reconstitute a desired sense of mutuality between the 'Mngosi' narratorial/authorial voices and their readers.

The next example, too, is symptomatic of the kind of social commentary and authorial distancing regularly enacted in the 'Mngosi' column:

> If you are famous please do not go around making other people miserable. Maybe I should say if you are famous don't think everybody in this sunny rainbow country has to know you. This ex-soccer star, or should I say soccer legend, visited some bundu [remote place] somewhere in KwaZulu. He went to a supermarket to grab fewnyana things. At the till he did not want to wait to queue, so he went upfront. One angry lady asked: 'Yewena bhuti wekhanda elikhulu – I don't care a hoot ukuthi uwaubani get in the queue. Uyezwake fame or no fame navo iqueue'
>
> (*Pace* 1996).

This trivial anecdotal account nicely brings out the way the 'Mngosi' writers switch from one linguistic code to another and in so doing show off their linguistic prowess and present themselves as multidimensional persons. In this didactic, fable-like piece, which sounds almost like an aphorism, the combined speakers set up an 'oral' narrative situation by addressing the reader directly. Their anecdotal account of the deliberately nameless ex-soccer star who felt his celebrity status entitled him to jump a supermarket queue is intended to take him down a notch or two and to convey a moral message to the readers, who, along with the 'Mngosi' writers, are cast into the role of social gatekeepers and are made responsible for maintaining social order. Interpolating vernacular usage into the overall English medium through code switching, the columnists seem to position themselves ambiguously, at once alongside their readers and a cut above them, although their final comment seems equally fitting on both counts: 'know your place, brother; even if you are a soccer legend, you too must queue.'

The 'Mngosi' writers insist on referring to themselves as the 'Pace Gang'. Given the central role of criminal gangs in historically structuring and organising processes of urbanisation and township life in South Africa, this self-ironic allusion is presumably not lost on their readers. While the 'Mngosi' writers clearly wish to distinguish themselves from criminal gangs as social deviants, they appear to be quite comfortable acknowledging the centrality of criminal gangs to urban African cultural identity by paying homage to them (Kashane 1999). By foregrounding their own sociohistorical authority through this acknowledgment, they again both distance themselves from and endear themselves to many of their readers even as they align themselves with a more esteemed role model, that of the traditional oral storyteller and/or poet.

In this essay I have examined some of the ways in which consumer magazines function as significant indicators of and contributors to the dynamics of cultural change in South Africa. Facilitating the formulation, dissemination, and authorisation of new and revived linguistic and cultural repertoires for and by black South Africans, within the broader context of a growing and increasingly more integrated consumer culture in South Africa, they afford us insight into the similarities and differences manifest in Western and African social entities, which are all, it would seem, typically 'driven by a tension between role-breaking, resource consumption, supra-social achievement, and structural innovation on the one hand, and personality assimilation, ordered collective action, and institutional reproduction on the other' (Coplan 1994: 42).

Finally, consumer magazines enable black South Africans successfully to recuper- ate traditional forums and social practices alongside modern, literate cultural options as part of what Orvar Lofgren (1996) calls 'the microphysics of learning to belong' in urban environments. By showing how they give black South Africans access to a vast 'marketplace' of global and local commodities, routines, linguistic practices, and aspi- rations, both trivial and esteemed, I hope I have gone some way toward suggesting a revised view of consumer magazines as viable cultural tools that generate options for individual personhood and collective sociability in the new South Africa.

Notes

1   The author thanks Seth Motsepi, former third secretary with the South African Embassy in Tel Aviv, for patiently sharing his linguistic proficiency, cultural knowledge, and sense of humour in translating the 'Mngosi' column.

2   Generally I am concerned with what middle-class people are typically assumed to 'do' or 'aspire to'. Following Pierre Bourdieu (1984: 230–31, 260, 321; 1985), my use of the term *middle class* refers here to the upwardly mobile lifestyle preferences and social practices manifested by increasing numbers of black South Africans who may not necessarily qualify statistically for admission to this socio-economic stratum. In terms of economic capital and/or production, many of them may best be classified as belonging to the working class or petite bourgeoisie, but through various cultural activities they engage in, they tend to af- filiate themselves with and are in turn affiliated with a desired sense of ease, respectability, and belonging typically attributed to those occupying the middle position. In this sense they conform to accepted views of the middle classes as people who seek to distance themselves from necessity and basic material consid- erations as primary concerns, striving overtly for cultural capital (knowledge, culture, and education) and social esteem (Bourdieu 1984; Wilkes 1990: 121), often manifesting a keen interest in style itself (Lury 1996; Swartz 1997), and at all times aspiring for ways of life that 'speak . . . of a world better than they have' (Wilkes 1990: 128).

3   *Ebony South Africa* was owned jointly by the African American publisher of *Ebony* (USA), John H. John- son, and a South African partnership comprising Keith Sandile Kunene, Hugh Masekela, and Welcome Msomi.

4   See also studies on the large-scale migration to white towns and the permanent establishment there of large numbers of urban(ising) Africans in Philip Mayer and Iona Mayer 1974 [1961]; P. A. Pauw 1963; and Allie A. Dubb 1974. More recently David B. Coplan (1985) and Alan G. Cobley (1990: 65–68, 75–91) have examined a wider range of urban social practices, such as popular music, dance, and other modes of performance, and the rise of a black petite bourgeoisie respectively.

5   I am greatly indebted here to David Kerr's (2000) exploratory paper on the sociocultural history of the *kgotla* in Botswana.

6   The 'Mngosi' page has been reformatted twice, once in mid-1996 and again late in 1999. In 1996 it changed from bright yellow to a more subdued black and white full-page spread sans subtitle, the title appearing us black typeface and the word Mngosi in bold, multicoloured typeface. One of the anecdotes

was transposed from below the headline to the upper left side of the page and was printed as part of the headline. Photographs of the writers were placed in a circle on the upper right of the page, enclosed in a pale blue comic-like bubble whose vector, the oblique protrusion connecting photographs or illustrations of speakers or thinkers to their speech or thoughts (as noted by Kress and van Leeuven 1996: 67), pointed to the name 'Mngosi.' The number of anecdotes was reduced from seven or eight to six. Toward the end of 1999 the 'Mngosi' page layout was again redesigned into a more sophisticated, high-tech image. This comprises less text (only four or five anecdotes) and allocates more space to full-body shots of the seven members of the *Pace* Gang, who for the first time are assembled in a group shot. The colour of the typeface used for the word *Mngosi* changes every month, but the overall pose of the *Pace* Gang as a group, their clothes, and the colours thereof remain constant, although the stances of the individual writers are slightly modified from month to month.

References

Alland, Alexander
    1977 *The Artistic Animal* (New York: Anchor Books).
Anderson, Patricia
    1991 *The Printed Image and the Transformation of Popular Culture, 1790–1860* (Oxford: Clarendon Press).
Arnheim, Rudolf
    1969 *Visual Thinking* (Berkeley: University of California Press).
Beetham, Margaret
    1996 *A Magazine of Her Own? Domesticity and Desire in the Woman's Magazine, 1800-1914* (London and New York: Routledge).
Bok, Edward
    1921 *The Americanization of Edward Bok: The Autobiography of a Dutch Boy Fifty Years After* (New York: Charles Scribner's Sons).
Bona
    1989a 'How to Check Your Newborn Child', August, 114–16.
    1989b 'Word Puzzle', August.
    2000a 'Checking Up on Mom's Cherub', April, 124–25.
    1993 'Word Puzzle', October.
    2000b 'Word Puzzle', April.
Bourdieu, Pierre
    1984 *Distinction: A Social Critique of the Judgment of Taste,* translated by Richard Nice (London, Melbourne, and Henley: Routledge and Kegan Paul).
    1985 'The Social Space and the Genesis of Groups', *Theory and Society* 14 (6): 732–44.
Casalis, Eugene
    1965 [1861] *The Basuto, or Twenty-three Years in South Africa* (London: James Nisbet).
Chapman, Michael
    1985 *The Drum Decade: Stories from the 1950s* (Pietermaritzburg: University of Natal Press).
Cobley, Alan G.
    1990 *Class and Consciousness: The Petty Bourgeoisie in South Africa 1924–1950* (New York and London: Greenwood Press).
Cohen, Barney
    1992 Interview with author, July.
Cook, B. L.
    1977 'Picture Communication in Papua New Guinea', Educational Broadcasting International, June.
    1980 'Effective Uses of Pictures in Literacy Education: A Literature Review', *Literacy Review* 2.

1981 *Understanding Pictures in Papua New Guinea: What Kinds of Pictures Communicate Most Effectively with People Who Can't Read* (Elgin: David C. Cook Foundation).

Coplan, David B.

1985 *In Township Tonight: South Africa Black City Music and Theatre* (Johannesburg: Ravan).

1994 *In the Time of Cannibals: The Word Music of South Africa's Basotho Migrants* (Johannesburg: Witwatersrand University Press).

Davis, John

1994 'Social Creativity', in *When History Accelerates: Essays on Rapid Social Change, Complexity and Creativity*, edited by C. M. Hann, 95–110 (London and New Jersey: Athlone).

Davis, Natalie Zemon

1975 *Society and Culture in Early Modern France* (Stanford: Stanford University Press).

Drum

1999 'Let's Make Our Own Jobs' (letter), 23 July, 2.

Dubb, Allie A.

1974 'The Impact of the City', in *The Bantu-speaking People of Southern Africa,* edited by W. D. Hammond-Tooke, 441–72 (London and New York: Routledge and Kegan Paul).

Duncan, H. F.

1977 'Illustrations', *Read* 12 (1): 18–23.

Epskamp, Kees

1992 'Cross-Cultural Interpretations of Cartoons and Drawings', in *The Empowerment of Culture: Development Communication and Popular Media,* edited by Ad Boeren and Kees Epskamp, 79-94 (The Hague: Center for the Study of Education in Developing Countries).

Even-Zohar, Itamar

1994 'Culture Planning and the Market: Making and Maintaining Socio-Semiotic Entities.' Paper presented at the Dartmouth Colloquium, 'The Making of Culture', Dartmouth College, 22–27 July.

1997 Culture Repertoire and the Wealth of Collective Entities: Parameters for Contrastive Culture Analysis.' Available online at http://www. tau. ac .il/~itamarez.

1999 'The Making of Repertoire, Survival and Success under Heterogeneity.' Paper presented to the V l ASS Congress, Dresden, 6–11 Oct.

Even-Zohar, Itamar, ed.

1990 'Polysystem Studies', special issue of *Poetics Today* 11(1).

Ferguson, Marjorie

1983 *Forever Feminine: Women's Magazine's and the Cult of Femininity* (Aldershot: Cower).

Finlayson, Rosalie, and Sarah Slabbert

1997 'We Just Mix – Codeswitching in a South African Township', *International Journal of the Sociology of Language* 125: 65–98.

Finlayson, Rosalie, Karen Calteaux, and Carol Myers-Scotton

1998 'Orderly Mixing and Accommodation in South African Codeswitching', *Journal of Sociolinguistics* 2 (3): 395–420.

Finnegan, Ruth

1967 *Limba Stories and Storytelling* (London: Oxford University Press).

Garvey, Ellen G.

1996 *The Adman in the Parlor: Magazines and the Gendering of Consumer Culture, 1880s to 1910s* (New York and Oxford: Oxford University Press).

Geertz, Clifford

1983 'Local Knowledge: Fact and Law in Comparative Perspective', in *Local Knowledge,* 167–234 (New York: Basic Books).

Geshiere, Peter
1997 *The Modernity of Witchcraft: Politics and the Occult in Postcolonial Africa* (Charlottesville and London: University Press of Virginia).

Geshiere, Peter, and Francis Nyamnjoh
1998 'Witchcraft as an Issue in the "Politics of Belonging": Democratization and Urban Migrants' Involvement with the Home Village', *African Studies Review* 41(3): 69–91.

Giltrow, D.
1977 'When Is a Picture Not Worth a Thousand Words?' *Read* 12 (1).

Goodman, Sharon
1996 'Visual English', in *Redesigning English: New Texts, New Identities,* edited by Sharon Goodman and David Graddol (London and New York: Routledge and the Open University).

Griffith, J., and L. E. Miner
1972 'Methodological Considerations in Visual Literacy Research', *Audiovisual Instruction 5.*

Hawthorne, Peter
1997 'A Slice of the Cake: South Africa's Affluent Blacks Share the Wealth with Stock Incentives and Community Ownership', *Time* , June 2: 31.

Hewes, Gordon V.
1978 'Visual Learning, Thinking and Communication in Human Biosocial Evolution', in *Visual Learning, Thinking, and Communication,* edited by Bikkar S. Randhawa and William E. Coffman, 1–20 (New York and London: Academic Press).

Hofmeyr, Isabel
1993 *'We Spend Our Years as a Tale That Is Told': Oral Historical Narrative in a South African Chiefdom* (Portsmouth, Johannesburg, and London: Heinemann, Witwatersrand University Press, and James Currey).

Jakobson, Roman
1960 'Closing Statement: Linguistic and Poetics', in *Style and Language,* edited by Thomas A. Sebeok, 350–77 (Cambridge, MA: Harvard University Press).

Kashane, Force
1992 Interview with author, July.
1999 Telephone conversation with author, December.
2000 Cited in 'Going the Gospel Route' (unsigned article), *Pace* July, 58–59.

Kerr, David
2000 'Media Democracy in Botswana: The *Kgotla* as Myth, Practice and Post-Colonial Communication Paradigm'. Paper presented at the Seminar on the Political Economy of the Southern African Media, University of Natal, Durban, April 24–29.

Kopytoff, Igor, and Suzanne Miers
1977 'Introduction: African 'Slavery' as an Institution of Marginality', in *Slavery in Africa: Historical and Anthropological Perspectives*, edited by Igor Kopytoff and Suzanne Miers, 3–81 (Madison: University of Wisconsin Press).

Kress, Gunther
1997 *Before Writing: Rethinking the Paths to Literacy* (London and New York: Routledge).

Kress, Gunther, and Theo van Leeuven
1996 *Reading Images* (London and New York: Routledge).

Kunetse, Daniel P.
1989 *Thomas Mofolo and the Emergence of Written Sotho Prose* (Johannesburg: Ravan).

Laden, Sonja
1997 'Middle-Class Matters, or, How to Keep Whites "Whiter, Colors Brighter, and Blacks Beautiful"', *Critical Arts* 11 (1–2): 120–41.

Lofgren, Orvar
  1996 'The Nation as House or Motel? On the Ethnography of Belonging', *Anthropological Newsletter,* October 33-34.
Lury, Celia
  1996 *Consumer Culture* (New Jersey: Rutgers University Press).
Manoim, Irwin Stanley
  1983 'The Black Press 1945–1963: The Growth of the Black Mass Media and Their Role as Ideological Disseminators'. M. A. thesis, University of the Witwatersrand.
Maspero, M. F., and E. Kennedy
  1979 *I See: A Report on Experiences in Producing and Using Audio- Visual Aids for Population Education at Village Level* (Rome: FAQ).
Mayer, Philip, and Iona Mayer
  1974 [1961] *Townsmen or Tribesmen: Conservatism and the Process of Urbanization in a South African City* (Cape Town and London: Oxford University Press).
McEwan, M. J., and L. Malan
  1996 '"We Are Waiting/This Is Our Home": Literacy and the Search for Resources in the Rural Eastern Cape', in *The Social Uses of Literacy: Theory and Practice in Contemporary South Africa*, edited by Mastin Prinsloo and Mignonne Brier, 197–2 12 (Bertsham: Sached Books).
Myers-Scotton, Carol
  1993, *Social Motivations for Code Switching: Evidence from Africa* (Oxford: Clarendon Press).
—ed.
  1998 *Codes and Consequences: Choosing Linguistic Varieties,* (New York and Oxford: Oxford University Press).
Ngcongco, Leonard
  1989 'Tswana Political Traditions: How Democratic?' in *Democracy in Botswana,* edited by J. Holm and P Molutsi, 42–47 (Gaborone: Macmillan).
Nicol, Mike
  1991 *A Good-Looking Corpse* (London: Secker and Warburg).
Ohmann, Richard
  1996 *Selling Culture: Magazines Markets, and Class at the Turn of the Century* (London: Verso).
Okpewho, Isidore
  1979 *The Epic in Africa: Towards a Poetics of the Oral Performance* (New York: Columbia University Press).
Olson, David
  1994 *The World on Paper: The Conceptual and Cognitive Implications of Writing and Reading* (Cambridge: Cambridge University Press).
Opland, Jeff
  1983 *Xhosa Oral Poetry: Aspects of a Black South African Tradition* (Johannesburg: Ravan).
Pace
  1990 'Family Planning', May, 69.
  1991/1992 'Mngosi with the Pace Gang', December/January, 2.
  1992 'Mngosi with the Pace Gang', July 2.
  1996 'Mngosi with the Pace Gang', March 2.
  1997a ' Mngosi with the Pace Gang', April 4.
  1997b 'Mngosi with the Pace Gang', August 4.
  1999 'Mngosi with the Pace Gang', December 4.

Pauw, P. A.

1963 *The Second Generation: A Study of the Family Among Urbanized Bantu in East London* (Cape Town and London: Oxford University Press).

Preston-Whyte, Eleanor

1974 'Kinship and Marriage', in *The Bantu-speaking Peoples of Southern Africa,* edited by W. D. Hammond-Tooke, 177–210 (London and Boston: Routledge and Kegan Paul).

Rabkin, David

1975 '*Drum* Magazine (1951–61) and the Works of Black South African Writers Associated with It.' Ph.D. thesis, University of Leeds.

Sampson, Anthony

1956 *Drum: A Venture into the New Africa* (London: Collins).

Schapera. Isaac

1938 *A Handbook of Tswana Law and Custom* (London: Frank Cass).

Shapin, Steven, and Simon Shaffer

1985 *The Leviathan and the Air-Pump: Hobbes, Boyle and the Experimental Life* (Princeton: Princeton University Press).

Sheffy, Rakefet

1997 'Models and Habituses: Problems in the Idea of Cultural Repertoires', *Canadian Review of Comparative Literature* 24 (1): 35–47.

Silverstone, Roger, Eric Hirsch, and David Morley

1992 'Information and Communication Technologies and the Moral Economy of the Household', in *Consuming Technologies: Media and Information in Domestic Spaces,* edited by Roger Silverstone and Eric Hirsch, 15–31 (London and New York: Routledge).

Smith, R.

1985 'Le magazine *Drum:* Voix des townships noires', translated by A. Viola, *L'Afrique litteraire* 75.

Spacks, Patricia Ann Meyer

1986 *Gossip* (Chicago amid London: University of Chicago Press).

Swartz, David

1997 *Culture and Power: The Sociology of Pierre Bourdieu* (Chicago and London: University of Chicago Press).

Swidler, Ann

1986 'Culture in Action: Symbols and Strategies', *American Sociological Review* 51: 273–86.

Teer-Tomaselli, Ruth

1996 'DEBI Does Democracy: Recollecting Democratic Voter Education in the Electronic Media Prior to the South African Elections', in *Connected Engagements with the Media,* edited by George E. Marcus, 377–421 (Chicago and London: Chicago University Press).

Tomaselli, Keyan G.

1996 *Appropriating Images: The Semiotics of Visual Representation* (Denmark: Intervention Press).

1997 'Ownership and Control in the South African Print Media: Black Empowerment after Apartheid, 1990–1997', *Equid/Novi* 18 (1): 21–68.

True Love

2000a Advertisement, May, 4.

2000b Advertisement, July, 17.

Tyler, Humphrey

1995 *Life in the Time of Sharpeville: Wayward Seeds of the New South Africa* (Cape Town: Kwela Books).

Van Beek, Walter, and Thomas D. Blakely
  1994 'Introduction', in *Religion in Africa: Experience and Expression,* edited by Thomas D. Blakely, Walter Van Beek, Dennis Thomson (London: James Currey).
Vansina, Jan
  1985 *Oral Tradition as History* (Madison: University of Wisconsin Press).
Webb, Vic, and Kembo-Sure, eds.
  2000 *African Voices: An Introduction to the Language and Linguistics of Africa* (Cape Town and New York: Oxford University Press).
Wilkes, Chris
  1990 'Bourdieu's Class', in *An Introduction to the Work of Pierre Bourdieu: The Practice of Theory,* edited by Richard Harker; Cheleen Mahar, and Chris Wilkes, 109–31 (London: Macmillan).
Williams, Rosalind
  1982 *Dream Worlds: Mass Consumption in Late Nineteenth-Century France* (Berkeley, Los Angeles, London: University of California Press).
Williamson, Judith
  1986 *Consuming Passions: The Dynamics of Popular Culture* (London and New York: Marion Boyars).
Worth, Sol, and J. Adair
  1972 *Through Navajo Eyes: An Exploration in Film Communication and Anthropology* (Bloomington: Indiana University Press).
Zimmer, A., and F. Zimmer
  1978 *Visual Literacy in Communication: Designing for Development* (Tehran and London: Hulton Educational Publishers).
Zondi, Musa
  1995 'Agencies Adopt Black Slang', *Sowetan,* May 29.

NOTES ON CONTRIBUTORS

David Attwell is Professor and Chair of English at the University of the Witwatersrand in Johannesburg. He is author of *J. M. Coetzee: South Africa and the Politics of Writing* (1993), he has more recently been working on black South African literary history.

Louise Bethlehem is a graduate of the University of the Witwatersrand and Tel Aviv University. She is currently a lecturer in the Department of English and the Program in Cultural Studies at the Hebrew University of Jerusalem, where she is also a Research Fellow of the Africa Unit of the Harry S. Truman Research Institute for the Advancement of Peace.

Jonathan Crewe is the Willard Professor of English and Comparative Literature and Director of the Leslie Humanities Center at Dartmouth College. His publications in Renaissance and modern literature include New Pelican editions, with introductions, of Shakespeare's *Coriolanus, Narrative Poems, Twelfth Night, Measure for Measure, Troilus and Cressida, Henry VIII*; *Acts of Memory: Cultural Recall in the Present*, co-edited with Mieke Bal and Leo Spitzer; *Trials of Authorship: Anterior Forms and Poetic Reconstruction from Wyatt to Shakespeare*; *Hidden Designs: The Critical Profession and Renaissance Literature; Unredeemed Rhetoric: Thomas Nashe and the Scandal of Authorship*.

Leon de Kock is Professor of English at the University of South Africa. He is the author of *Civilising Barbarians: Missionary Narrative and African Textual Response in Nineteenth-Century South Africa* (1996) and *Bloodsong: Poems* (1997). His other books include a translation of Marlene van Niekerk's prizewinning Afrikaans novel, *Triomf*, published in South Africa and the United Kingdom in separate editions in 1999, and in the US in 2004. He has published many articles on South African literary culture, including postcoloniality, and edited various collections of South African writing. He is Editor of *scrutiny2: issues in english studies in southern africa*.

Dirk Klopper is Professor and Chair of English at the University of Stellenbosch. His research interests include theory, romantic aesthetics, and South African poetry. He has published widely on the last in various South African journals. He is the editor of *Anatomy of Dark: Collected Poems of Arthur Nortje* (2000). He is Editor of the *English Academy Review*.

Loren Kruger is the author of *The National Stage: Theatre and Cultural Legitimation in England, France and America* (1992) and *The Drama of South Africa: Plays, Pageants and*

Publics Since 1910 (1999). She has published articles on South African topics in *Modern Drama*, *Public Culture*, and *South Atlantic Quarterly*. She is currently contributing editor to *Theatre Research International* and *scrutiny2* and Professor of Comparative and English Literature and African Studies at the University of Chicago.

Sonja Laden is a former lecturer in literary theory, comparative literature and cultural studies at Tel Aviv University, where she was involved in editing *Poetics Today*. She is currently a research affiliate of Culture, Communication and Media Studies at the University of KwaZulu-Natal. She has published numerous articles on Stephen Greenblatt and the New Historicism, and on the cultural functionality of consumer magazines in South Africa and in Israel.

Simon Lewis, Associate Professor of English at the College of Charleston, teaches African and postcolonial literature. Much of his scholarly work has focused on the representation of landscape in African colonial and postcolonial writing. He is the author of *White Women Writers and Their African Invention* (2003) and his new work looks at male writers in Africa and the construction of masculinity in respect of hunting and war. He is editor of the literary journal *Illuminations*.

Peter Merrington teaches nineteenth-century literature, British modernism, and creative writing in the English department at the University of the Western Cape. He has published articles on topics in Edwardian colonial and imperial cultural studies in *Theatre Journal*, *Journal of Southern African Studies* and elsewhere, as well as short fiction. He is preparing a book-length study of the performance genre of 'new pageantry'.

Pippa Skotnes is Professor of Fine Art at the Michaelis School of Fine Art at the University of Cape Town. Her creative work focuses on book arts and the creation of exhibitions. Her research has centred on rock art and the Bleek and Lloyd Archive of /Xam and !Kun narratives. She is the author and editor of several books including *Sound from the Thinking Strings* (1991), *Miscast: Negotiating the Presence of the Bushmen* (1996) and *Heaven's Things: A Story of the /Xam* (1999). She is currently working on the digital reproduction of the Bleek and Lloyd archive, with accompanying publication.

Patricia Watson Shariff lectures in the School of Literature and Language Studies at the University of the Witwatersrand. She was awarded the National Research Foundation President's Award for her Ph.D (upon which part of this chapter is based) in recognition of her research into gender and sexuality issues in rural societies in Africa. Her scholarly work focuses on popular media and development, literacy studies and information technologies, curriculum, and language policy.

INDEX

A

Abdurahman, Dr Abdullah, 124–125

Abrahams, Peter, 3

Achebe, Chinua, 171, 183

    Things Fall Apart (1958) 171

Adamastor, 10, 18

Adorno, Theodor, 160, 169

Advertisements and advertising, 218, 250–251, 257–258, 260, 263–265

African Connection Rally (1999), 60

African divination and healing, 140–141, 147–149, 158, 251–252, 258

African languages and literature, 4–5, 7, 18, 118, 120–123, 156–157, 171, 189, 219, 224, 232, 239, 264, 266, 268

    see also Black English writing

African National Congress (ANC),

    government, 17, 26, 174, 205, 210–211, 262

    movement, 15, 17, 121–122, 124–125, 129, 156, 174, 184, 204, 210

African nationalism, 14, 16, 76, 130

African Political Organisation, 121, 124–125

African Renaissance, *see* Slogans

African struggle and resistance, 7, 13–15, 17, 24, 120, 122, 126, 129–130, 137–139, 141, 145, 158–159, 161, 163, 169–170, 172, 184, 189, 205–211, 214, 218, 220, 226, 250

African tradition, beliefs and customs, 140–141, 145, 147–148, 171–174, 206, 209, 229–230, 238, 251–252, 255, 258, 265–266, 271

African tribes and tribal identity, 117–118, 120–123, 168, 207–209, 266

Afrikaans language and literature, 4, 6–7, 18, 25, 73, 124, 148, 180–184, 187–189, 218–219, 263–264

    Second Language Movement (1905–1925), 181–182

    Sestigers, 180, 183–184, 189

Afrikaner nationalism, 4, 59, 63

Afrikaners and Afrikaner identity, 3–4, 12, 16, 18–20, 25, 35, 37–41, 43, 46, 51, 61, 80–82, 130, 142, 165–167, 180–185, 187–190, 206

/A!kunta, 39

All Media Publishing Survey (AMPS), 256

Amnesty, 195, 205

Angel of History, 199–201, 203, 207, 209–210 *see also* Benjamin, Walter *and* South African history and historicism

Anglo-Boer War *see* Wars, South African War (1899–1902)

Anthologies, 2, 101

    A Land Apart (1986), 2

    South African Short Stories (1973), 3–4

    The Return of the Amasi bird (1982), 168

Apartheid, 3–9, 16–19, 22–24, 33, 94–98, 100, 104–109, 118–123, 137, 154, 159–160, 163–166, 170–172, 181–186, 189, 195, 197, 201, 203–206, 208, 211, 214–215, 218, 221, 227–230, 239, 249, 252, 265

K

N

T